E RISE

From a childhood in the celebrity-filled canyons of California to living in squalor in Manchester while playing in the band The Fall, to sitting front row in fashion shows as buyer for her own clothing store, to presenting prime-time television; Brix's journey required a fearlessness that has brought inspiration to many. A pioneering musical icon, she is one of a handful of successful female guitarists and songwriters, working not just with The Fall but with her solo band, Adult Net, and her current band, Brix and the Extricated. She lives in Shoreditch, London, with her husband, Philip, and her two pugs, Gladys and Pixie.

Twitter/Instagram: @Brixsmithstart
Facebook: @extricated

Further praise for *The Rise, The Fall, and The Rise*:

'Her book is open, honest, funny and warm, and highly recommended.' *Loud & Quiet*

'[An] enjoyably picaresque memoir.' Ludovic Hunter-Tilney, *Financial Times*

'She's one of those people who knows everyone and tells you everything – which makes for a vibrant, entertaining read, even when peppered with darker moments.' Kerry Potter, *Glamour*

'Brix Smith-Start's new memoir charts a remarkable journey . . . While her incredible story of career and life highs and lows beggars belief, it's also universal – this is a woman who's lived a full life, grown from her mistakes and learned to trust her gut. That's a lesson all of us can learn from.' *Red*

'[A] brilliantly weird and readable music memoir that brings a sun-soaked Californian perspective to early '80s Manchester and to the most enduring cult band in Britain . . . a funny and fascinating account of an idiosyncratic rock 'n' roll route through life.' *Caught by the River*

'Rich and evocative.' Fiona Sturges, *i*

'[An] extraordinary story.' Matthew Whitehouse, *i-D*

THE RISE,
THE FALL,
AND THE RISE

BRIX SMITH START

FABER & FABER

First published in 2016
by Faber & Faber Ltd,
Bloomsbury House,
74–77 Great Russell Street,
London WC1B 3DA
This paperback edition first published in 2017

Printed in the UK by
CPI Group (UK) Ltd, Croydon CR0 4YY

A CIP record for this book
is available from the British Library

ISBN 978–0–571–32506–1

FSC
www.fsc.org
MIX
Paper from
responsible sources
FSC® C020471

2 4 6 8 10 9 7 5 3 1

This book was written with truth and love.
I am especially grateful to
those people with whom I've had difficult relationships.
For those people, and those relationships
(no matter how hard they were at the time),
helped shape me
into the person I am today

CONTENTS

Part Three: The Rise

Epilogue

ILLUSTRATIONS

Plates

Laura and her grandmother at Disneyland
Laura looking haunted
Laura riding Scooter Pie
Laura and a turtle
The house in Chicago
Leah, Marvin, Brix and Nadia on holiday in St Barths
Mr and Mrs Smith on their wedding day
Mark and Brix at Blackpool Pleasure Beach
Brix channelling Edie Sedgwick
The Salenger family cruise
Brix's dad
Brix on tour
Steve Hanley, Brix, Simon Wolstencroft, Mark, Marcia and Craig
    Scanlon (© *Paul Cox*)
Brix and Michelle Lineker at Italia '90
Brix and Susanna Hoffs
Brix as an actress/waitress in LA
Brix, Nigel and his bulldog, Deadly
Murray Lachlan Young
Brix and Philip, soon after they met
Brix and Philip on their wedding day
Brix and Maggie
Marvin and Brix's mom
Brix and the Extricated (© *Kerry Curl*)
Marvin, Brix's mom and Philip on her adoption day
Gladys and Pixie (© *Gerrard Gethings*)

Text Illustrations

PART ONE
THE RISE

Me and Lisa at Bennington in our
Banda Dratsing days

DISNEY'S DREAM DEBASED

My face stung as my long hair whipped it repeatedly. The top was down on my grandmother's sporty convertible Mustang. Her tiny size 3 foot slammed the pedal to the metal as we bombed down the San Diego Freeway heading south. The metallic-green car was a slice of Americana and my grandmother loved it. It made her feel young again and sassy. It was just another textbook LA day. Grandmother and granddaughter breezing along on an adventure. The age gap between us evaporated. The temperature outside, a perfect 75 degrees Fahrenheit. Our lungs expanding like bellows, sucking in California smog, orange blossom and exhaust.

My grandmother rarely called me by my birth name, Laura. She called me 'Dolly'. I often wondered why. I guessed it was because she loved to dress me up.

Every weekend she would take me shopping to Saks or Neiman Marcus and buy me adorable outfits. Sometimes we'd get matching tops. This seemed to give her great pleasure, as it did me. My grandmother loved groovy clothes. Her favourite sweater was emblazoned with the words 'Rich Bitch' written across the front. Her own children had been boys. Three of them. Steve, the eldest, was my father. Then came his brothers, Gary and Fred. I suspect my grandmother longed for a little girl. When her first grandchild was born – me, a girl – she was thrilled. I was doted on and spoiled by both my wealthy Jewish grandparents, living the dream in the opulent splendour of Beverly Hills. I feel now, they spoiled me as a reaction to the guilt they felt about my father.

Steve Salenger had always been a difficult child and had now become a problematic, troubled adult. I was foisted on my doting grandparents weekend after weekend, as my father shirked his divorced-dad duties. The fact that he was eccentric, explosively angry and undependable did not go unnoticed by his parents. In old childhood photographs of me, I have a sad, haunted look.

My grandparents forever thought of excursions and ways to take me out of my obvious misery. I depended on them for everything emotional and, though I wasn't yet aware of it, they were also supporting me financially.

We turned off the freeway at Harbor Boulevard and took the side roads, passed seedy motor lodges and bad Mexican restaurants. Then we saw it. The Gateway to Happiness – Disneyland. My heart soared as it always did, beating a little faster with anticipation. We drove through the entry gates and, as we did so, I saw the teenage parking attendant with bad acne waving his arms frantically.

'Grandma, I think he wants you to park over there,' I said.

She ignored me and kept driving. I guess she knew where she wanted to park.

On we drove through the vast parking lot. Slower now, 5 or 10 mph, meandering deftly around pedestrians. She drove directly towards the front entrance. This wasn't our usual route into Disneyland. We had a routine. We either parked under a letter/ character sign, like D for Dopey or P for Pinocchio, in the main parking lot, then walked to the tram, which circled the lot and deposited us at the main entrance. Or sometimes we employed my grandfather's tactic of parking at the Disneyland Hotel and taking the monorail straight into the park, bypassing the lines of tourists. We never needed to buy tickets anyway. My grandparents seemed to have bags and bags of them. I used to reach in and pull out fistfuls. Every one of them was an 'E' ticket. As many as I wanted. I never had to slum it on 'A' or 'B' rides such as the Main Street Trolley or the Swiss Family Robinson tree house. It seemed to me then, metaphorically, my whole life was an 'E' ticket ride.

On this day, my grandmother had a strangely determined look on her face. A look I had never seen before. She looked hard, almost angry. This was out of character. She was normally so placid and easy-going. She never ever raised her voice at me like my father did. She was the only grown-up I could truly count on. Grandma was my safe haven, my one constant amidst the acutely neurotic behaviour of both my parents.

But, even as a small child, I knew that some of Grandma's actions were 'off'. I became uneasy. Her eyes were focused straight ahead, her hands white-knuckled the steering wheel.

A mini-wave of anxiety coursed through my body. My stomach tightened. 'Grandma, what are you doing? You've missed all the parking spaces.' My voice was higher in pitch than usual. My larynx was beginning to constrict with fear.

She drove right up to the entrance, and through it. Fear swept over me.

Grandma continued on her course. She drove past the topiary – hedges painstakingly clipped into Disney cartoon characters – and past the giant circular flower bed where the flowers were groomed to create the shape of Mickey Mouse's head. She drove through the tunnel under the Disneyland railroad. My hands gripped the dashboard. We passed the Disneyland fire station where Walt Disney had his private apartment. The private residence was decorated like a garish brothel. It was from this vantage point that Walt Disney would stand and oversee the kingdom he'd created on the nights he stayed over.

We passed the town hall, where the Disneyland jail was located. The jail cells were discreetly hidden from public view, housing all manner of riff-raff including hippies, troublemakers, bad eggs and unhappy campers who misbehaved and broke the law of the mouse. We passed Great Moments with Mr Lincoln, where an audio-animatronic Abraham Lincoln would rise in his herky-jerky waxwork glory to recite the Gettysburg Address. (That was my grandfather's favourite.) We carried on driving, careening down Main Street, USA.

*At this point I started to scream. 'GRANDMA WHAT ARE
YOU DOING? You can't drive down Main Street! You are breaking
the rules! Turn around! YOU ARE SCARING ME!'*

*People scattered on both sides of us. Children dropped bags of
candy, which rolled into the gutters as mothers hurled their toddlers
to the safety of the kerb. Baby strollers, pushed at lightning speed,
were rammed up the side of the sidewalk, out of harm's way. Shocked
little fists un-clutched helium balloons. I watched them rise up on
the Anaheim jet streams, escaping the chaos below. Mickey Mouse
ear-hats littered the cobbles. Tourists stared open-mouthed as angry
fathers shook their fists at us. I watched all of this unfold in slow
motion. Embarrassment turned to panic as she drove on.*

*'Maybe Grandma got a special pass?' I prayed to myself. After
all, she knew the Disneys personally. My father dated one of their
daughters. I used to imagine what would have happened if they
had gotten married, Sharon Disney and my father. We passed the
Candy Palace and left behind the jolly strains of music coming from
the Dixieland jazz band. Tomorrowland blurred on the right while
Adventureland disappeared on the left. Now we were on a collision
course with Sleeping Beauty's castle. I tried to scream, but nothing
came out. We circumnavigated the landmark hub of Sleeping
Beauty's castle. I only just caught the briefest glimpse of the moat and
drawbridge at the foot of the castle. I could barely glance up at the
iconic spire, the one Tinker Bell flies from.*

*On hot summer nights, Disneyland puts on a firework display of
some magnitude. Children and adults alike watch in awe as Tinker
Bell flies from the summit of Matterhorn mountain to the golden
spire atop Sleeping Beauty's castle. As she does this she is lit from
behind by a backdrop of fireworks set to theme music from Disney
movies. Both the castle and Matterhorn are aglow. The collective
visual cortex of the crowd is imprinted with this 'picture postcard'
memory, in memoriam. Matterhorn mountain is an actual 1/100th
scale copy of the real thing. It's a snow-covered bobsled ride on which*

you are catapulted through internal tunnels blasted out of rock at 60 mph. It's Alpine/Bavarian-themed, and so large you can see it from the freeway. Every kid I ever knew growing up in Southern California used the 'sighting' of Matterhorn mountain to gauge the distance left to travel to the Magic Kingdom. The Matterhorn is an 'E' ticket ride. Four people share a bobsled: two in the front and two in the back. You sit on each others' laps. This is extra exciting when you are a teenager and you get to sit on the lap of your boyfriend or girlfriend, or someone you might have a crush on. As you wait in line, standing and inching along, you are housed in a Swiss-style wooden hut. The Matterhorn attendants are young adults, dressed appropriately in lederhosen. As you shuffle along the waiting line, yodelling music is piped through the rocks to 'get you in the mood'. In the background you can hear the blood-curdling screams of people already on the ride, hurtling through the tunnels and tipping over the precipices. At this point, as you are waiting, your heart is pumping with anticipation and your anxiety levels are amped. Some people get so anxious they panic and take the chicken exit, but the Matterhorn is a mega-popular ride

My grandmother swerved to the right and headed towards Fantasyland. I could hardly bear to watch any more. My hands were clapped over my eyes and I was peeking through my fingers. A rational thought flickered through my brain. 'The brakes, the brakes don't work! She can't stop the car!' But as I looked down at her tiny feet I saw this was not so. Even though I was way too young to drive, I at least knew, on some simple level, how cars worked. Grandma was not pumping the brake pedal to get the car to stop. Her foot was firmly pressed on the gas.

We took another hard right and drove straight towards the Matterhorn. Again we veered right, sharply. Now we were on a collision course for Submarine Voyage.

Submarine Voyage was located roughly on the border between Fantasyland and Tomorrowland. It was one of my least favourite

*rides – depressing and claustrophobic, it was inspired by the Jules
Verne book that later became the Disney movie 20,000 Leagues
Under the Sea. The submarine itself was located in a huge water-
filled lagoon. Twenty people or more at a time would board the
submarine and take their seats. A klaxon would sound, the hatch
would slam shut. Just sitting in those confined quarters was seriously
panic-inducing. The words 'Dive! Dive! Dive!' would sound over
the loud speaker as the submarine started its descent, sinking down
below the water's surface. Air bubbles began to rise from the water,
streaming upwards over the circular porthole windows. Somehow
the air pressure would make your ears pop. There was seemingly no
escape. If you tried, you would drown. For most people, being in such
close quarters and in a confined space triggers basic universal fears.
Panic. Disney certainly knew how to tick that box. As the submarine
went down below the waterline, it began to inch forward slowly.
Out of the circular windows you could see all manner of sub-aquatic
tableaux going on. In the dark foreboding depths, plastic fish swam
past the vessel, meandering awkwardly through fake-looking, dayglo
coral reefs. Ruins of shipwrecks lay like broken dreams on the bottom
of the lagoon floor. Sunken treasure, partially algae-covered, was
scattered haphazardly among the undulating synthetic kelp. Costume
jewellery, never to be worn, glinted weakly, as the searing Orange
County sun pierced the dirty water, illuminating it briefly.*

*Finally, after travelling at a snail's pace around the lagoon,
just when you thought you couldn't take any more, you entered
an underwater cave. This was seriously anxiety-inducing. Disney,
the master of manipulation, had dished out a double helping of
claustrophobia. The submarine trapped in a cave, Captain Nemo's
voice then boomed out of the loud speaker: 'Watch out for the giant
squid, watch out for the giant squid! Dive, dive, DIVE!' And
seemingly out of nowhere, a gigantic animatronic squid lurched at
the submarine. It wrapped its stiff mechanical tentacles around the
vessel and shook it violently. As the squid released its grip, and the*

submarine began its ascent, you passed two robot mermaids perched on rocks. Only their hands moved. They were waving goodbye. They seemed to say, 'Have a nice day. Everything will turn out fine in the end.'

I was always relieved to see those mermaids, but they also made me angry. Their gestures were too little too late. The damage to my childhood psyche was already done.

The Submarine Voyage and its menacing lagoon loomed large in the windscreen of Grandma's Mustang. By now I had resigned myself to holding on tight for dear life. I braced myself. There was nothing I could do to stop Grandma. She drove straight ahead, hunkered down, focused and unwavering.

At this point, the thought flashed through my mind that she was trying to save me by killing me. Maybe it was like the Danny Walpee situation, still fresh in my memory. Danny was a boy in my class at Westland School. We went through kindergarten and group one together. Danny's mother was dying of cancer. Danny had some emotional problems because of it. He often had accidents in his pants and needed to keep extra clothes at school. Sometimes children teased him when he pooped in his pants. His mother went into remission and the whole school rejoiced. Then, suddenly, she took a turn for the worse and died. Shortly thereafter I was at a classmate's sixth birthday party. My father turned up in the middle of the party, unexpectedly. This was odd, as on this particular weekend I was due to be with my mother. My father had a serious face on. He spoke quietly. He took me into a bedroom and sat me down. Looking at the floor he told me matter-of-factly that Danny Walpee had died. He explained that Danny's father had shot Danny with a gun. He then shot his sister Debbie, and their older brother Alan. Finally, his father turned the gun on himself. I cried.

As we neared the Submarine Voyage, I could see something was wrong. Barriers were erected in front of the lagoon, blocking off all access to the ride. They were yellow and black and written across the front of them, next to the multiple images of Mickey Mouse, were the words, 'DO NOT ENTER. Submarine ride closed for maintenance.'

My grandmother steeled herself and drove straight through the barrier. As the Mustang soared through the blockade, I saw with horror that the lagoon had been drained. Empty. All that was left of the basin, previously brimming with horrors, were small filthy puddles of water, evaporating at the bottom. The walls of the lagoon were nothing but rough, fake-barnacle-encrusted cement. The menacing creatures of my fears, once so animated by the shadowy depths, lay inert and forlorn like cheap carnival detritus.

Our car flew into the desolate pit, slamming us against the far side of the wall. The only thought in my head was that my grandmother's Mustang was ruined.

WORDS OF WISDOM

These are some of my favourite words of wisdom, sayings I like to live my life by, passed down from my elders:

1) 'Listen to your gut instinct.' (Mother)
2) 'It's about the journey, not the end result.' (Stepfather)
3) 'Two minds are better than one.' (Anon.)
4) '*Auf der Lungen. Auf der Zungen.*' (Roughly translated, 'speaking without a filter'.) (Stepfather again)
5) 'Nothing is better than something that's bad.' (Father, biological)
6) And my all-time favourite, 'This too shall pass.' (Grandmother)

I've applied these golden rules to all the artistic endeavours in my life. Songwriting being a prime example. I can't tell you how many times I've been asked about the creative process and how it worked between Mark E and myself. People seemed fascinated with how we came up with such Fall classics as 'Cruiser's Creek', 'Hit the North' or 'LA'. In fact, forget the songwriting. People just wanted to know how our relationship worked full stop. We were polar opposites yet there was a shared energy, which intrigued people on a multitude of levels. And it all started with a gut instinct (Mother).

Inspiration is a mysterious thing. It's not so much about the environment, although this can be a stimulating factor. I feel it's more about tapping into a free-flowing stream of consciousness, listening, channelling and trusting without censorship from the ego. ('*Auf der Lungen. Auf der Zungen.*')

For me the quickest way to tap into that stream was to pick up a guitar and start strumming a chord sequence. Just three chords could start me off. I would put together chords in a pleasing pattern, until I felt a tingling in my body, and an emotional connection in my heart. It felt good. It made sense. It sounded good. It stirred me. I called this the skeleton of the song. Usually, this became the verse.

Then on top of these chords, I'd start singing a melody, feeling my way into a sympathetic match, or a pleasing mismatch to the chord sequence. I rarely used words at this point. That's where Mark E came in. He was, and is, one of the greatest poets.

Sometimes words, lyrics, or more frequently song titles would pop into my mind, as in the case of 'Terry Waite Sez', but I never forced it. After working through the verse of the song, with the chord structure and the rough melody, I'd start on the chorus. The chorus has to rise to the occasion. It has to lift the song to a higher emotional plateau – a climax, an aural orgasm.

The final thing for me was inserting the bridge between the verse and chorus. If this was done right, the verse would become an emotionally high starting point, the bridge would then bring you down, and the big, glorious, explosive chorus would (we hoped) blow you away.

Prestwich, Manchester, was where Mark E and I resided for the majority of our married life. It was a small, semi-detached house in a working-class Jewish neighbourhood. Mark E grew up in the next street, Dorchester Avenue, where his parents and younger sister still lived. This house was the subject of the song 'My New House' on the album *This Nation's Saving Grace*.

When we decorated the house, we decided to paint the outside a dark slate-grey, and the inside a calming dark blue-grey. I thought this was sophisticated. I seemed to have an instinctive understanding of the power and vibrational qualities of colour. This was long before I made a career of it in fashion.

Our furniture was basic. The dining-room table and chairs were black ash. Our Wesley-Barrell sofa was beige with a floral pattern, and looked 'posh'. Upstairs, we had two bedrooms. Well, three if you counted the tiny box room, where we kept papers, junk, microphones and instruments (including the three-string violin used on the song 'Hotel Blöedel' from the album *Perverted by Language*, my present husband's favourite Fall song).

The box room was also the location for our cat Frau's dirty little protests. She would pee on Mark E's microphone to pay him back, I decided, for being away so often on tour. We only had one bathroom and it was vile. The bathroom suite was avocado colour. I spent a good many nights puking into the hideous commode, which made me want to puke more.

The final room in the downstairs of our house was the kitchen. The kitchen was white and had a faux-brick vinyl floor. The kitchen also had a back door, which led to the small, ugly, unloved garden. Because at some point the foundations of the house had shifted, there was a gap underneath the back door, and sometimes after a rainstorm we would come downstairs to find an invasion of slugs sliming all over the kitchen floor. Even the slugs hated that garden. Mark E poured Morton salt on them, and watched them shrivel. He found this funny, and endlessly fascinating. I found it cruel, but I hate slugs and couldn't even step into the kitchen knowing they were there. So I kept mum. It was the beginning of a bad habit, keeping mum. I was soon to learn that the hard way.

Typically I would sit in the living room with Whitey, my favourite guitar. It was a white hollow-body Rickenbacker. I would start composing the skeleton of a song. Then, excitedly, I'd bring the red-hot inspiration to Mark E, who would be pacing the dining room with his headphones on. He was always pacing due to the excess energy from speed. Mark would then listen to it and offer only guttural grunting noises as comment. Like a maniac, he would then reach over to a stack of scrap paper and rifle through it until he put his hand on just the right sheet. Bingo! He would produce the perfect lyrical accompaniment. The pile of scrap paper was actually a massive collection of lyrics, poetry, cut-ups, and snatches of ideas.

How Mark E had already written the perfect words for the yet unwritten song I will never know. It was beyond coincidence. It was one of those synchronistic moments that reassure you that you truly are at the right place, at the right time, and on the right path.

We'd put together the two parts of the song and run through it. We'd do this five or six times before committing it to tape. We had a portable Sony cassette recorder. Mark E used it to grunt ideas into. That was the way he wrote, on his own, having never been taught to play a musical instrument.

All of us in The Fall became translators and interpreters of Mark E's grunting. Although it was unintelligible to most, it made perfect sense to us. It conveyed the purity and clarity of his intentions, and it felt important to capture this pure inspiration on tape. Mark was a big believer in first takes. There's a magic to a first take. This is one of the reasons musicians speak about 'demo-itis'. Quite often, the demo tape of the song is the best ever version of the material. It has an excitement which can lose its raw edge in the studio. We used many demos and first takes of songs on Fall records. Mark was big into truth and obsessed with non-perfection. Often during recording, I'd make a mistake on a guitar part, and want to go back and re-record it. Mark would never let me. I can now see he was right.

With the song finished and committed to the memory of the cassette recorder, we usually went our separate ways within the house. Mark E stayed downstairs, connected by headphone wires to the stereo, drinking scotch, snorting speed and chain-smoking Marlboro reds. Jigging around until the sun came up.

At this point in our marriage, I was happy to live and let live. His addictions did upset me but I told myself he needed his space and time to be creative. So I'd take myself off to bed, collecting our cats, Frau and Oscar, along the way. I'm a woman who needs her sleep. If it got too late, I had an inner overdose alarm that would wake me and I'd go down and check on him. This seemed normal at the time. I would often find Mark E passed out and unconscious on the floor in the living room next to the stereo. The headphones were still on, and his face had a moustache of sweat and a death-calm pallor, the record rotating on the stereo, scrape-scrape-scraping against the run-out groove. I'd drag him up the stairs and tuck him in bed – thanking God every time that he was breathing.

In the morning when we finally did wake, we'd go downstairs and make a cup of Tetley tea. Mark takes it strong, with a little milk. I like it weak. Too strong and I'll feel sick. We might pop a frozen potato waffle into the toaster or fry up a Danish back-bacon sandwich with white bread. Then we'd pack up our instruments and notes and the cassette recorder and call a taxi to take us to the rehearsal room to meet 'the lads'.

It was in the rehearsal room that the lads would hear the new song for the first time. I would play the tape once, then play it live on the guitar. They would then improvise their own parts. While this process was going on, Mark E was always in the nearest pub.

After the songs had settled into shape we'd start getting ready to go on tour . . . again. The long and winding road. Drugs, food poisoning, injuries, breakdowns and antics. Exhaustion. Who knew what might happen? It could be the making or breaking of a band . . . or a marriage. It's about the journey, not the end result (Stepfather).

PEANUT

My first nickname was 'Peanut'. It was given to me by the nurses in the hospital where I was born. I was 5lbs 3oz and looked like a peanut. Charming. I was born in Los Angeles, California, at the Cedars of Lebanon hospital at 8.30 in the morning, 12 November 1962. The name on my birth certificate said Laura Elisse Salenger.

My mother, Lucy Salenger, and my biological father, Steve Salenger, had just the one child from their union. They were divorced before I was two. I have only ethereal snatches of memories of us living together as a family unit; piecemeal tableaux of scenes and feelings that are severed from any cohesive timeline. These fragments of my memories are part of the wardrobe of my early childhood psyche.

Most days, my mother was not at home. She was holding down two jobs. She was trying to make it as a fashion model but worked a day job at a brokerage firm to pay the bills. I was left in the 'care' of Carmen, our Mexican maid. Carmen was the first person I remember not liking. Carmen was mean. She must have had a hard life and been very unhappy. Maybe she hated America? Perhaps she disliked children? It's possible that she had left her own children behind in Mexico. Whatever the case, her presence facilitated my earliest memories of fear, anger and injustice.

During the day, Carmen would turn up the heat to sweltering in our small upstairs duplex apartment. Why she would put the heat on at all, since we lived in LA and it was 80 degrees outside every day, I have no idea. Perhaps she was trying to get me to sleep.

Once the heat was up, she would deposit me in my crib and shut the door. This is how I remember spending my earliest days: imprisoned behind the shiny baby-blue guard rails that surrounded my cot. I shook the bars and cried out. I kicked away my baby blankets, 'Blue Boy' and 'Pinky', to try to escape the suffocating heat. Finally I lay there for what seemed like hours, sucking my thumb, waiting for my mother to get home and rescue me. I knew that if my mother found out, she would be angry and would stop her from doing it. Somehow I knew that Carmen was going to get caught.

Occasionally my mother would ask Carmen to do some shopping for groceries. Carmen would truss me up in sweaters, shoving my little arms into the sleeve holes and angrily pulling the garment over my head. She would grab hold of my arm and virtually drag me down the street to the supermarket. Unfortunately this meant walking through a subway underpass. It was dark and it stank of human urine – the antithesis of life in the light; the shadowy underbelly of sunny California. I was especially scared of the people who 'lived' down there.

This was the first time I ever remember feeling the strength of my own gut instincts.

One day Carmen dragged me to the market. When we reached the tunnel, I put on the brakes. I planted my feet firmly on the ground and refused to budge. Carmen pulled and pulled but was unable to dislodge me from the imaginary anchor I had sunk into the sidewalk at the gaping mouth of the tunnel. I was using the power of my will. Even at three years old, it seemed I had a strong one. Carmen began to scream at me in Spanish but I just stood there, holding my ground. She began to make a scene. I was aware of people staring. Then Carmen lost it. She grabbed me violently and yanked down my pants. In full public view, she spanked me hard on my bare bottom.

She then proceeded to drag me kicking and screaming to the market and back.

I remember wailing with rage and humiliation. I hoped some kind person would intervene. I wanted to punish Carmen and I wanted someone to tell my mommy.

I don't remember my father living with us. He came periodically to collect me and take me out. I remember the energy between my mother and father as strained and fraught with tension. They spoke to each other through gritted teeth. I never remember them touching each other, let alone kissing.

I knew that they both loved me, though. I was the one thing that united them. Whenever there was some crisis in my upbringing, they came together. Later in my childhood, I spent quite a lot of time plotting ways to manipulate them into situations that would force them together. I hoped, however irrationally, to fix their marriage and unite us as a family.

Later, when I could communicate more clearly, my mother used to ask me questions about what Carmen had done to me. I told her about the tunnel incident. I also told her that Carmen forced me to eat 'Spanish' salad, which burnt my mouth. It transpired that she never fed me any 'normal' food, only radishes. I am sure my mother felt guilty about leaving me with childcare and having to work full-time. I imagine all parents must worry about what goes on behind their backs. That day in front of the tunnel, I learned a lesson that by standing my ground I could make a point.

One day my father appeared at the apartment with a present for me: a tortoise. Where he got it I have no idea. It was big. Not as big as a Galápagos tortoise but big enough. I loved my tortoise. He was slow and gentle. He looked at me with wise blinking eyes. When I touched his head, he sucked in his neck and hid deep inside his shell. His shell was his home, his safe place. I remember wishing I had a shell.

My mother asked me what his name was. Without thinking I blurted out, 'Sammy.' My mother took out some red nail polish and painted S A M M Y on his shell.

'Why are you doing that, Mom?' I asked. 'So he doesn't get lost.' I would sit on a small patch of lawn in front of our 1960s duplex and watch Sammy munch contentedly on blades of grass, the arid LA heat warming his shell and my skin. One day, I ran inside quickly to grab a sandwich for my lunch and when I came back out, Sammy was gone. I never thought Sammy would leave me. I loved him so much, and we had a bond. I hoped the red nail varnish would bring him back home to us, that the person who found him would know he was my Sammy. I cried for weeks over my Sammy. Then my mother, feeling sorry for me, took me to the Farmers Market to cheer me up. I loved the Farmers Market, a historic Los Angeles landmark and tourist attraction. It is known for its fresh produce, sit-down eateries, food stalls and vendors. It dates back to 1934. It's vibrant and full of energy and is a colourful backdrop for all manner of LA life.

There is a seedy glamour about it. It's very old-school LA. You can see a real cross section of life there: from big Hollywood movie stars doing a spot of food shopping, to down and outs nursing their drinks in brown paper bags. Every time I go there, I can feel the desperation rising from the tarmac like a heat haze. LA is full of desperate people trying to make it in the entertainment industry. You can feel their crushed dreams raining down like the confetti from a busted piñata. Those crushed dreams are like a malaise. They hover and waft through the air. They drift like a fog. They meander through LA and shroud the Valley. They collect in the canyons and hang above the beaches, permeating the atmosphere wherever you go. For every single success story in LA, there are thousands and thousands of sad tales. Ambition and hopelessness go hand in hand, and are seemingly magnified; almost as if one were living them through the lens of a camera.

As my mother and I passed through the Farmers Market, something caught my eye: a pet store. Even then I had a deep bond with animals and couldn't resist. I pulled my mom into the shop. The first thing I saw was a round plastic terrarium containing a mini-palm tree and two tiny turtles. I had to have them. I begged and whined. My mom relented and bought them for me, knowing how distraught I'd been after Sammy's disappearance. I took them home and played with the turtles all day. I named them Cuff and Link. I kissed their tiny heads repeatedly. After nursery school, for the next few days, I played with my turtles all afternoon until dinner. They were all I could think about. Then one of those nights I fell asleep, like all the others. But when I woke up, two weeks had passed. I awoke to find my mother weeping tears of joy over my bed. Apparently, I had contracted salmonella from the little turtles and had nearly died. I remember nothing about it. Later my mother told me that for days I had a raging fever of over 104 degrees. I had been delirious and then unconscious. It had been *so* serious that, for two months after my illness, my mother had to collect specimens of my faeces to take to the California Department of Public Health. I was only four, but I felt embarrassed about my mother carrying around my poop in tinfoil.

Shortly after the turtle incident, my mother and I moved to 555 Huntley Drive in the flats of West LA. Huntley Drive is a street made up of modest single-storey bungalows lined with towering cypress trees. Our rented house was dark and gloomy. The only good thing about the house was the backyard. There was an avocado tree and two Santa Rosa plum trees. Santa Rosa plums are the sweetest plums in the world, with a delicate purple flesh. When I bit into them the juice would burst into my mouth and dribble down my chin, staining many a T-shirt.

My first fashion memory occurred in that house. For my fourth birthday, the first proper birthday party I ever remember, my grandmother bought me a groovy black patent leather swinging shoulder bag and a matching miniskirt. In that outfit, I felt like a big girl, which was great, as I was about to start kindergarten. My mother and father, to their credit, saw that I had some youthful talents. From a very young age, I had a flair and passion for the arts. I loved painting and drawing, making up stories and acting out plays that I would invent. I also loved music. Along with guns, clocks and vicious dogs, one of my father's other fixations was banjos. He loved playing banjos, guitars and listening to bluegrass music. My father made his own banjo out of spare parts and showed me how to play it. I learned to strum and pick around the age of five. My little fingers could only hold down one string at a time.

My parents chose to put me in a 'special' school, the Westland School. Westland is a private independent progressive school. It is the polar opposite of the 'normal' LA County public schools. I'm sure my parents realised that I needed to be nurtured. I suspect that they knew I would probably flounder in a public school.

The school sits high above the LA basin, perched on a ridge on Mulholland Drive, straddling both the city of Los Angeles and the Valley. At the time, it was known as a 'free' school. It was called 'free' because there were no normal rules. You called the teachers by their first names and there were no tests. The children were encouraged to express themselves creatively. Although there were classes, which were called groups, most of the ages mingled together.

My mother had recently quit her job in the brokerage firm. She stopped modelling when her agent told her she was too smart to be a model. She got a new job. A job that would change her life. It would change mine too. Cataclysmically. But I didn't know it yet. My mom became a researcher at CBS, on the prime-time news show *Sixty Minutes*. To celebrate her new job, she went out and swapped our sad old Ford station wagon for a 1963 lemon-yellow Porsche convertible.

The Porsche was technically a two-seater. In the back, behind the main seats, were two 'dog' seats. My mom used to cram all the kids that rode in our carpool into that tiny little spitfire of a car. One kid in the front seat and three smooshed in the back. We had to take turns. I don't remember there being any seatbelts. Those were the days of bucket seats, TV dinners and pay phones that cost a dime. Those were the days when we would start our mornings with Instant Breakfast or Tang because the astronauts drank it. They were also the days of hippies, riots, the Vietnam War and Charles Manson.

I loved school. We were encouraged to let our imaginations run wild and to play freely. I remember one time setting up my own pretend shop. I filled it with imaginary clothes and charged imaginary money. I find it intriguing that I played shop as a kid, then when I grew up I actually *did* open my own shop, START, with my husband Philip Start. It makes me realise how important child's play is, and how budding intentions can manifest into reality.

Sometimes on lovely days, our teachers took us out for hikes. Because the school was located on a mountainous ridge above LA, it was surrounded by scrubby, rocky nature trails and an abundance of wildlife. We learned the names of every plant and animal on the trail, including the century plant, the yucca plant and witch's hair, my favourite, because it was a garish orange string-like vine that strangled all the other plants in its vicinity. We had to be careful, though. The California chaparral is rife with rattlesnakes.

I remember my father's first new girlfriend, Ava. My father had a seemingly never-ending supply of girlfriends and then (later) wives. Most of them were nurses from the hospital where he worked as a psychiatrist. Ava was a statuesque Swedish blonde with a foreign accent. Although Ava was nice enough to me, I resented her. I wanted my father all to myself. My father spent only two days a week with me. Saturday and Sunday. He would come to pick me up from my mother's house in his fancy convertible Morgan. It was English racing green.

My father was at the height of his masculine beauty. He was a newly certified MD, specialising in child psychiatry. He always smoked a pipe, even when driving the Morgan with the top down. He was a supreme poseur and dressed like an off duty Don Draper, wearing 1960s leisure wear, styled within an inch of its life: deep midnight navy V-neck sweaters over white turtlenecks and slacks.

This was his suave Beverly Hills playboy doctor phase before his fashion went west and turned to 'cowboy'.

I was besotted with my father. I thought he was the most handsome man in the world. He told stories in a big loud voice. Everyone was riveted and charmed by him. Beguiled, mesmerised. Especially the ladies. I loved my father and he loved me. I could tell. He called me 'Lulu'. I don't think he really knew what to do with me on our weekends together. So he did what so many other California divorced dads did in the sixties. He took me to theme parks. When we weren't at theme parks he palmed me off on my doting, wealthy grandparents, Oscar and Ethel Salenger.

SCOOTER PIE

How many gallons of blood her heart pumped each minute, I have no idea. All I know is she had a big heart. Huge, in fact. After all, she weighed half a ton. Scooter Pie was my everything: a sixteen-hand bay mare, with a white stripe down her nose and four black socks. An unlikely pair we made, this gargantuan animal able to kick, crush or trample you to death, and this six-year-old girl, weighing (a below average) 40lbs.

My father taught me to ride. According to him, it was 'before I could walk'. My riding lessons consisted of him screaming at me, whip in hand, tears streaming down my face while I rode diligently around the ring (in our backyard) on my first pony, Maxwell. Whether or not I disagreed with his harsh methods, it matters not, I can now ride any horse, confidently. Horse riding is wonderful preparation for life. To be able to control, command and, most importantly, communicate with a beast which does not speak with words is one of the greatest lessons I have ever learned. (Later I would have to communicate with many beasts of the male human variety, and communication on this instinctual level got me through most of it.)

My father and his new wife, Maggie, moved to an area of LA called Malibu Canyon, contained within the suburb of Calabasas (today made famous by the Kardashians). We all know of the glittering glamorous Malibu Beach, which runs along the Pacific Coast Highway of LA. Well, just behind Malibu Beach are mountains and behind those mountains, tucked away, is Malibu Canyon. A winding, vomit-inducing, venomous road resplendent with twists, turns, tunnels and sheer cliffs leads you (nauseous, in my case) to an idyllic little 'Westernesque' community, hidden in an isolated pocket, away from the harsh klieg lights of Hollywood. Isolated communities – this one was called 'Monte Nido' – are weird. They usually contain eccentric people hiding from something with a bulging hornets' nest of life's little, and maybe not so little, secrets. This one was no different.

I spent most weekends of my childhood, between the ages of five and nine, at my dad's and Maggie's house in Calabasas. As I said, my father was a Beverly Hills psychiatrist. How a man so mentally unbalanced and troubled could help others unravel their demons was way beyond my comprehension. A mercurial genius, with good points as well as bad, he was a compelling master of manipulation and possessed an incredibly rich imagination – so much so, in fact, that I often wondered whether he could distinguish between fact and fantasy.

Not by chance was it that my future partners, Mark E. Smith and Nigel Kennedy, were eerily similar on so many levels to my father. It would take me many, many years and many, *many* shrinks to unravel this seriously unhealthy and ultimately destructive urge to form life relationships with men whom I perceived to be in my father's mould.

My stepmother, Maggie, on the other hand, was and is a wonderful woman. Born on the Great Plains of Iowa, to a rural farming family, she has the down-to-earth wholesomeness and hard-work ethic that makes you rejoice in humanity. She was a cardiac nurse and met my father at the hospital where they both worked. Today, I thank God for her. Like a soothing balm, she dampened down the moments he became incandescent with rage, putting out the fire that would definitely have left my 'hide tanned'.

He had a nuclear temper. Legendary, in fact. He seethed and vibrated, as if inhaling the fumes of the devil rising straight up from the bowels of hell. Standing above me, belt in hand, gritting his teeth and grinning like a coke addict coming off a three-day binge, he sucked his words through his teeth while he held the belt. It's no wonder I spent most of my weekends trying to be 'invisible', keeping well out of his way.

Being an only child, I was left to my own devices 90 per cent of the time. I spent the majority of my weekends playing outside, in nature, with my best friends. My friends were everything to me. They were my protectors and my teachers. They taught me about love (the unconditional variety), they taught me patience, how to watch and listen, and they taught me about trust, helping me to appreciate honesty. They showed me how to experience joy, and what it meant to be at peace. They also took me on wonderful adventures. My friends were the animals. To this day, I have a strange obsession with kissing 'muzzle' fur. Nothing is so delightful as the velvety-soft, whisper-thin hair that lies between the nose and mouth of a dog or horse. As you get close to the animal, they breathe in your scent and you breathe in theirs. This requires absolute mutual trust. In that moment one feels true peace and connection on a soul level. I feel love. When we truly trust another, our fears evaporate. To live a life without fear is to know freedom absolute.

This is one of the lessons Scooter Pie taught me. She listened to all my worries, while munching away contentedly on alfalfa. Sometimes, I'd manoeuvre her next to the corral, climbing up on the fence and slipping on to her bare back. Peering out from the barn, we would spend afternoons in the narcotic California heat, watching the evolution of the changing day and just being.

My father was a collector. A collector of the bizarre. Along with the banjos and guitars, there were antique clocks (our house was always tense with ticking and bonging). Then there were the tobacco pipes. That collection included a tobacco pouch that he told us was made from a woman's *breast* which I remember him claiming he stole from an anatomy class in medical school. He had many canes and walking sticks. His favourite was fashioned from a *bull's penis*. It looked like a glistening, gnarled piece of brown wood, like a tree branch from a horror story. It was topped by a shining, sterling silver bejewelled grip. But his scariest collection of all was the one he was most obsessed with: his collection of weapons. He collected guns. He had a .357 Magnum, a Smith & Wesson and many, many others whose names, thankfully, I never got to know. He also had an African blow-dart gun, a nasty tube through which you'd blow poison-tipped darts, and an array of bows and arrows, including a lethal crossbow.

I'm sure my father had wished I was born a boy. He might not have said as much, but I could just tell. He taught me to ride and shoot and hunt and would force me to do hours of archery target practice in our backyard. (I can *assure* you that this did not come in handy later in life.) Consequently, wanting to please my father, I became a tomboy. While I adored Barbie, I hated baby dolls and anything girly-girl.

Besides the weapons, my father had his loyal henchmen: Klaus and Heinz, his beloved German shepherds. Klaus and Heinz were attack dogs 'trained' by my father. The dogs instilled fear in almost everyone who set eyes on them, everyone but me. I spent hours 'communicating' and playing with them. Together we jumped fences, played hide and seek, and often they'd accompany me on long meandering treks along the creek at the foot of our property. We spent hours playing naturalists, David Attenborough-style, investigating the wonders of the land.

One day, Maggie took the dogs to the beach in Malibu for a long walk. Apparently Heinz took a dislike to another dog walking on the beach. An ugly fight ensued, ending with Heinz ripping the eye out of the other dog's head. Heinz had to be put down as he was deemed 'dangerous'. Eventually Klaus went on to die of natural causes, never harming anyone.

And eventually my father replaced them with three Rhodesian ridgebacks, Simba, Bantu and Imbira. But that would happen way in the future. By then he was married to wife number five, at a time when I hardly knew him, our relationship having long since become fractured and broken beyond repair.

CHILD OF A CHILD PSYCHIATRIST

At some point in his formative teen years my biological father, Steve Salenger, spent a summer on a dude ranch learning to be a cowboy. He learned to ride, rope and break horses, shoot guns and bows and arrows. This Jewish boy from Beverly Hills morphed himself into a Western character in the mould of Daniel Boone, Davy Crockett or the Lone Ranger. Heroes from his youth.

This also affected his fashion sense. He always wore cowboy boots, even to his psychiatric practice in Beverly Hills. He adorned himself in turquoise jewellery and Navajo rings, and wore a silver belt buckle with a steer's head engraved on it.

Not only did he fashion himself into a cowboy, but he also decided I should be one too. At around four years old, he bought me a pair of fancy red cowboy boots and fringed suede chaps. I always wore my hair in braids or pigtails so that it fit neatly under my cowboy hat. We would wear our Western gear not just for riding but in everyday life too. I wore those red boots to school with short shorts.

I was around four or five when my dad and stepmother Maggie moved into their new house in Calabasas, off Thornhill Road, down a private driveway that ended in its own private basin – a sort of a mini-valley. It was a dark wood California ranch house that had land encircling it, and a creek running alongside.

The interior of the house was decorated in Chinese Modern – walls painted turquoise, offset with black furniture. We had four bedrooms and two bathrooms. Our living room was clad in stone – big slabs of grey boulders everywhere, like a room made of rock.

My father began to assemble a collection of horses. He began to turn our ranch house into a mini-suburban homestead.

I loved horses from a tiny age. 'Horse' was my second word ('seal' had been my first). The first ambition I remember having was to be an expert rider. I wanted to grow up to be either a rodeo rider, show jumper or jockey. My father told me I would never make it as a jockey because I'd grow so tall 'they'd have to cut my legs off at the knee'. I only grew to 5 feet 2 inches in the end. I'm perfect jockey height, as it happens.

First came Scooter Pie, the sixteen-hand bay mare he picked up at a county fair. He was assured by the previous owner she was safe for a small child. She cost $100. Scooter Pie was so big I had to be lifted up on to her, or else I had to climb the corral posts to get my feet into the stirrups and claw myself up into the saddle. When I fell off, which was often, I always had the wind knocked out of me.

Next came Duchess, my father's horse, his pride and joy. A neighbour sold her to my father because she was too spirited for him to handle. Of course, this was no problem for my father, the psychiatrist cowboy. Duchess was an elegant palomino Arabian mare. She had a blonde body, a white mane and tail. I would spend hours talking to her and she would kiss and cuddle me. Whenever I cried after having been yelled at by my father she would dry my tears with her muzzle. I dreamed of riding Duchess but my father would almost never allow me to. If I did it was under his strict supervision and only as a special treat. Duchess was a highly strung animal and would jump at a piece of blowing paper or a clap of thunder. My father insisted she was too dangerous for me to ride and she probably was, but I felt such a deep connection with this animal. I believed she was my protector. My father would dress Duchess up in idiotic Western gear with a fancy rodeo saddle and golden festooned bridle, and himself like John Wayne in *True Grit*, while I looked like some kind of Annie Oakley effigy. Then atop Duchess and Scooter Pie we would parade around the neighbourhood.

The third equine addition to our mini-ranch was Smokey. Smokey was a greyish-black, nasty, evil, angry troll of a Shetland pony. But Smokey was darling to look at, so little and cute. You just wanted to throw your arms around him and cuddle him like a stuffed animal. God help the person that tried. No sooner would you start to sweet talk him then he would pull back his gums, bare his teeth and start kicking like a mule with his hind legs.

Smokey came into our lives cheaply. As we passed by in our car we saw a man selling him along with his adorable cart and harness. Wow. This pony could pull a cart. The ultimate party entertainment. My father and Maggie loved having the neighbours round for barbecues and yard parties at our house on Thornhill Road. Now we could give all the neighbourhood kids rides in our shiny new cart with Smokey pulling.

My father hadn't counted on that Smokey was Beelzebub with fur. Now that I look back on it, it's sad, as he was obviously mistreated and abused by his previous owners. Maybe once my father realised this, he thought he could 'fix' Smokey like he 'fixed' all the children he treated in his psychiatric practice.

A few months previously, there had been dreadful wild fires that swept across the Santa Monica mountains and down into Malibu. We had to evacuate our house. We packed all our belongings into our Volkswagen camper bus and headed to my grandparents' apartment. While Maggie, who was pregnant at the time with my half-sister Karina, and I headed off to the safety of the huge mansions and perfectly shorn hedges of Beverly Hills, my father stayed behind and saved our homestead from catching fire. He told us later he used the garden hose to drench the house and keep it wet. When the water ran dry, he fetched buckets from the creek. Helicopters circled overhead dumping huge amounts of fire retardant over everything. He said the flames burnt all around the property and the ground was so hot it singed all our corral posts. He saw wild animals panicking and rabbits hopping through the brush with their tails on fire. He evacuated the horses and the dogs to the neighbour's house, which was on higher ground and clear of brush. Many people lost their houses in that fire, including some of my school friends who lost everything. I gave some of my clothes and toys to them to help them start to rebuild. It was devastating.

Because of the fire, the entire canyon in which we lived was turned to ash. It seemed post-apocalyptic. Live electrical wires and downed phone lines lay like deadly voltage-snakes hissing among the char. All of the birds flew away. The creek running by the side of our house was the only thing unchanged. New buds and mosses appeared almost instantly after the fire. The frogs still croaked and the tadpoles still swam. Even though my father claimed, at one point during the fire, the creek boiled like a witches' cauldron.

Although wild fires can be devastating, they are regenerative and revitalising. They help the earth to be more productive, the trees to produce more seeds. Some national parks set controlled fires periodically to keep this cycle going (although this one was caused by a careless smoker). Death, birth, rebirth, death, night, day, day, night. From the ruins of this rugged wilderness came the rebirth, reinvention – rebuilding the ecosystem into something stronger, healthier and more majestic. Little did I know, later in life, how much 'sense' this cycle would make to me, and how much comfort I would take from it.

After the fires were all put out, the Los Angeles County department of forestry decided to start re-seeding in earnest. Every few hours, large noisy helicopters circled overhead, scattering vast quantities of seeds for the winds to blow across the barren mountainous landscape. The helicopters came so often they went mostly unnoticed by us.

A few months after the fires, my father and Maggie had one of their now famous neighbourhood barbecues. They cooked hotdogs, and the *pièce de résistance* of the whole spread was a massive bowl of sangria. The adults dipped their cups into the bowl over and over again as if it were the font of eternal youth.

Later, my father hitched Smokey to the cart. He entrusted me with the driving whip, with which I would crack or tap Smokey's behind to keep him on the straight and narrow. I was excited to be in control of the pony rides. I felt like a big girl, a proper frontier woman, despite being about seven. I was the master of the pony and I was proud.

Beforehand, my father had given me a long lecture on responsibility, so I knew this was a big moment for me. Smokey was hitched to the gleaming red metal cart as I sat in the seat bench waiting for my first passenger to be helped into the space next to me. The kids stood in line waiting their turn. The first little girl was scared and gripped the side of the cart tightly. Off we went, Smokey trotting away like a good boy, circling the basin of charred land around our house. Back we came, safe and sound. This went on for about twenty minutes. My father was all puffed up with the pride of it all and high as a kite on his sangria. Another great party at the Salengers'.

On about my seventh passenger, a nervous little girl, we were halfway round the house, when a re-seeding helicopter chopped loud and low overhead. Smokey screamed in fury. He reared up on to his hind legs, snapping one of the harness straps securing him to the cart, then bolted. The cart unbalanced and tossed us on to the ashen yard. The little girl smacked her head on the ground. I watched in horror as Smokey made a beeline for my father's party, heading straight for the crowd and the sangria bowl, dragging the twisted red metal cart upside down, clattering behind him.

This was my father's chance to be a hero. This was when all his 'cowpoke' training came home to roost. He ran into the house and grabbed his lasso. Chasing Smokey, he ran after him swinging the rope in wide circles above his head. Even with his busted cart holding him back, Smokey outran and outsmarted my father. Finally my father trapped him between the VW bus and the garage and got that idiotic lasso around his neck.

The party ended shortly after that. Parents took their crying children home. My father and Maggie cleaned up the scattered debris and the remnants of the festivities, while I hid in my room and waited for my father's wrath. I was sure I was going to get all the blame for this disastrous day, and it was only a matter of time before my father, gritting his teeth, would barge through my bedroom door, cowboy belt in hand.

Somehow, I managed to escape punishment, but Smokey did not. Shortly thereafter, two men turned up. They led Smokey slowly across the creek to the big corral owned by our neighbours, the Kingmens.

'Hey!' I yelled. 'Where are you going? Can I come?'

'No,' my father said. 'You don't want to see this.'

Their faces were sombre and their mouths set in grim lines.

'What are you doing? Where are you taking Smokey?' I asked.

'Get in the house, Laura,' my father said.

I sat in the den watching reruns of *Scooby-Doo*, twisting my hands with anxiety. About half an hour later, my father re-entered the house without the two men. I heard their truck drive off into the distance. I snuck out of the house and jumped across the stones in the creek, to scramble under the Kingmens' corral fence. Smokey was nowhere to be seen. Then something caught my eye. A small reddish-brown patch. I realised it was Smokey's blood. It had soaked into the ashen ground of the Kingmens' corral. In the middle of the pool of blood were Smokey's testicles: sad grey gelatinous sacks, already starting to shrivel in the shimmering relentless heat of the soporific California sun.

INTERVIEW WITH A VOMPIRE

I find vomiting both heinous and hilarious in equal measure. My life is splattered with vomiting stories. As I write this now I would describe myself as borderline bulimic. For instance, if I go to a swanky fashion party and drink three glasses of champagne (or more), I often go home and make myself puke. 'Nothing is better than something that's bad' (Father, biological). I stick my fingers way down my throat and jiggle them against my uvula until . . . up it comes. I have it down to a fine art now. I hate having things in my stomach that make me feel uncomfortable and, most of all, I hate feeling out of control.

Long ago I used to vomit because I felt guilty for eating too many calories. I used to vomit as a reaction to anxiety, and before that I used to vomit in the hope that my father would love me more.

It all started back in my father's ranch house in Calabasas. As a child I was extremely skinny. Boys in my class nicknamed me 'Bag of Bones'. I was a finicky eater. Very fussy and annoying. I liked only what I liked. My favourite foods were chocolate milk made with Nestlé's cocoa powder, and McDonald's hamburgers. (A far cry from now, where I try to stick to an alkaline–organic–vegetarian diet.) My mother, worried by my thinness and pickiness, took me to see Dr Levin. He was a Beverly Hills paediatrician whom I detested because he was always looking at my vagina. 'He's just being thorough,' my mother insisted. Dr Levin told my mother to let me eat whatever I wanted and not to make a big deal of it. He said I would start eating when I felt like it. Unfortunately, Dr Levin never had the same conversation with my father.

One weekend while staying at my father and Maggie's house, I woke up to the smell of cooking. My father had decided to let Maggie have a lie-in and had donned his chef's apron and was all geared up to make me and himself breakfast.

Maggie was an excellent cook, having grown up on a farm in Iowa. She knew about healthy seasonal food and taught me how to cook, bake and sew, although sewing sure is no part of my skill set. I enjoyed Maggie's cooking and homemaking. My father, on the other hand, was a 'creative' cook. Turning his bizarre artistic flair into culinary concoctions was the stuff of my nightmares.

On this particular morning eggs were on the menu. Eggs were not my friends. I didn't care if they *were* laid by the hens out back and fertilised with Rooster Cogburn's sperm, they were/are icky, slimy and mucoidy, with scary dark spots in their yolks. If I were going to eat eggs, they'd have to be cooked with precision: fried in butter and well done, almost crispy. If one speck of that gloopy albumen touched my mouth, my child gag reflex would kick in.

On this day my 'iron chef' father decided to experiment. Instead of frying the eggs in butter, he decided to use a brand-new exciting product to cook them in: PAM. PAM was an alternative to butter and oil and it was 'non-stick', so no mess and no scrubbing the skillet after. Happy day – not really. My father delivered the plate of shiny eggs to the table with a flourish. 'Eat them all up,' he ordered. 'I want to see a clean plate.' I cut a little piece off the white bit of the fried egg, and tentatively placed it in my mouth. Uggggggghhhhhhhhhhh! It tasted like burnt plastic. 'Dad, this egg tastes funny, like plastic.'

He threw down his cooking utensils and stomped into the dining room. 'Laura! I've had enough with you. You eat those eggs and clean your plate or I'm gonna throw you on the ground and shove them down your throat.'

With tears streaming down my cheeks, I shoved the eggs down my own throat. I swallowed them whole, without chewing. I was frightened of my father and his explosive anger and I didn't want him to be angry with me. I wanted him to love me.

The problem was (I realised later, after much therapy) that I was angry at him. My little indignant four-year-old body was stiff with fury. 'Nobody is *ever* going to make me do something I don't want to do again,' I reckoned. Silently, I snuck into the bathroom and, without even trying, vomited up all the eggs.

And so it began, my on-off relationship with bulimia, and my association with food as a means of control.

SUNSET BLVD

The PCH, Pacific Coast Highway, is a glorious living monument to the glamorous LA lifestyle. A long stretch of sun-bleached highway that runs along the ocean, past Santa Monica, Pacific Palisades, Malibu beach and beyond. Beautiful people in expensive cars, living charmed lives, drive on it. It's a great place to make you feel insecure, unless you are one of those people. I was one of those people, growing up in a privileged home.

Sandwiched between the sea and the cliffs, jaw-dropping houses sit, perched atop stilts, wedged into the mountainside. These are the houses of the 'holy'. The Hollywood 'holy', that is. Power moguls both old and new. The men and women who rule the city and run the world through the movie, recording and television industries: directors, studio presidents, actresses and agents, A&R people and lawyers. The houses hang, Zen-like, above the humming highway, and seemingly defy gravity. Their owners' eyes are drawn over the glittering expanse of Pacific Ocean blue, past the horizon . . . to the ends of the earth. The city of Los Angeles sits atop a multiple fault zone. At any given moment, should an earthquake occur, these modern mansions and quaint casitas could slide down the cliff and smash into dust on the road below. It's as if the people that own these properties feel invulnerable, omnipotent and charmed.

I believe there is something magical and spectacular about this road. For me, it's the road of dreams. It's the road of hope and ambition. A strong energy surges from the road, sandwiched betwixt the sea and mountains. It never fails to inspire me. Anything seems possible when you drive this road, anything at all.

If you head north on Pacific Coast Highway towards Malibu and take a right on Chautauqua, going up the hill, you reach Pacific Palisades and intersect with Sunset Boulevard. If you then turn right on Sunset Boulevard going east, you will begin a journey you may recognise. This iconic drive has been captured countless times on films and television shows and depicted in many photographs documenting the Golden Age of Hollywood in all its glory and seedy opulence.

The motion of the car along the drive is sexy on the tarmac. Undulating and soothing, as if one is navigating the curves of every starlet whose collected sighs of pleasure still hover in the balmy air. The wind is sweet on Sunset Boulevard, as it wafts through your hair, in your convertible with the top down. Your radio, tuned to KROQ – all rock all the time – sets the sonic scene.

The air is an intoxicating mixture of exotic concoctions: the decaying remnants of night-blooming jasmine, combined with the morning scent of Mexican orange blossom, interspersed with the scent of the salty sea and the ever-present fug of smog. I call this 'Eau de LA', the smell of home. Palm trees tower over your head, sentinels at the gate, waving to you and beckoning you towards forbidden adventures. Then, of course, there are the mansions. Flanking the road on both sides, most are hidden by massive gates, leaving your imagination to run wild as to who or what lies behind them. Some of the mansions are famous, or infamous: the homes of movie stars and murderers; the scenes of drug overdoses and suicides and endless tales of Hollywood folklore.

As you carry on down Sunset, different canyons and neighbourhoods jut off either side. Soon after leaving Pacific Palisades, you pass the exit to Rustic Canyon. This is where my father and Maggie would move after the Malibu Canyon ranch house. The future scenes of my teenage dramas would play out here, at the house on Haldeman Road, including my first experience with hard drugs, the neighbourhood paedophile who assaulted my little brother, my first stalker, numerous infidelities, witchcraft and delinquencies and, finally, the violent scene that would ultimately destroy the relationship between my father and myself.

As you continue down Sunset Boulevard you will pass Paul Revere Junior High School – where I went to school for a year, in 1975 and 1976, at the age of fourteen.

Just after passing Paul Revere on the right, you will see the turn off to Mandeville Canyon on the left. This is one of my favourite canyons and where I secretly wished I could live. I've had many friends over the years who've lived there, and it is utterly spellbinding. Each house is unique. The winding road meanders through the canyon and the individual houses lie tucked away in their own mini-enclaves of foliage-rich acreage.

You might catch a glimpse of a Spanish maid dressed in a white uniform shift dress, wheeling the empty garbage cans back from the road. She enters the wrought-iron gate, leading to the pink Spanish-style haçienda, dripping in bougainvillea, owned by her employers. Passing the ferns, palm fronds and birds of paradise plants, she wheels the garbage cans by the spare silver Mercedes-Benz SLK that her employers keep just for the use of their house guests. She enters the heavy wooden double doors and pads across the reddish-brown handmade tiles that perfectly complement the rough-plastered walls with adobe finish. She makes her way to the kitchen and then to the massive built-in (custom) sub-zero fridge-freezer, which cost her employers more than she makes in a year. She reaches inside the refrigerator and pulls out a can of Lily's Kitchen organic dog food imported from England. She scoops out two golf-ball-sized portions and pops them in a sterling silver dog bowl and places it on the tiled floor for the resident overweight black pug dog.

If you keep driving east, you reach Brentwood. Brentwood is where my aunt Susie and uncle Fred lived with my cousins Lisa and Jill Salenger. Brentwood is a community of wealth and grace. Steve McQueen and Ali MacGraw lived around the corner from my cousins' house, which I loved, as they were both among my first fashion idols. My cousin Lisa and I used to sneak around to the McQueens' house in the hopes of getting a glimpse of what seemed to me at the time to be the coolest couple in the world.

At least superficially devoid of the heinous brash taste and gauche trappings of wealth that pockmarked other desirable LA neighbourhoods, Brentwood felt discreet. That was until O. J. Simpson lost the plot and tarnished the land. He lived on the next block from Aunt Susie and Uncle Fred on the now infamous North Rockingham (Aunt Susie lived on Cliffwood). Later on, in the early nineties, when I was on my 'break' from The Fall, when all the OJ drama kicked off, Brentwood became a 'no go' zone; jammed with lookie-loos and endless news crews. It seemed like Brentwood had become the focal point of the world. I remember Aunt Susie grumbling and cursing OJ under her breath but I sat riveted, glued to the TV.

If you keep driving down Sunset Boulevard past Brentwood, you will then come to an area known as Bel Air, probably one of the most sought-after gated communities on this earth. Guarded 24/7 by its own security force, it takes privacy and wealth to a whole new level. After Bel Air you pass Westwood, the home of UCLA and my home when I was invited to re-join The Fall for the second time. Then if you keep going . . . a little further, another mile or so, you finally . . . reach Beverly Hills. The home of my grandparents.

BEVERLY HILLS GRANDPARENTS

I would describe my grandfather as having a style. Much like my father, he had a very unique fashion sense. He *always* wore cashmere socks, every single day. He wore a knit zip-front cardigan, usually grey or olive in colour, with leather panels down the front. His trousers were wide-legged and high-waisted. His eyes were protected from the searing California sunshine by blacked-out wraparound shades. On his finger he wore a thick gold ring in the shape of a baseball glove, a diamond baseball glittering in its centre. He forever had a Cuban cigar jammed in his mouth.

Whenever my grandparents wanted to keep things secret from me, they spoke in Yiddish. My grandparents had a lot of secrets. Even to this day I cannot pin down what my grandfather actually did for a living. As a kid I must have asked him a hundred times, and I never got the same answer twice.

What I do know is he was a lawyer and in the property business. He bought and sold buildings all over LA. I heard from my uncle Fred that during the Depression my grandfather had cornered the sugar market and had been making a million dollars a year. He had been something of a celebrity. His portrait hung along with movie stars and moguls on the famed walls of the legendary restaurant the Brown Derby, in Hollywood. I had seen pictures of him in the company of Eleanor Roosevelt; Martin Luther King had been a dinner guest at my grandparents' Beverly Hills mansion on Palm Drive. My grandfather counted some of the greatest sports team owners of the day, like baseball impresario Bill Veeck, among his friends.

One day, I remember driving with my grandfather in his silver Cadillac, on the way back to my mother's house. He kept randomly pointing out buildings, informing me that he owned them. They were extremely nondescript buildings – nothing glamorous like a restaurant or a fancy apartment building. They were warehouses and garages, for the most part industrial. One time, he stopped in front of an old-fashioned-style car wash – the kind of car wash that Walter White buys in *Breaking Bad* to launder money. 'I started the car-wash business,' my grandfather blurted out. 'I built the first car wash in Southern California,' he boasted.

'You mean you *own this car wash*, Grandpa?'

'No, Kid, not any more.' (He always called me 'Kid'. Unless I was creating a drama and then he called me 'Sarah Bernhardt'.)

I later found out that one of my grandfather's companies was actually the first one to make an automatic car wash: 'the wash mobile'. One of his other companies also made sleds for the US government to test rocket engines along a test track. And still another company made the original seaweed for Disneyland's submarine ride.

Every morning he would get dressed and go out to his club. The Friars Club of Beverly Hills was a private showbusiness club started in 1947 by comedian Milton Berle, 'Uncle Miltie'. It was housed in a modernist, almost windowless building designed by Sidney Eisenshtat. The building stood at 9900 Santa Monica Boulevard in Beverly Hills. The club basically shut down for lack of members in 2007 and its building was demolished in 2011. Its former members included such Hollywood luminaries as Dean Martin, Frank Sinatra, the Marx Brothers, Bob Hope, Sammy Davis Jr, Al Jolson, Judy Garland, Lucille Ball and Jerry Lewis, among others – basically 'the Hollywood Mafia'.

When I asked my grandfather what he did all day at the Friars Club, he told me he played cards. When I asked what he played, he told me gin or gin rummy. I was confused, as I knew gin and rum were drinks. I imagined he sat in a room with all of his cronies, gossiping around a round table. A red pendulum light hung overhead, illuminating the surface of the table with a hazy circular disc of light. The table was covered with green baize cloth, the room dim and thick with cigar smoke. It was perpetually night in that room, even though outside the streets of Beverly Hills were bathed in sunshine. Maybe he did business deals there? Maybe he gambled a little? Whatever the case he obviously loved it there and always came home with a spring in his step.

The Friars Club, which was open seven days a week, seemed to me to be very much a 'men's' club. They opened their doors to children and families only on Sunday mornings for brunch. These Sunday morning brunches were feasts of legendary proportions, bacchanalian in scale. The dark hallway would open up to a magnificent room. The room was angular and vast, high-ceilinged and dripping with modernist crystal chandeliers. It was dim, and opulently atmospheric. At the far end of the great cavernous space was a massive stage. This is where I supposed the fabled 'roasts' were held. Roasts were what the Friars Club was known for to the outside world: big lavish dinners to honour and pay tribute to a famous celebrity. The member being 'roasted' would sit at the head of the table, while all the guests would rip into him or her. They would tell stories and anecdotes about the celebrity's life, all the while having a laugh at the celebrity's expense.

On Sunday mornings, however, the room was transformed into a banquet hall on an epic scale. The brunch tables ran the length of the room and were adorned with ornate, gargantuan sculptures carved out of blocks of ice. The gaping-mouthed ice fish sculpture stood sentry over the heaping platters of 'lox'. Smoked salmon, from both the belly and the side of the fish, gleamed under the chandeliers. Smoked white fish, bagels of every variety – poppy seed, onion, egg and sesame seed – all lay piled up. One platter of bagels even had the inside part of the dough already hollowed out. (No doubt to save calories for those Beverly Hills waistlines.) Little balls of whipped cream-cheese speared with fancy toothpicks, with furled coloured cellophane ends, were ordered in towering cream-cheese pyramids. Next to them sat the condiments, beef-steak tomatoes, red onions, capers, chopped white onions, lemons and even iced individual butter pats stamped with the Friars Club insignia. There were herrings in both cream and vinegar sauce, giant bowls of chopped liver and chicken liver, and bread of every variety, including speciality bread like matzo, rye and challah. There were copious amounts of deli platter meats – pastrami, corned beef, roast beef, smoked turkey breast and (the always to be avoided) beef tongue.

If you felt like a light bite, you could help yourself to hot or cold cereals. Mounds of every variety of fresh fruit known to mankind lay piled up on a platter for your pleasure. If you were having digestive difficulties you might partake of the stewed fruit. I remember once overhearing my aunt Susie make a comment to Uncle Fred, 'Fred, would ya look at those stewed prunes, they're as big as my breasts!'

The food tables were manned by waiters dressed in white, each wearing a chef's hat – those big, puffy, tall hats that remind me of soufflés risen above their ramekins. The waiters were always Mexican and the chefs were always elder African American gentleman.

At the back of the room, in front of the stage, lay another massive table for hot food. It also ran the entire length of the room. The hot food table was covered in shiny sterling silver domes, housing all manner of delicious steaming concoctions. These included eggs Benedict, French toast, pancakes of every known type (including pancakes infused with chocolate chips, strawberries or blueberries), waffles, bacon (always both smoked and Canadian), sausages (always English, and Spanish and American), omelettes (always prepared on the spot to your specifications by the tall-hatted chef), and an odd collection of Jewish delicacies like noodle kugel, knish and matzo-ball soup.

I would sometimes completely forgo the savoury food and make a beeline for the dessert spread. And what a spread it was! Like something out of Willy Wonka's kitchen. I was like a pig at a trough. I'd hoard the chocolate-covered strawberries, which were as big as my fist. I'd go for the biggest ones first. The strawberries were dipped in dark chocolate and then double-dipped in white chocolate. I'd layer them up with different flavours of ice cream. I'd ladle out hot fudge sauce and then smother that with whipped cream. Finally, I'd sprinkle chopped roasted nuts on top and finish it off with a maraschino cherry. I'd help myself to a slice of cheesecake and/or pecan pie. Sometimes, I was unable to stop myself. So I'd go for the chocolate mousse too.

My half-brother Jon and my half-sister Karina and I referred to the Friars Club as 'the pig-feast'. Once in a while we oinked under our breath while we ate. We had zero control over what we consumed and seemingly no limits. We just went for it, Roman-style, and paid the price later.

Sometimes at the Friars Club we'd be lucky enough to hang out with the big guns – the now late and once great Hollywood luminaries and their progeny. Once we sat with Joel Grey (from *Cabaret*) and his family, including Jennifer Grey, his daughter. She was the same age as me. Of course, when she grew up she went on to star in *Dirty Dancing*. Nobody put Baby in the corner. (At least not in the Friars Club, anyway.) Later in life we ended up dating the same guy, but not at the same time.

I remember being taken, more than once, to meet Milton Berle. He was *the* big cheese at the Friars Club. My grandparents proudly led me to the table where he sat with his entourage. They grabbed me by the elbow and thrust my tiny arm out to shake the hand of Uncle Miltie, the legend. When we walked away, I heard my grandfather mutter snidely under his breath, 'His face is so tight, it looks more like his *tuchas* [Yiddish for ass].' Plastic surgery was normal in Beverly Hills. It was never talked about openly (except the obvious nose job) but everyone loved to gossip about everyone else's 'work'.

My grandfather was obsessed with sports. Over time, he owned two professional baseball teams. The first was the Milwaukee Brewers. Later, it was the Sacramento Solons. He was extremely proud of his baseball teams. He had a desktop photo of my father in his youth, along with his brothers, Gary and Fred, all dressed up in the Brewers uniform. They were sitting in the dug-out, 'kibitzing' with the players. All through my childhood, my grandparents took me to professional sports games. These were some of my favourite childhood memories. We would sit together and sing the communal fight songs. We would eat hot dogs, peanuts and crackerjacks. They had season tickets to both the Los Angeles Dodgers baseball team and the LA Lakers basketball team. Our season tickets for the Lakers were practically courtside, behind Jack Nicholson's.

My grandparents were my only childhood constant. They were always there for me. My grounding rods amidst the growing eccentricities of my father. It seemed like I spent more time with my grandmother than I did my own mother.

My grandfather and eight of his siblings escaped from Russia in 1921. It was by all accounts a harrowing journey. They made it to the fabled shores of America, entering through Ellis Island. When they arrived, like so many other immigrants, officials changed their family name, Americanising it from Zelenger to Salenger. They made their way from New York to Chicago, where their father was already living in a two-room apartment. They were poor and spoke little English, and took turns sleeping in a bed rather than on the floor as there weren't enough beds for all the children. They fended for themselves on the streets of Chicago, never losing faith that someday they would be living the American Dream. Years later, when they'd both made it, my grandfather, together with his brother, Uncle Jack, bought a hotel. It was an imposing vacation lodge in Minnesota called Breezy Point. They bought it from the man who owned Marvel comics. As a kid my grandparents would show me pictures of Breezy Point and tell me wistful tales about spending summers there.

To me Breezy Point looked exactly like the lodge in *The Shining*. It reminded me of an old-school-style summer camp, only bigger and grander. The main lodge, all three floors, was a huge log cabin. It had been crafted painstakingly with wooden pegs instead of nails. The interior boasted high peaked ceilings made out of massive tree trunks, and wood-panelled doors. Deer heads, with spiky antlers and glazed-dead eyes, hung from the walls. Ornate medieval chandeliers made from black wrought iron were suspended from gigantic overhead beams. It was quite some set-up. Besides the main lodge there were cabins and bungalows. There was also a main house where the Salenger family lived in the summer, separate from the hotel. Breezy Point was on a lake, stocked with fish, on which you could sail and canoe, complete with a sandy beach.

My uncle Jack was a real character. He was always referred to as the 'rich one' in the family. It seemed to me that the entire family deferred to him for all pressing matters involving money. Maybe it was because he was so generous? My father, who was always strapped for money and pled poverty at every chance (especially to my mother), always used to borrow large sums of cash from Uncle Jack. Maybe his own father, my grandfather, didn't want to lend to him any more? Uncle Jack never had children of his own.

Back in Russia, before our family escaped the pogroms and the slaughtering of the Jews, Uncle Jack was known to have been a master forger. It was his incredible talent for forging documents that allowed our family to escape. He manufactured the false identity cards that got them past the Russian authorities and into Europe, en route to the US. As with my grandfather, I never knew what Uncle Jack did day to day. One thing I did know, he owned a printing plant. He lived in Chicago in a towering high-rise apartment on the Gold Coast overlooking Lake Michigan. He was a bachelor most of his life, and always had a Las Vegas showgirl type on his arm. He was short and stout, just like my grandpa, and looked like an ageing elf. Every time there was a family dinner, he used to slip me $100 bills under the table. Sometimes I liked to see him only for the money. (I always felt bad about that.) He used to give me boxes of bizarre joke toys, like fake vomit, plastic dog poop and wind-up chattering teeth (apparently his printing factory produced the labels for the boxes of the tacky humorous knick-knacks). I can't tell you how many times I threw down the fake vomit on the floor of my classroom. I would stand above it, gagging and retching, hoping to be excused from school.

There was, though, something very shadowy about the history of Breezy Point Lodge. I have never managed to get to the bottom of what happened. When I asked my grandmother why we never went, why they didn't own it any more, she told me, 'Dolly, something awful happened. It burned to the ground, then we sold it.'

THE PINK MANSION

It lay nestled between the girding loins of Beachwood Canyon; half-way up the mountain between the sky and the HOLLYWOOD sign, encased in its own crumbling fantastical compound and surrounded by lush overgrown gardens. In the decaying remnants of a sumptuous, debauched and lost Hollywood sat the pink mansion. The pink mansion was the best house I had ever lived in. My mother and I moved there when I was six. I remember exactly because Deanne, our 'housemate', gave me the book *Now We Are Six* by A. A. Milne for my birthday. The house was so big we couldn't afford to rent it all, so we had to share it. We split the main part of the house with Deanne, a single woman. We kept it separated into two parts, only really coming together in the kitchen. Apart from that our paths rarely crossed. Above us on the top floor of the mansion, with their own private entrance, lived a couple. I used to spy on them doing naked yoga.

Separate from the house was another building altogether: the guest house, which was also pink. A rock star lived there – 'Jim'. He threw wild parties, with much nudity and drug taking. I know, because I spied on him too. Jim had washing lines strung between the sycamore and oak trees in his part of the garden in front of the guest house. Hanging on the washing lines were sealed glass jugs, filled with coloured liquid. They were the colours of the rainbow and they transfixed me. He also had a vast collection of *Playboy* magazines taking up half the space of his large living room.

I spent a lot of time observing everything and everyone, while living in the pink mansion. It was truly an enchanting, otherworldly environment. The pink mansion had extensive, mature gardens. The centrepiece of the garden was a cavernous rectangular swimming pool, also pink. In the centre of the pool stood a magnificent stone fountain. The fountain was dry. The swimming pool was empty. Its cement was cracked, and in disrepair. Slimy brackish water lay in stagnant puddles at the bottom. I think it had been empty since the 1940s. Very *Sunset Boulevard*. To even get to the swimming pool, you first had to navigate the maze. The maze was made of hedges, an actual labyrinth. There were entrances at all four corners of the rectangle surrounding the pool. But once you got into the openings, it was hard to find your way to the pool.

It was a tricky maze, especially for a six-year-old who was dwarfed by the towering, overgrown hedges. Branching off from the outside of the hedges were various garden paths. The paths would regularly lead me on my childhood flights of fantasy. I would spend hours playing in the creepy solitude of the magical garden, letting my mind run free, immersed in a total world of my own making. Riding the paths on one of my many imaginary horses, I would canter around the whole property.

My favourite path led to the back of the house, to the walled garden and koi carp pond. Here was the most sublime patio area. It was accessed from the inside of the mansion, through sliding glass doors which opened off the ballroom. The patio was paved in glittering stones. To me they looked like they were embedded with crystals. High stone walls engulfed the entire area, which was elliptical. The stone walls were dripping with passion flowers and night-blooming jasmine. The scent was intoxicating.

The koi, though, were long gone. Presumably they had met their maker years ago.

The dark, wood-panelled ballroom was the scene of some of my greatest childhood productions. Being an only child I had an inordinate amount of time in which to entertain myself. My favourite game was called 'cruise ship'. I'd set out all the occasional chairs into rows. On one chair I'd put my beloved cat

Matilda. (My mother and I had rescued her from the street, where we found her shivering and abandoned underneath our car.) Next to Matilda, on the other chairs, sat lines of imaginary people – all passengers on my cruise ship. I'd spend hours serving them drinks and hors-d'oeuvres, then singing and dancing for them. Matilda loved it when I played my child-size guitar and made up songs for her. The guitar was a present from my father. Matilda was a terrific audience. She even allowed me to drape her relaxed body over my shoulders, pretending she was my fur stole and I was a movie star.

My bedroom was crescent-shaped and protruded from an alcove at the front of the house. Back in the golden days of Hollywood and the glory days of the mansion, I suspect my bedroom would have been used as a charming sunroom from which some grand old movie star (like Gene Tierney) would sit and observe the labyrinth garden. Big curved glass windows looked out over the Hollywood Hills and the incandescent glow of LA at night. Directly in my line of view was the iconic Capitol Records Building. It was shaped like a towering stack of records. At Christmas they would put lights on it and it would transform into a giant glittering Christmas tree. I was fascinated by the building. Years later I would go there for a meeting. The A&R team were interested in signing my solo band, The Adult Net. I remember walking down the halls and savouring the moment. It felt like walking into a storybook.

The huge glass panes in my bedroom windows started to pose a problem for me. They made me anxious. It was as if they were actually windows into my imagination. Although they framed the reality of the physical world, somehow, in my mind at least, the physical and imaginary had become one. I had terrible fears that I would wake up and Superman would swoop down from the sky, flattening himself against my window, standing outside on the tiny sill, trying to get in to take me somewhere I didn't want to go. I was worried that he would take me away from my mother. That I wouldn't see her again. 'But, Laura,' my mother said, 'Superman is a good guy, he's here to save you, and, besides, he's not real.' I didn't see it that way. He looked pretty real to me on TV.

I had the real sense as a child that I never really belonged anywhere. As if it all might evaporate in an instant. I felt lonely, like a visitor. I had my first 'recurring dream' in that room. I slept on the top bunk of my bunk bed. Each night for weeks, I'd dream I was flying. I would float, fly and tumble through space, becoming one with the stars and the galaxy. I loved these dreams. They made me feel free. I felt like I would leave my body every night, and go on adventures.

One night, as I was dreaming, I hit the floor with a resounding thud. I woke up, face-down in agony. Something hurt, deep inside me. I stumbled into my mother's room, which was connected to mine by a door. My mother had heard the thud and woken up. She invited me into her bed, to cuddle. I moaned with pain. No matter how I tried, I couldn't find a position that was comfortable. After an hour of whining quietly, my mother placed her cool hand over my forehead and found it warm. She checked my temperature; it was elevated. She knew it was the sign of a broken bone. She called my father at his apartment. He told us to go to the hospital and he would meet us there. Doctors' families always received preferential treatment. We spent the rest of the night together in the hospital. Mother, father and daughter. United at last, by my childhood crisis. I was in pain – it was a fractured clavicle – but for once I felt complete.

My mother was a beautiful single woman. At one point during her modelling days, we used to do campaigns together. But my mother put her modelling years behind her to work her way up at NBC News, as a researcher. Later she got the job on *Sixty Minutes* as an associate producer. Her new position was prestigious but required her to travel. She began to live her life to the full. This included dating.

While my mother was travelling she left me in the care of an ever-revolving line of teenaged babysitters. They had to be sixteen or over, and have a car and driver's licence. My mom let me come to the interviews and choose which babysitter I liked. I always went for the prettiest ones, with long straight hair and groovy styled clothes. One of them, Kathy, was a singer-songwriter and taught me how to play guitar. She showed me chords and practised with me every day. We would sit outside in the magical garden and sing. We made up songs about the plants and the birds and the Vietnam War.

My mother began to travel even more. In her spare time, she began to work in the press office for Robert Kennedy in his presidential campaign. She loved politics and started to make inroads into that world.

One day, my mother grabbed my hand and dragged me through the glass doors from the ballroom to the patio. There we stood staring up at the sky, holding hands, our feet planted on a carpet of over-ripe passion fruit, newly fallen and split with sugar, disgorging their seeds on the crystal-embedded stone. Together we watched Apollo 11 orbit the Earth for the first time. I was wearing a badge with the pictures of the astronauts pinned to my T-shirt. The rocket streaked across the sky. A bright white light arcing overhead, it looked no different to a plane. But it was. I waved.

One night, I woke, sitting up straight in the top bunk of my bed. I had an uneasy feeling. I clambered down the wooden ladder to the floor and crept into my mother's room. What I saw stunned me. My mother was in bed, and on her couch was a strange man I had never seen before. His name was Marvin. He had a beard.

CHER WAS MY BABYSITTER

My teenage babysitters would come and go at an alarming rate. Often, my mother would get stuck without one and, having no other option, she would have to take me to work with her. My mother worked at CBS Television City. Television City was (and still is) a vast studio complex, located on Fairfax and Beverly, close to the heart of Hollywood. A variety of TV shows were taped there in the late sixties and early seventies, including game shows like *Hollywood Squares* and talk shows like *Dinah!*, *The Merv Griffin Show* and *The Mike Douglas Show*. Soap operas like *The Young and the Restless* and (later) *The Bold and the Beautiful* were also taped there. (I had tiny parts on both soaps after my first stint in *The Fall*.)

One of my favourite shows to come out of Television City was *The Carol Burnett Show*. As a child, I felt a real connection to Carol Burnett and her off-beat sense of humour. She was both hilarious and strong and wasn't afraid to make herself look idiotic for laughs. I also adored Lucille Ball and Joan Rivers. I followed their careers rapturously and found them inspiring. I'm sure I must have seen every episode of *I Love Lucy*.

As we would pull up to CBS Television City in my mom's yellow Porsche there were always long lines of people waiting to get into one of the many shows being taped there. I felt special skipping the queues and heading straight for the main doors with Mom. For a while, my mom would take me to her office at *Sixty Minutes* and I would play quietly under her desk.

One day, I looked up at Mom and said, 'I'm bored.' It was then my mother had a brilliant idea. She took my hand and marched with me off to the nearest soundstage. There were many to choose from. On one particular soundstage, rehearsals were going on for *The Sonny & Cher Comedy Hour*, a prime-time show featuring the two of them doing skits, singing and dancing. They sang their hit song, 'I Got You Babe', at the end of every show. Sometimes they brought out their darling daughter, Chastity, who was then a toddler. They bounced her in their arms while singing 'I Got You Babe' and seemed to me to be the happiest and grooviest family ever. The *Comedy Hour* also featured guest stars such as Glen Campbell, Truman Capote, Barbara Eden (Jeannie from *I Dream of Jeannie*, which I loved), Tony Curtis and many more. Everyone got into the act, doing silly (usually naff) comedic sketches. It was family-oriented entertainment.

My mother opened the door to the soundstage, walked me into the empty theatre and plonked me down. No one else was sitting in the audience. I sat riveted for hours, watching Sonny and Cher go over and over their lines, through their schmaltzy shtick and blocking out their scenes. Since they were rehearsing, Cher was usually wearing street clothes. Even in street clothes, she radiated glamour. I had never before (or since) seen a woman look so good in denim. Cher is my jeans idol. She wore faded Levi's with fringed buckskin waistcoats, daringly buttoned silk shirts and turquoise and silver jewellery. Feathers hung, here and there, from her hair. Her style was a cross between Native American rock star meets supermodel plus south-western Chic. Her long glossy hair had a life of its own. It fell to her waist, shivering and rippling like curtains of satin. Reflected under the huge studio lights, it sparkled like sunlight on water. Her nasal laugh reverberated off the soundstage walls.

This was my first lesson in the art of power-dressing. Like an exotic bird, complete with her feathered headdress, Cher would float on to the stage. Thousands and thousands of glittering beads, painstakingly hand-sewn to her Bob Mackie gowns, bedazzled me and sent my vision into refracted rainbows. I sat gobsmacked and tingling. Cher's transformation from normal woman to superstar was an education in attitude. I could see that the 'gown' transformed Cher. I understood, with every fibre of my being, that when you felt spectacular in your clothes, you radiated it. It was obvious to me that the show was a vehicle for Cher. She was the star. Sonny hardly got a look in. Cher had all the best lines while Sonny took the fall and played the fool. I watched them banter and bicker and argue. I began to see how argumentative and prickly they were when working together. Their relationship was nothing like the happy family they portrayed at the end of the show.

But what really stood out for me was their amazing work ethic, perfectionism and professionalism. I sat there like a sponge, absorbing everything. I was learning what it took to make a big studio-production TV show. I was bitten by the bug, there and then. I learned so much by watching and observing Cher at work. Cher was the best babysitter I ever had, and she didn't even know it.

BIG ROCK RANCH

As a kid, I had a natural resistance to authority and structure. I didn't like being told what to do. I loathed the idea of having to wear a uniform to school or anywhere else for that matter. I was selfish with my time. I spent so much of it on my own. I found spending time with other kids irritating. I preferred to be with animals, like the horses and dogs that were kept at my dad's house in Malibu Canyon.

I was furious with my mother when she decided to structure my summers.

One day, towards the end of the school year, my mother informed me that I would be attending Big Rock Ranch Summer Day Camp for six weeks. I remember having a tantrum and then sulking for days. Why did I have to go to day camp? When school is out for the summer, kids should be *free*, I reasoned. 'That's what summers are for, Mom,' I argued. Actually, the thought of going somewhere new and having to make friends filled me with dread. I hated the feeling I always got on the first day of school. I had that anxiety because I was shy and introverted. In situations where I felt comfortable, I flourished. But it took me ages to settle in. None of my homes were what you might call stable. I lived with my mother during the week but saw her for only about three hours a day. On the weekends I was carted off to my father's house. But with Maggie and their new child, Karina, I felt like an outsider – and, if I'm honest, a bit of a burden. A lot of the time, my father would just dump me at my grandparents'. If my grandparents were busy he might ask Aunt Susie and Uncle Fred to look after me for a night and let me play with my cousins Lisa and Jill, whom

I adored. Now those were kids I loved playing with: Lisa and Jill were whip-smart. Lisa had a rock collection, a pet rat, Roger, and every Barbie on the market, and Jill was hilarious, with a wicked sense of humour.

My first day of camp was in the summer of 1970, on an early July morning. I glared at my mother as I exited the front door. I clutched a brown paper lunch bag and tried to hide my nerves. My stomach knotted with childhood stress as I stepped up into the minivan and took a seat next to a bunch of kids I didn't know. The driver was a man in his late teens or early twenties who had long hair, hippy-style. 'Hello, Laura, welcome to the Big Rock Ranch bus. I'm your driver, Rick.' As we drove down Pacific Coast Highway, with the ocean on one side and the cliffs on the other, Rick blasted the radio tuned to KHJ.

As the first week went by, I began to look forward to the bus ride to camp every day just to hear my favourite songs. I loved 'Me and Bobby McGee' by Janis Joplin. I loved the Carpenters' 'We've Only Just Begun', and the gorgeous 'Close to You'. Freda Payne's 'Band of Gold' was infectious, and I remember being moved by Simon and Garfunkel's 'Bridge Over Troubled Water'. I also loved Crosby, Stills & Nash, Creedence Clearwater Revival, the Jackson Five, Stevie Wonder and, of course, Diana Ross and the Supremes, whose Christmas album I already had.

Once I settled into camp life, Big Rock Ranch turned out to be fun. It was deep in the heart of Topanga Canyon by a land-mark boulder called Big Rock. It was situated high up amidst the California chaparral and surrounded by scrubby oaks, towering sycamores and yellow grasses.

We had all sorts of activities during the day, including swim-ming, go-karting, arts and crafts and, best of all, horseback riding. As I had been riding since I was a toddler, I was one of the best rid-ers and horse handlers at the camp, regardless of age. Some older kids came to camp and were designated 'horse helpers'. These were the cool kids. They spent all day with the horses getting them tacked up and grooming them, and helping the campers mount up and dismount. They were also allowed to exercise the horses and take them out for trail rides. I wanted to be a horse helper. I wanted to hang with the cool kids and the horses. This was where I belonged and I lobbied for it. Their hands were stamped with the letter H. Boy, did I want that hand stamp. The problem was that horse helpers had to be five feet tall. I was two inches too short. I argued with the main horse counsellor. I told her, 'Who cares how tall you are? I have a sixteen-hand horse at home.' Still they refused.

I hung around the stables all day and helped where and when I could. I did everything from shovelling manure to soaping the saddles. Each week I'd check the measuring stick to see if, maybe, by some overnight miracle, I'd grown the required two inches. It was in the tack room of the stables at Big Rock Ranch where I had my first kiss.

The last day of camp that summer was an incredibly special day. My father did the nicest thing he'd ever done for me, before or since. He made a dream come true.

Having been obsessed with horses and riding my whole life, I adored watching cowboy shows on TV, like *Bonanza* and *Gunsmoke*. I was fascinated with the Old West and how the cowboys used horses to travel across the country instead of cars. I loved riding and longed to experience the adventure of trail riding. Somehow I managed to figure out that Big Rock Ranch in Topanga Canyon was just a few canyons away from Malibu Canyon, where my father lived. I came up with a fantasy plan. I asked my father if he could pick me up from camp on horseback! Foaming with excitement, I managed to persuade my father to take a day off work. I said, 'Dad, you could ride Duchess, and lead Scooter Pie? You could travel by trails between the canyons. You could arrive at three, going-home time, and we could ride back together.' Unbelievably, he said yes. I was so excited that day I could barely contain myself. I told everybody who would listen that my dad was picking me up by horseback. The camp owners didn't believe me. One called me a liar to my face. 'You'll see,' I said. 'I am not a liar.'

At the appointed time all the buses gathered to take the remaining campers home for the rest of the summer. I waited. An hour went by. And then like a mirage he appeared, riding Duchess, his golden Arabian, and leading Scooter Pie, my big bay quarter horse. I started to cry. I was so happy. I mounted Scooter Pie and we rode off into the orangey glow of the California afternoon, leaving behind the sour owners and their dusty summer camp. Five hours later we arrived home, saddle-sore but elated. For I knew then, without a doubt, that my father, in his own way, loved me.

BOMB

Often, when you receive really shocking news, when you first hear, let's say, of the death of a friend or a public figure, you remember the *exact* time and place where you were when you heard it. Sometimes, though, the shock of what you are being told is so strong your mind goes blank. The world begins to spin. As a means of self-preservation, you shut off and shut down any recollection of the moment. This is what happens to me when my mom dropped a nuclear bomb on my world.

His name was Marvin. He was the man with the beard whom I discovered on her couch when I walked into the living room that night in the pink mansion. I can remember nothing about where she told me the news or how, but the news was this: she and Marvin were in love. We, as in she and I, were moving to Chicago to live with this bearded Marvin professor guy.

First of all, I didn't even really know Marvin. I had only met him a handful of times, if that. He had a beard. I didn't trust men with beards. It made me think they were hiding something. He was a divorced dad with two little daughters, Nadia and Leah. He was a professor at the University of Chicago. I did not want to leave LA or my dad. I was feeling very loyal to him after he had picked me up from camp on horseback. I did not want to go and live in Chicago, as there was no ocean or beach. Worse, it was supposedly bone-breakingly cold in the winter.

I wanted my mother to be happy, but I was *furious* that she hadn't taken into consideration *my* feelings. In fact she hadn't even consulted me at all. This new life-changing plan was presented to me as a fait accompli. I begged to stay in LA with my dad. I came up with a long list of reasons why I should. All of them sat at the bottom of the vast pool of good reasons not to leave LA gathering dust.

With them, some of my sunny optimism also eroded – the precious childhood protection shield that had sealed me off from the harsh realities of life. My bubble had been compromised and, as innocence leaked out, melancholy seeped in. The memories of the last months I spent in LA were vague. It was almost as if I was going through the motions of life, underwater and on tranquillisers. The thought of saying goodbye to everyone and everything I knew was overwhelming. The thought of moving to a new city, starting a new school and living in a new house was also overwhelming. (Actually, I was told the 'new' house was an *old* house, built in 1893. Nothing in LA was that old, except the historical Spanish missions.) I was overwhelmed by anxiety.

One day before I left LA, I was playing outside the log cabin my mother and I now lived in in Mar Vista. I remember being in my own world and looking at the sidewalk in minute detail. I tried to imprint every unique characteristic of sidewalk on my mind so I would not forget any of it. I was worried that Chicago sidewalks might corrupt my memory. I looked closely at the flecks of glass embedded in the grey cement, glinting and glittering as I squinted. 'This must be the most beautiful cement anywhere,' I thought. 'I love you, LA,' I said, out loud. Just then I heard a voice.

'Are you talking to the sidewalk, little girl?'

I looked up and there, standing above me, was a teenage boy. He was wearing a white T-shirt and jeans, and clutching a bag in one hand and a skateboard in the other. He had long straight brown hair. His eyes were big and dark. 'Do you wanna buy some pot?' he asked.

Oh my *God,* he's a pusher! My mom warned me about drug pushers. And scary men in cars that offered candy to little girls. I turned and fled. Running down the street as fast as I could back to the safety of the log cabin. I locked the door, and hid. As I hid behind the door of my bedroom and tried to calm my pounding heart, I would never have imagined that, in just a few short years, my own experimentation with drugs would begin.

CHICAGO (NOT) MY KINDA TOWN

The sky was grey and the air smelled like farts.

'Sulphur,' Marvin told me. It was the faint smell of the steel mills, wafting its windy way down from South Chicago and Gary, Indiana. The lake was huge and dark. It was so big I could not see the end of it. It was unappealing. There were shoals of dead fish floating on top.

'Alewives,' Marvin called them.

'Ugh,' I said.

LA had seemed alluring and glamorous to me. The weather was always perfect and the air, even if it was smoggy, smelled of gardenias and jasmine, patchouli and coconut. People on the streets were happy and LA life had an optimistic bounce. My passion for LA and the heartbreak I felt at leaving it would inspire me, years later, to write the Fall song 'LA' and the Adult Net song 'Waking Up in the Sun'. They were love songs to a city, my real home, and the loss of my childhood innocence.

Chicago, on the other hand, was another story altogether. The Midwest was so buttoned up and conservative. Everyone seemed to look and dress the same. Trench coats, accessorised with briefcases. A visual palate of varying shades of beige. I was not about to move to this city without a fight, so I concocted a plan. A master-plan. I was going to make my mom and Marvin pay for their decision to make me move to Chicago. They would be well and truly sorry for ruining my life. I decided to be as unpleasant and withdrawn as I possibly could. I tried very hard to always communicate only monosyllabically. I suspected I could crack my mom and eventually get my way, but Marvin was another story.

He was an unknown quantity. My mom got very little attention from me; Marvin got virtually none. But when I paid him attention, I was openly hostile. I would look him dead in the eye and tell him, 'I hate you.'

My new home was on South Ellis Avenue, a classic three-storey stone house in the Kenwood/Hyde Park area of Chicago's South Side. Hyde Park had once been Chicago's wealthiest area, containing some of the greatest, most grand and gracious houses of all time, including a few by Frank Lloyd Wright. These properties were much different to the fake Tudor, adobe faux-Mexican or pretend Georgian mansions in Beverly Hills. Our new house was big and tall and stood in a row of three houses all looking very similar, as they were built by the same architect, for a rich family. All the residences retained period features, and when you entered them it felt like you were stepping back in time.

The house was massive. You walked up stone steps and through cement pillars to the huge wooden door, and rapped the solid brass knocker, in the shape of a hand holding a golden ball. The interior of the house was all dark oak wood, carved and sculpted at every turn. The dining room was wood-panelled and fitted with bevelled glass and mirrors. All the sinks were hand-painted with ornate decorations, like fine Wedgwood porcelain. The kitchen was huge and had a butler's pantry. In the summer we would sometimes eat on the screened porch at the back, overlooking the garden. There were two staircases leading upstairs – a sweeping main one at the front of the house, and a second, simpler staircase at the back for the servants. Two more floors rose above this one, and a basement lay below. There were six bedrooms and multiple bathrooms. All the bathtubs had feet, with claws.

The moment I entered Marvin's house I felt distinctly uneasy. It was old and there was a creepy atmosphere. Even in the summer, there were spots in the bedrooms, staircases and especially the downstairs bathroom that were inexplicably freezing all the time.

One night, shortly after I arrived, I was awakened by a loud rapping on the wall above my head. I was petrified. This continued on and off throughout the time we lived there. On another occasion, a schoolfriend swore he saw a woman dressed in Victorian clothes enter the downstairs bathroom. There was no one else in the house at that time. The most terrifying event occurred on the main stair-case between the second and third floors. In broad daylight, I was climbing the stairs when a huge, spinning orb of blue-white light emerged from the window above my head and shot past me. I was so scared I stopped going to the third floor altogether. At the time my mother would not believe the house was haunted, and chalked my visions up to the upheaval of moving and her divorce from my father. But she believes me now.

On the morning of my first day at the Laboratory School, I thought I would either throw up or have diarrhoea I was so nerv-ous. I sat in the kitchen of Marvin's house, now ours, trying to eat a bowl of Rice Krispies and drink a glass of orange juice. I watched as Marvin sat opposite me and tucked into a modest-sized cof-fee cake and dipped juicy strawberries into sour cream and then raw sugar. I don't remember my mother eating. This is probably because she didn't. If she did it would have been only a small pot of zero-calorie natural yogurt and a cup of coffee with Cremora.

The Laboratory School is part of the University of Chicago, with classes from nursery school through to twelfth grade. It's con-sidered one of the best preparatory schools in the country, and is highly academic, rigorous and intellectual. Westland was all about art, music, acting and writing. I was ill-prepared for the Lab School. I didn't even know basic things like my multiplication tables. I didn't 'get' math at all, and hated and feared it as a subject. I had never had a science lesson in my entire life, unless you call nature hiking 'science'.

My self-confidence took a huge knock that September. I was low, anxious and uprooted, and now I was dumb to boot. I was also the new kid, the oddball Californian girl who lived with her unwed mother and a bearded college-professor lover. I was coming into this school at the bottom of the pecking order. Now it would be time to see what I was made of.

Somewhere, at the edge of my conscious mind, I realised this was an opportunity for me to reinvent myself. I *had* to do it, to adapt to my new circumstances. The Laboratory School felt like one giant experiment. I was not one of the control subjects, I was a variable. How this new chapter in my life would turn out would be a direct result of the choices I made. I realised that, although seemingly everything I knew and loved from my old life had been taken from me, I still had one thing. Me. And the power to choose who I would become. I was nine years old. I remember my mother, looking directly into my eyes and telling me, 'You can be anything you want in life. You can do anything you want to in life, nothing is impossible.'

TAPESTRY, BOYS AND DRUGS

During the first year my mother and I lived in Chicago, I was terribly homesick for LA. I missed everything and everyone, especially the weather. I'm sure now I was suffering with depression, even at that young age. I didn't know how to alleviate the sadness I felt, or even express it.

After school one day, I found myself in the shopping precinct in Hyde Park. I meandered through the shops and ended up in the record store. As I pawed through the record bins, I came across the album *Tapestry*, by Carole King. While reading the list of song titles on the back of the LP, a miraculous thing happened. I remembered every song almost word for word and every single melody. In that moment of recollection, the memories of the songs were vivid and transported me back to the time when I first heard them. I was back home in LA again, happy and carefree. The memory of the music was a powerful tool. It actually shifted my reality and in doing so relieved the deep sadness I'd been feeling since I moved to Chicago. I bought *Tapestry* with some pocket money my mother had given me for emergencies. I took it home to the living room on South Ellis Avenue and proceeded to listen to it over and over again.

The meaning of each song seemed to relate to my new life and my emotional situation. I felt as if every word had been written for me. I had found an escape hatch. The next album I bought was *Pearl*, by Janis Joplin. I identified with the pain and passion in the delivery of Janis's vocals. I could feel the misery of her whole life and the despair she felt coming through the songs themselves. Then I moved on to the Carpenters. I marvelled at the crystalline clarity of Karen's voice and the clean, unfussy hooks of the melodies. Their tunes were infectious and I could not get them out of my head. Then I saw them on TV and I was stunned to see that it was Karen who played the drums.

I spent every afternoon after school in those early years in Chicago listening to those records and being carried to a better-feeling place. Music was saving me, healing me, giving me something to look forward to. My mother and Marvin also had their own record collection. Thank God they had pretty good taste. They had everything by the Beatles, including *Rubber Soul*, *The White Album* and *Abbey Road*. I never thought, in my wildest dreams, that in less than twelve years I would actually be recording my own records in the legendary Abbey Road Studios. My mom particularly loved the California sound of the Mamas and the Papas, Crosby, Stills & Nash, the Beach Boys and Creedence Clearwater Revival. Marvin had a slightly more 'intellectual' taste in music, favouring artists like Leonard Cohen, Dory Previn and an odd mishmash of musical soundtracks like *Fiddler on the Roof* or *Cabaret*.

Marvin also had an extensive collection of classical music. In fact that's pretty much all he really ever listened to. Every single morning the radio in our kitchen would be turned to WFMT, the classical radio station. The music of Beethoven and Bach particularly resonated with me. The rock stars of the classical world. I systematically devoured them all. I listened to our family record collection over and over again until I had completely digested each recording.

Oddly, this is a peculiar pattern I still have to this day. When I love a song or an album, it's all I want to listen to. I actually *crave* listening to it. I also do the same thing with food. Often I have the exact same meal for months until I'm sick of it and the thought of it makes me gag.

By the time I was thirteen and got to eighth grade, I began to push the boundaries of authority, both at home and at school. Having always been something of a tomboy, I found it easier and infinitely more preferable to hang out with the boys. The boys were uncomplicated and fun; they didn't play games or exclude you like the girls did. And, besides, the boys had way better taste in music than the girls. They talked about music every day, all day, and I was pulled into their conversations, as it was my passion too.

Andy, Roger, Steve, Peter and Chris were the boys I hung out with. Most of them had older teenage brothers who turned them on to all kinds of bands, new and old. For these boys, it wasn't just about the catchiness of a song, it was about the quality of the musicianship. They loved Led Zeppelin, Jeff Beck, Jimi Hendrix and Eric Clapton. It wasn't long before I was included in their gang and invited to spend afternoons at their houses after school, listening to music with them. The boys seemed to relish turning me on to great bands and virtuoso players. They also educated me on something else too.

Drugs.

Reefers, doobies, jays and weed, grass, bud, herb, bong hits, water pipes, apple pipes and roaches. In the words of Jimi Hendrix, 'Are you experienced?' Yes, I was becoming just that. And fast.

I remember sitting in the bedroom of Andy's house after school. His family's modest middle-class town house was perfectly proportioned and compartmentalised. The walls of his boxy, hormone-soaked bedroom were adorned with posters of *Star Trek*, Zeppelin and Hendrix – the three 'Jims', Kirk, Page and Hendrix.

We turned on, tuned in, and zoned out.

Pot in those days was very different. There was none of the hydroponic scary paranoid weed around. The weed was gentler, and you could gauge your high from where the grass originated. Maui Wowee, Kona gold, Thai stick, Acapulco gold, or homegrown were weed types we regularly consumed.

First, we'd take a few tokes of the reefer to get us prepared, and then don our headphones. We both plugged into the turntable/stereo and cranked up the volume. Next, we'd kick back, close our eyes and within moments we were in another dimension. The pot made the music come alive for me in a different way. The sound became colour. Visualisations of abstract particles dancing on vibrational frequencies created patterns resulting in glorious spacescapes in my mind. I felt I understood the music from the interior of its inspirational seed – an understanding so pure it seemed to resonate from the spark of creation itself, emanating from the divine nugget within the heart of the creator.

SHRINK

After my pot-smoking musical afternoons with the boys, I'd walk the nine or so blocks back to our house in a dreamlike daze. Ravenous with the munchies, I'd sit down in front of the TV and catch the last of the afternoon movies. I loved all the Elvis movies like *Viva Las Vegas*, *Spinout* and *Jailhouse Rock* or old Gidget movies, which reminded me of home. They were set on the beaches of Southern California and celebrated surf culture. These movie genres appealed to me because they were perforated with great pop songs and were highly stylised. The groovy clothes and poppy colours lifted my spirits. The movies themselves were 'feel good' and helped me to block out the dispiriting melancholia of Chicago. As I sat in front of the TV, I'd chow down on a huge bowl of Breyers vanilla-bean ice cream covered in Nestlé's Quik chocolate powder.

When I finished that, I might make myself a toasted cheese sandwich. For sure, I wasn't counting the calories. Beside being stoned and having the munchies, I was also starting to use food to comfort myself, to fill the deep hole of sadness, the nagging source of angst that had been growing steadily inside of me since we moved. Inevitably I began to pile on the pounds.

At about 7 p.m. both my mother and Marvin would return home from work; Marvin from teaching his classes at the University of Chicago, and my mother from her new high-powered job as the Commissioner of the Film Office for the state of Illinois. I knew they were so absorbed in their lives they'd probably never even notice I'd come home stoned. As I began to settle into school and teenage life, our family life began to work itself out too. Of course, I was still angry about moving to Chicago, but I was slowly taking my foot off the nasty pedal of punishment I had directed at my mom and Marvin. Things were less barbed, but they were still far from idyllic.

Marvin's two daughters, Nadia and Leah, spent time with us periodically. They bounced between their mother's house in Boston and ours. Nadia, four years younger than me, was a sweet, gentle, intellectual girl who was easy to be around. Leah, eight years younger than me, was a spitfire. She and I rankled each other. Even though she was much younger, she was tough and stubborn. The way our family dynamic worked was that Nadia and Leah stuck together and formed a team. My mother and I took our own side. Marvin, for all intents and purposes, was the peacekeeper stuck in the middle. It was always them against us, the Zonis against the Salengers. Our family was a mini-war zone. If I am honest I was a manipulator and a stirrer.

At some point Mom and Marvin realised we needed the outside help of an objective observer. They could see I was angry and struggling and came to the conclusion that we should all go to family therapy. This decision whipped up my anger even more. Admitting there was a problem made me feel weak, and sharing it with a stranger made me feel vulnerable.

Our family therapy sessions took place in the office of a shrink with the hilarious name of Royal Butler. Over the years I've seen many, many different shrinks and tried a smorgasbord of therapy. Some have been successful while others were a complete waste of time. Royal Butler was shrink #1. He was a tall, slim man who wore a cowboy hat – I know this because he placed it on the side table next to his chair – cowboy boots and a fancy silver and turquoise stone belt. This was most disconcerting as his choice in accessories was distinctly similar to that of my biological father. As we entered his medium-sized bland office, he rose and greeted us, extending his hand to shake Marvin's. I looked at the floor and did not meet his or anyone else's gaze. After beckoning us to sit on the proverbial couch, Royal Butler took his place in his leather shrink chair, lounging back pompously. He sat relaxed, with his rangy legs outstretched, and his ankles crossed, showing off those fine, hand-tooled leather cowboy boots. I remember trying not to speak. 'Why should I talk?' I thought to myself.

'Fuck all of you,' I said out loud. 'I don't want to be here.' I seethed through gritted teeth. When forced to talk, it was to proclaim how much I hated *everyone*. My mother and Marvin took the sessions seriously. God bless them, they really wanted to make some constructive changes in our family. Unfortunately, with such a sullen, foot-dragging teenager determined to scupper any advancement, no progress was ever to be made.

After two or three sessions, mercifully, they gave up. To everyone's relief we never went back. It appeared I'd won.

Eventually, my mother and Marvin decided to formally marry. This was good news to me. I was ashamed that they were 'shacked up', unmarried. Their status became a talking point for kids at Lab School, who quizzed me and teased me on their then unconventional relationship. I just wanted to be normal. Their unwed status had made me feel defensive because I was put in a position of having to justify their choice. By now, though I was loath to admit it, Marvin was slowly growing on me. He was patient and, even in the face of my hate campaign against him, only ever showed me love. He was the opposite of my biological father, whose erratic rage and irrational behaviour had made me frightened of fathers and gun-shy of grown men in general.

I spent every school term in Chicago. But in the summer and during the Christmas holidays, I would fly back to LA, ensconcing myself at my dad and Maggie's house and spending time with my half-siblings, Karina and Jon. I looked forward to those vacations with every fibre in my body. I lived for them. They were the daydreams that got me through the drudgery of the school year. Even so, every time my mom and Marvin drove me to O'Hare airport and walked me to the jetway, I cried. I was torn apart; a casualty of love and divorce.

THE GRASS IS ALWAYS GREENER

As per my parents' custody agreement, I spent the summer between my sixth and seventh grades in LA. I was twelve, going on thirteen. By now, my father, Maggie and the kids had moved from Malibu Canyon to a new house in Rustic Canyon, a tiny, wealthy neighbourhood with some of the most appealing and interesting houses in LA.

Each house is unique; some of them architectural benchmarks. My favourites were the California canyon dream homes – homes that seamlessly integrated with the natural environment in which they were built. For instance, the architects would build a house around pre-existing trees so that the trees actually grew through the house. Or use already-standing boulder formations to create the walls within the structure, blurring the boundaries between the outside and inside. These houses were creative, modern approaches to architecture, dramatic and organic in their uses of space, light, glass and wood.

Rustic Canyon felt like the pearl in an oyster, tucked into a pocket of hills between Malibu Beach and Santa Monica Beach (technically, it's on the outer edges of Pacific Palisades). The residents of Rustic Canyon formed a proper community. Everyone knew each other and looked out for one another, no matter what the eccentricities of the residents were. It was a community of powerful creatives. Our neighbours included legendary songwriters, Oscar-winning actors, TV stars both old and new, record company moguls, screenwriters and authors, entrepreneurs and top showbiz lawyers.

Our new house was gorgeous, and my father had spent a lot of money remodelling it. The house sat at the end of a private road.

In fact, the whole of Rustic Canyon was *private*. We lived in the centre of a cul-de-sac, with high redwood fences surrounding our property. We had a pool shaped like a keyhole, complete with pool house. The interior of the main house was stuffed with my father's collection of eccentricities: the fifty or so antique clocks, constantly ticking, binging and bonging away at all hours of the day and night, recreating that palpable tension. One of my father's most recent purchases was a bizarre, antique music-box console, housed in a Victorian wooden cabinet that took up the entire side of a wall. This music box had metal discs with perforations in them. He would load these giant discs, which were each as big as a small table, into the console. Then the music box would play strange, mechanical, creepy calliope music, bringing the tinny, haunting sounds of another era into a new century. Around the same time, he also bought a player piano. Once turned on and loaded up, this piano would play songs all on its own. The keys of the piano would actually be depressed and move of their own accord as if a ghost were sitting there playing the songs. Of course, he still had all of his banjos and guitars, which were mounted and hung on the walls. He kept his gun collection and poison blow darts in a special place in his and Maggie's walk-in closet, located in their bedroom.

My father then started a new collection. He had begun amassing an assortment of pinball machines. He also bought a brand-new Pong console table, which was one of the earliest and most iconic video games. It was arcade quality. This new collection made me a very popular girl in the neighbourhood. Once the kids learned about it, everyone wanted to hang out at my house. I made a lot of friends and, consequently, had an awesome summer.

Most of the house was on one level, but my father's office was accessed by a wrought-iron spiral staircase that led down to his private domain. The office also had its own private entrance at the front, and contained the pipe collection and the tobacco pouch my father said was fashioned from a woman's breast. He told us so many stories we didn't know what was real and what wasn't. His office, also home to the dreaded bull's dick cane, was painted grey and wood-panelled. There was a fireplace with a mantel above and book shelves to either side. Hidden inside one of the shelves was a magic button. When you pressed the button, the book shelf would swing open, revealing a secret room. The secret room was like a dirt cave: no floor, no walls, just a subterranean space backing into the hill at the rear of our property. God knows what my father did in that room. Mostly I think he used it as a wine cellar for the rare wines he was now consuming with great gusto.

Again, I made friends with the neighbourhood boys, my pin-ball pals. Because we were all still too young to drive, and it was California, we used skateboards to get around. I skateboarded everywhere and learned all kinds of tricks. The ultimate fun day was when my skater friends would locate a vacant house for sale, with an empty pool. Skater community kids from all over the area would congregate at the uninhabited house and skate the drained pool. I was always way too chicken, but I loved to watch the long-haired boys in their Hang Ten T-shirts skate the shit out of those pools.

As the end of the summer approached, I felt a familiar knot of anxiety growing in my stomach. The thought of going back to Chicago and the Lab School and facing yet another year of family tensions was abhorrent. I came up with a new scheme for staying in LA. I sat down with my father and Maggie and told them I wasn't happy in Chicago. I asked them if I could live with them and go to school in LA. I must have painted a horrible picture of my life in Chicago. Whatever I told them, I convinced them to let me stay. I also knowingly and manipulatively pitted my father against my mother and Marvin. Here was a way for my father to win.

The pain I inflicted on my mother came back at me like a karmic boomerang to pierce *my heart*, with a guilty blade of *my own making*. I understood this only years later, when my mother and I had grown close again. That was after the *real* troubles with my father had begun.

TWILIGHT ZONE AND HALTER TOPS

We spent a lot of time with a family called the Flickers. The dad, who was (weirdly) also named Marvin and had a beard like my stepfather, was a shrink too. He was big and gentle, soft-spoken and kind. He carried a man bag. His wife, Carole-Anne, was a psychotherapist. The Flickers had three daughters: Briar, Amy and Laura. Amy Flicker became my best girlfriend. The Flicker household became my safe haven. I loved spending time at their house in the Santa Monica Canyon. It was an inviting Spanish-style house – big and rambling with a gorgeous pool in the backyard. It was an eye-opener for me to spend time with a family that was not dysfunctional: eccentric, yes; chock full of characters, yes – but generally mentally healthy and, above all, loving. Amy and I got along famously. I had many, many sleepovers at the Flickers' house. One of my favourite activities was to binge-watch back-to-back episodes of *The Twilight Zone* TV series. Little did I know how watching that show would inspire me in the future.

After I joined The Fall, I found out that Mark E. Smith was also inspired by *The Twilight Zone*. I suggested to Mark that we use the image of the spinning vortex from the show as the backdrop for our stage show. We recorded music from the opening segment of the show, where Rod Serling speaks and the do-de-do-do music starts, as our stage intro tape. The spinning vortex image would become an iconic symbol forever associated with The Fall.

Amy's mom, Carole-Anne, would fry up American sausages for us to snack on. Then, in the afternoon, after *The Twilight Zone* was over and the sun began to sink towards the sea, we'd ride our bikes to the Santa Monica Mall and buy material to make sexy halter tops.

While we were there, we loved to scour the record store. We bought records by Elton John, Steely Dan, the Steve Miller Band, Cat Stevens, and Abba. Late at night, after Amy's parents would turn in, we would skinny-dip in their pool under the stars.

Amy's older teenage sister, Briar, was super-cool. She turned us on to great music. Her taste in music was a little more rebellious and dangerous. Pretty soon I was into the Rolling Stones and before long I became completely *obsessed* by David Bowie.

BARBIE CLEANED UP MY BARF

The Crossroads School was a Hollywood microcosm. Exactly like the Westland School, the children at Crossroads were the progeny of the showbiz elite. Their parents were 'A-list' actors and directors, producers and moguls, rock stars, comedians, lawyers and, of course, shrinks. At one end of the spectrum, we had the child actors, pop stars, and mini-virtuoso musicians who had been especially head-hunted for the school. These were talented kids, there on their own merit and probably on some kind of scholarship. At the other end of the spectrum we had the rich, spoiled, fuck-up kids that wouldn't or couldn't fit into the LA school system: the ones who had everything handed to them on a plate, including brand-new BMWs and Porsches for their sixteenth birthdays complete with customised licence plates. Finally, in the middle, and making up the majority of the school, were kids like me: slightly off-beat and creative, from affluent West LA families.

The school was located in the industrial part of Santa Monica, a strange no man's land surrounded by Mexican restaurants. I made friends easily; with Amy Flicker to show me around and introduce me to her friends, the transition was seamless. LA was and always has been a town about the body beautiful, with major emphasis put on one's physical appearance. At this point I was thirteen years old, almost fourteen, and my body was changing. I was becoming a woman, and this made me awkward and insecure. I felt fat all of the time. All my friends were skinny and I was feeling the pressure.

My father also began to add to this pressure. He informed me that I might actually be beautiful one day, *if* I lost weight. He decided to reward me $5 for every pound I lost, and then when I had lost ten he would buy me a whole new wardrobe. I began to experiment with dieting. My bulimia began to resurface. I hated looking at my body. I struggled with the binge-and-purge syndrome. I felt unattractive and worried. I feared I would never have a boyfriend and that I would turn out ugly. Even though I didn't really believe in God as such, I still prayed that I would be attractive and skinny when I grew up and have big tits. A tall, slim-hipped woman with large breasts – that was my ideal of a woman's body. It came directly from Barbie. When I was a teenager, I wished I would grow up to have the body of Barbie.

I had many different Barbie dolls and used them as a means to experiment. I cut off their hair, made them clothes and scribbled pubic hair and nipples on to their anatomically incorrect bodies. My cousin Lisa and I took our Barbie and Ken playtime seriously. We acted out all manner of scenarios. We made Barbie go on dates, have sex and get into fights. We threw them in the pool, forcing them to 'go swimming naked' and maimed them by running them over with their own dune buggy or camper van or, as Lisa and I used to call it, their 'fuck truck'.

Our Barbies had differing personalities that changed daily depending on our moods. Sometimes they were hot and sexy but prudish: the 'prick-tease Barbie'. At others they were complete sluts. Some of our more epic Barbie play sessions would last a whole weekend, interrupted only by sleep. We constantly humiliated Ken in front of Barbie by forcing him to show his 'mangina'. We were sure Barbie preferred the rough and rugged GI Joe to the witless, emasculated Ken. Imagine my shock at finding out that one of my new school friends at Crossroads was . . . the daughter of Barbie. Barbara – 'Barbie' – was her mother and . . . Ken was her uncle. She was the niece of Ken. What's more, her grandparents owned the Mattel toy company and were rumoured to own the circus too.

My friend, whom I will call Susan, out of respect to her privacy, was a real 'tom girl'. She loved surfing and skiing and wore checked shirts or Lacoste polo shirts over tight but flared Sassoon jeans, which hid her perfect body. She had definitely inherited her mother's genes. Sometimes Barbara came to school, to pick up Susan and her younger brother. All the kids would try not to stare. It was hard, though – I mean, it was freakin' Barbie! Barbara had red hair just like the original Barbie and was *very* young for a mom. She was stunning and fun-loving. Effortlessly glamorous, she drove several fancy cars and I particularly remember a saucy convertible. The story going around was that Susan's grandparents had decided to create dolls in the likeness of *both* of their beloved children, Barbie and Ken. To say I was a little bit weirded out – that Ken was actually Barbie's brother – would be an understatement. Especially as we had made them do unmentionable things together.

In another stranger-than-fiction twist of fate, Ken and his real wife and kids bought and moved into the house across the street from my father's and Maggie's, in Rustic Canyon. I didn't realise this was *the* Ken until Susan told me her uncle moved to our street.

On Halloween, Barbie threw a lavish party at her massive gated mansion in Bel Air. She suggested that Susan invite a few friends over to go trick-or-treating. I was thrilled to be spending the night at Susan's. The thought of actually staying in Barbie's house for real – was surreal. A group of kids from Crossroads School all met up at Susan's, and hit the neighbourhood hard, armed with silk pillow cases for swag bags to collect our Halloween treats, plus fresh eggs, toilet-paper rolls and cans of shaving foam. All of this booty was given to us by the coolest mom in the world, Barbie. That night I ate my body weight in chocolate.

My father had a rule that I could eat as much Halloween candy as I wanted within the first twenty-four hours. After that I had to *hand over the rest* so he could take it to the children at the hospital, who were too sick to trick-or-treat. Although I realised that my father's rule was seemingly implemented with good intentions, there was also something about it that triggered feelings in me of deprivation and of being controlled – volatile psychological issues.

I gorged myself on my favourite jumbo-sized candy bars as we climbed the big sweeping streets and gentle hills of Bel Air. After a brilliant night of trick-or-treating, we made it back to Susan's and slipped behind the massive gates that protected her house. Barbie's party was still going strong. I didn't engage with any of the guests but, when I saw the food Barbie had put out, I decided to tuck into a deli platter. I had only eaten candy the whole night. Maybe I should put some healthy food in? I reasoned. I had a pastrami on rye with a dill pickle. We said goodnight to Barbie and went upstairs to sleep. I was excited to sleep with Susan in her waterbed. I had never slept in one before. It was comfortable and warm and very, very soothing. In no time I was asleep.

A few hours later I woke up. I was boiling hot and could feel vomit rising in my throat.

I struggled to get up. For a few seconds I was disoriented and forgot where I was. 'Oh shit, I'm at Susan's and I'm gonna barf.' I tried to push myself up from the undulating mattress and make a run for the bathroom. Where was the bathroom anyway? I couldn't remember, there were so many rooms in this house. I wondered if I was seasick. Then the memories came flooding back: Mars bars, Marathon bars, KitKats, Reese's Peanut Butter Cups and Milky Ways and finally the *healthy*, the pastrami sandwich and dill pickle.

A hideous inventory of what I had consumed the night before came roiling, wrecking-ball-style, into my mind. Unable to rise from the bed I turned sideways and attempted to vomit over the bed frame on to the floor. Unfortunately, I only partially succeeded. The majority of my vomit ended up between the waterbed mattress and the frame. Down the crack, probably pooling at the bottom of the bed where it's nearly impossible to clean without draining the bed. Dark, sticky, chocolate vomit that looked like mud and smelled like pastrami.

'*Ughhhhhh*,' Susan yelled. 'Did you barf?'

'Susan, I'm so sorry,' I managed to say, in between gags.

'I'm going to sleep downstairs,' Susan announced.

I was left alone to sleep with the disgorged contents of my own stomach. In the morning I felt truly sick. First of all I still felt the after-effects of barfing. Mostly, though, I was dreading having to fess up to Barbie. I had *disgraced* myself at Barbie's house. My feelings crept up the notches of the emotional ladder, passed embarrassment and inched dangerously close to mortification.

Barbie entered the bedroom, with Susan behind her.

'Laura threw up in the bed last night,' Susan reported. 'I had to sleep on the sofa,' she continued.

I started to stammer. I hung my head. 'I'm so sorry, Barbara. I feel terrible. I'll clean it up.'

'Don't worry, the maid will clean it,' Susan said, matter-of-factly.

'But, Susan,' her mother reminded her, 'today is the maid's day off.'

Barbie looked at me, with her limpid empathetic eyes. 'Please don't worry, Laura,' she said. 'I'll clean it up.'

'You'll clean it up?' I stammered.

'Sure,' she sweetly replied. 'I don't mind. In fact, once, when Susan was really sick, she threw up so hard I had to clean her vomit off the ceiling!'

Mercifully for me, Barbie had a sense of humour and much kindness.

My dad came to collect me in his car. I couldn't tell him what I had done. I was too shame-filled. I couldn't admit to him that, because of his rule, and the deep psychological buttons it pushed in me, I had eaten myself ill, and that Barbie had cleaned up my barf. As I got into my dad's car, I willingly handed him the bag of leftover candy, for the sick children at the hospital.

That year, he didn't even need to ask me for it.

BACKWARDS AND FORWARDS

After finishing the seventh school year at Crossroads, it was back to Chicago to spend the long hot summer with my mother and Marvin. Chicago was sweltering and very humid. The Midwest is plagued with thunderstorms so violent they can knock out your electricity. Tornadoes are not uncommon either. Luckily, our house was equipped with a lightning rod, had a basement for shelter, and my mother was an excellent food shopper, buying in bulk, just in case. She also had a pharmaceutical cabinet that could rival any drugstore. We were in good shape, come what may, acts-of-God-wise.

Hyde Park was an upper-middle-class oasis that was largely surrounded by the ghetto. Both the City of Chicago Police and the University of Chicago Police patrolled the streets of our residential community. As a precautionary measure, I had to wear a rape whistle on a chain around my neck whenever I left the house. So did my two stepsisters, Nadia and Leah. If someone *were* to attack us, we were told to blow the whistle hard. My mother drummed into me the importance of being street smart. I was taught not to look people directly in the eye when passing them on the street. The sound of sporadic gunfire in the distance was common. As shots rang out, our family would 'hit the deck', dropping to the floor until the gunfire finished. New Year's Eve was particularly hairy. There were so many guns being shot off at midnight that it was like being in the middle of a Western.

My mother was consumed by her job. She was responsible for making Illinois a major film-production centre, and, in years to come, attracted *The Blues Brothers*, *Ordinary People*, *Risky Business*, *A Wedding* and many others to the area. Sometime she'd take me with her to the location where the movies were being shot. I got to meet everybody and watched how movies got made.

My mother and Marvin had dispensed with traditional babysitters. Instead, we had an ever-changing cast of Marvin's students who, for extra pocket money, helped Mom and Marvin with anything they needed, including keeping an eye on me, Nadia and Leah. Marvin's students loved and even worshipped him. He was one of the most popular and respected professors at the university.

We also had a housekeeper, Mildred. She was an elderly black woman from Belize. I adored Mildred. She became my confidante, the keeper of all my secrets. She even answered the phone by saying, 'Miss Laura's residence', in her lilting Belizean Creole accent.

For the first few weeks of the summer, my mother had enrolled me on the Art Institute of Chicago summer programme. I actually looked forward to going, and once there I learned how to make an animated film. The rest of the summer was spent lazing around. I'd climb on to the roof by slipping out of the window of the third floor and slather myself with Bain de Soleil tanning oil, baking my skin in the morning sun while listening to Fleetwood Mac or Pink Floyd. Then in the afternoon I'd wander down to the lakefront and hang out with some of the boys I'd gone to school with at Lab the year before. We'd smoke pot, naturally.

As the summer ended, my father informed my mother, Marvin and me that, for reasons never made clear, he felt it best that I spend the coming school year in Chicago.

So it was back to the Laboratory School, once again. But this time it was to the eighth grade, the 'middle school'. We had a bit more freedom and I actually enjoyed it. I got involved in the school theatre and played coronet in the brass band, and sang in the choir. I also took operatic vocal training.

I made a new best friend, this time a girl, Gabrielle Frahm. We became inseparable. Gabrielle was one of the prettiest girls in school. Blonde, freckled and whip-thin, she excelled in ballet and gymnastics. She loved fashion and everything European. Her parents had fabulous taste in absolutely everything. Her mother's wardrobe was to die for. We used to go into her closet to worship at the altar of Nancy's clothes. These included iconic pieces by Yves Saint Laurent, Kenzo and Chloé.

Gabrielle was rebellious, like me. We got into all kinds of trouble. Having a friend like Gabrielle made eighth grade fun. We amused ourselves by making a series of elaborate and creative prank phone calls after school. A couple of times, we even hitchhiked to and from school for thrills. But we were very choosy about whose car we got into. My mother's street-smart lessons were still in the forefront of my mind, and I still wore the rape whistle around my neck, as a reminder of what could happen. Unbelievably I was actually starting to fit in.

THE KING IS DEAD

16 August 1977 is indelibly stamped on my memory. It's the day that Elvis Aaron Presley died. I was sitting on the lanai of my uncle Gary's house in Maui with my cousins, Samantha, Matt and Mikey, and my half-brother and sister, Jon and Karina. We were watching TV when the news broke. It was a big deal. Hawaii loved Elvis. The world loved Elvis. I loved Elvis. I had never known the world without Elvis.

It's obvious to me now that my father and Maggie were having marital problems. They had arranged a holiday for just the two of them during the month of August and had shipped me and Jon and Karina to stay with my uncle and Aunt Sydney in Maui. This was fantastic, as I got to spend time with Uncle Gary, whom I adored, and I got to hang out with my cousin Samantha, a few years younger than me. Best of all, we were in Hawaii. Elvis was dead but I was reborn.

Without my parents around to nag me I stepped up to the plate, as the oldest cousin, to take some responsibility for the others, as well as for myself. The first thing I did was put myself back on a diet. I was in a bikini every day and wanted to feel good about it.

Since I had spent eighth grade in Chicago, my dad agreed to let me stay in LA for ninth grade. I had decided, yet again, to change schools. I wanted to try something new. I had never attended a public school before, and lots of the kids I hung out with from Rustic Canyon raved about the local public school, Paul Revere Junior High. I was so happy to be back in LA. I loved the lifestyle and felt so free, but I wasn't so happy to be back in the presence of my father. Over the years, his behaviour had become more erratic.

His anger was flashpoint-nuclear. To me, and my friends, he was downright scary. My neighbourhood friends stopped coming over, especially the boys. The boys had increasingly become the focus of my dad's rage. None of them wanted a run-in with him. I was fast becoming known as the girl with the crazy dad. I remembered a conversation when my dad and Maggie lived in the old house in Malibu Canyon. He pulled me aside and told me, 'Laura, I want you to know that I have a disease; it's called multiple sclerosis. In a few years' time I could be in a wheelchair. I want to prepare you mentally for the possibility that you may have to push my wheelchair and change my diapers.' I became very upset and worried about my dad from then on. I could tell he had no feeling in one of his hands. He asked Maggie to button his shirts for him. He walked with a limp and used a cane (not the bull's dick cane; that was just for show). I couldn't tell if he was drunk or not. He walked lopsided, as if he was plastered, but it's possible it was the MS. He loved red wine, and when he was drunk he was loud and vulgar. The sicker he got, the meaner he became and the more crazy his behaviour. He was, however, thankfully not confined to a wheelchair and, as far as I know, never in need of a diaper.

I started to avoid my father. I hid in my room in the pool house. I timed my comings and goings so as not to coincide with his. I walked on eggshells. As my father got crazier, Maggie and I grew ever closer. I had a feeling that Maggie was grateful to have me around. My father was often violent, but I believe that my presence somehow helped to keep it in check. Maggie and I had each other's backs.

The last week of August 1977, Maggie asked me if I would babysit Karina. I was spending all day, every day, at the beach, topping up my Hawaiian tan, showing off my newly honed beach body. Karina was seven. She was an extremely pretty child, and we always got along well. While Karina and I were at the beach I met a really cute boy, a couple of years older than me, who was also babysitting his little brother, the same age as Karina. His name was Damian and he had the looks of a teen idol. He flirted with me at the beach and asked me on a date, my first real date (I was almost fifteen), to a restaurant and a movie. I couldn't believe it. I had always felt fat and awkward. Now, since my weight loss and the dark tan from Hawaii, I was feeling good about my looks for the first time.

I was so excited about being asked on a date that I practically floated up Mesa Road, the exhausting steep hill that rose from the beach to Rustic Canyon. When I told Maggie about meeting Damian, she was happy for me. When I told my father, it was another story. I got the third degree. My father asked endless questions about Damian and his family. He tried to find every possible reason for me not to go on my date. He acted as if Damian ran a satanic sex cult and my virgin body was to be used as a sacrifice. Unbelievably, my father told me I could *not* go on a date unless I was *chaperoned*! I mean, what was this, the Middle Ages? He insisted that he be the chaperone.

I managed to convince him to drive us to the restaurant and wait in the car while we ate. The mental image I had of my father sitting at a nearby table and watching our every move was beyond cringe-making. The ride to the pizza parlour was fraught with tension.

My father barely talked to Damian and when he did, it was to grill him and pepper him with intimidating comments. We were not allowed to go to the movie. I mean, what was he thinking? That I would fuck Damian in public like an oversexed animal?

KARATE KID

Paul Revere Junior High looked like the typical American school one might see on TV. It had a billboard out in front announcing upcoming events. The school was made up of a cluster of buildings that were connected by outdoor walkways and dotted with what felt and looked like semi-permanent trailers as classrooms. Since Paul Revere was a public school it had kids from all kinds of economic backgrounds. In California, the law specified that kids from poorer communities were to be bussed into wealthy ones so all the kids could mix. Mix they did not. My new school was made up of rich surf kids from the Pacific Palisades and Brentwood, and underprivileged Latino and black kids from East LA.

This was scary shit.

I had two sets of friends at school. One set was made up of two girls from my neighbourhood, Tolley and Lisa, whom I had met on the bus to school. Tolley was tall and thin, with freckles and a wicked sense of humour. We are still friends to this day. Lisa was hot – jailbait hot – with icy-blonde hair and giant baby-blue eyes. We spent most afternoons together and loved listening to Led Zeppelin, smoking pot and dabbling in witchcraft. Lisa's mother was a witch, complete with cloak, dagger and powders to use when casting spells. She belonged to a Southern California coven. Lisa lived with her divorced mother and was totally unsupervised. She had an older boyfriend, who lived in a suburb and drove a red pick-up truck. Lisa was the first girl I knew who had given a guy a blow job. She told us how great it was when this guy came in her mouth – it felt and tasted like warm nectar running down her throat. Later that year, Lisa ran off with one of her father's best friends.

One day, Tolley and Lisa got tickets to see the Ramones supported by The Runaways at the Santa Monica Civic Center. This concert was a milestone in music history – one of the most iconic and brilliant double bills. I was so excited. I loved the Ramones. The Runaways were girls. They were the first all-girl group I knew about. They didn't just sing, they played their instruments and they were good. Their song 'Cherry Bomb' had cracked the charts and they were holding their own against all the male-dominated bands. Joan Jett was the guitarist and looked vaguely like a female Elvis. Their singer, Cherie Currie, looked just like Lisa.

Of course, when I asked my father if I could go to a concert with Tolley and Lisa, he said no. He hadn't even heard of the Ramones or The Runaways, it was the concert part he objected to. I was furious and, to this day, I still regret not sneaking out of the house and facing his wrath later. Tolley and Lisa felt bad for me. They sympathised with me and called my father 'the Psychopsych'. They bought me a T-shirt at the concert. It was a lovely gesture but small consolation. Years later, I would see the Ramones every chance I got. I would end up meeting all of them, at some point or another. One night in New York City, at the Peppermint Lounge, I snorted heroin and threw up on Joey Ramone's leg. He was extremely gracious about it.

One day at Paul Revere, I was on my way to class when I was surrounded by a group of Latino boys. They began to close in on me and encircled me, saying awful things. They told me they were going to gang rape me and, as they inched ever closer, I began to really fear for my safety. Thankfully, a teacher happened by and witnessed the incident and broke it up. I was incredibly shook up. I went home and told my father about it. Even though he was difficult, I knew he'd protect me and know what to do.

My father enrolled me in private self-defence classes at Ed Parker's School of Karate. Ed Parker was famous. He had been Elvis's bodyguard. Elvis was so inspired by Ed Parker and karate that he even started incorporating karate moves into his stage routine.

After just a few lessons, Larry, my Kenpo Karate teacher, who was a black belt to the third degree, informed my father that I was a natural at martial arts. He suggested that my father enrol me in the group classes to study karate properly, a move beyond simple self-defence.

I was the only girl in my class and was expected to spar with boys and men. I soon worked my way up to yellow belt and then orange. One of the boys in my class was the chubby, shy son of Carl Wilson, the lead guitarist in the Beach Boys. Of course, growing up in Southern California meant the Beach Boys were akin to God. Everyone got excited when Carl came to watch the sparring. Every time I had to spar this boy, I'd kick the bejesus out of him to the tune of 'Good Vibrations' running through my head.

I learned that martial arts were a mental, physical and spiritual art form – a way of thinking and a way of life. Knowing karate gave me the confidence and the discipline to avoid physical confrontation. We were taught to fight only when absolutely necessary, when all else failed, when every other option was exhausted.

I began to walk around school with more confidence. I no longer lived in fear of the gangs and went about my business peacefully. Until, one day, towards the end of the year, as I exited the restroom and stood over the row of sinks to wash my hands, a gang of five mean girls surrounded me. They called me a 'fuckin' white bitch'.

'Please leave me alone,' I asked.

They began to spit on me.

'You don't want to be doing that, girls,' I said, hinting that I wasn't going to be a pushover. 'You don't want to mess with me,' I warned them.

I felt a hand grab my shoulder from behind. Without thinking, I pinned the hand to my shoulder with my right hand, and held it firm. I used my left elbow to smash up hard into her jaw.

This was exactly what I'd been taught to do in my very first self-defence lesson. I heard a crack. The girl fell backwards, momentarily unconscious. Then a full-scale fight broke out. I kicked, fought and punched. In a blind fury I used every move I had ever mastered. I kept my face covered. I blocked any blows to my head while my legs doled out a series of furious roundhouse kicks. Everything was a blur. I felt like I was in a scene from a Bruce Lee movie. Two more of the mean girls went down. Then I felt another hand on my shoulder. Thinking it was an assailant, I kicked backward with one of my legs, hoping to catch the person in the kneecap. I made contact. Bingo!

All at once the room fell silent. Out of the five initial mean girls, I had managed to take down three. When I looked at the floor, I saw that the person I had just kicked in the knee was a teacher, Mrs Nagle.

All six of us were told to write down *exactly* what had happened. Everybody's parents were called, including my father. One of the girls was sent to the hospital with a suspected broken jaw. All of the girls' accounts of the fight differed *dramatically*. They hadn't had time to get their stories straight. The principal knew they were lying. My father arrived in the principal's office fresh from treating neurotics in Beverly Hills. He was wearing a three-piece suit and walking with his cane. The stomping of his boot heels on the linoleum floor told me he meant business. As I sat on the seat outside the principal's office I heard shouting and pounding coming from within. My father's voice boomed through the thin walls. The door opened and my father took me by the arm. 'Let's go, Laura,' he said. His face was red. His passion was up. We got into his car and I was almost too scared to ask.

'What happened, Dad? Did they kick me out?'

'They threatened to kick you out,' he said. 'But I told them if they did, I would assemble a serious legal team and sue the shit out of them.'

It felt good to have my dad stand up for me and to stick it to the school. I was not punished. I wasn't even disciplined. I returned to Crossroads School the next year. My public school days were over. At least I gave it a go.

THE DAD RASH

Tenth grade was one hell of a year. The year of my breaking and the year of my making. The year my innocence was annihilated. The year I wrote the epitaph to my relationship with my father. The tenth grade was the winter of my discontent. A week or two into the school term, after I started back at Crossroads again, my father and Maggie sat me down and told me they were separating. They assured me that my place in their home was secure. I would continue to live in the house and finish the school year at Crossroads. Afterwards, we would see where we were before deciding what school I would attend next year. My father's behaviour had become increasingly bizarre. He was a human pressure cooker, liable to explode at any moment.

That autumn a killer called the Hillside Strangler was on the loose in Southern California. Everybody was paranoid about him, especially my father. Not since the Manson murders had the Southern California population been so freaked out en masse. The nightly news reported on little else. I was put under strict curfew. I was allowed only to go to and from school. No going out after school, or at night.

One day in early autumn, my brother Jon and I were sick with the flu. We were both home from school. Bored out of our brains, we sat in the dining room drawing pictures together in our pyjamas. The phone rang and I answered it. 'Hello,' I said.

'Hello, Laura,' said a man whose low, slow voice I didn't recognise. I assumed it was a friend or colleague of my father's.

'Hello,' I said. 'Who's this?'

'I love the blue pyjamas you are wearing,' the man said.

'Who is this?' I demanded.

'Are you going back to bed . . .?' the man asked lazily. 'Can I join you?'

I slammed the receiver down. Oh my God, someone's outside watching me! I ran around the house closing all the plantation shutters and pulling down the blinds.

'What's a matter, Laura?' my little brother asked. 'Oh, Jon, a weird man was on the phone asking me strange questions.' Jon tilted his head and thought about it for a moment and then out of his five-year-old mouth came these words: 'You mean the man that calls me sometimes and asks about your tits and what size bra you wear?'

It turned out this creep had been calling the house for a month or two and asking my brother a series of bizarre and disturbing questions about me. My brother had been carrying on an innocent conversation with this man. When anyone else would answer the phone, the guy would hang up.

My father took me straight to the police. He was worried the caller might be connected to the Hillside Strangler, or one of his schizophrenic teenage patients out for revenge.

The police were monitoring all calls. I was driven to school by my dad and could no longer ride the bus. I was fifteen at this point, and just a month or two shy of getting my driver's licence. My father said I could drive the old brown Volkswagen if I passed the test. I was living for that moment – the less time I had to spend with my father, the better. I avoided him as much as I could. He had convinced himself that I was sexually promiscuous. He had zero facts to base his belief on. Maybe he was freaked out by his daughter growing into a woman? I began to question my father's sanity. I'd yet to have a real boyfriend; I'd never been in love. I was at that point, still, very much a virgin. But I also began feeling awful about myself.

The police informed my father that they had managed to trace the phone calls coming from my stalker. They were being made by a neighbour. It turned out that a man in his early twenties was living across the street and working as a 'manny'. He lived in, and looked after the children of Ken, as in Barbie's brother. My father spoke to Ken and the 'manny' was fired and threatened with legal proceedings. No legal proceedings were ever initiated because by that point my father had an awful lot on his plate. Worrying about punishing my stalker was way down on his to-do list.

Just before the Christmas school break, my father informed us that he was moving out in the new year. He and Maggie were in therapy together, trying to fix things, but at the moment *he* needed some space. I was allowed to stay with Maggie and the kids in the house.

Maggie took Jon and Karina and headed off to Iowa to spend Christmas on the farm with her mother and father and eleven brothers and sisters. It was just me and Dad alone in the house. The next morning I was due to fly off to Chicago to visit my mom and Marvin for the holidays.

That night, Dabney Coleman, the actor and father of my friend Kelly who had been in my class at both Paul Revere and Crossroads, had arranged a special treat for Kelly and me. He had bought us two tickets to see Queen in concert, and arranged a limo and driver to take us there and back. The concert was breathtaking and we came back on a high. Kelly planned to spend the night at my house. Her mom would pick her up the next morning, before my dad drove me to the airport. As our limo pulled up in front of our house that night, I noticed a little yellow Porsche parked outside our walkway. I wondered whose car it was.

Kelly and I pushed open the big door and walked inside the house. I was practically foaming at the mouth with excitement and couldn't wait to tell my dad what an amazing show we'd seen and what an incredible performer Freddie Mercury was. What I saw when we opened the door stunned me and left me speechless. My dad was sitting on the floor on the Persian carpet in front of a roaring fire. There was an open bottle of red wine and two glasses. Sitting next to him was a petite young blonde woman whom he introduced as Angela. She was British. They were barefoot. They were giggling and flushed. His words were slurred and his lips were the colour of red wine. Apparently, Angela was a nurse at the hospital where they both worked. They were discussing hospital politics, or so they said.

The moment was beyond awkward. My father looked like the kid who had been caught with his hand in the cookie jar. Looking back, it seems obvious that he must have wanted to be caught.

I began to hope that perhaps it was just a mild flirtation, a mid-life crisis thing. 'Maybe I read too much into the situation?' I thought. Anyway, Angela would go home soon, and that would be that. He would never let her sleep over with me and Kelly in the same house, no matter how much he fancied her. That would be reckless, not to mention tacky.

As we were brushing our teeth, bent over the double sinks, surrounded on all sides by 1970s orange mirrored wallpaper, the central heating system switched on. The heating in the house was connected by a series of air vents. The vents didn't just carry the air, they also carried sound. All at once Kelly and I looked at each other. Our mouths agape, toothbrushes hanging, eyes bugging. It sounded like my father and Angela were having loud, grunting, rutting, moaning sex in his and Maggie's bed. I felt sick.

The next morning I could not look my father in the eye. I tried to forget what I heard and put it out of my mind. I went to Chicago and spent the Christmas holidays with my mom and Marvin. I never told anyone what happened. I held it inside and churned with guilt.

When I returned to LA, my father had moved out. I continued to go to Crossroads and also to my twice-weekly appointments with Vicky, my shrink, whom I had been seeing for a year or so. Finally, I began to talk to her. After months of sleeping on her couch, burying my feelings, I began to unload. I told her about the night of the Queen concert. I felt a loyalty to Maggie that I did not feel to my father. We had bonded through the crazy nastiness of their situation. Vicky said Maggie deserved to know the truth. It wasn't fair for me to have to lie; to keep a secret that wasn't mine.

I summoned up my courage and I sat Maggie down. I asked her to please not breathe a word of what I was going to tell her to my father. I was scared of how he would react, of what he would do to me. I explained that I was telling her this out of loyalty to her.

My father and Maggie had arranged a visitation schedule. He came on Tuesday nights to take me, Jon and Karina out to dinner. We also saw him one night during the weekend. We usually went to his very sad new apartment in a hideous complex in Brentwood. It was a place for lonely people. More often than not, Angela was there. We discovered she wasn't actually a nurse. She was, in fact, an actress.

I used to dread those Tuesday-night dinners with my dad. He would pick us up around 7 p.m. We would usually go somewhere cheap for dinner, like Pioneer Chicken or for a pizza. My father was a crazy, fast driver consumed with road rage. He swore constantly and smoked cigars with the windows rolled up. He raged on and on about Maggie and my mother. I started to develop hives and a rash on my chest and neck just thinking about my father, let alone being near him.

Other than the designated days he was assigned to see us, my father was not supposed to be around. One afternoon I returned home from school. I parked the Volkswagen on the street and unlocked the front door of the house. Nobody was home. Jon and Karina were still at school, Maggie was at her job as a property developer. The housekeeper, Mercedes, was out on an errand. As I walked into the living room, my father stomped up the spiral staircase from his office below. 'Hi, Dad,' I said, nervously, sensing something was wrong. 'Why are you here in the afternoon?' I asked.

'You are a liar,' he seethed at me. 'How dare you tell Maggie that I fucked Angela when she wasn't here? You are delusional. You imagined everything. You are crazy and need to be institutionalised.'

As I attempted calmly to explain that I wasn't crazy and that I had heard him with Angela, and that I had a witness, he lunged at me. He grabbed me and started squeezing. My words were stifled. The room swam. My legs gave way.

When I came to, my father was hugging me hard. Rib-breakingly hard. He was telling me he loved me, over and over again. I was beyond freaked out. 'I'm sorry, Daddy. I did lie to Maggie,' I said, just to get out of the situation and away from him. I thought I had just witnessed him losing his mind. I believed I was in danger. I would have said anything to save myself.

Finally, my dad left the house. He never mentioned the incident again. He never apologised for losing his temper. He went away believing that we had made up, had come to an understanding. How could he not realise that something inside me was irrevocably broken. For ever. I sat alone, shaking, until Maggie got home. I was covered in a rash.

THE SWORD OF DAMOCLES

After his outburst, my father was told by Maggie not to come within a hundred yards of me or the house. She threatened him with a restraining order if he did. I still lived at Maggie's, for the time being. The pool house was rented out to a young hotshot lawyer called Brandon James. Brandon was fun. I hung out with him a lot. He turned me on to Roxy Music and class A drugs.

One night Brandon invited me to the Whisky a Go Go nightclub in West Hollywood to see Penetration and the Balls, a punk double-header. As we drove there in Brandon's open-top Alfa Romeo Spider we smoked a joint. After the show we went to his friend's house in Beverly Hills, where a small party was going on. We all sat around the palatial living room. I was sixteen, the others were in their mid-twenties. I felt like a fish out of water, a little high-school kid hanging out with grown-ups. I told Brandon I felt tired and wanted to go home. He said to wait just a bit.

Then, all of a sudden, someone brought out a big glass plate covered in lines of cocaine.

'Snort some of this,' Brandon said. 'You won't be tired any more.'

'I don't want to,' I said. 'I'm scared. What will happen?'

'Just try it,' Brandon urged.

So I did. I perked up immediately. I started to chat and felt like one of the group. All the recent troubles with my father disappeared. I felt trouble- and problem-free – until it wore off. Then I wanted more.

Despite Maggie's warning, one day after school I found my dad standing inside the house. He had found a hole in the basement and scuttled in on his belly. Unbeknownst to us, he'd been doing this from time to time, taking objects he wanted from the house for his new apartment. He had always complained about how 'hard done by' he felt in the divorce from my mother. His new separation from Maggie brought on more anger. Maggie decided it would be safest if I moved out of the house for the rest of the school year. My therapist, Vicky, was so appalled by what had happened with my father, she offered me a safe haven if I needed it.

When the Flickers heard what was happening with my father, they welcomed me into their home. Since both Marvin and Carole-Anne Flicker were therapists, they thought my father would be forced to be on his best behaviour. He would not risk bringing shame down on himself. The whole shrink community would be watching. I was looking forward to living with the Flickers and being in a stable home and spending time with Amy. I wanted to escape the war zone.

My father thought that Maggie had poisoned me against him and that we were out to ruin him. He was happy to have me live with the Flickers, away from Maggie, and insisted I report to him weekly. I was allowed to drive only to and from school and to and from my therapist. My father calculated the exact mileage of these journeys on his car and threatened to check my mileage. If I exceeded his limits, he threatened to take my car away.

I decided I needed to detach emotionally from my father. My fear of him had grown as he became even weirder, especially about my sexuality. When we met he grilled me about boys and watched me like a hawk, slinging unfounded accusations at me, all the while flaunting his concubine in my face. I wanted to be my own person; it was time for me to grow up. I decided that I would lose my virginity. I figured that if I did I would be grown up. It was also a way to get back at my father.

I remember having a covert meeting with Maggie one afternoon at Moonshadows restaurant in Malibu. Unless my father was having us followed, he would never find out. Over a big piece of chocolate cake, I told Maggie that I wanted to lose my virginity. I asked her to help me find a doctor so that I could go on the pill. She agreed.

But how to proceed? I had no boyfriend. I wasn't in love with anybody. My first time was not going to be some glorious celebration of young love. It was not going to be with my high-school sweetheart nor the man I intended to have children with. Instead, my first time was going to be a coldly calculated agreement between myself and some male of my choosing. In some ways this was quite sad; in other ways it was actually quite liberating.

The person I chose was older, twenty-seven. I was still just sixteen. I wanted someone with experience. No awkward fumblings for me. I wanted a man who knew what he was doing. He was a musician in a famous band whose records I listened to. That was another side of the younger me – seeking out famous, wealthy men who bolstered my ego. If I could have whomsoever I wanted, I must be pretty hot stuff. I found this rock star's number in the phone book. I called him and introduced myself. I drove to his apartment in the brown Volkswagen my father had given me. We sat down and talked. I explained to him what I wanted. He was more than happy to comply. He was gorgeous, sexy, kind and gentle. The deed was done. I never saw him again except on the movie screen. I may have lost my virginity, but I found my strength. Little did I realise at the time that I would have to spend many years learning to find my deeper strength in healthier ways.

DISOWNED

Back in Chicago, my mother did not realise the severity of my situation in LA. When she discovered that I was *living* at the Flickers' house, and not just visiting, she jumped on a plane and came to take me home to Chicago. After having conversations with everybody involved in my life, including Vicky, the Flickers and Maggie, my mother reached the conclusion that my father had gone 'over the top' and that she needed to get me away from him. Immediately.

My mother arranged a meeting with the three of us in a Hamburger Hamlet restaurant on San Vicente Boulevard in Brentwood. My father entered though the glass doors of the restaurant. He walked in with his cane, his gait lopsided and his jaw set. He slid into the seat opposite us. I didn't realise it then but this would be the last time I saw my biological father for many, many years. I also did not realise that for the next twenty or so years, I would try to fix our relationship by choosing men with personal qualities similar to my father's. I would make countless mistakes. Thankfully all of them would ultimately lead to my healing and becoming the person I am today.

My mother spoke to my father in a quiet, calm tone – the way you would talk to a wounded animal that might turn on you. My father, who was puce with rage, spat out his words and pounded the table with his fists to emphasise his points. His main demand was that I was to have no further contact with Maggie – none at all.

This was completely unacceptable to me. Maggie had been in my life for twelve years, since I was four years old. I told my father I understood how he felt but I would not be dictated to. I would continue to speak to Maggie if I so wished.

With that, my father stood up. He took a long hard look at me. Glaring and grinding his teeth, he seethed out the words I will never forget. 'I disown you,' he hissed. 'You are no longer my daughter.'

BECOMING BRIXTON

I wanted to become a different person. I wanted to reinvent myself and move forward. Laura had been disowned. She was unloved by her father. Laura was a broken, sad, damaged girl. Laura was the person I no longer wanted to be.

At the Laboratory School's 'U High' – the University of Chicago's high school, attached to the Lab School – I hung around with kids who felt marginalised. Our collective pain and eccentricities seemed to unite us. We were struggling to come to terms with those supposed flaws – gay/straight/bi; black/white; fat/thin; depressed/manic; and on and on – and who we thought we were. Around this time, I began to develop a passion for all things British. It had started with the Beatles. But now I watched every British television show I could find on US TV. I couldn't get enough of the British accent. I watched series and dramas – *Dr Who* in the Tom Baker years; *Poldark* and *I, Claudius* – and comedies: *Monty Python*, *The Two Ronnies* and Dave Allen. I watched the David Frost interviews too.

Once, David Frost called our house to speak to Marvin. He was doing some research for an upcoming interview with the Shah of Iran. I nearly fell off my chair. I begged Marvin to let me listen in to the conversation just to hear David Frost's accent. I loved British sports too, and avidly watched football, motor racing and Wimbledon. I was fast becoming an Anglophile, and my dream was to visit the UK.

I began listening to mostly British music. I was bucking against the mainstream and reaching for the fringes. At the time, the bands I liked were The Clash, The Jam, The Undertones, Siouxsie

and the Banshees, Adam and the Ants, The Police, Blondie, the
Buzzcocks, the Ramones, Cheap Trick, the B52s, Gary Numan,
U2, the Sex Pistols, Elvis Costello, Madness, The Specials, the
English Beat and Marianne Faithfull.

I still loved the sound of the sixties and adored psychedelic
pop. I still listened to The Byrds, The Doors, the Mamas and the
Papas, Simon and Garfunkel, Hendrix, The Seeds, The Yardbirds,
Spirit, Love, The Strawberry Alarm Clock and The 13th Floor
Elevators. I must have listened to the album *Sunshine Superman* by
Donovan every day for an entire year. I would have never believed
that I would one day record Donovan's song 'Hurdy Gurdy Man',
become friends with him, his wife Linda and their kids, and holiday with them.

Out of all the new music I had heard up to that point, *one*
band stood out for me above the rest: The Clash. After school,
we used to have impromptu 'punk music' parties at each other's
houses. My favourite song was 'Guns of Brixton' by The Clash. I
asked for it again and again. I asked to hear it so many times my
friends started calling me 'Brixton'.

Brixton was a way cooler name than Laura. It was a strong
name. The prefix, Brix, sounded like what you'd build a house
with – a sturdy, solid, grounded name.

MY FIRST PROPER JOB

My first proper job was working in fashion. I worked in downtown Chicago, at the famous Water Tower Place, in the iconic boutique Fiorucci. Since I was at school all week and studying for my exams, I could work only weekends. Fiorucci was like fashion theatre. It was bonkers. It smashed the mould of traditional retail, it ripped up the rule book and glued it back together with glitter and leather. Fiorucci was the hottest store in Chicago in 1980. Staffed by artists and performers, every day was like an ever-changing art installation. The other sales people, who were super-cool and fabulously freaky, took me under their wing. I got an education in more than selling.

I was introduced to the Chicago underground club scene – a whole way of life I never imagined existed in the stuffy Midwest. Even though I was still underage – I was seventeen; the drinking age was twenty-one – I frequented after-hours clubs and illegal music venues in such places as abattoirs, abandoned factories and gay bars (my favourite), where I would dance all night long to the best music.

One day at Fiorucci, I was asked to do something very different. Instead of helping out on the shop floor or assisting the heavy-hitter sales people, I was asked to *be* the window display. The visual merchandiser dressed me head to toe in a red Lycra leopard-print cat suit. A mini-stage was erected and placed in the gigantic main windows, facing out into the busy atrium of Water Tower Place. From my stage, I was to go-go dance in the window. This was groundbreaking stuff. I was actually a human art installation; a bizarre fusion of fashion art and entertainment, come to life in a shopping centre. Out-of-towners eating hotdogs stopped and gawked at me. At first I felt embarrassed and awkward, standing there in my cat suit, watching the tourists wipe mustard off their mouths. It was like being a fish in a fishbowl or an animal at the zoo. People's judgements ricocheting through the windows could have withered me, if I had let them. The experience might have caused me to flee in floods of tears.

Instead I embraced it. I struggled at first to conquer my fears and insecurity about what other people thought. Eventually, I got into it. My initial technique was to shut out the world and groove to the music. The music was my life raft, the sonic vehicle that allowed my mind to escape and set my body free. By the end of the day, I actually felt *comfortable* and began to *interact* with the shoppers. This was the very first time I was *consciously connecting to an audience*. That day, I began mentally to separate the insecure teenager I was in real life and replace it with an entirely new person on stage. On stage I felt free and empowered. Old Laura was gone. I stepped up, stood in my light, and let it rip. It felt good.

At Fiorucci, I learned a lot about selling, which, unbeknownst to me, would come in handy later in life, especially when it came to jeans. I was good at it and had a natural affinity for it. Styling people was rewarding. Empowering people through fashion was satisfying. I loved working with colour and understood how powerful a tool colour is. It can actually change a person's mood. If used correctly, it's like fashion Prozac, it can lift spirits and help you have a better, more positive day. If you get it wrong, though, it can make a person look ill.

Towards the end of my senior year in high school, some of the boys I knew in Hyde Park, who had been my after-school musical buddies, decided to put together a band. They needed a singer and thought of me. The leader of the band was a guy called Wayne Braxton. Wayne was older than us, and had never gone to our school, but I knew him through people in the neighbourhood. He was a proper musician. Our band did cover versions of hit songs of the moment as well as rock and roll classics. Our first gig was playing at a party in Rockford, Illinois. I was excited to play in Rockford as it was the home of Cheap Trick. I had a schoolgirl crush on the singer, Robin Zander.

I can remember rehearsing for the gig in Wayne's basement, but the only songs I recall from the set were 'Roxanne' by The Police, 'Hanging on the Telephone' by Blondie and 'Mony, Mony' by Tommy James and the Shondells.

Although I had sung in the choir and had some operatic vocal classes, I have to be honest, I had no confidence as a singer. In fact, singing live on stage filled me with fear. My voice was OK – I had decent pitch – but I'd yet to discover how to engage emotionally with an audience. Singing in public did not come naturally or easily to me. I longed to stand behind a bass guitar like Paul Simonon of The Clash. Being a woman and playing bass guitar, or any guitar, seemed about the coolest thing in the world to me. Too bad I couldn't *really* play.

I didn't realise then that it didn't matter. Punk had changed all of that. In less than a year I'd be writing my own songs and playing in my own band. In three years' time, I would be in England recording the first song that I'd ever written. I'd be playing guitar and singing a duet on an album for The Fall.

LONDON CALLING

Mercifully at last, I graduated high school. I applied to only three colleges and got into my first choice, Bennington. Come the following autumn, I would be going to Vermont and living in New England. That summer, though, I would be visiting the original England. In celebration of my graduation and acceptance into Bennington, my mom and Marvin decided to take me and my stepsisters on a family holiday to Europe. I was beside myself to be going abroad for the first time. I'd amassed savings from working at Fiorucci, and was planning on spending all of it on cool European clothes and underground music unavailable in the US.

Our first stop was London. As the wheels of the big 747 touched down on the tarmac at Heathrow airport, I was overcome with a very strong feeling. I turned to my mother and said, '*This* is where I'm going to live.' Without even having put a foot on the ground, I instinctively knew I belonged here. How or when I could make this happen, I had no idea. Without knowing why, I felt I was home.

We visited museums during the day and had tea at the Fortnum & Mason department store. We shopped at Harrods, and marvelled at the food hall, the fish sculpture and the amazing pet department. At night my stepsisters and I would stay up late and watch TV. There were only three channels. Two of them were broadcasting at night, but only up to eleven or *maybe* twelve. The other had a static test pattern permanently stuck on the screen, with a bizarre picture of a clown and a girl. One night, the two programmes were hardly scintillating: we had a choice of watching either a middle-aged woman making jam, or cricket.

I'd never even heard of cricket. They didn't show it on US TV. It seemed so quintessentially English. The players, all men, wore chic white clothes with V-neck sweaters. The bowler (pitcher) wiped a red ball on his white pants before he threw it, staining the white trousers red. It was kind of like baseball, but seemed a thousand times more complicated and boring.

Marvin took me shopping to Kensington Market and to the Garage in Chelsea to buy the coolest clothes. As I walked down the King's Road, I couldn't get the Elvis Costello song '(I Don't Want to Go to) Chelsea' out of my head. I bought a red leather biker jacket, just like Chrissie Hynde wore on the cover of The Pretenders' album. Marvin also took me down to World's End. I was desperate to visit the Vivienne Westwood shop. I bought a head-to-toe pirate outfit just like I'd seen Adam of Adam and the Ants wearing.

After three days in London, we took the train and then the hovercraft to Paris. Paris was a magical city to look at but I found it very stressful. It was not – how shall I put this – a friendly place. For me, speaking no French was a huge handicap. I felt embarrassed and stupid not being able to communicate. Europe felt so sophisticated, and I felt America was crude and crass by comparison.

While in Paris, I begged Marvin to take me on a pilgrimage to the Place des Victoires to the flagship Kenzo store. Going into the Kenzo shop in Paris was like walking smack into a screaming forest of rioting flowers. The colours, the textures, the energy were breathtaking. The cut, folds and volume of the fabrics, combined with clashing patterns, was beyond visually and mentally stimulating. I am so grateful I had an hour in that space, at that time, to experience fashion and retail magic. Marvin, bless him, saw how blown away I was and treated me to two dresses. Both of them were iconic pieces – covetable examples of Kenzo's textured-floral-Russian-bohemian signature style.

About a hundred croissants later, we left Paris and arrived in Venice, the most romantic place I'd ever seen in my whole life. A real-life Disneyland. I fell in love with the city and Italy in general.

At this point, I remember family tensions starting to build. We had been in each other's company for far too long. In such close quarters I was starting to feel frisky. My teenage hormones were kicking in. I couldn't stop looking at all the European boys and men and wondered what it would be like to be with one. I was soon to have an experience with one, but it wasn't the kind I imagined.

Our family trip was coming to a close. We were to leave Venice by sleeper train and spend the last week of our trip back in England. My mom and Marvin were going off to spend time together in Istanbul. Nadia, Leah and I were going to stay in Surrey with their aunt Ros and uncle Cyril, from their mother's side of the family, whom I'd never met.

The overnight train from Venice to Calais, in those pre-Eurostar days, was elegant. It was wood-panelled and evocative of another era; it had a dining car. In Calais we would disembark and take the hovercraft across the English Channel. Then we would board another train into London. Nadia and Leah and I shared a sleeper compartment. Tempers were starting to fray. We were on top of each other, literally. I decided to take a walk down the corridor of the train to get away and smoke a cigarette. I met two French guys in their late teens, who started to flirt with me. I was flattered, and relieved to have something to take my mind off bickering with my stepsisters. Since I couldn't speak any French and they couldn't speak English, communication was difficult. But before I knew it, they grabbed me and dragged me into a nearby empty sleeper compartment. They started to grope me and tear at my clothes. I kicked and fought and yelled in English. My old karate moves came in handy. Somehow, I managed to scramble away unscathed and intact.

When I woke up in the morning I was dreaming groggily that Nadia was trying to take my necklace off me. 'What are you doing?'

I asked, half asleep. I cracked my eyes open to see not Nadia, but the train conductor standing at my bedside with his hands down my nightgown, fondling my breasts while I slept. 'Get off. Get off. Get the fuck off!' I started screaming. I was so shocked I hauled back with both my legs and kicked him in the chest, causing him to smash backward into the door, which sent him packing.

Plans had been made for us to stay with Aunt Ros and Uncle Cyril. They were pensioners who lived in Croydon, along with an annoying little poodle, Louie. Uncle Cyril was an ex-military man and Aunt Ros was his American wife. Uncle Cyril watched cricket all day long. He was fairly uncommunicative. We were bored out of our minds in Croydon, and I got the feeling that Aunt Ros and Uncle Cyril couldn't wait to see the back of us. I longed to go into London and get my teeth into the city.

One of my mother's best friends, the artist Andrea Tana, and her husband, the legendary restaurateur Dan Tana, had moved to London from LA about ten years previously. I had been very close to their daughters, Gabby and Katie. I decided to give them a call and see if I could stay. They welcomed me with open arms to their gorgeous house in Kensington. Gabby, Katerina and I hung out, and the girls introduced me to their English friends and took me to parties and clubs.

One party was at the top of the old Biba department store in Kensington, a place called the Roof Gardens. It was an amazing party. I saw a good-looking man out of the corner of my eye and noticed him staring at me. He came over and asked me out there and then. It turned out he was the keyboard player in a very famous prog rock band, and another pop band, which had just had a number-one record. We left the party and he drove me around London in his Porsche with the top down. We went to his mews house off Wigmore Street and had sex. Then he dropped me back at the Tanas'. I felt wild, free, happy and sexy. For the first time I was beginning to understand how great life could be.

MIND CONTROL

The human mind is a powerful and complex thing. What we choose to think about determines how we consciously feel. How we consciously feel is the be-all and end-all of our existence. Obviously, there's a lot more going on in our minds. We have little control over the non-conscious part and its occasional eruptions into our feelings. But we can control the rest, however small a part of our total mental processes. So we make choices about what to think about.

I slobbed out for the second half of the summer after returning from Europe. I was glued to the TV watching the wedding of Charles and Diana. I recognised all the London landmarks and longed to be among them again in the thick of the celebrations. I spent lazy days hanging with old school friends on the Point by the lakeshore. Chicago was hot and humid. Like seals, we sunned our bodies on the hot rocks. Our Sony Walkmans disconnected us from reality. I revelled in my last summer of freedom before college.

At night I'd use my fake ID to get into underground clubs to see bands or just to dance to good music. Part of the ritual of going out to clubs was getting dressed up. I wore leopard-print coats, vintage trench coats, PVC jeans or miniskirts. I wore my red leather jacket and all the gear I'd bought in London. I was beginning to get into rockabilly music and loved the style of the Stray Cats. I started to wear pointy cowboy boots and girly styled zoot suits. My favourite clubs were Exit and Metro. Cabaret Metro would become a historic place in my life. In that very club in less than a year and a half, I would see The Fall play and meet Mark E. Smith on a night that would change my life for ever.

I always remind myself to live in the moment. One cannot change the past nor can one relive it. Agonising over mistakes one may have made only makes one feel worse. Learn from those mistakes, forgive yourself and move on.

One night, I was in an Irish pub in Chicago. I was there to see a local punk band made up of some kids from Hyde Park. While at the pub, I ran into a guy I knew from U High who was in the year above me. His name was J, a musician who had just finished his first year at university. I had always gotten on well with J, although we were just acquaintances. J was 'camp' and theatrical. His energy was manic and his style was eccentric. J also lived in Hyde Park, so when the gig was finished he offered me a ride home. I accepted. When we got to our neighbourhood he asked me if I wanted to come over to his house and jam, to play some music together.

'Sure,' I said. 'Sounds like fun.'

J's basement was like an old-fashioned rumpus room. There was a place to chill out with a sofa and a TV, and an area set up for music. He had a couple of electric guitars and amps and a drum kit. I perched myself down on one of the amps while J fiddled with stuff in the corner. Then he approached me with a guitar lead in his hand.

'Have you ever seen a lead like this?' J asked me. One end of the lead was coiled around his arm and the other end he swung in the air theatrically. 'Put your hands behind your back,' J said.

I thought he was goofing around, so I did it.

J grabbed my arms and tied them together tightly at the wrists, binding them behind my back. I still thought he was being bizarrely playful. He stood back and looked at me strangely. His eyes were glazed and he looked possessed. I realised too late this was not a game and I was in serious danger.

Then everything spun out of control. He pushed me to the ground and ripped off my jeans and raped me. Anally. I tried to fight but it was no use. My hands were tied behind my back. I screamed, even with his hands clamped over my mouth. I bit him but he seemed to feel nothing. Finally, I stopped fighting. I just willed it to be over.

My grandmother's prophetic words gave me strength in the moment. 'This too shall pass.'

It was brutal. It was painful, embarrassing and humiliating. I was shocked and in absolute agony. He was a psychopath. I had totally misread him. I assumed wrongly that he was gay. The thought never entered my mind that he could be dangerous and could attack me.

Somehow I stumbled out and made it home. The first thing I remember clearly is sitting on the stone steps outside Mom and Marvin's house in the early hours of the morning, alone, curled into a ball, rocking back and forth and weeping. The internal pain I felt in my body was akin to being violated with a red-hot poker. Rape was something that happened in an alleyway or when a stranger jumped out of the bushes with a knife. 'Date rape' was not part of the cultural consciousness.

At that moment, I needed to make a choice. As I saw it, I had two options. I could wake up my mom and Marvin, tell them what had happened and go to the police. I knew who did it and where he lived. We could begin a long-drawn-out procedure, involving doctors and lawyers. I felt that I was somehow to blame. I think that the specifics of the assault were even more mortifying. I couldn't face telling anyone or going through months or possibly years of reliving it.

The second choice I had was to shut it out, completely. I could chalk it up to experience and learn from it. If I told no one and didn't talk about it, I believed it was possible to make it go away – block it out and move on. I made a pact with myself there and then while sitting on those steps. I would never think about it again. I refused to let it affect me. I wouldn't let it ruin my life or my future relationships with men. If I let it affect me, then I would be a victim. If I were a victim, then he would have won.

So I picked myself up and opened the door to our house. As silently as I could, I hobbled upstairs to my bedroom and cried myself to sleep. I never told anyone what happened to me. Not my mother, not Marvin, nor either of my husbands. Writing this now is the first time I've ever openly acknowledged it.

For all these years my unconscious mind has kept my secret safe, even from me. It lay buried somewhere deep within the complexities of my brain. I successfully managed to shut down the conscious memory of the rape and I refused to let it devastate my life. Some people might call this denial. For me it was survival.

BENNINGTON

Bennington College was a picture postcard. Set in rural Vermont, it was quietly impressive and extremely isolated. On the surface, it looked storybook quaint. The social focal point of the campus was a white, patrician New England-style commons building, which boasted a grand old clock perched high on its roof. Above it, a charming bell tower, complete with widow's walk and gabled crow's nest, cast a shadow over the sweeping green lawn of the exclusive school. The lawn was dramatic and generous in proportion. It was flanked on either side by substantial 'Vermontonian' clapboard houses, weathered and stoic. Their bedrooms served as dormitory rooms. Their genteel living rooms were the scenes of both civilised coffee hours and wild, debauched parties. The houses all had names, old, waspy American names. They were in honour of the founding families and the original benefactors of the school: Dewey, McCullough, Stokes and Swan, Kilpatrick, Booth, Leigh and Welling, to name only a few. The vast rolling lawn and the line of charming houses created a visual corridor, a vista that led your eye and drew you physically to 'the end of the world'.

At the far end of the lawn, opposite the commons building, the earth abruptly and dramatically fell away. It looked to all intents and purposes like 'the end of the world', a sheer drop into nothingness. As I stood on the lawn, observing my new surroundings and trying to orient myself, my internal compass began to spin in circles. There was a definite otherworldly energy about the place. A dark yet creative life force seemed to emanate from the ground itself, as if the campus rested on an intersecting nest of ley lines or a time warp.

Some said Bennington was built on a sacred Indian burial ground. They claimed that the Native Americans, who were in touch with the energies of the earth, found the site of Bennington extremely powerful. Supposedly, 'the end of the world' was one of the few naturally occurring geographical places where all four winds met at the same time. I often felt as if I could see into two dimensions at once, the present and the past. A few times, while walking on campus, I caught my reflection in a pane of glass. My reflection was shadowed by another reflection, of a girl who was not there. It was as if the veils between dimensions were paper-thin at Bennington, and the creative channels from a collective consciousness could penetrate all of us with clarity and precision. We were all sensitive and intuitive students, who were isolated, corralled and distilled into this energetically intense environment. I personally felt like I was plugged, metaphysically, into a hotline of inspiration.

Bennington College was a private liberal arts college founded for women in 1932. In the 1960s it became co-ed. By the time I got there in 1981, there were two and a half girls for every boy, and half the boys were gay. Competition for the few straight boys was fierce.

In high school, kids who were different (like me) were marginalised and ostracised. In Bennington they were idolised. Bennington College was a place to let your freak flag fly. Creativity was your currency. How talented you were amounted to your social stocks and shares; individuality and eccentricity were money in the cool bank. Internally, we referred to Bennington as 'an insane asylum for the rich'. It was the most expensive private college in America. A multitude of kids were heirs and heiresses to great fortunes. These included the heirs to the Campbell's soup fortune and Benson and Hedges cigarettes. One of the Getty girls was in my class, along with Princess Farahnaz, the ex-Shah of Iran's daughter.

I remember looking over the dappled courtyard during orientation and seeing a girl I thought looked super-cool. I had an instant girl crush and decided to make friends with her. Her name was Lisa

Feder and she came from Brooklyn. She had short curly blonde hair, cut into a coif, and wore ankle-length trousers and a vintage short sleeve shirt, with rolled-up sleeves, rockabilly-style. We became best friends almost instantly. I lived in one of the modern dorms called Noyes, with a very strange roommate. Her name was Michelle and I think she had some sort of serious depression. For her art project, she menstruated in fresh white knickers, for all six days of her period, and then tacked her knickers, crotch spread open, framed on a white background. She left school soon after, unexplained, but I heard she became quite a successful artist later in life.

Soon Lisa moved in with me and another girl, Caroline. Caroline was a pothead. She was so bad she used to 'wake and bake'. Sometimes she'd take a bong hit in the middle of the night and fall back to sleep again. In the morning, the first thing she did was to sit up in bed, reach for her water pipe and smoke another bowl.

Lisa and I bonded over music. We both had similar tastes but, being from NYC, she was slightly more switched on than I was. We started to dress like rockabilly girls or alienated post-punk teens like Echo and the Bunnymen or The Cure. We took our lovely clothes that our moms bought us and sold them on campus for drugs. Then, with the remainder of the money, we went to the local Salvation Army store in Bennington and bought old rain macs and vintage shirts and trousers. We also loved dyeing our hair. We both cut our hair like boys. I had an undercut and a long fringe that flopped in my face.

I was technically at Bennington as a theatre–literature major. I loved my creative writing classes and poetry workshop. We had some seriously talented writers in our class, including Donna Tartt, Bret Easton Ellis, Jonathan Lethem and Jill Eisenstadt. Even then, they were extraordinary.

Bennington was isolated. Left up to our own devices, we went stir-crazy. There were only six hundred students in the whole college, including graduate students. Sometimes we just had to get away. Usually we would have a night out at one of the local bars, like the Villager. 'The V' was in North Bennington, a short walk from campus. North Bennington was as creepy a town as I have ever seen. It bordered on sinister. To go there felt like stepping back in time. Every time I went, I felt like I was walking into an episode of *The Twilight Zone*. Students used to joke that the residents of North Bennington had one eye, two teeth and were all cousins.

Aside from our nights out at local bars, we made periodic weekend pilgrimages to New York City. This involved taking a Greyhound bus from Bennington to Albany, New York and then a second bus from Albany to the Port Authority in NYC. Our weekends in NYC were always epic adventures. One weekend, Lisa, Skinny Vinny, whom I had known since Lab School, and I decided to go to the city with almost no money and no place to stay. We only had just enough cash to get there. Somehow Lisa managed to get her hands on a large bag of marijuana. We figured if we could divide it up and sell small bags of it, we could make enough money to see us through the weekend. I thought this was a spectacularly bad idea, but the others were up for it so I went along.

The first night we ended up in the Red Bar in the East Village. We started chatting to people. The first person we tried to offload some pot on turned out to be Steve Rubell, the legendary owner of Studio 54, who had just been released from jail for tax evasion. The next person was a really sweet guy called Eric Ambel. Eric was the guitarist with Joan Jett and the Blackhearts. He had recently left the Blackhearts and started up his own band, the Del Lords. We became friends and, almost immediately, lovers.

Having nowhere to sleep, I assumed that if the worst came to the worst we would either stay up all night roaming around aimlessly or buckle under the pressure and knock on Lisa's mom's door in Brooklyn. Instead, Vinny had a mad idea. He knew a superintendent of a local apartment building and thought if we asked him nicely, he might let us sleep on his floor.

We made our way to the apartment building, and Vincent introduced us to Earl, a middle-aged black man. Earl took us down to the basement of the building where he stayed. It was a lair, a hovel, which was wallpapered floor to ceiling with pornographic pictures torn from magazines. I had a strong sense of foreboding. What were we getting into? Earl said we couldn't stay with *him*. But, he could do one better. He took us up to an apartment at the top of the building, whose residents were away for the weekend. It was a gorgeous apartment and we made ourselves at home, without touching or moving anything. Of course, I couldn't sleep. Anxiety plagued my mind. I had visions of the residents coming home early. I listened for the sound of the key in the lock and imagined them finding three rag-tag interlopers staying, Goldilocks-style, in their home.

The next day we hung out again, with Eric Ambel and his friend John Aiosa. John also worked with Joan Jett. The next night Eric and John took us to an after-hours bar. John always had a plentiful supply of cocaine and we stayed up all night. Every time one of us started to fade, John would shove another mini-spoonful of coke under our nostrils and we'd perk up again. By the next day, we were the worse for wear. Exhausted, strung out and shaking, we made our way to the Port Authority bus station and back to Bennington. Naturally, we didn't have the funds to get back to school, so I sold my Sony Walkman at the terminal for just enough cash to get us back.

January and February are bitterly cold in Vermont. Bennington ran a special programme during those months, called 'non-resident term'. Over this period, school was not in session. Instead we were expected to get a job in the 'real world'. We could either do something we were interested in doing in the future, or we could just have a working or internship experience.

I decided to go back to Chicago, where it was also hideously cold, and take a job at Marshall Field and Company. Marshall Field's was a massive landmark department store, smack in the middle of Chicago's downtown 'Loop'. I was to start working with the window-display team. I learned how to dress, style and install a themed shop window. I was the lowest person on the totem pole and was treated as such. I swept floors and papered tables in the design room with brown butcher's paper. My most time-consuming and painstaking task was to brush out and comb the mannequins' wigs. We were never allowed to call the mannequins 'dummies'. They were only referred to as 'girls'. They were treated with reverence. Mannequins made by Adel Rootstein were the Rolls Royce of models and cost over $1,000. Each night when I would put them away, I had to cover their faces in silken bags to protect the artistry of their make-up.

The whole time I worked at Marshall Field and Company I dreamed of being a rock star. My work station in the design room was plastered with tear-outs from magazines of my favourite musicians. I remember having a classic photo of the Ramones wearing ripped blue jeans and leather jackets, and Debbie Harry in her Dr X T-shirt.

Working with the mannequins all day long did not help my body image. In fact, it brought up underlying issues of insecurity. The 'girls' were physical perfection, and I could not help comparing myself with them. I remember one day actually despairing that one of their upper thighs was the same size as my arm.

I learned a hell of a lot at Marshall Field's. All my window-display experience would come into its own in the future, when my husband Philip and I opened START boutique in East London. I would create some fantastic window displays amounting to retail theatre. But, of course, I wasn't to know that at Field's.

Back at Bennington I took courses in theatre arts, acting, Alexander technique and visual arts classes, as well as music. I had a particularly inspiring class called 'Stringed Instruments'. We played everything that was stringed. It got me thinking: I had always wanted to play bass guitar, figuring that with only four strings it couldn't be too hard to learn. I knew I'd never be able to master the classical guitar this late in the day. But bass? Now here was a possibility.

I took the book money I had left over for the month and went down to the second-hand store. As if it was meant to be, just sitting there waiting for me was an old black electric Carvin bass. It cost $50. I took it back to my dorm room and started messing around. The strings were fat and hard to press down. They made a dull ping when I plucked them and resonated with a hollow sound that died away fast.

I had no idea about where the notes were, so I walked over to McCullough House to see a guy who was considered to be the best guitarist at school. His name was Ian Gittler. Ian showed me the basics – E, A, D and G strings and where the notes were on them. He showed me how to fingerpick and pluck to create a rhythm. He assured me that the most important thing was to practise.

I sat on my dorm-room bed and played for hours. The bass guitar became an extension of my body. My fingers blistered, on both hands, but the joy of playing overrode any pain. Effortlessly, a song fell into place. It was so natural and easy, I didn't have time to question where it had come from. First came the melody and the basic structure, then the words followed, fully formed. The entire song took me less than an hour to write. The song was called 'Edie', and it was an ode to dead style icon Edie Sedgwick. Edie had been a socialite and 'It Girl' in the sixties. She was famously a muse of artist Andy Warhol. I used to model myself on Edie and emulate her. I asked Lisa to listen to my new song. She sat on the bed opposite to me and listened intently. Afterwards she said three words: 'Brixton, that's amazing!'

'Edie' would go on to become the second single I released with my solo band The Adult Net.

BANDA DRATSING

Right there and then we decided to form a band. We looked like a band anyway. We certainly had the attitude. We walked around all day, pretending we were rock stars. Lisa had a guitar too, a red Epiphone. She could barely play but had mastered a standard bar chord pretty well, and that was enough. After all, the Ramones used only three chords and their songs were brilliant. That in itself gave me more than hope.

We started to practise all the time in our dorm room. Our band needed a name. We toyed with The Rage, but settled on Banda Dratsing. 'Banda' and 'Dratsing' were two separate words in the made-up language Nadsat, taken from the book *A Clockwork Orange*, which we both loved. 'Banda' meant band, and 'Dratsing' meant fighting. Fighting Band.

The next two songs I wrote came to me as quickly and easily as the first. One of the songs was called 'Can't Stop the Flooding'. It later became the Fall song 'God-Box' (Mark rewrote the lyrics). The third song I wrote was originally called 'One More Time for the Record'. It was renamed 'Hotel Blöedel' and became the first song I ever recorded with The Fall, on the album *Perverted by Language*. The album version of 'Hotel Blöedel' remains exactly as I wrote it. Mark added a spoken word over my verse and a haunting three-string (out of tune) violin. That was our first proper collaboration and remains one of my personal favourites.

But back in 1982, two girls playing bass and guitar in their dorm room was hardly going to set the world alight. To be a real band we needed a drummer, to take it to the next level.

Claus Castenskiold was a year above us in school. He was devastatingly handsome. Supposedly, he was the descendant of Danish royalty and was rumoured to be a prince. He was extremely popular at school, and the subject of many a crush. He stood over six feet tall. Not only did he have sculpted cheekbones and cropped hair but he had a lazy, entitled, European swagger about him.

Claus came to Bennington to study painting. He was one of the most promising talents in the art programme. His paintings depicted figures and buildings that were psychedelically angular, as if viewed through the fractured fragments of a broken mirror. They were off-kilter and disturbing. It made one fear for the state of mind of the artist. Claus would go on to paint album and single covers for The Fall, including *Perverted by Language* and 'Oh! Brother'.

Luckily for us, Claus was also a talented drummer. He kept a full drum kit at school. We decided to pluck up our courage and ask him to be in our band. Amazingly, he accepted.

We started to rehearse at night in an old red barn, which was part of the admissions building on campus. The three of us playing together felt marvellous. We were a power trio. Having a live drummer was a musical game-changer for me. I was able to hook my bass notes around a solid beat, which completed some kind of electrical circuit in my mind and body. I felt high and completely energised.

Almost immediately we started to plan our first gig. Our debut would take place at the canteen in the students' union. We rehearsed a few nights a week, and started to spread the word: Banda Dratsing was playing live.

On the day of our gig I was so nervous I couldn't eat. My mind was laser-focused on the show. All other aspects of life were completely shut out. As we took the stage, my brain emptied of all thought. My hands shook as I started to play, but in no time at all I switched on to autopilot. My rehearsing paid off. The music flowed through me, and I became the music. Any nerves I had evaporated as I grew in confidence. We ploughed our way through eight songs and left the canteen to rapturous applause.

After the show I was physically tingling all over. My mind was zinging. It was one of the best feelings I had ever known. A girl named Lisa Martizia came to congratulate me and asked me why I was still at school. 'Brixton,' she said, 'you should be doing this for real.' *The seed was planted.*

A few days after our triumphant debut, Ian Gittler, the guy who'd showed me the notes on the bass, asked if I had seen the graffiti about me in the boys' bathroom? 'No, Ian, why would I go in the boys' bathroom?' I said. 'Let me show you,' he said. Ian took my hand and led me in. I was almost too scared to look. I imagined it said something awful and smutty. I kept my eyes clamped shut. 'Look,' he said. 'Open your eyes.' There, written in bold black magic marker above the boys' toilet, were the words 'BRIXTON IS GOD'.

LEAVE OR DIE

I truly believe I am guided by the force of the universe. I know this is a bold statement to make. I also believe in signs. I see signs all the time. When something seems to me to go beyond a mere coincidence, I pay close attention. I use my gut instincts or inner guidance system like a dowsing rod to feel out the direction I take in life.

My second year at Bennington was an unmitigated chain of disasters. One incident after another drove me to the conclusion that I had to leave Bennington – and not just Bennington, but college altogether. I felt this *so strongly* that I now believe the universe was *shoving* me towards my *destiny*.

As the first term of my second year wore on, each incident became progressively more dramatic. Until, finally, as Christmas approached, and I headed back to Chicago in shame, I heard these words in my head: '*Leave or die.*'

Instead of living on campus, in one of the old-school New England-style dorms or the modern ones like Noyes, I'd made the choice to live in a shared house off campus. My roommate was an odd girl called Julie, who was from Scarsdale, New York. Julie became extremely possessive of me. She followed me everywhere and was inappropriately jealous of my other friendships. At first I thought she was insecure and lonely. One day, when I returned from school, she called to me from the bath and asked me to bring her something. When I went in I saw that she was in the bath with all my lingerie swirling around her. I moved out.

Bennington had a rule that you needed to change roommates every term. This meant Lisa and I could no longer room together.

I moved into Swan House, one of the old Vermont houses on campus. Then a large double studio opened up in Sawtell House, one of the modern dorms next to Noyes. Somehow Lisa and I managed to convince the housing committee to let us live together again. Our new room was perfect for rehearsing. It was a big open space in the basement. We loved our new room. We practised our instruments and listened to records with the sound blasting, while dancing to the music. In that room, I remember first hearing Culture Club's 'Do You Really Want to Hurt Me', Tears For Fears' 'Mad World' and Visage's 'Fade to Grey', as well as becoming infatuated with Depeche Mode.

We were always up on what was happening in the UK music charts and tried to listen to everything we could. Lisa and I continued to make periodic trips to NYC for weekends. I still hooked up and remained friends with Eric Ambel and John Aiosa. We had endless nights partying in the city. I remember a particularly scary incident in the Gramercy Park Hotel. In New York, in those days, you could dial a number and a town car would arrive to deliver drugs. You could literally order off a drug menu. We were staying with Eric and John. We were on a two- or three-day bender and had been up for most of the time. At a certain point, round about the middle of night two, my system could take no more and I 'wigged out'. I started shaking, consumed by sleep deprivation and severe anxiety. I had to be calmed down by John. I ended up being comforted by him and then sleeping with him behind Eric and Lisa's back.

Mercifully, I learned my limits with coke. It was unpleasant to feel *so* out of control and it frightened the bejesus out of me.

Back at school I started dating a guy named Mark Norris. Mark was tall and extremely good-looking; a sweetheart of a man. We had a tempestuous on-and-off relationship. I remember being quite high-maintenance and possessive. These are not great qualities to foist on a boyfriend.

They came from my own insecurity. Back in those days, every relationship I had was an emotional rollercoaster. I was addicted to drama. I pushed many a man away with this behaviour. In the times that I pushed Mark away, he found solace in the arms of his other on-campus girlfriend, Donna Tartt. He bounced between us. (Since I really liked Donna, I felt happy for them when she and Mark were together. Of course, in my 'high drama' moods I was prone to jealous rages but somehow I didn't feel jealous of Mark being with Donna.)

I continued my course studies and practised with Banda Dratsing, much as I had done during the previous year. But something inside me felt different. There was an undercurrent of panic, an ungrounded energy swirling around me. I couldn't explain it. I couldn't quite put my finger on what was causing it. I only took notice of it after a series of *bizarre accidents*. At first I chalked up *the accidents* to a run of bad luck. But in the end, the synchronicity of the occurrences shook me to the core and changed the course of my life.

The first incident seemed innocent enough. In art class, we were assigned a project to create a sculpture out of cardboard, and were given two tools: a Stanley knife to cut the cardboard and a hot glue gun to stick the pieces together. I decided to make a sort of wigwam, which was actually an alien spacecraft. It would be human-sized and I would be able to sit inside. We had a massive art studio in the VAPA (visual and performing arts) building. It was gloriously modern, made of wood, glass and concrete. This impressive architectural structure was open twenty-four hours a day so we could work on our art whenever the muse struck us.

One night, very late, I decided to go and finish my sculpture. An architect I am not, so I was having trouble preventing the wigwam from collapsing. In my frustration and fatigue, I had an accident with the hot glue gun. Somehow, I managed to shoot a wad of burning glue all over my arm. The pain was spectacular. I ran screaming to the medical centre. Thankfully, there was a nurse on duty. She informed me I had second-degree burns and held my arm under streaming cold water for half an hour. She explained this was to prevent the glue burning deeper into more layers of skin. After that, the nurse cleaned my burn and bandaged it up. I went back to my dorm and tried to sleep. It was agony.

The next incident took place on Halloween. I was due to go to a party in one of the old dorms with Mark Norris. Before the party we had sex. I remember feeling wild and whipped up. The dark energy of Bennington was coursing through me. At the party I ran into Tyler Scott, a sexy gay man of whom I was very fond. He was dressed as a vampire. I guess he was really embodying the character because, before I knew it, he had pushed me up against a wall and was telling me he wanted to drink my blood. He kissed me deeply and passionately on the neck. I felt thrilled by the role-playing. The kiss got even deeper and more intense. He sunk his teeth into the delicate skin on my throat. I shivered.

He drew blood.

A few days later I was in my dorm room, changing. As I pulled off my turtleneck jumper, I felt pain where it grazed my neck. Then I remembered *the bite*. I ran to the mirror and sure enough, there was an angry welt where Tyler Scott had bitten me. It was greenish in colour and very sore. I ran to the Bennington College medical centre again, suspecting it was infected. I told the doctor that I had been bitten. He turned to me, and with a quiet, calm voice asked, 'What bit you?'

'A guy bit me,' I explained. 'At a party.'

He looked at me, his eyes widening in a dramatic way, trying to make sense of what had happened. In the gravest voice, he asked, 'A human bit you?'

'Yes,' I said. 'What's the big deal? Is it infected?'

'Don't you know?' he said raising his voice, barely disguising his panic. 'Human bites can be deadly. This one is very infected. We are going to have to deal with this right now before we send you to hospital. This is very serious.' His face was full of horror. The doctor explained that the germs in the human mouth are extremely dangerous. He took my blood, to test it to see how serious the infection was. Then he told me to lie down on the table.

'What are you going to do?' I asked.

'I'm going to cut it out,' he said. 'This is going to be very painful, but we have no choice.'

'Can't I have a painkiller?' I pleaded.

'No,' he said. 'There's no time left. You've already waited too long to get here. You're just going to have to grit your teeth and deal with it.'

At that point, an amazing thing happened. A crystal-clear thought sprang into my head. It wasn't spoken to me in words. It was a thought but not in my own voice. The guidance was so clear, calm and reassuring. I had no idea where it came from. I didn't question it or even try to analyse it. One can argue it was my higher self. As bizarre as that might seem to some people, I chose to believe it was an angel. The thought told me to separate my mind from my body. It said, if I could detach myself mentally from my physical being, I could rise above my body and feel no pain.

With zero emotion and freakishly no fear, I watched the doctor, with shaky hands, slice into my neck, cutting around the infected area, and gouge out the bite.

I felt *nothing*.

Just a few minutes before, the simple act of removing a sweater had been painful. It was incredible. The doctor asked me how I had done it. How I had remained silent and unflinching. I explained how I had separated myself from my body and felt no pain. He was amazed.

After the bite had been excised, he called the nurse, who came in with a bowl of steaming-hot salt water. She soaked compresses in the salt water and applied them to my neck for an hour. She told me it would help draw out the poison. The doctor also gave me a massive injection of antibiotics. He didn't wait for the blood-test results to come back. He was taking no chances. He also prescribed antibiotic pills. Twice a day for the next week I had to return to the medical centre to have the salt-water compresses applied to my neck. When the results of the blood test eventually came back, I had indeed contracted a very serious staph infection. That doctor had most probably saved my life.

The third incident happened a few weeks later, and it was also very serious. I had been having an on-and-off flirtation for a year with a guy named Brian Peeper. Brian had a long-term girlfriend and I'd been seeing Mark, but nothing could stop the sexual tension from building between us. The fact that we were sneaking around only added grist to the mill. I was besotted with Brian. Because we couldn't spend a lot of time together, whenever we did, I behaved like an idiotic schoolgirl, literally intoxicated by our meetings.

One night, when Brian's girlfriend was in New York, he invited me over to his dorm. We hung out and smoked a joint. At some point he informed me that Amanda was due back any minute and I had better leave or risk getting caught. Amanda was a beautiful, feisty, popular girl, and I feared her wrath. I left Brian's dorm and dreamily walked back to mine. Bennington was prone to fogs and mists. Swirling mists hovered above the ground like sinister vapours.

The next thing I remember was feeling stunned and hearing a thud as my head hit a cement wall. I did not know what had happened or where exactly I was when I came to. All I knew was that I needed to get back to my room and get help. I staggered to my feet and half-crawled and half-walked to my dorm. When I got there, Lisa was in, thank God.

'Oh my God! Brixton, what happened to you? What did he do to you?' she said.

'He didn't do anything. What are you talking about, Lisa? Why am I covered in red paint?'

'That's not paint,' Lisa said. 'It's blood!'

'What happened?' I asked, bewildered.

'I'm calling an ambulance,' Lisa shrieked.

I remember nothing else from that night. I woke the next day in the hospital, with a bandage around my head. I had serious concussion and a deep graze where my head had collided with the wall. I had fallen into a cement basement, outside Brian's dorm, and whacked the back of my head on the wall as I fell. The cement wall had sheared off some hair follicles. I would forever have a bald patch to remind me of this time.

When I got back to Bennington, rumours were rife. The predominant theory was that I jumped off the top of Sawtell House in an attempt to commit suicide.

Less than two weeks later, I started to feel unwell. I was nauseous on and off and extremely claustrophobic. Even a low-ceilinged room was enough to set me off. I was also moody. The slightest thing sent me into a full-blown rage. One afternoon, Lisa and I arranged to meet in our room to tidy it up. When Lisa, who had spent the night with a couple she was seeing, turned up late, I went nuclear. I threw things, kicked walls and shouted. I felt bad about it afterward, but I was literally unable to control it at the time. When you suffer concussion all kinds of symptoms emerge, including depression, frustration and rage. Your personality can change.

The morning after the fight, Lisa and I went to breakfast together in the cafeteria on the first floor of the commons building. As I walked up the stairs and into the cafeteria I was overwhelmed with claustrophobia. The smell coming from the kitchen of cooking eggs was revolting. I gagged and ran out of the building and sat on the steps in the fresh air. I really felt unwell. I thought perhaps I had the flu. The next morning I woke up and was ravenous for maple walnut ice cream. Normally I'm a chocolate person. Or chocolate chip, but maple walnut? Never. I went to the kitchen and managed to find some. This was was Vermont, after all, and maple (especially syrup) is big there. I ate a huge bowl and went back to bed. As soon as I lay down I was overwhelmed with nausea. I ran to the sink and threw up. I couldn't even make it to the toilet. Either I had the stomach flu or there was something really wrong from the concussion.

That night I had my weekly phone conversation with my mother in Chicago. She asked me how I was feeling, and I told her. She listened, asked me a few questions and then said, 'Do your breasts hurt?'

I felt them there and then while standing at the pay phone. They hurt. 'I think you might be pregnant,' my mother said. 'You'd better go to the doctor and be tested.'

I was absolutely dumbstruck. Being pregnant was something I had feared. It could mean your life as you knew it was over, and it was stigmatising, if not marginally scandalous.

Swallowing my embarrassment, I went to the medical centre (once again) and asked for a pregnancy test. The same nurse who had helped me through the burn and the bite took my blood. 'My,' she said, 'you've had a rough time.'

By then, I didn't actually need the test results to know that I was pregnant. Once my mother had said it, I knew it was true.

I felt ashamed. I didn't want to tell anyone. Pregnancy gossip would spread around the campus like wild fire. I had only three weeks left until the end of term, when we would break for the Christmas holidays. Those were three long weeks.

I knew I would never keep the baby.

It wasn't even an option for me.

I kept my head down for the last few weeks of school. I was low and depressed, racked with shame. I counted down the days until I could leave. I remember telling Lisa about the pregnancy but swore her to secrecy. The chain of incidents over the term had left me with hostility to Bennington. It just didn't feel good to me any more. I didn't feel safe there. I believed that school could not teach me what I needed to learn. Only life could teach me that. I felt I had absorbed everything Bennington had to offer. It was as if I had been 'hothoused' and my learning there was freakishly accelerated, time-warp-style. I instinctively knew it was time to leave. I knew dropping out of school would upset Mom and Marvin but I was willing to take the risk. I had to do what I believed in. I had to follow my gut instinct. Who knew what might be around the corner? When one door closes, another one often opens. Leap and the net will appear (except, apparently, when leaping into a basement).

A DATE WITH FATE

My tongue must have been silver-coated or my enthusiasm infectious because I convinced Lisa to take a term off from Bennington to come to Chicago and play music with me. We moved into the third floor of my mother's and Marvin's house and set up a makeshift rehearsal room. I'd dropped out of school. This was real now. We were a band.

People who are lost or are struggling with a transition in their lives sometimes ask me how I have managed to reinvent myself time and again. The simple answer is that I've always followed my passion. Even if the choice goes against everything I know is right in my head, I follow my heart. When I've tried to follow my head, I inevitably hit brick walls.

What I've learned is that life should feel good for as much of the time as possible. When things feel good and you are enjoying them, the journey itself becomes fulfilling. I believe that if you do what you love you will succeed, on some level. When I'm feeling stuck, I take solace in this quote: 'Your talent is your best security.'

Lisa and I needed a drummer to complete the band in order to play live gigs. Claus would not leave Bennington, so we decided to advertise for a new drummer in the *Chicago Reader*. The ad said, 'Drummer wanted to join two girls, bass and guitar, for a power-punk-garage trio. Influences: Joy Division, The Clash, Blondie and the Ramones.'

We got a few responses and decided to go with a goofy, nerdy intellectual named Rob Clarke, mostly because we liked the way he looked. Rob was the first person to tell me about the newly opened Haçienda club in Manchester. He told us the club belonged to

New Order and their manager. He said it was the coolest club in the world and there was nothing like it. Unimaginably, in less than six months I'd be walking through its doors.

As many days a week as we could, we rehearsed with Rob. I remember him being adequate, but not a patch on Claus in either drumming skills or attitude. This was my first taste of inter-band dynamics and the pitfalls of personality clashes and ego battles – it would not be my last. Far from it.

Practically every night after rehearsing, Lisa and I would hit the clubs. We saw every great band that came to town. Sometimes we'd just go out dancing and socialising, returning home to Mom and Marvin's house, sweaty and elated, in the early hours. Lisa and I were becoming well known, and people seemed to love our energy and attitude. Of course we were still underage but the promoters and club managers turned a blind eye.

Late one night while on our way home, we passed by our favourite record shop, Wax Trax. It was still open, so we decided to go in and have a look to see if anything new had come in from the UK. We loved it because they imported foreign records that were not yet released or might never be released in the US. We were always looking for discoveries and quite often bought records for their covers alone. We headed straight for the import section and started pawing through the bins alphabetically. When we got to 'F', Lisa snatched out an EP. It was smaller than an album and contained six tracks. It was called *Slates*, by The Fall.

'Oh my God, Brixton,' Lisa said. 'Have you ever heard The Fall?'

'No, I've never even heard of them. Who are they? What are they like?'

'They're the *GODS* of the East Village! They are so cool.'

'Let's get it,' I said.

Life is about duality. The tide had turned. The chain of bad incidents that had befallen me just months before came to be replaced by a series of amazing synchronistic events. If I hadn't

gone through the horrendous events that drove me to leave
Bennington, I'd never have been standing in Wax Trax holding
fate in my hands.

We went back home and I put *Slates* on the turntable. I couldn't
get to the record player fast enough. What I heard was unlike anything I'd heard before. The sound of The Fall was unique. It was
uncategorisable. The bass and the drums were instantly hypnotic.
The singer was not singing and not speaking, but delivering a powerful fine line between the two. The guitars were barbed and crude
but at the same time they created a lush, doleful soundscape. The
sound was simultaneously naive and genius. The lyrics were nearly
unintelligible. *Slates* was like an aural Rorschach test.

Because I couldn't understand all the words, my mind filled in
meanings particular to me. The music dragged up my own subconscious thoughts in an effort to make sense of what was being
sung. My interpretation of the songs was actually a window into
my own psyche, telling me far more about myself than I would
garner from reading the lyrics on a page.

I couldn't get enough of this record. I became obsessed with
it. The songs were infectious in a way that I had not experienced
before. They were intellectually contagious. I found myself thinking deeply about them for days, trying to make sense of it. Every
chance I got, I ran to the turntable to play the record again. I
was desperate to understand what was being said, what the songs
were about, not realising that part of the power of the music was
this precise effect it had in the brain of the listener. I scoured the
record sleeve for clues. There was a blurry nondescript photo of
the band on the front cover, but I couldn't tell anything about
them from the picture. Contrary to most of the other albums I
had, these musicians were shrouded in mystery. The shadowy pho-
tograph piqued my interest even more. The elimination of ego
reinforced the importance of the music. Strange notes and lyric
scraps were scrawled in freehand writing on the sides of the cover.

The scribbled words and typed bits of description were no help at all and seemed to render the meaning of the lyrics even more cryptic. What was meant by 'Real Bert Finn stuff'? What was a 'wet lib file'? Or 'starring "gent" and "man" in Asda mix-up spy thriller'? Or even 'Religion costs much – but irreligion costs more'?

The Fall's music was more challenging than any music I had ever listened to. It made demands on my intellect. By comparison, most of the pop music I had been listening to puddled into pools of banality.

One night, exactly two weeks after we had bought *Slates*, Lisa came running into the bedroom clutching the *Chicago Reader*, shrieking, 'Brixton, look! You're never going to believe this . . . The Fall are playing in Chicago on Saturday, at the Metro!'

The shocking coincidence of the timing was not lost on either of us. It felt that it was meant to be.

On Saturday 23 April 1983, Lisa and I paid the $6 ticket price and entered through the front doors of Cabaret Metro, 3730 North Clark Street. The room was full and we mingled with the other concertgoers, some of whom we knew from clubs. The scene was fairly small in Chicago in those days, so even if we didn't know everyone's names, we recognised quite a few people – one of whom was a guy we referred to as 'Mop Top'. He was adorable and aloof. We'd seen him around but never actually spoken to him. Although Lisa and I had tried to catch his attention numerous times, he'd always ignored us. On this night, however, the opposite happened. Mop Top, whose real name we found out was Bill, made a beeline for Lisa. It seemed Bill had clocked us before, but had not had the confidence to chat to us. Bill and Lisa started talking, and hit it off. Before I knew it, Lisa asked me if it would be OK for her to go out with Bill after the concert. Of course it was OK with me. I was happy for her but, to be utterly honest, I have to admit I felt a pang of insecurity. Lisa and I had never been separated since she came to Chicago. She had never left my side. As Lisa and Bill moved off to get acquainted, I was left on my own to watch the show. The concert started and I was transfixed.

The first thing that caught my attention was the pulverising bass line. Immediately, I locked in with the music, rocking back and forth as if in a trance. I felt the music in such a visceral way. At last, I got to see what the band looked like. I was stunned. They looked normal! They were five normal-looking English blokes. I had expected posing and posturing, because that's what I was used to. These guys were the antithesis of rock stars. They were anti-fashion too. There were no gimmicks or contrivances. A manufactured commercial band this was not. This band were a law unto themselves: mighty and brutal, unforgiving, honest, and utterly brilliant.

The bass player was a tall man who played hunched over his instrument. He made no eye contact with the audience at all. He too rocked back and forth to the music as if in a state of abstraction. His punishing bass lines were flagellating, mesmerising and savage. Because I played the bass, I was most focused on him. I wanted to absorb everything I could from watching this man. I stood there like a sponge, rooted to the spot, swaying like a bewitched heathen.

The singer was an odd character. He was lanky and skinny, with a head of nondescript brown hair. He had huge eyes and dimples in his cheeks. He seemed angry, as if a simmering rage lay just below the surface. He looked dangerous to me. I remember thinking that I wouldn't like to be friends with this guy. There was something a little scary about him. His stage presence was unlike anything I'd seen before. He stalked the stage, snarling out words, spitting the lyrics out with hiss and vitriol. At points he almost sang, but his singing was raw and keening. I can only describe it as a percussive type of sing-speak. He periodically turned his back to the audience, which was jarring and felt like an act of defiance. Try as I might, I still couldn't decipher the lyrics. They were even harder to understand live than on the record.

There was only one guitar player. I had expected two. He was standing off to the left side of the stage and appeared to be in his own world. He was also detached from the audience. The noises coming out of his guitar were something equivalent to alchemy. It wasn't 'normal' guitar-playing. In fact, I'd never heard a guitar make sounds like that before. I noticed he was a lefty. I think he was playing a right-handed guitar strung upside down. It was battered and blue. He was also stooped over his instrument, so much so that I couldn't get a look at his face. The noise from his single guitar filled the sonic holes in the room, like a sauce immersing the ingredients of a soup. At times it was abrasive and atonal, at other times it was melancholy and beautifully tragic.

There were two drummers. I had only seen that once before, when I saw Adam and the Ants. Watching and listening to The Fall, the two drummers reached another level. They worked their kits like voodoo hit men. One drummer was young, tall, baby-faced and good-looking. He seemed to be playing what I would call more traditional or lead drums. His power was immense, his rhythm ferocious and unapologetic. The second drummer was an animal. I can only describe his style as tribal. While the first drummer focused on the whole kit, this one, the animal, worked the floor toms, cow bell and snare rims. He was swarthy with unkempt curly black locks. He had piercing dark eyes and heavy brows. He looked Romani. The way he interwove his beats with the main drummer was nothing short of brilliant.

I recognised all the songs from *Slates* as I stood there, in the middle of the crowded floor, in the Metro. I was slack-jawed, mind-blown and utterly transported. The world evaporated around me. In the hour and a half that I saw The Fall for the first time I felt as if I had left the planet.

After the show, Lisa was nowhere to be seen. I assumed she had left with Bill, and that I would see her in the morning. I wished she were there so that we could discuss the brilliance of what we'd just experienced. On my own, I decided to head downstairs to the Smart Bar. This was the bar attached to the venue. It wasn't about getting a drink, I wanted to prolong this wonderful night. I didn't want it to end. But without Lisa to bolster my confidence, I felt insecure, awkward and shy. It would have been far easier and less challenging to get back into my car and head home, but I didn't. I felt compelled to go to that bar no matter how uneasy I felt.

The bar was crowded. The lighting was dim. I started to wade my way through the sea of people to try to find someone I knew. Everyone was talking to each other. I meandered, pretending to look for my friend.

Then all at once, BANG! I bumped into a man walking back from the bar. He was carrying a beer in each hand. 'I'm sorry,' I said. As I looked up, I recognised the lead singer from the band. I had smacked right into the lead singer. I was so flustered I didn't know what to do, so I blurted out, 'That was such a great gig and I love your music so much, but your lyrics really irritate me because I can't understand them!'

He looked at me. He bent down and spoke softly into my ear, so I could hear him above the din. 'Why don't we sit down and discuss it,' he suggested.

We sat at a table. It was loud in the bar. I asked him his name. 'Mark.' He asked me mine and I told him, 'Brixton.' He looked at me incredulously, 'Brixton?' and laughed. I tried to have a sensible conversation with him, but it was nearly impossible. The background noise was clamorous, and Mark had a very thick accent. It wasn't an accent I was used to. It was Mancunian, but it sounded more like German to me. I remember feeling a bit stunned, sitting there with Mark. We couldn't really communicate with each other but there was a strange and tangible energy between us. There was electricity, in fact, more than that. I can only describe it as magnetic. If felt inevitable, like the force of two magnets connecting. We sat there staring at each other. I didn't want to go but I was feeling awkward, and I didn't want him to think I was a groupie simply after him, looking to hook up. As hard as it was, I stood up and pushed my chair back, and muttered something about it getting late and that I needed to go. He looked at me and said, 'Would you like to come to a party with me?'

'Whose party is it?' I asked. 'Where is it?'

'It's at someone's house. They are throwing it for the band,' he said. 'We can get a taxi.'

'OK,' I replied. 'But we don't need a taxi. I can drive. I have a car.'

My gut instinct told me that if I had left and gone home, I might have regretted it for ever. 'What the hell,' I thought. 'This is an adventure.' I couldn't believe that I was actually going to a party and hanging out with The Fall.

I wasn't initially attracted to Mark. I was fascinated by him. This guy was obviously hugely intelligent and creative. I observed him as we walked to my car. I worried I might not be able to think of anything to say to him. I didn't want to say anything lame, so I let him do most of the talking.

He loved my car. It was a 1966 Ford Futura. Even though I wished it were flashier, Mark commented on the cool retro-ness of it, and the fact that it was Prussian blue. As we got in the car, Mark asked me what I did. I turned and looked him in the eye. 'I'm a musician,' I said.

'Do you have any tapes of your music?' he asked.

Of course I did. I was told once that you should always carry a demo tape of your music because you never knew whom you might meet.

'Can I hear it?' he asked.

Nervously, I popped it into the cassette player. It was a rehearsal tape of Banda Dratsing, with me, Lisa and Rob. It had three songs on it. Mark listened silently for the duration of the tape. The anticipation of what he would say next was excruciating. This was the first time a professional musician, or anyone who was really in the music industry, had heard what we were doing. I shifted in my seat and steeled myself for criticism, constructive or otherwise.

The tape finished. Mark sat in silence for a beat. I was practically hyperventilating but trying to remain cool.

Mark turned to me. 'Who wrote those songs?' he asked.

'I did,' I said shyly.

Then, what he said next took my breath away. 'You're a fuckin' genius.'

I sat there stunned.

There was a part of me that didn't trust Mark or what he said. After all, I'd known him all of one hour. Did he have an agenda? Was he telling me what I wanted to hear in order to placate me so he could carry out a different plan? Like getting me into bed?

Although I had vowed never to think about the rape again, I'm sure it was in my subconscious. I was now wary of men, slightly distrustful. As much as I fought these feelings, I was not the happy, free, trusting person I once had been. I did my best to push these negative thoughts away. I wouldn't let them infect this moment and spoil the joy I was feeling. We drove to the party. As we chatted, mostly small talk, I was trying to get to grips with Mark's thick Northern accent. Inside I was still reeling with what he'd said about my songs. I was trying very hard to remain cool and nonchalant, as if this type of thing happened to me all the time. I had the feeling I was being discovered.

What was odd, though, was that somewhere inside me, all of this felt so familiar. There was a feeling of almost déjà vu. It was as if I knew this would happen. I found it difficult to explain any of this rationally.

The party was in an apartment. It was crowded. I knew no one. It was very man-heavy. Mark introduced me around. I met the rest of the band. They took little overt notice of me but I did catch them clocking me slyly with raised eyebrows. I wondered if it was common for Mark to pick up girls at a gig and 'pull' them. None of the band spoke to me that night, except muttering a 'hello'. I was dying to talk to the bass player, whose name, I found out, was Steve Hanley. Steve was in a conversation with an American man who had Steve backed into a corner and was dominating both him and the discussion. I noticed that Steve hardly spoke and seemed very shy and quiet. He didn't seem approachable, and I didn't have the confidence to try.

The most talkative person at the party turned out to be Pat, The Fall's American tour manager. Pat was a plump fellow from Hoboken, New Jersey. He was a fun-loving, beer-drinking kind of guy. Mark went to Pat and asked him for some pills. Pat removed a plastic bag full of colourful capsules. He twisted off the two ends of a capsule, poured the powder out on to a glass coffee table and divided it into three small lines, then handed Mark a rolled-up $5 bill. Mark snorted the powder then offered me the note, so that I could partake.

'What is it?' I asked.

'It's caffeine,' Mark informed me.

'Just caffeine, like in coffee?' I questioned.

'Yes.'

I tried the tiniest bit. My nose burned and my scalp tingled. It was speed. 'Ugh,' I thought. I'd hated speed ever since I'd tried home-cooked Ritalin at Bennington while cramming for finals. A few months later The Fall would pay homage to Pat, their tour manager, in a song entitled 'Pat – Trip Dispenser'. In the lyrics, Mark remarks on his 'imitation speed' and refers to Pat as 'the Spine-Fuhrer of Hoboken', which I found hilarious.

After much beer-drinking and fake-speed-imbibing (but not by me), the party began to thin out. I offered to drive Mark back to his hotel. I was a little nervous as to how this would pan out. I had firmly made up my mind not to get out of the car and go into Mark's hotel. That would just be asking for trouble. I did not want

Mark to confuse me with a groupie. I was a musician and wanted to be treated and respected as such.

But, of course, I was torn. I was feeling the frisson of electricity. How could I not? I didn't want to get carried away. I had to keep a cool, calm head. Tomorrow, Mark and The Fall would be heading off to another city on the tour. I was determined not to become a road statistic. I decided I would have to be direct with him, and if and when the appropriate time came I would tell him, in no uncertain terms, that nothing was going to happen between us.

As we drove up to Mark's hotel, I saw it was in fact a motel. It was very budget and old-school, with a lot of character. I stopped the car and said goodbye and thanked him for everything.

Mark sat rooted to the spot. He shifted in his seat. He seemed to be searching for words. There was a moment of awkwardness. Then he asked, 'Won't you come up for a drink?'

'I don't want to drink,' I said. 'I'm driving home. Plus, I'm not sure it's appropriate that I come up to your room. You might get the wrong idea. I'm not a groupie.'

'I promise nothing will happen,' Mark replied. 'I will be a perfect gentleman. You don't even have to drink. I swear. I'll even buy you a grape soda.'

It was the grape soda that convinced me. Although, to be honest, I didn't need much arm-twisting. I didn't want to go home, but I knew saying goodbye and going home alone was the appropriate, intelligent choice to make. Grape soda was such a nerdy, safe, insipid drink. I hadn't had one since I was five. Anyone who would offer a drink as innocent as grape soda was trustable, I figured. I could tell he really wanted me to come up. I felt he didn't want this night to end, and, truly, neither did I.

Mark's motel room was basic, Americana-kitsch décor. It had twin beds, an old-fashioned TV with rabbit-ear antennas and a retro colour scheme of burnt orange, avocado and brown with white walls.

'This is how real bands tour,' I thought to myself. I had naively envisioned all bands living like rock stars on the road. I never thought about all the hard grafting and economies that cult bands had to endure. It was an eye-opener and it only served to reinforce my respect for The Fall as musicians.

Once in the room, we sat down and I sipped my grape soda. We talked and talked. I had to ask Mark to repeat himself so many times, because of his accent, that it became hilarious and we started laughing. What was apparent to both of us was that we were click-ing. Even without perfect verbal communication, we understood each other intuitively. The dynamic of our combined energy was intoxicating. Like two pieces of a puzzle fitting together, we both felt pressure by the fact that we had limited time together. We were trying to find out as much about each other as we could.

Up to this point in my life I had managed to seduce a few older male rock stars. It made me feel desirable and connected to the rock world. This time it felt different. So much about Mark was alien to me, and we were opposites in so many ways. But his energy felt familiar.

As the night began to fade, and the morning sun rose, both of us became sad. We didn't want to leave each other. We simulta-neously started to dread the approaching hour when Mark would have to leave Chicago for the next date on their tour. After talking all night, we were both tired. We lay down on one of the twin beds, fully clothed, and fell asleep in each other's arms. After a few hours we awoke to a bright, sunny Chicago day. As the sun shone in through the motel blinds, our eyes locked. Wordlessly we removed each other's clothes and made love.

I had found my soulmate.

MEET THE PARENTS

I felt like a stunned mullet. Proverbial bees and tweeting birds flew around my head in circles. I was love-struck. How I drove home safely, I'll never know. I had left earth and was orbiting planet bliss.

What had happened in my life over the previous eighteen hours was unbelievable. I now understood what it meant to experience joy in one's life. I had experienced only momentary fragments of joy before this. But this feeling was all-encompassing. Now I felt hopeful about my future; hopefulness that crystallised my intentions. The confirmation I had received from Mark about my songs was literally life-affirming. Knowing that I had the seal of approval from someone whose music I admired lit the fire in my being and gave me the confidence boost I needed.

Lisa sat in rapt silence with hanging jaw and bulging eyes, as I told her what happened after the show. We both talked about how 'it was meant to be', including Lisa going off with Bill. Lisa asked me how I had left it with Mark. She also asked me what his last name was, and I realised I didn't know. I told Lisa that we had said goodbye at the motel. We left it until the last possible second. We had gotten up that day and spent the last of the morning having breakfast in a coffee shop.

I was sad to see Mark go and I'm sure he was sad to leave me. He asked for my number and said he would call me from his hotel in the next town. 'We'll see,' I thought to myself, as I was trying to keep my emotions under control. All I knew was that Mark was one of the most interesting, intelligent gentlemen I had ever met. The way his brain worked, and his perspective on the world, was unlike that of anyone I had ever come across. It had seduced me.

Every time the phone rang, I jumped. Finally, around 8 p.m., the phone call I was waiting for came. We talked for an hour. Mark had an idea of how we could see each other again soon.

He was going to re-route the tour.

The Fall had a day off after their next show. Instead of staying where they were in Minneapolis, Mark decided to turn the bus around and come back to Chicago so that he could spend twenty-four hours with me.

He returned to Chicago and checked into the same motel he had been in before. I wanted to show him around Chicago. I wanted to give him an insider's tour. I even took him home to see where I lived and to meet my mother, Marvin and Lisa. My mother could not understand a single word of his Mancunian accent. I translated. Mom and Marvin are wonderful people and truly non-judgemental. If they had any misgivings about Mark, they never let me know. I think they were pleased I was so happy, for the time being at least. Even though Mark was not a nervous or fearful person, he was anxious about meeting my mom and Marvin. There was the normal awkwardness with first parental meetings, and he was absolutely on his best behaviour. I think Mom and Marvin were relaxed with Mark because they didn't expect our relationship to amount to anything. If they *had* known what the future held, my mother would have certainly given him a more thorough grilling.

The twenty-four hours Mark and I spent together seemed to redefine time. My memories of that day are dreamlike. The shimmering moments have hung, sun-filtered and ethereal, in my mind to this moment. The bulk of that day, though, was over in a click of the fingers. I felt as if we were existing on two different dimensions simultaneously, both physical and non-physical – real time and magic time.

The final part of The Fall's US tour was to be based out of New York. They were due to play a very prestigious and super-cool gig at the Speed Trials, an art-music movement that was the brainchild of some amazing kids, including members of Live Skull. It was an underground 'no wave' series of concerts that included performances by Sonic Youth, the Beastie Boys, Swans and Lydia Lunch. It took place at the White Columns.

After spending the last twenty-four hours together, Mark and I could not bear to be separated. Mark invited me to fly to New York and hang out with him for the six or so days they would be based there. I remember walking him to the van where all the other members of The Fall were waiting to set off. We delayed our parting until the very last second. We kissed deep and long, outside the open door to the van while the others looked on. There was no way we could hide our relationship. Nor did we want to. It was a *thing* now. The momentum of our passion was unstoppable and totally undeniable.

I have no idea what the rest of the band thought. I'd like to assume they were happy for Mark. A happy singer makes for a copacetic band. What I hadn't realised was that Kay Carroll, who was Mark's long-term girlfriend and the band's manager, had left only two weeks previously. It had been very upsetting to all involved, and the band members were very close to Kay and very loyal to her.

Mark and Kay's break-up had been immensely traumatic and ugly. The story I later heard was that things had been going south in their relationship for some time. They had grown curt and angry with each other. They rowed all the time. Kay was a strong, outspoken woman who was considered 'hard' and didn't 'take any shit'. Apparently, somewhere near Denver, Mark had 'gotten off' with a hotel receptionist and Kay had found out. Naturally, she went bonkers. A day-long fight ensued, after which Kay disappeared. She never turned up to continue on to the next city on the tour. Instead, she took what she was owed from the tour proceeds and left, leaving the band high and dry.

While Mark had invited me to come to New York and join the band there, he told me he could not afford to pay for my plane ticket. Luckily, I had saved up some money from my summer jobs. I told him it was no problem and, frankly, I couldn't think of a better way to spend the money. I was so excited. The adventure continued.

When I told Mom and Marvin I was going to New York, they grumbled. Of course my mother didn't want me to go. We disagreed over it, but in the end she knew she couldn't stop me. I was determined.

I have wonderful memories of those heady six days in New York. We were totally loved up. Honestly, I'd never been so happy. We spent every hour together. Considering we hardly knew each other and we were very different, we got along fabulously. Hanging with The Fall in the East Village was an education into the coolest inner sanctum of the New York music scene. The Speed Trials was a very special event. It was populated by cutting-edge artists, musicians and performance artists. Creativity and self expression dripped off the walls at the White Columns. I remember few details, though. I was completely focused on Mark and everything else was blurred. We spent most of our spare time in the hotel, shagging like rabbits.

As the end of our blissful six days drew closer, we both became sad and a bit panicky. I dreaded saying goodbye, and possibly never seeing him again. Or, if we did manage to meet again, I was worried it wouldn't be the same. Time and distance have a way of eroding a fledgling relationship very quickly. I kept wondering if he was feeling the same way. I fretted that I was more in love with him than he was with me.

I needn't have worried. And I didn't need to be insecure. He was besotted with me. Actually, he was like the cat that got the cream. I didn't know it yet, but I was his saviour as much as he would be mine. The day before we were to fly in opposite directions, separated by a vast ocean and thousands of miles, Mark looked into my eyes and asked me to move in with him. He had a plan. He would bring me over to England as a solo artist. He would produce me and get me a record deal. That way I could continue on with my music and we could be together. Marriage was brought up at this point. We actually spoke about getting married after only seven days of knowing each other. Mark informed me that he wasn't a rich man. He told me he had £1,000 in the bank. 'Don't worry,' I said, 'I only have $700.' Like it even mattered at that point. Money was the last thing on my mind. I didn't even need to take time to weigh my decision. This was my dream come true.

I dreaded having the conversation with Mom and Marvin. I knew they would lose their minds. I also felt bad for Lisa. I would be leaving our band in the lurch. I had convinced her to move to Chicago and now I was moving to another country. But I knew instinctively that I had to make the move. Leap and the net will appear. *This was it. This* is what was *meant to be*. This was my fate and all the winding paths on my life's road had led to this point. Once the decision was made, the sadness that had been surrounding our imminent separation evaporated. We set a date: 18 May 1983. That was the day I would fly to England and start my new life. It was exactly two weeks away. At the time, that seemed an eternity.

I flew back to Chicago, sat Mom and Marvin down at the kitchen table and told them what I had decided. Naturally, they freaked out. My mother practically choked. She seethed and ranted and pleaded. Our argument lasted three days at least. She was totally horrified. Really, who could blame her. I was going to move in with a man I had known a week. Marvin was boiling mad too, but he let my mother deal with the family crisis. If anyone could change my mind it was her.

Lisa, to her credit, took it very well. She knew it was the right thing for me to do. Like the great friend she still is, she told me that, with my talent, I would really have a chance to make it as a musician, especially over in the UK with Mark as a Svengali. She told me I deserved it. 'Go, Brixton,' she said. 'You're gonna be a rock star, I just know it! I can feel it in my bones.'

PART TWO
THE FALL

Burger Queen. Smiling through the tears,
from the ballet *I Am Curious, Orange*

PETER PAN'S FLIGHT

Anticipation caused my mouth to become dry. My feet shuffled slowly.
We inched forward in a line. My pulse quickened. I could smell all
manner of things: freshly buttered popcorn, spun-sugar Flower Bomb,
clouds of cotton candy, clean babies, and teenage toxic sweat. My
senses became heightened. I felt my pupils dilate. My own breath,
loud now in my head, became the tide.

In . . . out, in . . . out, inhale . . . exhale. The rhythm of my
breathing, adding to the tension.

Seven more, to my turn.

Five more.

I moved forward.

She was blonde and milk-fed, healthy and Southern Californian.
She had Swedish blood. Or was it Danish? She wore some sort of
Alpine get-up. Her hair in neat clean braids, wound in big generous
circles, round her ears and pinned. 'Like Heidi,' I thought.

She was my hostess, I trusted her. Her hand brushed my shoulder as
she directed me to sit. The small boat slid into place and stopped in front
of me. The sails were dull gold, and static. I sat alone in my own boat
for two. It was important that I took everything in, with no distractions
or cross talk. This was my experience, and I wanted to absorb every
detail. The safety bar clicked into the locked position over my knees. She
jiggled the bar with her hands to make sure it was really locked.

My boat shot ahead . . . then slowed . . . then it gently tilted up.

I was flying. We were flying. It felt normal. Natural, of course I
could fly.

I flew often in my dreams. When I decided to, I would simply lift
off the ground with a thought, an intention. No biggie, no drama.

I didn't need the boat either. I didn't need a vehicle to help me.

Now, however, I was awake, and the boat served as my Merkaba.
My vehicle of ascension. It made it easy for me. I sat back and let it
simply carry me.

The window was flung open on the top floor of a large house. It
was welcoming and beckoning. The window was seemingly too small
for my boat to fit though. I felt momentarily anxious, but it passed
quickly. A warm yellow light, like a beacon, lit the interior of the
room. We magically sailed through the window with inches to spare.
My flying boat was picking up speed now. I swivelled my head to
try to take it all in. I knew we were not in America. It was night.
We were in a children's bedroom. Three single beds were lovingly
turned down. One belonged to a girl and had a canopy above it. 'A
princess bed', my mother had called it. The other two beds were for
boys. The walls of the room were slanted and angular and rose up to
the eaves. This room had once been an attic. The walls were papered
in bold stripes, like giant sticks of seaside rock candy. A fluffy dog
sat sentry in front of the white door, which was shut tight. An oval-
shaped rag-style rug in terracotta covered the wooden floorboards. A
cuckoo clock, a tartan blanket, storybooks and a toy horse on wheels
decorated the room. ABC blocks lay scattered on the floor.

We entered the room through one window, flew quickly above
the scene and exited through another open window at the back of
the room. I sat back. The view was beautiful. This was England.
I just knew it. I rose above the rooftops and chimney pots. It was
twilight. It was witching hour, and the purple light permeated,
filtered by vibrating black dots of darkness. The colour spectrum was
disintegrating before my eyes. It was dream time.

Still at top-floor-window height, we flew between the buildings,
tall houses and winding streets. The windows glowed. I could
almost see inside. I imagined the people who lived behind those
windows were safe and carefree. I heard singing and now I could
make out the words. 'We can fly . . .we can fly . . . we can fly.'

We rose over spires and a courthouse, over towers and old-fashioned street lamps, still lit by candlelight. I saw the domed globe roof, a landmark cathedral in the distance.

I knew its name.

The river, which was illuminated turquoise against the growing darkness, slithered through the city like a snake.

I recognised the river.

We rose up again.

Now we were above the bridge, which was also lit up.

Its gateway arch was flanked by two regal towers, and it felt somehow majestic, royal.

It too was familiar.

All at once the city shrunk, as we climbed higher. Now it was nothing more than pinpricks of light against a black backdrop. The lights twinkled and glittered. So pretty. The boat tilted up and I gasped, as my face hit a pocket of stars. As above, so below. The lights of the city, a call and response to the stars in the sky.

The boat dipped down again and swooped. Rising disproportionately high above the city was the big friendly clock tower. As the boat circled around it on a cushion of air, I spoke its name. 'Ben. Big Ben. London . . . I love you, London. I love you, England,' I called from my boat, as we sailed into the stars, my voice breathless with emotion and wonder. My words carried away, on the backs of the notes, of the ever-present celestial music.

England had come and gone too quickly. I had wanted to alight from the boat, but I was too high. 'This is where I want to live. I must get back there,' I said to myself. The wind had other ideas. My boat was propelled by determined gusts. I was momentarily disoriented. We tipped backwards, and then up. I saw black. All at once I felt the confines of space. I felt the solidity of a wall in close proximity. The wall of the room? The wall of the universe? One and the same?

I braced myself for the crash.

There was no crash, because there was no solid wall. It was simply a barrier of densely vibrating particles. An energetic threshold. My boat shook for a moment as we crossed into the new dimension.

The depth of stars was beyond comprehension. I could only equate it to a thicket of fireflies on a humid Southern summer night. I pushed the stars away with my hands. I scooped them out of my path so I could get a clear view.

I needn't have bothered. The star clusters had only been an overture to the main attraction. The stars acted as a cloak of disguise shielding and protecting the ultimate destination. Of course I had been disoriented. That had been part of the plan. The creator had built this into the journey. It was partly psychological. It was meant to separate the wheat from the chaff. Others might not have been as wide-eyed and trusting as I was. They might not have persevered. It would have been understandable to turn back. It would have been easy to have seen the stars as impenetrable.

The stars were supposed to be a diversion, not everybody was meant to pass through them. They protected the essence of it all. Only those who were given the key would be able to pass through. The key was the suspension of your beliefs.

As the stars disappeared around me, I circled above an island. It was green and lush. At some point in time the earth must have belched, and the jagged peaks of land shoved their way through the earth's crust, passing through the sea and forming volcanic spires in the sky. Waterfalls ran from high cave mouths. Sparkling streams, lit by the internal crystals embedded in the rocks, meandered their way through the rugged terrain. Two enormous rainbows flanked the island on either side.

I was filled with almost unbearable happiness.

I knew this was the place of bliss. The destination of every childhood dream. This place was the answer to every question in the world.

But if you were looking for answers, you would not find them here, because here, there were no questions.

Then it was gone. I turned round in the boat, trying to catch the last glimpse of the place. It was gone. I panicked. I scrambled to imprint every detail in my mind. It had evaporated, and I struggled to hold on to strands of the vision. The threads of the knowledge I had just been given were fading fast. I clawed at the memories. Time seemed to speed up, it felt like a jump cut in a film. The first thing I saw were trees. Palm trees and fern fronds of a tropical variety. My head filled with the sounds of birds and the forest. Someone was playing a wooden flute. I was closer to the land now. My boat was flying over a lagoon. I recognised the terrain as similar to that of the place of bliss. This new land was forged from the same rock, but here there was strife.

A group of swarthy pirates had made their camp on the shore, while a pretty girl in a blue nightdress stood in front of them on a rock. Her little brothers watched the scene unfolding. The girl's hands seemed to be tied behind her. These were the children whose London bedroom I'd first flown through. They'd made it here safely. We'd been on this journey together, I realised.

Across the water, there was a battle going on.

A small fierce boy holding a sharp blade was duelling a mean-looking angry man – the king of the pirates – holding a sword. They stood precariously on a plank. Below them in the water was a crocodile, its jaws yawning and gaping. The aperture of its mouth was huge and it was ancient in its patience.

I knew this was a warning. What did it mean? I couldn't understand why the boy and the pirates were fighting. What was the struggle about? The crocodile had been most disturbing. It sat in the water simply waiting for someone to put a foot wrong, to make a mistake, to lose their bearings.

The sound of the birds was replaced by the tension of a ticking clock. Immediately my stomach clenched. I was sense-memory slammed back to my father's house. Before I could dwell on the thought, my boat swung round. Sitting on a stony ledge were three

Native Americans. They were playing drums and chanting. At once I felt safe again. They would guide me home. The 'Indian' had been with me for as long as I could remember. He was always there when I needed him. He had taught me to interpret signs and navigate paths. He dried my tears with his wisdom. It was through his voice I was able to hear the animals speak and the grasses grow.

As the boat turned again, on the final bend of its journey, I passed the three children and the fierce boy standing on the deck of a big ship. Presumably, the pirate ship. The children held the ship's spoked steering wheel in their hands.

'Set the course for England,' I heard the fierce boy say, before the doors swung open and I was blinded by sunlight.

MANCHESTER OR BUST

20 May 1983. I knew virtually nothing about Manchester. My mother told me that it was a city in the north of England, whose heyday had been during the Industrial Revolution. Apparently Manchester was famed for its manufacturing of cotton and textiles. My mother said she thought it was a depressed place. Her description did nothing for my mental preparation. She was still fuming mad at me for leaving. I know she thought I'd gone insane. Running off with a man I had known for only six weeks. Moving to a foreign country, and worst of all, becoming a college dropout. 'Do you have a round-trip ticket?' she asked me. No, I didn't. Mark had bought me a one-way. What did I need a round-trip ticket for?

'What do you need a round-trip ticket for?' she said, incensed. 'In case he turns out to be a drunk or wife-beater!'

'Oh, for fuck sake, Mom.'

'I'll buy you the other half of the ticket,' she said. 'That way I'll know that if something happens you can always come back.'

I never intended to go back. In my mind, I'd made a decision and I was going to make it work. There was no alternative. Failure was not an option. I was going to move to Manchester. I was going to live with the man I loved. I was going to become a rock star. Mark was my Svengali. He was going to produce all the songs I'd written for my band. Furthermore, I would return to Chicago after conquering the world. I would headline my own show in a massive theatre, maybe even the Metro, where I'd met Mark.

But I never expected Manchester to be so grim. Glowering Victorian red-brick buildings lined the sides of the streets. They looked like mean structures, where horrible atrocities had been

committed in decades past. The sky was toxic: heavy, with omi-
nous grey clouds. The few people I saw, as we rode in the back of
the taxi from Piccadilly train station to Prestwich, seemed joyless.
Nobody smiled. Everybody looked so poor. All their clothes were
drab. Where was the colour? I felt like I was watching the city
through a black-and-white film clip, a Pathé post-war newsreel.

Although it was May, I didn't see leaves on the trees or one single
flower in bloom. Left behind were the skyscrapers of Chicago and
the yachts bobbing on the glittering waters of Lake Michigan. As
we drove along, Mark pointed out all the must-see sights of his
beloved city. 'Look, Brixie, there's the Boddingtons Brewery! There's
Strangeways Prison! Over there is the new modern *Guardian* newspaper printing plant. That won an architecture award, that did!'
(The Sears Tower it was not.) As we drove out of the city centre all
I could see were squat little buildings with the words 'Cash and
Carry' spray-painted on the front of the windows. I didn't know
what Cash and Carry meant, but I had a feeling it wasn't glamorous.
It was a long way from Bloomingdale's, that's for sure.

Mark loved his city. He was proud to be a Northerner and
it gave him great joy to show me his world, and the things that
inspired and influenced him. He was passionate and protective of
Manchester; like a lioness with her cubs.

I loved Mark and everything about him. I was going to have to
find the beauty in this place if I was going to survive here. I was an
optimist. I would have to skew my perspective and start looking
through his eyes. I knew nothing of the rivalry between the North
and the South. I didn't understand why Mark referred to people
who lived south of Birmingham as 'Southern bastards'. I hadn't yet
heard the Fall song 'The North Will Rise Again'. It would be years
before I co-wrote the song 'Hit the North'.

We drove through Prestwich, my new neighbourhood. It was
'a Jewish neighbourhood', Mark informed me. 'You'll feel right
at home.' It didn't look like home. It felt alien. Cortinas and

Vauxhalls replaced the Cadillacs and Mercedes Benzes that were so commonplace on the streets of both LA and Chicago. We pulled up in front of Mark's place on Rectory Lane. Suitably, his building was an old rectory. I wasn't sure what a rectory was, but it looked like a gothic church.

'Wow,' I said. 'This looks so cool. I had no idea you lived in a place this big.' (At last, I felt a ray of hope starting to glimmer.)

'No,' he said. 'I don't live in the whole building, just one of the flats at the top. It's only £20 a week.'

Mark grabbed my one suitcase and I carried my guitar, a cherry-red Gretsch solid body, very light and very rare, given to me by Eric Ambel. We walked through the front door and up the stairs. The long straight stairway up to Mark's flat was covered in sparse, scrappy carpeting, swirling with 1970s clashing colours and nylon threads fraying around the edges. The walls of the hallway were smeared with dirt. There was a strong odour of urine. There was a shared landing at the top of the stairs that separated the two flats at the top of the building, one door on the right and one on the left. The door on the right belonged to Mark's neighbour, a woman who Mark informed me ran a 'knocking shop' out of her flat. The door on the left was Mark's.

We entered the flat and were greeted by a drove of cats. They were meowing and hungry and obviously happy to see Mark. I dropped to the ground, stroking and patting them. The main cat was called Frau; she was a Burmese. She was smart and affectionate and social. I grew to love this cat very much. The other cat I remember was striped yellow, Primrose. 'Primmy' for short. I assumed she was named by Kay Carroll, Mark's old girlfriend and The Fall's former manager. All her belongings were still in the flat, exactly where she had left them.

I didn't expect Mark to be so poor. Once I got past the cats and got a good look at the flat, I was shocked.

'Shall I make you a cuppa?' Mark asked.

He walked to the kitchen, which was only as big as my shower back home in Chicago. There was only room for one person to stand. The oven, or 'cooker', was a filthy white enamel-type appliance. This took up most of the space. It had two spiralling electric hobs and a grill pan layered in grease – the remnants, it seemed, of every meal ever cooked on it. Our oven back home had been a state-of-the-art, restaurant-quality industrial range.

'Do you take milk?' Mark asked me.

'Yes, please.' I noticed what I assumed was Mark's refrigerator. It sat on the floor opposite the cooker and looked like a white cube. It was no bigger than a cardboard box. I assumed he kept his freezer somewhere else. This was the smallest fridge I'd ever seen.

'I'll get the milk,' I said, squeezing into the kitchen and opening the door on the front of the box. It was warm and it was empty.

'Where do you keep your milk?' I asked.

'Out the window,' Mark said.

'What do you mean, "out the window"?'

Mark pushed open the sooty window at the back of the kitchen to reveal a cement ledge where perched precariously were a small bottle of milk, a pack of Danish back bacon, a carton of eggs and a loaf of Hovis white bread.

I was incredulous. Perhaps this was a traditional resourceful British custom? After all, back home in Chicago we had a walk-in butler's pantry (much larger than Mark's kitchen) where we kept all our non-perishables that weren't chilled. My mother had told me that in England and Europe people traditionally did their food shopping every day. They bought fresh vegetables from the greengrocer and meat from the butcher; they didn't 'stock up' at the supermarket, once a week, like we did.

'The fridge broke ages ago,' Mark said, 'and I never bothered to get it fixed.'

I drank my tea and continued to look around the small flat. The carpet was patterned with a swirly purple and black design, not dissimilar to the carpet on the stairs and the landing. It was hideously retro. The sitting room was small and shabby. The double-seat settee was a sludgy lime-beige, and threadbare in places. The chair, which was cack-brown, had springs poking through its fabric. There was a hi-fi system on the floor, with stacks of records lined up next to it. There were piles of Mark's lyrics, books and papers everywhere. There was a small table with two wooden chairs facing a window at the back of the room, that looked over the rain-soaked streets and twinkling lights of Prestwich. The bedroom was behind the living room and opposite the kitchen. The bed, which had recently been vacated by Kay Carroll, was old. I don't think the sheets had been changed for a while. The floor was scattered with clothes, including Kay's knickers, which were . . . how shall I put this? . . . worn. Mark hadn't bothered to get rid of Kay's stuff before my arrival. I wanted to erase all memory of her and make only new memories of us.

There was no closet in the bedroom – only a small wooden antique wardrobe that still contained Mark and Kay's sparse belongings. I set about collecting all Kay's dirty knickers and threw them in the dustbin. I took her clothes from the wardrobe and small chest of drawers and folded them up. I put them in a pile and covered them with a blanket so I couldn't see them. It tortured me that I would have to sleep in the same bed that they had had sex in. I had to wash the sheets immediately. This was my home now. The shock of the transition from my old life to my new one was beginning to wear off. I would embrace this new life. I would scrub this flat until it gleamed. I would make it into the loveliest home it could be. I was going to look after Mark and make him happy. I was going to change his life for the better. We would work together as a team to create a wonderful life. We would make important music that would leave its impact on the world. And what's more, we would have fun doing it together. I stripped the bed and collected the sheets in my arms. 'Where is your washing machine and dryer?' I asked.

'I wash me clothes in the bathtub,' Mark explained. 'I hang them here to dry.'

I looked at this weird contraption leaning against the wall in the bathroom. It was a fold-up metal rack that opened up into an A-shaped frame where you could drape wet clothes.

Oh my God. The words 'third', 'world' and 'country' came to mind, but I pushed them away. I threw the sheets into the bathtub and turned on the taps. I waited for the water to get hot. 'Mark, there's no hot water!' I yelled.

'You have to turn on the immersion heater, love.'

'What's an immersion heater?'

He led me to a cupboard door in the wall outside the bathroom. He opened it to reveal a small tank, some pipes, and a light switch. He explained that if I wanted hot water, I would have to flick the switch a half hour before I needed the water.

'Mind, though,' he said, 'the hot water runs out very quickly, so if you want a bath, you will have to boil a kettle or two.'

'Do you have a shower?' I asked

'Of course,' he said. He then proceeded to show me a bizarre hose-like contraption that you attached to the mouth of the tap.

'You mean, you don't have a normal shower?' I was aghast. How the hell was I going to condition my hair? I waited for the immersion heater to get warm. I scrubbed the sheets and hung them out as best as I could. I found another set of linen in the bottom of the chest of drawers and made the bed. Then we crawled into it.

I was exhausted from my trip and all the upheaval, but I was ecstatic. I was madly in love. I was living in my very first apartment. In England, no less! I had turned my whole life into an adventure. Even though I would be living in a much more modest style than I'd been accustomed to, I didn't care. I knew I'd made the right decision. When you feel like that, and you follow your heart and your passions, you can achieve anything.

I didn't get much sleep that first night, as we spent most of it shagging. I woke up the next morning practically levitating with joy. Mark presented me with a homemade 'full English breakfast' which he had cooked himself. It consisted of a mug of Tetley tea with milk and sugar, two fried eggs, fried bread, grilled Walls sausages and something mysterious. Mark had promised me that if I came to live with him in Manchester, he would make me breakfast in bed every morning. And he certainly lived up to his word. It looked delicious, except for one thing – the round purple salami-like thing on the plate.

'What is this, Mark?' I asked.

'It's black pudding.'

I had assumed that black pudding was made out of chocolate, like an American pudding.

'It doesn't look like chocolate. What is it made of?'

'Oh, it's not chocolate,' he said, laughing. 'It's dried pigs' blood.'

I didn't want to hurt his feelings. It was extremely sweet of him to cook me the breakfast. Still, there was no way in hell I could eat the black pudding. I couldn't even put it near my mouth. I was struggling not to retch. It smelled like death. I didn't want to be ungrateful, but I knew myself well enough, and I knew how sensitive my gag reflex was. It would be far better to leave it on the plate than vomit up the entire breakfast. So I ate everything else on the plate. Mark's feelings weren't hurt. It was one of those things you could chalk up to cultural differences.

After breakfast, it was time to brave the dreaded shower and start the first day of my new life in Manchester. I was a long way from home now. It dawned on me that I knew no one at all in my new country. Not a single person. There was nobody I could call if I needed help. I had no close family here, no Grandma, no Aunt Susie, no Maggie.

This had been a momentous day.

1983

Shortly after arriving in Manchester, I accompanied The Fall on a tour of Germany and Austria in June of 1983. I was the roadie. I wanted to make myself totally indispensable, one of the boys. I carried equipment, tuned all the guitars, and helped them in whatever they wanted – like doing the lights. I loved watching them every night and being a part of it.

It was the first time I had ever been to Germany, or Austria. It was amazing to be travelling around with them and staying in *Gasthauses*. They were playing anarchistic student venues and, most nights, the students would cook us dinner. No matter the town, it was *Bratwurst* and potato salad. Nobody but me could speak German. I was not fluent by any means but I had studied it for three years in the Lab School.

The one word we all knew was 'goulash'. I remember Paul, Craig and Karl ordering 'Goulash Zuppa' every time we went to a restaurant. I assumed it was because they knew exactly what they were going to get. In reality they ordered it because it was cheap and they were broke. After the complimentary *Gasthaus* breakfast, on which they gorged in the morning, they could only afford a can of beer and a bowl of goulash soup – which came with free bread – for the rest of the day.

Mark had control of all the gig takings. He carried the tour cash around with him in a carrier bag. When I first saw the bag full of money I was gobsmacked. Mark explained to me that no one would think of looking in a crappy old plastic carrier bag for cash. He kept the lads on meagre wages, and kept his hands firmly round the neck of the carrier bag. The Fall hadn't done any really big money gigs yet, and the cash that was earned had to be eked out. Beside the wages, there were endless miscellaneous expenses that had to be accounted for. The band needed a cash flow for its running costs, and Mark always made sure there was enough money to get out of any predicament that might arise.

I think the guys in the band were fairly nervous and wary of me in the beginning, but they were used to Mark creating chaos and shifting the sands underneath them. Marc Riley and Kay Carroll had just left. They were down one guitarist and one manager-girlfriend. But by this time it had been established that the members couldn't do anything about personnel issues. Everything depended on Mark's whims, so they accepted it. It was obvious that Mark and I were besotted with each other. They figured that if Mark was happy, then everyone would be happy. With me there, Mark was treating everyone better and being less vindictive.

The lads kept their distance from Mark and, by extension, me, since we were already such a unit. I could even feel it within the confines of the van. Saying that, they were pretty welcoming, considering that I was foisted on them. As we travelled, I got to know them better, although there would always be some distance in my relationships with the members of the band. I would later learn that this is how the band functioned.

Karl Burns was not refined in any way, and he had no social grace. He was extremely crude and used shocking language – every other word was 'cunt'. At the same time, he could also be warm and funny. You never knew what you were going to get with Karl. Drummers bang things for a living. It's like Bam-Bam in *The Flintstones* – another level of brutalism. Drummers are primal creatures and a law unto themselves. Karl had a unibrow and pulled a lot of girls. But what really stood out was his talent; he was magnificently skilled.

The other drummer, Paul Hanley, was closest to my age. Paul was adorable, and much more civilised than Karl. He was cute and he loved pop music. He was easy to get along with, just super-normal. I probably palled around more with him than anybody. He was a voracious reader of music magazines and knew every song in the charts. I don't ever remember seeing him take any drugs. His style was more simplistic than Karl's, which was more tribal. Together they interwove both their personalities and beats.

The guitarist, Craig Scanlon, was incredibly introverted, even on stage, but not in a sour or dour way. He was quietly brilliant, a sensitive soul. There was a depth to him, but he was very shy. He was the kind of person that couldn't look you in the eye, and making conversation with strangers wasn't easy for him. But he had a very dark, left-field sense of humour, which I often couldn't grasp. The songs he wrote were moving and complex.

Craig, Steve and Paul were very close. Paul and Steve were, of course, brothers and they had been friends with Craig since they were children. Marc Riley, the guitarist whom Mark had fired at the end of 1982, was also their childhood friend and part of their faction in the band. Steve and Craig were deeply vexed at his ousting.

When Marc Riley was in the band, he was the lead hydra head of this unit. I think that camaraderie threatened Mark, and I think he helped to break up that unit to counterbalance the scales. It was Marc versus Mark. Marc was the only one who would stand up to Mark and not take his shit. Riley rubbed Mark up the wrong way and it culminated in a brawl in Australia. That was it, Marc Riley was gone.

But the spectre of Marc Riley would continue to loom – he really got under Mark E. Smith's skin. Even after he'd gone, Mark continued to bitch and moan about him.

The European tour manager's name was Scumech. He was a trendy and Mark referred to him as a 'dickhead'. For some reason, Mark took great offence at Scumech. Perhaps it was because he would keep the tour money in his briefcase and handcuff it to radiators. He was robotic, which also annoyed Mark. He had the façade of being hip, but was actually quite bureaucratic, in a German way. Of course, that drove Mark crazy.

In the van on the tour, suffering from severe sleep deprivation and spent adrenal glands, I had a tendency to become hysterical. It happened often when we were cooped up and travelling from place to place during a long journey. The trigger was someone saying something random, and slightly humorous. Mark had two names for it: Deutsch Hysteria and Van AIDS. 'Oh no, Brix has Van AIDS.'

In one university town *Gasthaus*, Karl Burns was in his room and for some reason decided to lift up the mattress of his bed, and he found an old woollen Nazi blanket with a swastika on it. He freaked out and called us all in to have a look. We assumed the owner of the *Gasthaus* had been from a Nazi family. We had been told it was illegal to have any Nazi memorabilia. The band was fascinated by the swastika blanket; Mark was completely obsessed with history and wars. Everywhere we went it was all about the war(s). This happened there, that happened there. But World War II was his main war to geek out over. He used to watch *The World at War* over and over again – a twenty-two-and-a-half-hour documentary series. I think one of the reasons he was interested in me was that I was Jewish. By being with me it gave him a direct connection to the war, and to history. He always called me a Jewess. He used to tell me that he used to think all the Jewesses in Prestwich were really sexy. There are so many lyrics in songs like 'Who Makes the Nazis?', 'Fortress/Deer Park' and 'Wings' that reference the war. I would soon have a major role in his next song – it would be the first time we co-wrote something together.

We were on our way to a gig in Holzkirchen when our van broke down outside of Dachau. When we saw the signs for Dachau, I felt my pulse rise with foreboding. Just being so near a concentration camp made me feel sick and desperately sad. I couldn't believe our van had broken down there. I began to fret, realising we had to spend the night and find a *Gasthaus*. We were on our own without the tour manager. We had been due to rendezvous with him in Holzkirchen. The *Gasthaus* we stumbled upon was called Hotel Blöedel, after the family's name who owned it. We found out later that *Blöedel* in German also means an 'ignorant person', like a village idiot. We got to Hotel Blöedel in the middle of the night. We had to ring on the doorbell and wake the owners from their sleep. The whole thing felt very surreal. The owners spoke no English. We attempted sign language and scraps of my German to explain our broken-down van and how many rooms we needed. Thankfully they were not fully booked and we had somewhere to sleep. As we entered the *Gasthaus* an unexplainable feeling of dread swept through me. I began to have Hansel and Gretel anxieties. As we walked down the corridor of the house I noticed shoes lined up outside the doorway of every room. When Mark and I got into our room there was a really awful smell, so bad I remember gagging. It was rancid. Mark thought perhaps something had died in there. The place felt unsafe. We smoked some cigarettes and just left others burning – a nicotine incense to mask the odour. We went to sleep. During the night Mark had a nightmare. He dreamed someone was cooking heroin in a giant silver spoon behind the big armoire in the room. He woke up shaken by his dream. In the morning we were awakened by the sound of blood-curdling screams. We sat up in bed and Mark turned to me and asked, 'What the fuck is that?'

I flung open the curtains to look outside and saw a woman, a typical German blonde Fräulein-type – Helga-esque, a shot-putter with braids – walking across the grassy yard behind the hotel carrying what looked like a large, clear plastic bag of blood. At first we thought we had stumbled on a murder. We seriously freaked out. We stood at the window of our *Gasthaus* room, gasping and bug-eyed, repeating, 'What the fuck?' But it turned out that Hotel Blöedel had its own slaughterhouse. That morning they were slaughtering the cows. Needless to say I did not eat breakfast. The eerie feeling of ghosts in the area and the disturbing events of our night in the *Gasthaus* would serve as inspiration for the song 'Hotel Blöedel'.

Mark and I got married immediately following the tour in July. I had to stay in the country, and only had a tourist stamp for six months, which did not allow me to do paid work. That was not the reason why we got married, though. We had actually first mentioned marriage a week after we met. Our connection was so intense and we loved each other.

When we got married I was just twenty years old and had known Mark less than six months. He was twenty-seven. Our wedding was in the registry office in Bury, Lancashire, outside of Manchester. Mark's parents suggested that we have the reception in the Eagle and Child pub, and that we serve sausage rolls, salt and vinegar crisps and pickled onions to our guests. Karl Burns was our best man. I had no maid of honour, no friends and no family there. I didn't know anybody at my wedding apart from the band and Mark's parents and sisters. The thought of Mom and Marvin coming over to Manchester and seeing where we lived, in that hovel of an apartment, was more than I could bear. The night before the wedding, when the reality of being without the support of my family on the big day hit, I called my mother in tears. I said, 'I changed my mind, please come. I need you.' My mother said, 'Honey, it's too late. I can't get there in time.'

Mark's father drove us to the wedding in his Eastern European box on wheels. His dad, who's now passed on, had amazing hair, like a pompadour, a kind of a quiff. He was quite good-looking, and he was a plumber. Mark, his dad and his grandad all used to go down to the same pub, three generations of Smiths. His mom was sweet and quite welcoming and warm to me. I wore a strapless white watermarked taffeta Laura Ashley gown that I bought off the rack. There was no fanfare. It was as simple a wedding as could be. We went back to our flat afterwards and everyone came around. We played records and partied.

Around this time The Fall were recording *Perverted by Language* but were one song short. Mark asked if they could use one of my songs, a Banda Dratsing number called 'One More Time for the Record', which was on the demo tape I had played him in my car that first night in Chicago:

> And it's painless
> Sitting in Subterranea
> Ancient reference
> To Mesopotamia
> And it's quiet again
> Hidden fragments, surface now . . .

I had no idea what the song was about until years later. Generally, I write from my subconscious, and the complete understanding of my words and emotions may only make complete sense with hindsight and an objectivity gained from distance. This particular song was about history repeating itself. It's about past lives and about reliving things over and over again. In the early days when I wrote songs, I didn't realise that I was channelling from a collective consciousness. I didn't know where those songs were coming from. They would come to me in chunks, written without thinking. They would just come right through me, and I would tingle when I wrote them.

I was overjoyed that one of my songs would go on a Fall album. Then Mark asked me to play it. I said, 'But I don't really play guitar.' Of course, when I write I play guitar, but I thought of myself as a bassist. He said, 'No, you play so good, you play like Lou Reed.' 'Are you kidding?' I said. 'No, you have to play and sing it.'

You would think that if a singer says, 'Here's this woman I met in America, who's now my wife, and she's going to play on our album', somebody might get really upset and be angry about it, or at least want to have a discussion. As far as I know, the band were OK about it.

We were in a generous-sized studio. We had a room for the drums, a live room, and then there was a room for overdubs where you would do your vocals. I went into the vocal room where they had set up an amp. My guitar was plugged in and I had a microphone, so I could sit on the chair, play my guitar and sing. I sat down and started rehearsing, running through it with the producer. I rehearsed it maybe five times, at which point Mark stopped me rehearsing and said, 'That's it, you're done.' They took my rehearsal and used it, and that's what was on the finished recording. I always felt I could have done it better, but in truth Mark had captured something magical, raw and intimate.

Then he took the three-stringed violin. It was untuned – we had no idea how to tune it – and he played those haunting scrapes before adding his vocal part of the duet. Mark wrote lyrics based upon the gory experience of the slaughterhouse ('A reasonable smell of death'), and wove in a similar theme to my lyrics about time-hopping and the Civil War, and thus 'Hotel Blöedel' was born.

Before the album came out The Fall toured England that autumn. Instead of being just the roadie, I would come out and play guitar on a few songs, hiding in the back behind the speakers. I was very sensitive about joining them, and it was all happening by osmosis. They were already a fully formed unit and I did not want to steamroll into it. I was really nervous about the fans, and I knew it was a risk to go there. It could have been really terrible. People were talking about nepotism. Who's this American bitch/wife? I wasn't some girl banging on a pot or tambourine. But I immediately got the Linda McCartney treatment in the press. And their record label, Rough Trade, weren't keen on me joining the band at all. I kept out of the way, didn't push myself forward, and just eased into the band. Eventually I told them, 'I'm either part of this band or I'm not.' Very quickly, I was. To their credit, the band members accepted me, and I think they really grew to love playing with me.

Craig and I are so opposite in terms of how we play guitar. Craig as a guitarist is like no other in the world. He's a lefty, he probably uses a whole different part of his brain, thinks differently, and the two contrasting styles (his and mine) worked well together. I did these really clean, bonehead, surfy leads, and then strong rhythms. Craig was like Jackson Pollock. I think he was happy to have a foil to play against. We clung to each other in the madness. I had to figure out what parts I would add to their already existing songs, because what I would play hadn't been written. At that time The Fall already had a rich back catalogue, and the newer material consisted of long, sprawling, complex songs like 'Garden' and 'Tempo House'.

The person who helped me most was Steve Hanley, who would always tell me what he was playing. Steve and I were always connected. He was my grounding rod in that band. I would weave what I was doing around the bass line because I'd originally come to The Fall as a bass player and that's what I understood. I felt more confident with the bass than the guitar, and that dichotomy informed the guitarist I would become.

I listened to records at home to sort of pick out things on my guitar that went really well with what they were doing and develop this kind of lead guitar technique – very hooky, simple, powerful leads. All of the songs were equally hard to learn. 'Garden' and 'Smile' – which was a devastating drone thrash, despite the title – were powerful, hypnotic songs. I remember being on stage and playing those songs and being transported. Chills would run up and down my body and I felt as if I were being lifted off the stage. I was so immersed in the music that I felt possessed by it. At the most powerful times when we were so on point, it was religious. It blew me away.

The Fall ran as an autocracy, with Mark as the dictator. When it began in the 1970s it was very much a collective but, by this point – and especially with Kay and Marc ousted – the last remnants of democracy were gone. It was Mark's band. The final word on business and artistic decisions was his. There are good things and bad things about this, but it worked well to have a leader enact a singular vision, someone to edit and coalesce six people's egos and opinions. Every member of the band was also a songwriter, and someone had to unite the sound. One of Mark's major talents was to edit the elements together. This was the first proper group I had been in, so I thought it was completely normal. It was clear-cut for everybody. Nobody was chained to it. And sometimes it was not pleasant. Mark was the president of the cardboard-box factory, and if you didn't like it, then leave.

The Fall was run like an office. Wages were doled out weekly. Mark was Captain Kirk, and, by default, I was Mr Spock, second in command. If someone wanted to get something past Mark they would come to me because I was an easier route to the Mancunian Castro. I would slyly finesse whatever they wanted into my own speech to get it past Mark, whether it was issues of pay, or a key-board line someone really wanted back in a song. During this time, Mark trusted me and relied a lot on my instincts.

The downside of being in a rock band which worked like a corporate structure, especially with the board president married to a worker, was that it was far from what I'd dreamed being in a band would be like. We were creative but, at the heart of it, we were co-workers, and The Fall was our office. We each had our specific cubicle where we would perform our assigned function. I was in the riff and lead department.

During my tenure, I rarely went into any of the band members' homes. I knew where they lived, we'd go on tours and the van would stop outside of people's houses and pick them up. But, normally, everyone would be picked up before me and Mark. It was only on occasion that I ever got to see where people lived. Sometimes, I never did. Karl Burns, for instance, lived in a brutally poor area of Manchester called Moss Side, which was almost like a slum. Once in a while, the pick-up would be reversed and we'd have to go to get Karl. I would never see which door, or where he came out of. He would just appear on the street.

For songwriting, I would never go to Craig's house and jam, which would be the modus operandi for a normal band. I would write with Mark or I would write by myself, and bring it to Steve and Craig. Steve and Craig would write by themselves and bring it to us. Everyone wrote separately, and then brought it to the table, and then we would all collaborate. We never sat down and all wrote, unless we were in a rehearsal room or doing a sound-check, and something naturally evolved.

On that first tour I started to do backup vocals on some tracks, like yelling, 'Jew on a motorbike!' at the end of 'Garden' and singing the beginning of 'Wings', an amazing song about time travel and going into different dimensions. Mark loved me doing backing vocals in my annoying American accent. In my mind I considered them bratty backing vocals that contrasted well with the darkness of The Fall. A new song we started doing that showcased this was 'C.R.E.E.P.'. Everyone assumed it was about Marc Riley, but Mark's lyrics were a takedown of the previous tour manager, Scumech ('He is a scum-egg, a horrid trendy wretch'). Because the music was a pop contrast to what the band had been doing, it was assumed I wrote it, but it came courtesy of the Hanley brothers. We had this stupid Casio toy piano that we used to lug around and play.

The first song I brought in that we played on that tour was '2x4'. I would write the songs at home on the couch in front on the TV with my guitar unplugged. I wrote all the earliest songs for The Fall on my beloved cherry-red Gretsch. '2x4' had a great rockabilly rhythm. I played it to Mark and said, 'Look what I came up with.' He was like, 'Great.' He would take out his Sony cassette recorder, and we would record it at home. Then the next time we would go into the rehearsal room I played it to the guys. I brought in the skeleton of a song. They would add the flesh, bones and blood. Pretty soon, the song had just developed.

In England, they don't have '2x4's, which is a non-metric term for a wooden plank. That image is from watching so many cartoons as a child – Road Runner hitting Wile E. Coyote with a two-by-four. It was that kind of imagery. When I listen to the lyrics now, for his part, it's evident that Mark was talking about my family's perception of him. There's a line where he goes 'used table leg to club son-in-law'. He would always write songs about members in the band, but for some reason I thought that, as the wife, I was exempt.

Mark would make us do a song called 'Hey! Marc Riley' to the tune of 'Hey! Bo Diddley' and I would have to sing the chorus, 'Hey! Marc Riley', in my brattiest voice. It was mean, and I feel bad now (but it was a good song). I think it upset Riley, but Mark Smith was mad. When he gets mad, he writes songs about it. God only knows how many times I ended up being the brunt of it, where I never thought I would be. Everyone was paranoid about having songs written about them. It was part of his vengeance.

As the tour progressed, we had become a super-tight and powerful band. We got better each night. Just when we thought it couldn't get any better it would. We were so intuitively locked in, it was almost spiritual.

Mark always made the set-lists. There was no input from us, this wasn't a subject to be debated. If there was a song you really didn't want to play, there was no vote to get it off the list. It changed every night. We never had the same one twice. He liked to create chaos. There were so many songs that we all wanted to do, but Mark was against doing old stuff. But then out of nowhere he'd put in a song that hadn't been played in years and revive it for one night. We would fake it as best we could, and it would come out amazingly. My favourite record of theirs was *Slates* and I was dying to play those songs. I begged to do 'An Older Lover, Etc' and 'Leave the Capitol'. We got to do 'Middle Mass' a couple of times. I managed to get that in.

The live songs that I loved the most were the ones that the audience liked best, because I could feel their energy. Mark had a completely different philosophy – he would always want to be as challenging as possible. I wanted to please the crowd. By me pleasing them, I felt the energy rise between us. My favourite songs were the powerful ones like 'Smile'. It felt like standing in front of a freight train. There's nothing better than that. I would have been happy playing 'Totally Wired' every night. People would scream for songs. Mark purposely didn't give it to them, which was a good and a bad thing. It was frustrating, but also maybe why the band was so special.

Mark would never explain his set-list theory. I remember asking him once, 'Why aren't you smiling? Aren't you happy?' He said, 'I don't want to walk around looking like a bloody fool.' I think it was the same thing with the songs. It was almost like he didn't want us to be good or popular.

Before a show the band would pace, heads down, focused on what was going to happen. Sometimes Mark would order us to stand in a circle, and walk anticlockwise. There was something about the energy of walking anticlockwise, he said. Mark never had stage fright. It was antithetical to his character. Confidence was one thing that defined him: it's why he could be an incredible singer without necessarily having what traditionalists would define as a good singing voice.

He wasn't concerned about me hanging out with the guys in the band. There were times when men flirted with me, which got under Mark's skin and raised his hackles. He would stake his claim, marking his territory. He could get jealous and he could get possessive over me, but he wasn't riddled with jealousy and insecurity like I was. I was always wary of other women, which was a really negative and ultimately destructive thing. I would be prone to jealous streaks. If someone got too near him or too flirtatious, I'd stand up and let them have it.

In November we played the then unreleased '2x4' and 'Smile' for *The Tube* – The Fall's first appearance on national TV; John Peel, a guest presenter, had insisted we play if he was going to host. By now, I treated being in the band like being in the army. I took it extremely seriously. You could barely see me in the background on the show, which was very frustrating. It was a rare thing for a woman to be in a band in those days, especially as a guitar player, rather than lead singer or backup vocalist. I adored Poison Ivy from The Cramps and Chrissie Hynde. They, along with Lita Ford, Joan Jett and Nancy Wilson, helped pave the way for me and other women guitarists, but beyond them there weren't too many of us.

In December I recorded my first Peel session with The Fall – at Maida Vale in London, this really old, kind of haunted BBC studio where they did lots of classical music recording. We always used this one particular studio for the Peel session, and would work with a producer called Dale Griffin, who had been the drummer in Mott the Hoople. Queen's first tour in America was with Mott the Hoople and I was obsessed with Queen. I would always try to pick Dale's brain. I was fascinated by the bloated seventies supergroups. I wanted all the gory details of what it was like to be on one of those legendary tours. I wanted the filthy scoop on the sex, drugs and rock and roll. Unfortunately Dale was discreet. He was a gentleman and a professional. I never managed to get any of the real juice or good gossip out of him, no matter how much I wheedled.

We had so much fun doing Peel sessions. There was one big room and a separate control room. We went in and played live. I don't remember ever doing overdubs. Time was always short and we had a huge amount to do in one day. The live element and the mistakes are what set Peel sessions apart, made them special. A session lasted all day, from the early morning to well into the night. It was all mixed and done, there and then. We ate our meals out of the vending machine. I took power naps sitting upright in uncomfortable office chairs in the foyer. There actually was a canteen where the orchestra ate lunch and dinner. The food was inexpensive, subsidised by the BBC. For some reason I only realised this existed after I'd done four or more sessions.

Besides '2x4', the song we had been playing at shows and that I had co-written for that first Peel session was 'Pat – Trip Dispenser', the one about the American tour manager who tried to sell the band fake speed. It would go into a whole subgenre of Fall songs about amphetamines, like 'Totally Wired' and 'Gramme Friday'.

The entire band, except Paul, took speed at this point. Mark was in love with speed. That was his favourite drug, so he wrote about it. Speed made him feel good. There was always powder wrapped up in a small envelope. Everyone seemed to be on it. In my life I took speed maybe three times in total. Seeing as how Mark liked it so much I took it just to be part of the group, and to see if I was really missing something. But once I tried it again, I remembered how much I'd hated it since the Bennington days. My scalp tingled, my nose burned, I stayed up for days and it caused me anxiety. It also took ages to end, almost to the point where I feared it might never wear off. Speed will destroy your looks – it rots out your teeth and fries your brain. I am so grateful I never had an addiction to it.

Another song we recorded was 'Words of Expectation', an expansive bass-heavy harangue that could go on for almost fifteen minutes. It never made it on to a record. There are so many great lost songs that were never recorded for albums, only played live and then thrown away. And so many songs on records that were never played live, such as 'Hotel Blöedel', or classics like 'No Bulbs' that were relegated to B-sides. The Smiths are known for putting some of their best work on B-sides, but The Fall had been doing that since the 1970s.

Perverted by Language came out that December and was well received, and people really loved 'Hotel Blöedel'. When people saw that I was actually a writer, and that I was credited, they began to come around. I was no longer perceived as a hanger-on or groupie. Holding *Perverted by Language* in my hands, I couldn't believe my voice and guitar-playing were actually on it. It was mind-blowing. I was holding my first album, the first album I'd ever played on. I'd done it.

The other watersheds would happen later, like when I heard a song I'd written or played on on the radio for the first time. My favourite watershed was when I'd hear somebody walking down the street singing or humming a song I wrote.

At the time, *Perverted by Language* wasn't released in the US, so I sent copies to Mom and Marvin and my grandparents. I don't know if they listened to them, but my grandmother put a framed poster in her house, and Mom and Marvin never missed a show when we'd come through town.

It was great to have the record come out, but as a band we had moved on from it. Most of the songs on the album were from before I joined. We had written and were performing so much new material. All of the new songs we were doing would come out the next year. With The Fall it was a case of never luxuriating in what you had created; it was always full steam ahead, on to the next thing.

1984

For me, Disneyland is one of the greatest art installations in the world. During the hours I have spent at Disneyland throughout my life, my immediate troubles, and those of the world at large, have seemed to fade away. I feel safe and protected there, and unburdened. In Disneyland I allow myself to become immersed in fantasy. I am fascinated with the art and science of 'imagineering'. Walt Disney was an early pioneer in the use of sound and scent. He used them as a medium to manipulate a mass audience into the immersive and experiential world of his making. He created lifelike sets, façades and faux landmarks, which as a child I knew were fake but were still realistic enough to trick my mind into acceptance. As I grew older and became more aware of music and sound in general, I began to notice how the rides at Disneyland used sounds and ambient music (discreetly coming from camouflaged speakers in rocks) to subconsciously manoeuvre the public into becoming happy and excited. I also noticed that when something scary was about to happen on a ride the music would take a dark turn, and drop down to a minor key. It was all so clever and seamless.

When I was in The Fall, I would visit Disneyland with a Walkman in my hands. I would walk the park, recording all the ambient sounds, using the headphones as a microphone. Later I sampled those recordings, directly on to our records. I captured the music being piped through the artificial rocks and clockwork parades. I captured the screams and 'oohs' of the crowd, the joyous, sugar-fuelled squeals of children and the iconic 'themed' soundtrack music of the rides. I banged on and on about Disneyland to Mark. He'd never been there, nor did he have any desire to go.

But when we visited my grandparents in LA we stayed in their high-rise apartment above Wilshire Boulevard and, finally, after much persuading, I managed to convince Mark to accompany me on a walking tour of the park. I wanted Mark to experience Disneyland as I saw it. I hoped he could see past the ugly veneer of the general public, past the superficial theme-park element, and appreciate the elaborate installation of emotional puppeteering, the suspension of disbelief that Disneyland had to offer. It was only after I thought I had sufficiently indoctrinated him to my way of thinking that, at last, I led him to my favourite ride of all time.

The Matterhorn, the high-speed rollercoaster where, strapped into bobsleds, you careen around corners and precipices, through ice tunnels and caves – an Alpine, Bavarian extravaganza, the culmination of which results in your bobsled plunging into a pool of water underneath a cascading waterfall.

As we waited in line, we shuffled along to some piped-in yodelling coming through the hidden speakers. The juxtaposition of the screaming with the yodelling provided a brilliant layering of sound.

Mark is psychic and he knows it. He's a precognitive psychic, able to pick up snatches of future incidents before they happen. As we were waiting in line he said, 'This ride is evil.' He looked at me dead in the eye, and repeated, 'This ride is evil.' I said, 'Don't be ridiculous, I've been going on this since I was eight.' He freaked out and kept repeating, 'I don't want to go on it', like a mantra of fear.

'Stop being such a baby, just get on the ride, it's so much fun, you'll see. It's a rush.' His face was white. We sat down in the front of the toboggan and were belted in. We went through the ride, and I screamed, because I love screaming. It's a release. He was silent. His eyes were clamped shut the whole time. His pallor was deathly; tears of terror leaked from the corner of his eye.

When it was over, he said, 'That ride is fucking evil, Brix. It's evil. It's evil.' I told him to calm down and took him to It's a Small World, which is a baby ride where you go about 2 mph in a boat while you watch dolls from around the world sing and dance. It is actually pretty perverse and evil-seeming, with its high-pitched brain-infecting theme song. When we emerged from the tepid darkness and warm fetid waters of It's a Small World there was a very strange atmosphere in Disneyland. The air bristled with a palpable undercurrent of fear. The atmosphere pulsated with negative energy, panic and chaos. We stood staring and slack-jawed as a disguised underground elevator rose from behind a bush and a mini-fire engine emerged, lights flashing but its sirens ominously silent. A woman in a nurse's uniform stood on the running board of the fire truck and clung to the collapsed ladder on the back. Officials materialised out of nowhere. They were dressed head to toe in black with walkie-talkies and clipboards, like secret service agents. Scattering and fanning out, they cleared everybody away from the vicinity of the Matterhorn ride. The mini-fire engine drove up to the foot of Matterhorn mountain and the nurse got out and clambered over the tracks. The ride had been stopped. The bobsleds were still, the yodelling silenced. A cordon was put up. We were ushered away to another area. Nobody was allowed to go near the ride. In fact, an all-encompassing cordon was erected, blocking any visual access to the Matterhorn. Since the Matterhorn was the focal point, for all intents and purposes the park was closed.

Mark said, 'I told you it was fucking evil.'

As we were directed away, and turned the corner from Fantasyland to Tomorrowland, I saw a Mickey Mouse who had obviously been put out as a diversion to distract people from what was going on at the Matterhorn.

I asked Mickey what was happening. Mickey Mouse is never allowed to talk – he's only allowed to mime. I was momentarily shocked to hear a voice come from him. I knew something bad had happened then. The person in the Mickey suit said, 'There's been an accident on the Matterhorn. You need to keep moving.'

We went back to my grandparents' high-rise apartment in Beverly Hills. I said, 'I wonder if there's anything on the news.' We turned on the TV and were immediately greeted with the six o'clock headline: DEATH AT DISNEYLAND. A woman had either jumped or fallen off the bobsled, and had become trapped then crushed by an oncoming sled. It took mountain climbers hours to get her body off. The woman's name was Dolly. Which is completely freaky, because that was my grandmother's nickname for me.

Disneyland changed in one instant from 'the happiest place on earth' to the land of nightmares. I found the whole thing incredibly upsetting for many reasons. It shook me to the core and brought back vividly the childhood nightmare of my grandmother crashing her Mustang into the Submarine Voyage. I felt the last threads of my childhood innocence go up in flames, to be replaced by the world of adult anxiety and death. The duality of safety and danger had never been so black and white.

Mark and I wrote the song 'Disney's Dream Debased'. It tells the whole story. It would close *The Wonderful and Frightening World of The Fall*, which we'd record and release that year. I came up with the title as a reference to one of my favourite childhood shows, *The Wonderful World of Disney*.

Mark had been losing patience with Rough Trade and decided we had to look for a new record label. There were a few reasons Mark had soured on them, but the main one was that The Smiths had arrived. This was a huge bone of contention. When he was younger, Morrissey used to write Mark long, fawning letters. Mark has them all saved. Morrissey was obsessed with The Fall and Mark. Mark would never call him Morrissey and would refer to him by his first name, Steven. The rumour was that they named themselves The Smiths after Mark, and that they loved The Fall so much they wanted to be on Rough Trade. One of their first gigs was supporting us.

There was a real buzz around them, and Rough Trade were in a complete tizzy over them. I was oblivious. I wasn't privy to the record company politics, and I didn't know exactly what was going on. But Mark started to get really paranoid and kick up a fuss. He believed that Rough Trade were putting all their money into The Smiths. Maybe that's true – and quite rightly so, as it certainly paid off for them.

Grant Showbiz, who had worked with The Fall for a long time, both as a producer and front-of-house soundman, defected to do sound for The Smiths on tour. Mark was not thrilled about these upstarts poaching Grant, but he moved on, and we found another soundperson.

We put the word out with various people that we were looking to move labels. A weird thing happened when we were approached by an A&R man at Motown, who had been told to broaden their roster. Motown had opened a London office and they were probably looking at absolutely everything. Mark and I were invited down to their new office to meet them. We were so excited. We thought, 'God, if The Fall were on Motown it would be the weirdest juxtaposition ever – it would be so cool to be on Motown!' We took *Hex Enduction Hour* and *Perverted by Language* with us. We had a really good meeting, and the A&R man was warm and enthusiastic. We left with a positive feeling. We went skipping out of the office and didn't hear anything from them for ages. Then we heard, 'We don't think this is the right fit for us.'

What we figured was, one of the opening lines of 'The Classical' runs, 'Where are the obligatory niggers?' Perhaps they didn't understand the context in which Mark meant it.

We met Martin Mills and we loved Beggars Banquet. They never tried to take control artistically in any way. They encouraged us, enabled us. They were quite cost-conscious, but not as tight as Rough Trade. For a record company, they were nurturing. The set-up was slick and professional. It was a whole other world. It was super-indie. Besides that, we got along with all the bands that were on the label, so we'd go there and hang out with other bands all day. Beggars would take us out for meals. They actually had a press department, run by two super-smart women. They arranged our first proper studio photo-shoot, where we weren't just standing outside or jumping in the air. A stylist was brought in and I wore some club brand that doesn't exist any more called PX. I was ill and run-down from being on tour. I had some awful virus where you have sores inside your mouth. My whole face was swollen. I looked like a chipmunk. That's why there's no real close-up. Ulcers lined the inside of my lips, gums and the inside of my cheeks. I had to stop and repeatedly rinse my mouth during the photo-shoot with dissolvable Aspirin to kill the pain, but despite a mouth full of sores and chubby cheeks I still felt glamorous.

A lot has been said about my trying to project an image upon the band, to add a fashion element. Well, the band had no image, so it was a blank slate. When I got there, Mark was wearing polyester shirts printed with Spirograph designs. He was not only anti-fashion, he was non-fashion. They were normal blokes. The album art was the band's image. I never projected an image on to anybody except Mark, and that was just in the normal sense of the dynamic between husband and wife. I was looking after him. Mark's not the kind of man you could force to wear anything. We did share a lot of BodyMap clothes. He wore this black BodyMap parachute silk coat all the time that we shared, and also another one that was in bronze fake leather.

BodyMap was a cult 1980s brand – exalted and legendary today – and we'd become friends with the designers. I would later model in one of their shows during Fashion Week. The social scene surrounding BodyMap would factor heavily in The Fall's personal life. One of BodyMap's designers was David Holah, and at the time his boyfriend was the renegade ballet dancer and choreographer Michael Clark.

One night, Mark and I were watching *The Tube* and Paula Yates did a segment on a ballet dancer who had defected from the Royal Ballet. This punk wild boy, Michael Clark, was shown dancing through a supermarket wearing a tutu. He had a shaved head and a little Mohican, and he was jaw-droppingly gorgeous. He was an enfant terrible. We watched him and thought he was the coolest thing ever. A few weeks later, we were contacted by him. He was a massive Fall fan, and he asked to use some of our music to create a ballet for his troupe. It was called *Hail the New Puritan* and featured outrageous costumes by Holah and Stevie Stewart of BodyMap, and Leigh Bowery – the troupe also became known for nudity.

We went to see one of Michael's performances and met him afterwards. It was like we had known him for ever. It was such an easy friendship. There was no awkwardness. Mark and Michael got along in such a fantastic way, and I adored Michael. It was a beautiful union. He was mischievous and mercurial. He had a tense fire ignited within him. He was sexy in every way, one of the most sensuous creatures on this planet. It was a whole new scene that we were pulled into: punked-up, homosexual high art in London, as opposed to Manchester pub culture. With the fabulous nightlife we were now fully embracing came the emergence of a new drug, Ecstasy, among a small circle of elite club kids. A now very well-known fashion designer friend of theirs used to fly to Amsterdam and bring suitcases of MDMA back. It wasn't illegal then, because nobody knew what it was, and that was the first time that I remember people started taking it and dancing. There were also a lot of poppers around, and I would do amyl nitrate with them sometimes.

Mark thought Leigh Bowery was the modern Benny Hill. Bowery never ceased to amuse him; he had an extremely sarcastic sense of humour. He would say things that were funny, but they were also scathing at the same time. At first, I didn't quite get how brilliant he was. When you are around someone so much, you often don't see their brilliance until after they're dead.

One night, at the legendary club he started – Taboo – he had on clown make-up, and his face looked like it was covered in cold sores and scabs. It was wretched. 'Leigh, what is on your face?' I asked. He looked at me and said, 'Cornflakes.' He would glue giant mirrored sequins to his face and wear crash helmets covered in rhinestones. He was a clown, but also a walking art installation. I finally caught on that he was a genius, and not just some fun crazy guy. Leigh said, 'I'm doing a show at the Anthony d'Offay Gallery.' I asked, 'What do you mean "a show"?' I assumed he was just a club fixture. He replied, 'Yeah, I'm there for like a week behind glass.' We went, and there he was, sitting behind plate glass, on a chaise longue. I don't know if he ever went home. People would just come in and look at him like he was an exhibit at the zoo. No one was as extreme as Leigh. If it wasn't for Leigh, there would be no Marina Abramović.

Mark and I would accompany Leigh, Michael, David and their extended crew of friends to Taboo and wild gay bars like Bill Stickers and Heaven. I think there is a general misconception about Mark being some provincial, closed-minded Northerner. In reality, he was super-open and accepting of gay people, and it was a complete non-issue for him. He appreciated being around true creative people and artists, and this energy was feeding the music we were making.

But a really dark incident will always stand out when it comes to Leigh Bowery. One day, I went to his apartment in Angel to get ready before going out to a club. At this point, Angel, Islington, was a very sketchy neighbourhood. His flat was in a depressing, brutalist-style council tower block.

I went up in this grim lift and down a scary dark hallway to his apartment. Someone opened the door and it was like stepping into Narnia. The floor was covered in rocks. Not pebbles, but flat, black stones, the kind you use in hot stone therapy. The whole place was a work of art: Leigh's boyfriend Trojan's paintings covered the walls; there were large multicoloured lights here and there, poking out from among the stones, shining up the walls and creating a fantastical environment. But it was not a sober get-together – Leigh was off his face on drugs. It started out quite pleasantly, but at one point Leigh grabbed me and pulled me into his bedroom, which was very small and could barely fit the bed. He threw me down on it and – it is hard to describe, because there was no penetration – he acted out raping me. It wasn't like a dog humping your leg. I was trapped underneath him and he was gigantic, crushing me. He was yelling the whole time. I was a victim of his performance art. I was more forgiving at the time, and we would go on to work with him on a few projects, but I remained wary of him and a bit scared.

Our long-time music publisher, John Fogarty of Minder Music, introduced us to the producer John Leckie, who'd started as a tape operator at Abbey Road Studios, engineering for Phil Spector and working on John Lennon's solo albums. When we first met him, he was Rajneesh. He had recently walked off an ashram, where everyone had to wear the colours of the rising sun and was encouraged to have group sex. John had produced plenty of big rock albums, but he'd basically retired and was living in some weird community in Seattle or Portland or somewhere. He came back, and the first band he worked with was us. It must have been an extreme culture shock for John, going from Bhagwan Shree Rajneesh to Mark E. Smith.

We did two singles; 'Oh! Brother' was first (which was backed with 'God-Box', the original Banda Dratsing song, called 'Can't Stop the Flooding', which Mark had changed all of the words to). I thought it would be a massive hit. It made it to number 91 in the charts, which was at least a hit in terms of The Fall. I always had unrealistically high expectations that our singles and albums would do well.

'C.R.E.E.P.' came out next (the B-side was 'Pat – Trip Dispenser'). Now I was sure we would get on *Top of the Pops*. I was always pushing for hits. I strongly believed that by just injecting a tiny bit of commerciality into the mix, the pendulum would swing in The Fall's favour and get us played on the radio. At the time, Radio 1 was it, really. It was the make it or break it station. Of course, we had John Peel on our side, and he championed us with all his might, but it was all about cracking daytime radio. 'C.R.E.E.P.' was catchy, irreverent and a bit weird – kooky enough to be a hit. My optimism about our work never faded.

Around this time Mark was working on a small-press book of his lyrics and asked me to illustrate it. For 'Hotel Blöedel' I tried to render the origin of the song and drew a cow on its knees in the slaughterhouse, holding a machete in its hoof, with blood and cigarettes around it.

The drawing of C.R.E.E.P. is a strange monster guy, with lesions on his brain. I find it really creepy when men wear rings – so he's got a creepy paedophile hand, and then the other hand is a lobster claw, because creeps always pinch you in the ass. One leg is chewed off, and the other is a chicken leg, because he's just worthless. Behind him is a spinning vortex, from *The Twilight Zone*. Mark loved it – he thought of Rod Sterling as one of the greatest poets that ever lived. I thought the graphic was suitable since The Fall were coming from a different dimension to everything else that was out there.

We worked with Leckie on *The Wonderful and Frightening World of The Fall*, recorded at Focus Studios in London. He was a genius at getting those warm, old-school, analogue sounds. His favourite technique was to put a guitar through a Leslie amp, which is kind of organ amplifier. We also ended up working with him on the next two albums. They can be seen as companion pieces, and are seen by many as the best albums the group has ever done.

The Wonderful and Frightening World . . . starts off with a song Mark and I wrote, 'Lay of the Land'. The main body of it, the guitar part, was thrashy country rockabilly; it's the way I play rhythm guitar. E and A minor are my favourite chords; I put them in everything. I wrote the music for 'Lay of the Land' at home, and then I brought it into the rehearsal room and everyone added their bits. The spark of the song was the science-fiction TV show *Quatermass* (a cult show about cults). Mark and I sat down to watch it one night, and the characters were chanting, 'Lay, lay . . .' Mark was fascinated by ley lines. He was a bit of a witch, a psychic, a warlock – he understood energy intuitively. That's where 'Lay of the Land' came from. When we went to record it, every single person went into the studio and said, 'Lay, lay, lay, lay, lay . . .' We were all the disciples in a way. We were like the hypnotised masses behind Mark.

We finally recorded '2x4' and 'Copped It', which had been a live song from the band's 1970s era. I co-wrote 'Elves', which has an obvious riff lifted from 'I Wanna Be Your Dog'. It was meant as witty commentary, a send-up of punk, but also a homage to Iggy and the Stooges, one of Mark's favourite groups. Everyone thought we were trying to steal something from them, but it was so obviously cribbed it should have been evident.

In 'Slang King', Mark sang, 'This is Mr and Mrs Smith to whom you are speaking.' I loved being referred to. I felt loved by him, and it became a piece of history. Once you put it on a record, it's there for ever. It's obviously a direct allusion to us, but he is also sending up the heinous game show, *Mr & Mrs*, which we would sometimes watch even though we hated it. It was so bad it was good. A kitsch bit of British television history.

The favourite backup vocal I did – which sounded like an updated version of classic girl groups' 'la' – was for the song Steve Hanley wrote, aptly titled 'Stephen Song'. As with the recording of many songs, my part just evolved in the studio. While sitting in the control room listening to everybody else do their bits, hook after hook popped into my brain, and I'd spring up like a jack-in-the-box: 'I've got something! I've got something!' This was probably how I wrote 50 per cent of the time, these studio moments, almost like spontaneous improv.

Gavin Friday, the frontman for the Virgin Prunes, guested on a few tracks. At home in Manchester, Mark had played me the Virgin Prunes' 'Sandpaper Lullaby', and before long I became obsessed with it. So we got him to come in. He had this amazing sandpaper voice and . . . talk about style: at that point, he wore Doc Martens and dresses with raccoon *Blade Runner* make-up, and a big samurai ponytail. His band would play a lot of shows with us on the subsequent tour.

In 'Stephen Song', Gavin sings a throwaway lyric underneath the mix: 'Adult Net. Net of mesh.' I said to Mark, 'What the fuck is an adult net?' This was years before the internet, but something about the phrase really resonated with me. 'How cool.'

'No Bulbs', on the US version of *The Wonderful and Frightening World . . .*, was about the squalor of our apartment. We were quite aware it was a shithole. When we would come back from being on tour, our suitcases would explode and everything was a mess, and you couldn't find anything. One morning, Mark got up and started looking everywhere for a belt to hold his trousers up, because he was so skinny. He couldn't find the belt. He couldn't find the black strap. Then the light bulb went out . . . everything was breaking. 'Your home is a trash mount.'

When we finished the album, we knew it was good, but we didn't know it was a masterpiece. We didn't stop to reflect on it. It was business as usual: album, tour, album, tour, album, tour. We were never rich enough to stop working. We always had to have gigs booked. We lived hand to mouth. The band had to be paid their weekly wages. On the *Wonderful and Frightening . . .* tour, which went through the UK and Europe, we started getting booked into bigger venues and festivals. I also started to get fanatical boy fans who were obviously besotted with me – they would wait for me at the stage door. But, at the same time, more women also started turning up to the shows. The strange side of that was the emergence of Brix clones. People would come dressed like me. This was one of the reasons I constantly changed my look. It was actually quite flattering, but I had to consciously keep trying to evolve to stay ahead of them.

We performed 'Lay of the Land' on *The Old Grey Whistle Test*. It was my second time on TV but, again, not that anyone would have noticed. We were on a darkened platform in the background, while Michael Clark's dancers cavorted with their asses hanging out in front of us. It ended with them ushering out a pantomime cow and dousing it in milk. It was a brilliant performance, but maybe not the best PR stunt to sell the record – the exposed buttocks and the cow were, of course, the only thing the press talked about.

I felt very secure in the band. I counted on those guys in terms of camaraderie and musicality. Once you start playing with people you grow to understand how they play and how they think. Karl Burns was an exquisite drummer. He was a great, all-round musician. Sometimes he'd pick up the bass, sometimes he would sing in a deep, baritone voice. He could play guitar too. But as a drummer, he had finesse unlike anyone. Unfortunately this is when the core differences of who we were started to become more and more apparent. Karl had been in the very first incarnation of The Fall: he was on the first album, left, then came back a few years later. He was from the era when the band were not Mark's employees, under his complete direction, but a collective. There was a real duality to Karl. On good days, he was Mark's lapdog, his henchman. On other days, it was like he had a screw loose, and was out of control. He wouldn't show up to get in the van, if we were going on tour. He would keep people waiting. Of course, back then, there were no mobile phones, and Karl would simply go AWOL.

He was also extremely unhygienic. For a six-week tour he'd bring a plastic bag with one pair of socks – he didn't bring any change of clothes, nor did he wash his clothes the whole time. He stunk, and it drove me crazy. He wore Chelsea boots that had holes in the soles. We would fight quite a lot, but I actually liked him. We were just two diametrically opposed people. I would try my best to get along with him. Once, it was his birthday, and we were on tour. I got him a German chocolate cake, one of my favourites, and sang, 'Happy Birthday, Karl!' He looked at me – he often spoke in a monosyllabic way, like a caveman, and said, 'Oh? Ah? Oh?' – and then opened the box with the cellophane lid and he smashed the cake all over the hotel-room wall.

Mark educated me in all sorts of different styles of music. I had never heard of Can before. He had an equal deep love for proper sixties psychedelia, like The Seeds, as he did for truck-driver music. There were so many obscure bands, especially krautrock bands, I didn't know about. Mark also loved Frankie Valli and the Four Seasons. During one particular tour he played Frankie Valli and the Four Seasons every single day on the bus. 'Sherry' and 'Big Girls Don't Cry' over and over and over again – until one of the lads took the tape and hurled it out the window.

The tour was gruelling, but the shows continued to get better with each gig. After playing in Cardiff we went back to our budget hotel, and the car park was chained shut. We had to leave the van on the street. While we were sleeping, somebody broke into it and stole all of our equipment, including my special solid-body, cherry-red Gretsch, the one possession that really meant something to me. The thieves left only the bass cabinet, which is too heavy to move. We were all furious, but Mark was on a different plane of angry – one that wouldn't subside. We had to call Beggars Banquet to get them to hire us replacement gear for the next night's concert in Brighton. The theft triggered the first exodus from the band. Mark was beside himself with fury, and tensions continued to build.

The next night, we were playing on shit borrowed instruments, and Mark exploded after the show. We were in a club under the hotel, and Mark had got hold of a big fucking stick from somewhere. He was waving it around and threatening everybody. He was saying the reason the gear got nicked was because he had given the band too much control. He managed to piss Paul and Steve off so much that they both (separately) quit. Paul had had enough. If Paul didn't like something, he'd get up and go. He was a strong guy. He calmly informed us he was leaving, and he never came back.

I was broken when Paul left. One of the things that made The Fall so powerful and special was having two drummers. As though by telepathy, Steve also quit. He couldn't take the misery of being in the group, and his newborn son was very ill. Unbeknown to them, both brothers had left within twenty-four hours of each other.

Mark was fine about Paul going, but he was tormented about Steve. Still, Mark didn't want to have them back. He wanted to punish them. He said, 'Fuck it. Fuck them all.' I was beside myself that Steve was gone. I missed Paul, but I knew that no matter what, we couldn't get him back – but with Steve, I thought there was hope. I begged Steve to come back. I called him repeatedly, 'Please come back!' Steve anchored it all for me; he was as much the sound of The Fall as Mark.

Meanwhile, I worked on Mark, trying to get him to capitulate and bring Steve back. I was trying to be the peacemaker and deal-broker. Mark knew that Steve's playing was singular. Finally, he accepted that we really needed Steve, and that not all musicians are ancillary and disposable. We went to Steve's house, uninvited and unexpected, where he lived with his wife and son. It was great that Steve had a stable marriage; he seemed so reliable because of it. At the same time, on the road, he was more reserved than the other guys. (I hated it when the groupies would get on the bus.) Eventually, Mark, chastened for probably the only time I had ever seen, asked Steve to come back. Mark gave him a check for £1,000, and they went to a pub to hash it out. His permanent departure was changed to a temporary leave to care for his family – paternity leave, as it were. He ended up working at a petrol station during his sabbatical, and made more money than he would have if he were still in the band.

Every time a member of The Fall would leave, it felt like the rug was pulled out from under me. It caused me great anxiety and panic. I would learn, though, that these line-up changes, although traumatic, would often have a positive effect. They were like a forest fire raging destruction, but leaving fertile earth primed for new growth. Bringing new people in would reinvent and reinvigorate the band, and that's why The Fall would keep evolving and not stagnate, like the Rolling Stones. It makes you have to redouble your efforts to make it great. *This Nation's Saving Grace* was the result.

1985-1986

The thought of driving on the other side of the road in the UK filled me with terror. Even as a passenger I would sometimes become confused and momentarily freak out that the driver had made a mistake and was driving on the wrong side. In America I had driven since I was sixteen. I knew that to have a car meant freedom. Mark did not know how to drive, so I decided to face my fears and take the British test. I saved up a bit of money and thankfully Marvin made up the deficit. I bought a navy second-hand BMW 3 Series. Johnny Marr drove a BMW and I thought we should have one too. It was ridiculous. We were in competition with The Smiths, although they weren't even aware of it. Mark loved the car because it was German.

I drove up and down Cheetham Hill to practise. I failed the test. Mark said it was because I looked too posh, and I was driving a posh car – I was American, so they automatically had it in for me and failed me. The next time I attempted to look English. Really, really English. I put a fake Hermès scarf over my head, like the Queen, and wore wellies. I failed again. The third time I passed it, and when I did so I kissed the examiner, I was so relieved.

Mark loved having a car. I was the only one who could drive it, so that suited me fine. Being the designated driver empowered me. It was a blessing Mark did not drive. He was a man who liked his drink.

Our biggest purchase together was a house. It was around the corner from Mark's childhood home, where his parents still lived. It was very comforting to him to live a block away from his mother. We bought the house from a Baptist couple. They had kind, calm energy and there was a good vibe in the house. This was not a swanky Los Angeles type of dwelling. It was a typical British suburban semi-detached house, in a predominantly Jewish working-class area. The house was a massive step up from our shabby apartment on Rectory Lane. This was the first house either of us ever owned and the pride Mark felt at owning a house himself was immortalised in the song 'My New House'. Although Mark's lyrics are sometimes impenetrable, on this occasion he writes with transparent clarity. He sings, 'I bought it off the Baptists . . .' For some reason the fact that they had been Baptists gave Mark solace. The song is credited just to Mark, but I remember that he and Craig Scanlon wrote the music together – since Mark didn't tra-ditionally play an instrument it would be pretty hard for him to come up with *all* the music.

He often took sole writing credit for things. Like with the song 'Terry Waite Sez'. I actually came up with the title and wrote it. I was obsessed with Terry Waite, the Archbishop of Canterbury's envoy who was on the news every day. He was in Lebanon at the time trying to secure the release of hostages. I was very caught up in his story, which had echoes of the American hostage crisis dur-ing the Iranian Revolution – an incident my stepfather Marvin, an expert on the Middle East, had been heavily involved in. It was only after we released the song that Terry Waite himself got kidnapped. I remember hearing a rumour that a member of Terry Waite's family had contacted Beggars Banquet for the lyrics to the song, in case there were some psychic clues to his whereabouts hidden in the words.

Mark is notorious for crediting songs incorrectly. He would leave people off songs that they had primarily developed, and sometimes put band members' names on tracks they had nothing to do with. He'd give the information to the publisher, and we'd have no clue until it came out. He was sure to always have his name on everything, though. His 'solo' efforts gave us particular consternation. One of the only songs that didn't have his name on it was the instrumental I did, 'Mansion'. It was supposed to evoke the creepy theme song to the haunted house at Disneyland, and it would open *This Nation's Saving Grace*.

Before we started working on *This Nation's Saving Grace*, Simon Rogers was brought in to fill in for Steve, who was still on sabbatical. He had been recommended to us by Martin Mills. Simon had been in a strange band called Incantation that played Bolivian folk music, and was also signed to Beggars. He was classically trained, adept on any instrument. He was The Fall's first proper muso, and for me that was a great relief. Simon would come in and 'get' what we were doing and play anything proficiently. His technical prowess gave our shambolic energy a backbone of stability. This musical duality added a professional element and took *This Nation's Saving Grace* up a notch. Simon put the chaos into context.

Simon was primarily a guitarist, but he came in to play bass. I still thought of myself as a bass player, but Steve Hanley's shoes were too big to fill. Simon used his fingers instead of a pick to play bass, jazz-style. This was a different sound for The Fall. At first I thought it too passive, until I got used to it and realised that the subtleties and the tones he could get with his fingers added a new dimension to the songs.

Simon was a normal, stable person. Middle class, he was from Romford in Essex. I bonded with him. He didn't do speed and we would hang out while travelling together in the van. We talked for hours. He had a great sense of humour and he made me laugh. Simon played on the single 'Couldn't Get Ahead', which we did without Steve.

During the London sessions for *This Nation's Saving Grace*, Mark and I stayed at Simon's house. He lived in Hammersmith with his wife, Lucy Burge, the principal ballerina of Ballet Rambert. We loved staying with them. We slept on a futon in their living room. Both Lucy and Simon cooked, and it was all very civilised and comfortable. Simon had a small home studio in his spare room upstairs. We actually did a lot of work in that room for both The Adult Net and The Fall.

John Leckie was again the producer, and, thankfully, Steve came back to work on *This Nation's Saving Grace*. Steve brought in 'Bombast', which has one of his most amazing bass lines. Simon happily switched to guitar and keyboards. Karl could more than handle the drum kit by himself, but it was a shame that Paul was missing out on what we were creating, which I thought was leagues beyond *Wonderful and Frightening . . . This Nation's Saving Grace* is for me the best album The Fall have ever done. It was certainly the album I was most proud of, personally. There are some truly great songs on there. One of them is 'I Am Damo Suzuki'. I co-wrote Mark's ode to the Japanese singer from Can. When I listen to it now I can hear my then technical weaknesses as a player, but in saying that I can also hear complete freedom and a certain creativity that might not have been captured had I played it perfectly. Another song on the album was yet again inspired by one of our favourite TV shows: 'What You Need' melds two *Twilight Zone* episodes together. 'Spoilt Victorian Child' was Simon's first attempt at writing with us. It's got a blistering hooky riff which it took Simon ages to teach me. I had to really practise to get it right, but once I had it I loved playing it. I felt like Eddie Van Halen. 'LA' is a love song to my city. It's become a Fall classic now. I was very, very homesick, and I wanted to try to capture the feeling I had for LA in a song. I was heavily into the LA psychedelic music scene, both in the sixties and the eighties with the emergence of the Paisley Underground.

I could think of no better place in the world than LA. I loved all of it and missed the seedy, psychotropic glamour of Hollywood. I had a passion for Russ Meyer films; *Beyond the Valley of the Dolls* was my favourite. It featured an all-girl band, called the Carrie Nations, who were really sexy and wore evening gowns and played guitar. As kids, both my childhood friend and future Bangle Susanna Hoffs and I wanted to be those girls. I had met Susanna when her mother, Tamar, had worked on a movie in Chicago with my mom. The image of the Carrie Nations was so strong that it inspired both of us. That film made me want to be in a band and dress up. Seeing these powerful, sexual women playing instruments, rocking out, was a life-changer for me. In the middle of the song 'LA' I speak a line directly lifted from the movie. It's a tribute to the inspirational effect the movie had on me. I also meant it as a subtle link for the listener to connect the visual images from the film to my personal fantasies of LA and what it meant to me. The part I speak is, 'This is my happening, and it freaks me out.' It's a quote from the character Z-Man Barzell who screams it after freaking out on acid, tripping at his own party, at which The Strawberry Alarm Clock are playing 'Incense and Peppermints' live. This is also why 'Incense and Peppermints' became the first song I recorded for The Adult Net. It's all connected.

Mark's parts in 'LA' – 'White snow, scum-ball' – came from William Shatner's character in the cheesy cop show *T. J. Hooker*. He was busting a cocaine ring. A line of Mark's I really love is, 'Uncanny bushes are in disagreement with the heat.' To me these are some of Mark's most brilliant lyrics. In LA it gets so hot, you can almost hear the bushes complain.

I think 'Paint Work' is the best thing on the record. Mark and Simon started it in his bedroom studio, with Craig. I played an electric guitar that wasn't even plugged in, so it just made a scratching sound. Mark made a recording of it on his Sony cassette player, which he would always carry around with him in a plastic carrier bag. While watching TV, he accidentally hit record and erased part of the song and recorded the documentary he was watching. 'Fucking hell, the red light's on!' and he turned it off. It was irreparable and turned out to be a glorious accident. That's why it has such an amazing texture. We were never going to be able to replicate this on the record, so John Leckie put the original cassette with all of the re-recording and fucked-upness right on to the twenty-four-track, and we played live with it to fill in the gaps.

There are mistakes in a horde of songs in the whole catalogue: a wrong note here, a late drumbeat there. Mark was aware of this. The errors ended up not being mistakes at all, but what made the music so special.

During the recording process, Mark's complete control would be undermined on occasion by subterfuge and subtlety. People knew how to work around him and they used different sorts of psychological means to go sideways until the issue resolved itself. Nobody would directly confront Mark. Sometimes, when Mark was out of the studio, I'd have a word with John Leckie and ask him to add in a part of my guitar, or turn it up a little, and hope that Mark wouldn't notice. Sometimes we'd get away with it, he wouldn't notice. It depended on how much booze had been consumed.

We piggy-backed the album sessions to record the debut Adult Net single, 'Incense and Peppermints'. We also recorded 'Edie', the first song I wrote at Bennington. The band members used absurd pseudonyms on the recordings but, just as the lads hid behind their fake names, I was hiding behind The Adult Net. I wasn't confident enough to stand up with my own name and say, 'This is me. This is who I am.' I felt controlled by Mark and in his shadow. I also thought it was cooler to have this construct of a band, even if a group didn't really exist. I wasn't trying to be Madonna or Cher. I always viewed it as a small side project. I worried about putting too much into it and upsetting Mark. I was trying to be respectful to him. It would take me a long time to realise how limiting that state of mind and my situation was. I have always been empathetic and considerate of other people's needs. That, coupled with my own sporadic feelings of unworthiness, made it very comfortable for me to give away the primary power to someone else, and do my manoeuvring from slightly behind. Second in command in The Fall, hidden behind a name in The Adult Net.

My grandparents took my entire family on a cruise for their fiftieth wedding anniversary. They never learned how to decipher Mark's thick accent – he might as well have been speaking Swahili. I would have to translate his Mancunian into Beverly Hills for them. They took all twenty-two of us on a six-day cruise from LA to Acapulco. It was one of those cruises where cocktails would be served in the captain's lounge, and you'd watch the sunset surrounded by massive glass windows, as if inside a floating conservatory. The ship had a gym, skating rink, bowling alley, casino and beauty salon. You would have meal after meal. It was non-stop gluttony and bourgeois decadence: there were midnight feasts in case you hadn't managed to cram enough down your throat during the day. Of course, my biological father was on the cruise with Angela, now his wife. Aunt Susie, Uncle Fred and my half-siblings and cousins, and Uncle Jack, my grandfather's brother, were also all there.

The cruise ship was like the TV series *The Love Boat*, except instead of lovers it was filled with seniors. You've never seen anything weirder than Mark E. Smith on a fucking luxury cruise. He can't swim, and was panicked just being on the boat. He hates the sun. He will not sit in the sun, never mind sunbathe. He was also stuck with all of these bizarre rich people. We were the only young people there; the Grim Reaper was first mate. Every time the boat would rock, one of the octogenarians would die. Mark was fed up with my family, and the whole experience, and he escaped to the library. Every room had been given some kind of grand, nautical title, like the Pelican Perch Bowling Alley, and the Narwhal's Nebula Theatre. The library was christened Cruiser's Creek.

After *This Nation's Saving Grace* came out, we recorded the single 'Cruiser's Creek'. It started with a blistering riff I'd come up with that carried on throughout the song. I hadn't consciously realised yet that the riff was my forte; the sonic nursery rhyme that made The Fall songs of that era so catchy. I was proud that this was the second single in a row I'd written the music to. Mark's words elliptically germinated from our trip. When he wrote the song, I assumed it concerned the Salenger family vacation. But his miserable voyage made him reminisce about his brief time working at the docks in Manchester as a teenager – his only real job. He had been fascinated by the office parties there, and remained curious about office parties in general. Like how cubicle-dwelling co-workers would get drunk at the Christmas bash and fuck under the desk or on the copy machine. This mixture of the surreal and the mundane encapsulated Mark. He's not the kind of guy who likes black lace, garters and stockings. Mark's more a copy-machine kind of guy, much more excited to fuck you on a vibrating washing machine than pull you out of a strip club. So 'Cruiser's Creek' was about an office party that ended in disaster because somebody left the gas on and the whole thing blew up. Leigh Bowery, covered in polka dots, starred in the video, which was rarely played. Videos were never our strong suit – Mark was quite indifferent to them. One time he tried to have 'Hang Tracey Ullman' flash subliminally during one, but the record company made us pull it out. It was the one time he was excited about the prospects of the medium.

The B-side to the 12" of 'Cruiser's Creek' included 'Vixen', a song that was quite special to me. It was inspired by a TV documentary on foxes. I was a TV addict, and the problem would get worse and worse. It had started growing up in LA, with my mother always working. The documentary depicted an urban fox, living in the city with her cubs, and how she was such a solitary creature. In it, I sing, 'The vixen has no friends.' Writing it, I thought that it was about an animal, not a woman. But, subconsciously, I was really writing about myself. There were so many parallels between the vixen and myself. I identified with her and was even referred to as a 'rock and roll vixen' in the press. We never played 'Vixen' live.

A sense of isolation and loneliness in my life was starting to build. I wasn't just one of the gang in the band, I was an American in Manchester – not even Manchester, but the suburbs. When I was home, part of my daily routine was to go to the same newsagent and café. No matter how many times I visited that newsagent's over the years, they always treated me as an alien. They would hear my accent and ask, 'Are you on holiday, love?' When we would come back from tour, I would be physically and emotionally drained, and would spend days sprawled on the couch watching crap British TV while Mark would go to the pub with his mates. I had no real friends. Mark was my only lifeline to humanity. Our cats were my buddies.

Heaton Park was near our house, and that was an uplifting place for both of us. It was huge – Manchester's answer to Hampstead Heath or Central Park – rife with wild fields and varied terrain. Mark wrote a song about it, called 'Papal Visit', as the Pope had spoken there. It was within walking distance of our house and for Mark it was a special place, he really liked to go there. I had told him that, growing up, I rode horses and he said, 'Oh, they've got horse riding at Heaton Park.' Whenever I felt I needed to clear my head, I would make little pilgrimages to Heaton Park. There was indeed a riding stable there, but I only rode a few times. It made me sad: the horses were just little, battered old ponies and nags one step from the glue factory or a dog-food can. We spent a lot of time in the Woodthorpe pub, which was the only pub I enjoyed going to. Since it was on the edge of the park, it felt like an English country pub set in a big house. It was spacious, with a roaring fire in the winter.

The band had a high profile in the weekly music press, but we were certainly not the toast of Manchester. We had quasi-fame. But people were scared of Mark, I think, and they were afraid to approach him. There was a lot of whispering. Mark was the guy who could be relied upon for negative soundbites in the music press, and was known for firing people. The good aspects of his personality weren't broadcast for public consumption – his humour, his kindness, his devotion to his family.

Mark had three sisters. The eldest one was a sort of a biker chick. The middle one, Suzanne, was very attractive and artistic and did the cover imagery for *Grotesque* and some singles. The younger one was a strong character, wild and extremely loyal to Mark. Although I had a good relationship with all of them, and there was never animosity, there would always be distance. I never felt like I could call them for sisterly chats. That didn't happen, nor did they confide in me.

I lived for my marriage and the music. But other than those aspects of my life, it was empty, and I was so alone. I wasn't able to live a normal, youthful life: I didn't know what it was to have girlfriends, to go and have fun on a girls' night out, or to just hang out. I was uptight, in a weird way, and very focused, like an army sergeant, on the work we were doing. That's why I barely ever drank and hardly took drugs the whole time I was in The Fall. On tour I would have one or two glasses of champagne after a show, to wind down and celebrate a great gig. I enjoyed cocaine, but only took it rarely, as a special treat, and only then before a day off. I *never* drank or took anything before a show. I'm the type of musician who *must* play sober. I needed all my wits about me. The show and performance were all that mattered, and sometimes the rest of the band were so out of it I felt I needed to captain the ship.

Our marriage was fulfilling. We had a great partnership, but it was intertwined with work. On tour in the early days we would make an effort to be a normal couple. We would go out to restaurants, experience different cultures and go to parties. When we did go out to eat in Manchester, we'd go to a popular restaurant in Chinatown. Mark loved it because it was owned by these hardcore Chinese guys. One day there was a brawl and someone got their arm cut off with a machete.

Once in a while we'd go out to the fish and chip shop, which was actually a Chinese takeaway, referred to by Mark as 'the Chinky'. I bristle every time I hear that word. We usually ordered curry and chips. We never had a dinner party. When not on tour, Mark would go to the pub as soon as it would open, and stay until it closed. I would usually eat at home alone in front of the TV with our cats. The rare times Mark cooked, he always made exactly the same dish, every time. He would take a thin, cheap cut of steak and throw it in a pan, then he'd fry it with a bit of oil and butter, take two untoasted pieces of white bread, sop up all the oil and make a sandwich. There would always be stringy remnants of gristle in his teeth – he never used floss but would get a matchbook to pick it out. He also really liked frozen potato waffles. I cooked for him on occasion, but food was very secondary in our household.

Mark would drink very strong tea in the morning, up until 11 a.m., at which time he would switch to beer. As the night went on, the whiskey came out. The darker it got, the darker the liquid, the darker he became.

The tour for *This Nation's Saving Grace* started in 1985 and stretched into 1986. Our tour dates were usually broken into three- to six-week chunks. Touring was both physically and mentally hard, and Mark used to say America would make or break a band. The long distances travelled, the sleep deprivation and the endless hours in close quarters, were enough to fray anyone's nerves. If there were cracks in the foundation of the band, they would develop into canyons on those big open roads. Only the strongest units survived, and you were only as strong as your weakest link.

Being a tour manager is a very particular job. It's a cross between a babysitter, a scout leader, a whipping boy and a nurse. I often relied on the tour manager so much that when I'd come off the road I'd struggle to do even the smallest things for myself. I was so used to being told what to do – mollycoddled – that adjusting back into the real world after a tour ended would take me weeks. A tour manager was expected to wear many hats. They needed to get everybody organised, make sure we arrived on time, and dampen down any incendiary situations that might crop up – like marital spats or dealing with irate hotel receptionists when a band member wet the bed after a night of heavy drinking. To me it seemed like a hard, thankless job. I always felt sorry for our tour managers. They got the brunt of everything.

Up until 1985 our tour managers had all been men. When we toured America from 20 March to 7 April 1985 that changed. Someone at Beggars Banquet recommended a *woman* as our tour manager. Her name was K2, and she'd recently been on the road with Herbie Hancock. She had brown hair cut into a long mullet. She was Californian, pretty, confident and smart. I wondered how the dynamics of introducing another woman into the Fall fold might play out. I needn't have worried. Having K2 join us was like a breath of fresh air. She was totally professional and the band respected her. Things were relatively calm, bordering on civilised. We did one American tour with K2 at the helm. I hadn't realised how much I needed a dose of girly camaraderie. K2 was a welcome balance to all the testosterone whipping round the bus.

K2 lived in Mill Valley overlooking San Francisco. It was a beautiful wealthy area in the hills, across the Golden Gate Bridge. On 25 and 26 March we played our third and fourth dates, performing two nights in a row at the legendary I-Beam club in San Francisco, located smack in the middle of Haight-Ashbury. Haight-Ashbury had always held a fascination for me. We were taught in school that it was the birthplace of American counter-culture. I remember standing on the street before our soundcheck, staring up at the iconic Haight-Ashbury sign and trying to absorb the historic inspirational vibes surely wafting through the air.

After the second I-Beam show, we had a whole day off. We did not have to leave until night, when we were booked on the red-eye to New York. K2 suggested we spend the day hanging out at her house, swimming and relaxing in the sun, and then drive to the airport late in the evening. Her house was stunning. It was made of wood and glass, modern and rustic at the same time.

K2 had mentioned that she had a stash of 'primo' California weed, and I got the idea to make pot brownies for the whole band. I'm sure spending time in Haight-Ashbury must have subconsciously stimulated my desire to take drugs. I spent the morning cooking the brownies, then arranged them on a serving dish and handed them out to the band. I ate one and waited for it to kick in. After an hour I felt nothing so I ate two more. I remember going around asking everyone if they felt anything yet. They all said they did, but I still didn't, so I ate another. We were splashing around in the pool when it hit me. The water felt like liquid silk against my skin and the glinting sunlight bounced and reflected off the surface of the pool, strobing like shards of jewels under a halogen lamp. At first the sensations were pleasant and gently mesmerising. Colours were more intense, sounds became clear and vibrant, my skin was alive and tingling. But then it kept building and building. Within fifteen minutes, I felt higher than I'd ever been in my life. I felt so high I was sure I was tripping.

Ingesting pot makes you much higher than smoking it. It's much more intense, lasts longer and it's impossible to control. I was sure I'd overdosed. There was no talking me down. I became super-paranoid and began to panic. I could not control my thoughts. I felt like the high would never end, that I'd never be 'normal' again and would never come down. I began to worry about being hospitalised.

K2 took me downstairs and put me in the bed in her guest room. She tucked me in and turned on the television to try to calm me and take my mind off my freak-out. I had no idea how I would ever make it to the van for the drive to the airport later that night, let alone how I would get on the plane without being carted off or arrested. I was a gibbering wreck. It was then I knew that

God was going to punish me. I could feel it. I deserved it. How could I have eaten all those brownies?

Lying in K2's guest bed, I had a surreal post-modern moment. From the TV, I heard the familiar strains of the theme tune of *The Brady Bunch*. I loved *The Brady Bunch*. As a kid I probably saw every episode. I turned to look at the TV, hoping the happy family would anchor me back in reality. As I began to watch the screen, what I saw freaked me out even more. The Brady kids looked different . . . they were *old*. They were *grown-up*. They'd skipped puberty and morphed into adults. *What the hell happened to them?* I started to scream and yelled out for K2: 'I'm hallucinating . . . help me. Time has sped up. I'm seeing the future through the TV. The Brady kids are old, the Brady kids are old.' K2 ran into the room to see what I was going on about. She looked at the TV and started laughing. 'They *are* old, Brix, because you are watching a Brady *reunion*. This is what they look like *now*.' Somehow through the haze of my paranoia I could just about see the humour in the situation. I continued to lie in the bed, getting my head around the fact that Cindy Brady was a woman, and tried to stay calm. Eventually it was time to leave for the airport. Wrapped in a blanket, I was bundled into the van.

The drive to the airport was hair-raising. I was convinced we were going to drive off the dark cliffs on the winding stretch of highway. I gripped the seat hard and willed the van to stay on the road. I made a deal with God never to eat pot brownies again if He let us get to the airport alive, although it was a promise I would renege on more than once.

We did make it to the airport, but then my paranoia shifted from the van crashing to the plane crashing. With my head bowed and the blanket draped over me like a Russian babushka, I was escorted on to the plane by K2, whimpering and muttering and praying out loud. She sat next to me on the flight and held my hand. During the flight I must have passed out; I have no recollection of it. What

I do remember is being very disoriented when we landed. I was still stoned when we reached our hotel early the next morning. I slept during the day and prayed the pot would wear off before our gig that night. We were playing at Danceteria in New York, but I was so stoned I thought we were in Denver.

When it came time to go on stage that night I was *still* stoned. I remember telling the rest of the band that they would have to pull me through this one. I consoled myself by remembering a story I once heard about Jimi Hendrix putting Windowpane LSD under his eyelids and playing while tripping. 'You can do this, Brix,' I told myself. 'You've only eaten brownies. Don't be such a wimp.'

I made it through the show on autopilot and muscle memory. I don't think the audience could tell I was off my head. I'd got away with it. This was the one and only time in my musical career I have ever played stoned, even though I hadn't meant to. By the next day the high had finally worn off. We played a second night at Danceteria, and by then, thankfully, I realised we were in New York and not Denver.

In July 1986 we played the Festival of the Tenth Summer at Manchester G-Mex, a celebration of the tenth anniversary of the Sex Pistols' now legendary gig at the Lesser Free Trade Hall, organised by Factory Records. On the bill were New Order, The Smiths, The Fall, OMD, Pete Shelley and the Buzzcocks, Cabaret Voltaire, Luxuria, John Cale, John Cooper Clarke and Margi Clarke. It was compèred and hosted by Paul Morley and Bill Grundy. I was extremely excited to be playing. To share a stage with the Buzzcocks, New Order and John Cale was a teenage fantasy come true. Not only that, the bands were all put up in the Britannia Hotel and given day-rooms to hang out in. I remember once hanging around with a bunch of people, including members of The Fall and Johnny Marr, and there was stuff being smoked. The fire alarm went off and we all had to evacuate. I was sure the Britannia was on fire. It never even dawned on me that our smoking may have set off the alarm. As we were hurrying down the stairs to evacuate the hotel I ran into Morrissey. By this point I was having a full-blown anxiety attack, bordering on panic. The alarm was blaring and I was desperate to find Mark. I asked him, 'Have you seen Mark?' Morrissey responded in a dry, mean tone: 'He's probably upstairs, burning up in the fire.' He thought it was funny, but I had no sense of humour right then. I was really worried about Mark's wellbeing. I never spoke to Morrissey again. He was always so unfriendly, prickly and weird, whereas Johnny Marr was the loveliest, most friendly, genuine person.

New Order were down to earth and easy to be around. They always made me feel welcome. Even though I tried to act cool and nonchalant around them, inside I was a bit star-struck. Mark had known New Order since the Joy Division years. I got on really well with Bernard Sumner and Peter Hook. Steven Morris was a true eccentric; he was jovial and seemed like he really enjoyed life. Gillian was friendly. She was quiet and normal. We shared an unspoken bond of women players. There was a mutual respect and supportive connection between us. We didn't go to each other's houses or anything, but we hung out a lot at the Haçienda, which added some much-needed glamour and nightlife to Manchester. I looked up to them because I had been a massive Joy Division fan. *Unknown Pleasures* and *Closer* were the two albums I had listened to most at Bennington.

Obviously the Haçienda was New Order's club, but it felt like ours, too. We played there so many times that we were as close to being a house band as you could be. If we weren't playing there we would hang out at the downstairs bar, the Gay Traitor, which had secret catacombs and tunnels behind it, where all sorts of shenanigans went on.

We toured North America on the final leg of the *Nation's Saving Grace* jaunt. In Chicago, my mother gave me and Mark a bottle of sleeping pills. He could never sleep because of the speed, but for me it was the disorientation of being in a different hotel room every night. I developed a serious sleep disorder. I was beginning to get anxiety attacks on flights. I figured that, having flown so many times now, the law of probability would kick in and we were going to crash. I could hardly get on a plane without Valium.

My mother's pills came in the prescription bottle with her name on it. When we landed in Boston, immigration singled us out to be searched – this happened often, being in a rock group; when we came through customs carrying guitars and music gear we set off internal klaxons inside officials' heads; we practically had stickers on our foreheads saying 'Search me' – and the customs officials were aggressively questioning us about the prescription pills not in our name. This experience led us to write our version of a hip-hop track, 'US 80s–90s': 'Had a run-in with Boston immigration/to my name they had an aversion/Nervous droplets due to sleeping tablets . . .' In the airport the signs would read, 'Welcome to the United States of America', but we would always get tormented by security and feel like we were entering a police state. In the song Mark proclaims, 'I am the original white (big shot) rapper', and it's not hyperbole.

Throughout the tour, Karl's relationship with the entire band began to sour. I don't know what it was that Karl had over Mark, or why Mark was so connected to Karl. No matter what Karl did, Mark would let him back in. I suppose an element of their bond – besides the length of their relationship – was that Mark was as cerebral as Karl was animalistic, primal. Their duality created an odd balance, but also a creative schism. Karl unravelled to the point where he was barely a human being, and we couldn't work that way. He would miss gigs and go missing in action, and it hurt Mark. He was a mess. It was also extremely disconcerting for the band: a drummer is someone you need to count on, literally, and when he went AWOL it felt like we were on shifting sands. We needed to find a drummer we could rely on. Karl was obviously unhappy, and not able to be there for us, for whatever reason.

He was replaced by Simon Wolstencroft, who had been a part of early iterations of both The Smiths and The Stone Roses. His nickname was 'Funky Si', and he was a great guy to be around, a true pothead. He always had a spliff, was very laid-back, and he didn't get flustered by Mark at all. Things just seemed to kind of roll off his back. He always had girlfriends who looked like 1960s models. They reminded me of the girlfriends the Rolling Stones had. Mark would, of course, let Karl back into the fold years later.

At Bennington, I had been introduced to the work of Vladimir Nabokov. The books he wrote stayed in my psyche and became reference points throughout my life. I thought *Bend Sinister* would be a great title for an album. It would be the third album in three years we'd make with John Leckie and, sadly, our last with him. But I don't view the albums as a triumvirate, because the recording process was so distinctly different with *Bend Sinister*. It was a miserable experience.

A defining characteristic of Mark is that he is a self-saboteur. When things start to go really well he gets destructive, rips it up and starts again. He burns his own fields, so to speak. This is why The Fall remain fresh and ever-evolving, but the transitions are ruinous, and never carried out in a direct way that is upfront and honourable – or often even verbalised. Relationships were never severed in a professional manner: Mark's modus operandi was to psychically torture the victim until they would fuck off. I don't think this was a subconscious method either; it was another form of his creativity – making life into art. Mark created drama and chaos. He purposely made us feel wrong-footed and vulnerable, which caused us to work harder and infused tension into our music.

Our experience with John Leckie had been spectacular. He'd heightened our sound, harnessed our live power into the recordings, and the creative suggestions he would make had always been subtle and spot-on. Besides that, Leckie was the most easy-going, Zen person to have in the studio.

This time around, Mark constantly questioned Leckie. Mark was drinking heavily and he was angry. I suspect by then that he was starting to be unhappy in our marriage. He was in a bad state and was taking it out on Leckie, who was doing nothing wrong but making a great album.

I was also a victim of Mark's vitriol. We'd have massive fights in the studio, and I'd storm out. I would wander around for three hours and try to make them think I ran away, then would come back. I'd pull a Jan Brady. I learned this particular method of angry denial from watching episodes of *The Brady Bunch* as a child. In one episode Jan got so furious she stomped out of the house, slammed the door and ran away. I wanted to upset Mark and make him think about how it would feel to lose me. That's how I used to handle things. I had no other recourse. If someone won't listen to reason, how do you convince them to just act like a nice person and stop being vile?

Mark was relentless. He would argue with every single decision. If John would mix something one way or put something down, then Mark would argue against it. John would spend the day mixing something, we would all think it was fantastic, and then Mark would come in and attack the mix for no reason, other than to be contrary. I think the speed was beginning to rot his brain. What I considered brilliant, Mark was just turning into crap. The whole experience was confusing, because Mark's intuition as a whole with music was usually so right, whether or not it made sense at the time. Leaving in the mistakes, insisting on first takes, simplifying arrangements to the most elemental, tribal cacophony . . . cursorily these aren't recipes for brilliance, but herein the magic lies. But for *Bend Sinister* his edicts weren't coming from any objective musicality, but from a strange, angry place.

The resulting record isn't bad, by any means, but it could have been incredible. I love 'US 80s–90s', another example of my riff-writing. Heavier than the 'Cruiser's Creek' riff, 'US 80s–90s' was blistering and hypnotic. We were also influenced by the emerging rap music coming from America. On the other side of the song spectrum I loved the song 'Gross Chapel – British Grenadiers'. I found it otherworldly and sublime. The opener, 'R.O.D.', was me at my surf-lead best. I was basically doing a solo for the entire song. It was sad, haunting surf music. The initials stand for 'Realm Of Dusk'. I added the California beach to the dark dimension. I loved the simple guitar leads of the Beach Boys and really studied them. That Americana mixed with The Fall made a psycho surf sound, and I was quite proud of that mesmerising song.

'Riddler!' was more of a soundtrack. I was very into doing evocative soundtracks and soundscapes. I was beginning to explore that on this album. There's not a lot of me singing on the record, besides 'Terry Waite Sez', but my guitar is to the fore.

Mark asked me to shout 'banana, strawberry and exotic fruits' in 'Dktr Faustus'. I cringe when I hear it. I hated having to say those stupid lyrics. This was also the first album where Mark recorded with his idiotic megaphone. He began to use it all the time, on and off stage. It had buttons on top that would make different siren sounds, and he'd put it right next to your head and blast you. You wanted to kill him. He marched around playing the part of a clichéd old-school Hollywood movie director, directing us. Mack Sennett/Mark Sennett.

Just before *Bend Sinister* was released, I was asked to perform a session with Janice Long on Radio One. The Adult Net had released two more singles, but had yet to play a gig. I was so excited, because up until then The Fall had been doing Peel sessions – which never stopped being an honour. But I felt it was a huge step for The Adult Net to be on in a different time slot – a more commercial time slot. I craved commercial success. I had tasted cult success but wanted to bring both The Fall's music and that of The Adult Net to a wider audience. On the show I debuted 'Waking Up in the Sun', a kind of companion piece to

'LA', another song about being homesick, but cuter, sugar-coated pop with no *T. J. Hooker* lines.

Mark and I went on a holiday to Venice with my mother and Marvin. We stayed at a charming three-star *pensione* just off the Grand Canal, went to restaurants every night, and the Lido. It was always a bizarre juxtaposition to see Mark with Mom and Marvin, and even though we toured non-stop, he was so oddly out of place in so many locales, like the beach and Venice. But he fell in love with the city and it became one of his favourite places. We saw numerous art exhibitions and went to various openings. One of the museums had a special exhibit called 'Instruments of Torture'. Advertisements for it were plastered all over the city. Mark said, 'I'd really love to see that.' We said, 'Sure, let's go see the instruments of torture.' Stepping into the museum was like stepping into a horror film: exhibits included a medieval torture device that would hold open a person's mouth, allowing bathtubs of fluid to be poured into their stomach, which was then beaten with a board until it exploded; and something that looked like a huge ship's wheel that people would be pinned to and spun around – gradually stretching the victim until they were ripped limb from limb.

My mother and I made it through about four instruments of torture and became nauseous and fled the museum. Traumatised, we sat outside in the hot air. Marvin exited shortly thereafter. Mark relished it. He stayed in that museum for an hour and a half, examining every single mechanism while we sat on the steps. He said it was the best exhibition he'd ever seen.

We now had keyboard-heavy songs like 'Shoulder Pads'. Simon Rogers' role was shifting away from performing with us and into production. Mark said we needed a keyboard player. I said, 'What about Marcia?'

I had met Marcia Schofield in New York, briefly, when I was still a student. She was in a band, Khmer Rouge, with Claus. We were in Claus's sister's seventeen-room apartment on Park Avenue, with Picassos, de Koonings, and Rothkos on the wall, when Marcia came by. Her English husband, Phil Schofield, formed Khmer Rouge, and they had opened for The Fall in 1985. Marcia wasn't with Phil any more when she joined the band. With her on board, my life took a turn for the better. It suddenly struck me how hard it had been to be the only woman in this hardcore working-class Northern post-punk band. For three years I had been living with them on buses. I had become one of the boys, which was necessary for coping, but having Marcia to hang out with reminded me of the girlyness I had lost. Now we formed a gang; I had a partner in crime. I loved her keyboard playing. She was always great on stage. But, most importantly, I found a true friend. I leaned on her emotionally, and she probably leaned on me.

Craig had the most gigantic crush on Marcia. All the men would drool over her. She was a goddess, the physical opposite to me. I was petite and blonde; she was a dark Amazonian, voluptuous woman, almost six feet tall. Occasionally I would feel a tiny bit jealous of her because she was everything, physically, that I was not. But at the same time, I was out in front and rocking it, and we just got on so well.

Mark was savvy and knew her coming on board would give the band an image jolt, just like when I'd joined three years earlier. He loved being bookended by these blonde and raven-haired Jewish women. The Fall would land the cover of the *NME*, which featured just the three of us. I think Mark really quite fancied her. He also liked having her in the band because it kept me occupied, out of his way. Marcia's presence really changed my life.

Shortly after her arrival we toured America. It was our first time in a really fancy bus – its prior occupant had been Willie Nelson. There was kind of a lounge in the front, a bunch of tables, a big video screen and disco lights, then, in the middle of the bus, were bunk beds in nooks. In the back was a separate lounge with a circular coffee table and semi-circular brown leather banquette. This became the girls' zone. We couldn't handle it with the men any more. They were all up in the front smoking, drinking, playing cards; Mark dictating the bizarre shit to be played non-stop over the stereo system, like Frankie Valli and the Four Seasons. We would watch the same movies repeatedly – *This is Spinal Tap*, mostly.

Sometimes on tour you kind of lose your mind. With seemingly endless hours of travelling, especially across America, you get up to all kinds of things to break up the monotony. Our favourite game to play occurred at night. It had to be dark for it to work. Driving through small towns, we'd seal off our back section of the bus by closing the privacy partition. We didn't want the boys to see what we were up to. Marcia and I would then turn on the lights in our back part of the bus, and we'd pull down our pants, part the curtains, and press our asses to the windows so that, as we drove through these shit-kicker villages, the locals would see two lit-up asses driving past. We just howled with laughter.

Marcia also had a porn fetish. On tour in a city like Amsterdam, she'd go into the red-light district and buy hardcore pornography that you couldn't get anywhere else. I had never really seen porn, I'd only seen tamer fare like *Playboy* and *Penthouse*. I'd never seen a hardcore porno movie, and she didn't want to show me the one she'd picked up. She said, 'You don't ever really need to see this. I don't want to corrupt you.' I was fascinated, though. I really wanted to see what all the fuss was about. I made her show me the film, and it was so awful I nearly threw up. Even today those disturbing images are still branded in my brain.

Mark had been reading a bestselling book called *In God's Name* about corruption in the Vatican and the murder of Albino Luciani, better known as Pope John Paul I, who served thirty-three days in office and died. When a man referred to as 'God's banker' was found hanging under Blackfriars Bridge in London, suspicious looks were directed towards the Vatican. Mark became fixated on this incident and decided he was going to write a play about it, a

Grandma and me at Disneyland, with the Matterhorn in the background

'A sad, haunted look'

Riding Scooter Pie

Bonding with a turtle, post-Sammy

'There's a ghost in my house' – our home in Chicago

My new family. From left, Leah, Marvin, me and Nadia on holiday in St Barths

Mr and Mrs Smith on our wedding day

Me and Mark at Blackpool Pleasure Beach. 'Oh my God, your monkey is so cute!'

Channelling Edie Sedgwick

'Ahoy, Captain' – Cruiser's Creek, the Salenger family cruise

My cowboy dad

In full throttle, giving it hell on tour

The Frenz Experiment. From left, Steve Hanley, me, Simon Wolsten-croft, Mark, Marcia and Craig Scanlon

Me and Michelle Lineker at Italia '90

The garage days. Me and Susanna Hoffs

My time as an actress/waitress in LA

Me, Nigel and his bulldog, Deadly. No longer together, we remained close

Murray Lachlan Young – a vision

Philip and me, soon after we met
Our wedding of the century, 14 August 1999
A pre-wedding night hug from my beloved stepmother, Maggie
Marvin and my mom

Still got it. Brix and the Extricated live at the ICA

Adoption day, with my dad Marvin, Mom and Philip

Gladys and Pixie

proper musical. My attitude was, 'OK, honey, you go do that.' I wasn't expecting him to follow through, but somehow he pulled it all together. The wonders of speed!

Hey! Luciani, the musical, coincided with the release of our single of the same name. The play was performed five days a week from 5 December until 20 December at the Riverside Studios in Hammersmith. The entire band (and Leigh Bowery) were drafted in to become thespians. Mark roped in everyone we knew to be in it, including Simon Rogers' ballerina wife and some actors that we knew. Some songs were played live, some were pre-recorded. I played a couple of different characters: one was either the devil or the wife of Doctor Faustus, I was never quite sure, but I wore a David Holah–BodyMap-designed lace dress covered in skeletons and spray-painted red.

Alana Pillay also performed. She was a trans-woman in The Fall's circle, a talented gal-about-town they all dearly loved, and a Manchester cabaret legend who adopted the persona of Shirley Bassey to perform show-tunes. When I met her she was Alan and then became Alana full-time. I think Mark helped her out with some money when she decided on the gender transition. I'm not sure what she calls herself now, but I run into her from time to time and she's just as fabulous.

Poor Steve Hanley was forced to play the central role of the Pope. Steve is Catholic, so I don't know whether Mark was shaming him or honouring him. Steve is a man of few words, and had to stand there in full Pope regalia. The strange thing was, he actually looked like the Pope.

Hey! Luciani was non-linear and nobody understood anything about the play. It made no sense whatsoever. Even to me.

The climax for me was playing one of a pair of Israeli commandos, along with Marcia. Mark, of course, loved that Marcia was Jewish too. One scene took place in the jungle. We were in full army camouflage, and had massive sub-machine guns strapped across our chests – two fierce Jewesses hunting Martin Bormann, the Nazi. When we found Bormann, Marcia's line of dialogue was, 'The desert has addled his jungle mind.' And I responded, 'And mescal screwed his nomad's wits.' Then we sang the song 'Haf Found Bormann' in guttural tones.

I have never seen any filmed footage of *Hey! Luciani*. Very few photographs exist.

It's a shame, as I reckon it was brilliant – in many ways ahead of its time.

During that period Mark was firing on all cylinders creatively, despite my worry that he was beginning to become unglued.

1987–1988

1987 was the first year since I had joined The Fall that we didn't release a studio album. This wasn't some sort of grand plan, although it was probably a good idea not to keep flooding the market, so the fans could keep up. Even though there was no new album, we still released two singles, a compilation, and toured extensively throughout the year.

Our main tour that year was a co-headliner called Kings of Independence, with Nick Cave and the Bad Seeds. We took alternate turns headlining the bill each night. It was an epically fun tour. We all adored the Bad Seeds. Nick Cave and Mark had been friends for years. Marcia had recently been flatmates with Kid Congo Powers, whom we knew from his days in The Gun Club and The Cramps, both of whom we'd toured with. Kid was one of our favourite people: always good-natured and a laugh to hang out with on the road. I learned a lot about guitar playing from watching and emulating him.

I also had a very soft spot for guitarist Blixa Bargeld. People would laugh about the similarity of our names, Brix and Blixa. I flirted outrageously with Blixa, but it was only flirting. Marcia, on the other hand, actually had a fling with a Bad Seed, and my extremely good-looking rock-god roadie, who I also had a secret mini-crush on.

Like Amsterdam, Hamburg is legendary for its red light district. There is a famous six-floored brothel called the Eros Center, located on the Reeperbahn, very close to the theatre we were playing at. Marcia, being fascinated with porn, wanted to check it out. She convinced Simon Wolstencroft to go with her. I was not invited, so I stayed in my hotel room like a hermit, watching CNN and taking my sleeping pills.

I'd had no real desire to go to the Eros Center, but when they eventually returned from their excursion I couldn't contain myself. I was gagging to know what happened. I had never even been to a strip club, let alone an actual brothel. Marcia described it as vast underground car park where no women were allowed, except those who 'worked' there. I asked her what the women were wearing, and she told me most wore nothing but a belt and high heels. When she walked in, the women took one look at Marcia, taking in her Amazonian goddess physique, and yelled at her, '*Verboten! Verboten!*' She said they practically chased her out.

Very slowly, we began to introduce some new songs on the tour, including 'There's a Ghost in My House', the R. Dean Taylor cover. It was a hugely famous Northern Soul classic in England, and one of Mark's favourite songs. I'd never heard of it. But the song became quite personal to me, because the house in Chicago that I grew up in was filled with ghosts, and Mark was fascinated by all the stories that I would tell him.

We did the video for 'There's a Ghost in My House' at the Woodthorpe pub. We sat in a posh sort of room with a big fireplace. I played the ghost in a white minidress and black thigh-high boots and two-toned hair. I would disappear and reappear on screen, which I loved because it reminded me of one of my favourite childhood TV shows, *Bewitched*.

I had always expected our singles to be chart hits, but by this point I had given up. I didn't expect this song to do anything – yet it became our first single to break the top 50, and made it to number 30. It was weird: the ones we didn't write would be the hits. Beggars Banquet had a marketing idea. They did a limited-edition single of 'There's a Ghost in My House' featuring a hologram of a ghost disappearing on the cover. I think this novelty cover helped us at long last crack the top 40. When we first got the news of our

chart triumph I remember being in the van. We shrieked, celebrated and slapped the upholstery. All of us were thrilled.

The single had been produced by Grant Showbiz, who, happily,
was back on the scene since the break-up of The Smiths. Grant
was a lovely person, who also had the talent to simply get along
with Mark; Grant Showbiz had been with The Fall during so many
incarnations, it was like going back to the womb. Grant was like
family – working with him was different, but it was familiar and
lovely too. I trusted Grant, and still do.

He regaled us with stories about The Smiths' ultra-PC tours. He
told us about how a crew person once joked, 'What do you call a
dog with wings?' The punchline was: 'Linda McCartney.' He was
summarily dismissed. Everybody was forced to be vegetarian. If
you ate meat, you were fired. I heard lots of stories later about crew
members sneaking off for a burger or steak and chips. There was
a very different sort of madness in The Fall. Mark took it to the
other extreme. Years later, he would fire our sound engineer, Rex
Sargeant, for eating a salad.

I recorded an Adult Net album for Beggars Banquet. It was
called *Spin This Web* and was produced by Ian Broudie. Ian had
produced various bands, including Echo and the Bunnymen, and
was also starting up his own band, The Lightning Seeds. *Spin This
Web* was very electronic; we didn't use any live drums. I found it
difficult to sing with electronic music. It felt cold. I was used to
playing with a live band. The record was never released and I don't
have a copy of it, but it must be in the vault of a record company
somewhere, rotting. *Spin This Web* included early renditions of the
songs that would eventually come out on *The Honey Tangle*, like
'Waking Up in the Sun'.

Since The Smiths had split up, Andy Rourke and Mike Joyce
were playing with all sorts of people in Manchester. Funky Si was
friends with them. Johnny Marr was off working with Talking
Heads, and Morrissey was being Morrissey. I recruited Rourke,

Joyce and their ex-secondary guitarist, Craig Gannon, to play the first and only Adult Net show. The Adult Net was always a changing cast of characters, and I knew that getting the remaining Smiths would be a massive coup. I thought Craig Gannon was an exquisite talent, and I loved how he played guitar.

We played at the ICA in London. It was a packed house; the rest of The Smiths as my backing band was a major part of the draw. Every record company sent an A&R representative, but I was signed to Beggars and already had the album made.

I had never done a gig where I was the front person. I was so nervous that it took me a long time to settle into the set. When I played with The Fall, I was generally nervous for the first five minutes or so, or the first song. On this Adult Net gig my nerves lasted almost the entire set, nearly a full hour. The next day there was a review in one of the music tabloids which described me as a cross between Barbra Streisand and Josie from the all-girl cartoon band Josie and the Pussycats. For some reason I took this as a bad review. I was devastated; it made me even more insecure about my solo work, which was still relegated in my mind to a minor side project. Now, I realise it was an amazing review and super-cool. Being compared to Barbra Streisand and Josie from Josie and the Pussycats was the perfect combination. I should have been elated.

Mark was surprisingly indifferent about me playing with The Smiths. He couldn't have cared less about the backing band. But I suspect my getting a deal with Phonogram, plus a lucrative publishing contract with BMG, ate away at his ego. I worried that he began to feel emasculated, although I was only doing what I had intended to do since I was a teenager. This would become a major point of contention in our marriage, and would trigger all of the hidden faults that had been building up.

We recorded 'Hit the North' – our first stab at dance-floor fodder with the prerequisite remixes – with Simon Rogers, who

co-wrote it. It was fun, and a bit before its time, but it didn't replicate the success of 'There's a Ghost in My House'.

The video was shot in an old bingo hall in the seaside town
of Blackpool; the regulars were the extras. Simon's sister-in-law,
Emma Burge, directed it, and it was her first big music video
project. By this point I was familiar with most of the provincial
English towns, but going back to Blackpool reminded me of the
first time I went there, when my mother and Marvin came to
visit us early on in mine and Mark's marriage. I'd asked Mark,
'What should we do with Mom and Marvin?' He said, 'Let's take
them to Blackpool, it's great. You'll like it, it's like Disneyland
and it's by the seaside.' My family loves the beach, so we rented a
car and drove to the most heinous place I've ever been to in my
life. It was grim and freezing. They call the amusement park area
Blackpool Pleasure Beach. The rides were like the rides of doom,
rickety and old. How could Mark not be scared of these but be
tormented by the amazing technological breakthroughs of Disney?
Along the promenade in Blackpool they hang lights, grandiosely
called 'illuminations'. They do this in lots of seaside towns. They
looked like crude crappy candy canes in black and white. I've
seen backwoods country carnivals with better lighting decoration.
My mother turned to me and said, 'This is the night of the living
dead.' (Earlier we'd walked on the beach. It was the first time any
of us had been on a beach composed of jagged rocks rather than
soft sand. A man came up to us holding a monkey, its fur dyed
into rainbow colours. I blurted out, 'Oh my God, your monkey
is so cute!' I was beside myself seeing a rainbow monkey. Mark
screamed, 'Get away from the monkey!' My mom said, 'Get away
from the monkey!' I held up a coin and the monkey snatched it
from my hand and jumped on me. They thought it was going to
eat my face. The man stepped back and photographed me with the
Technicolor simian and charged £5 for the Polaroid. Mark should
have written a song about that damned monkey.)

In January 1988 we released the Kinks cover 'Victoria', and it made it to number 35 in the charts. I don't know why our cover versions had such crossover appeal, because we really reworked them into being Fall songs, put our own stamp on them. The video took on the appearance of some big-budget 1980s production, because we shot it on the set of a film version of Charles Dickens' *Little Dorrit*. The set was in Rotherhithe, East London, and we got to use all of the cast's wardrobe. I was feeling subconsciously insecure about my marriage. I was unable to articulate this, and it manifested itself in feelings of threat and jealously towards Marcia. I demanded to be the beautiful Victorian princess, in a corset and gown. Marcia was the obese maid, with warts and grey hair. It was my doing, and I feel bad about that now. Due to my insecurity, poor Marcia had to wear a fat-suit.

The Frenz Experiment came out the next month. 'Victoria''s success bolstered the album, and it reached number 19. We had finally gotten into the top 20. We played the massive HMV store on Oxford Street in London, and had an autograph-signing session like we were a proper band. There were life-size cardboard cut-outs of us. I felt like we had taken a huge commercial leap. The record wasn't a disaster, but I knew it was no *This Nation's Saving Grace*. In the grand scheme of things it was a fine album, but The Fall are judged by different criteria, and in my mind it is a creative low point.

The song 'Frenz' is credited to just Mark, as are half of the songs on the album. Every single one of those songs was a collaboration. It seemed to me that the deterioration of our relationship was reflected in my dwindling songwriting credits. The marriage was so intertwined with the music and the band that this was one facet of how our turmoil was expressed, and Mark was able to get the final word and appropriate the credits to suit him. Mark sings, 'My friends I can count on one hand, my friends don't count up to one hand.' I really like this plaintive song, a curious and gentle opener to an album, and it was revealing of both of us. We were mired in solitude, but whereas I really had no friends (except when we toured with Marcia), Mark's isolation came from a different place – he was surrounded by hangers-on. Now, I can count ten super-close friends that I call my 'vagina friends'. If something goes wrong with my vagina I can call any of them up and talk about it. By this point, Mark was paranoid – about me, the members of the band, and especially his friends. He was at a place of weird infamy and pseudo-celebrity, and he realised that many people just wanted to know him or hang around us because of who he was.

Mark had a few friends that I didn't like at all, and I felt they were using him. But, for whatever reason, he really liked these people. Some were raging drug addicts and amphetamine dealers. They didn't really care about him, they just wanted to be around him. Mark prided himself on having normal friends, real salt-of-the earth people. One I remember was a postman. He tried to cultivate this circle of normal guys. But Mark is a true artist and intellectual. These 'friends' might have kept him connected to reality, but as far as inspiring and engaging him on any sort of artistic basis, I don't see how that could have happened. Maybe I didn't like them because they never really warmed to me, or I seemed alien to them? I don't really know.

It was becoming clear to both Mark and me that our marriage was collapsing. The intervals between the mood swings would get less and less as the speed took over. He was a swinging pendulum, completely irrational. The material we were developing was subpar, and he was making everybody's life difficult. It wasn't just me. He was not pleasant to be around at all.

I told him that I didn't want him to do any more speed. That did no good whatsoever. You can't sever a physical addiction through reason. No one can make another person become sober. Then I started to try to ban certain people who I associated with supplying Mark with drugs from coming to the house. That didn't work either. I once dumped two wraps of speed down the toilet. That made no difference. The amphetamine and the alcohol were taking over.

One day, I looked at Mark and said, 'When you're an old man with no teeth lying in the gutter like a tramp I am not going to save you. I am not going to be there to pick you up.' It was cruel, but honest. The 'scared straight' approach didn't work either.

I have barely any memories of the actual recording of *The Frenz Experiment*. I don't know why this particular record is blacked out, buried somewhere in my subconscious. Marriage and musical strife went hand in hand, and this was the nadir. I was singing less and less, which was also the case on *Bend Sinister*, but at least there I still had a heavy voice in my guitar parts. What vocals I had on the *Frenz* record I had to fight for. But now my wings were clipped and I could not have flown. I was in a cage but I didn't realise that until much later – how I had allowed myself to be controlled. I could have developed as a musician even more, instead of being kept in the cage, playing my riffs.

For most of *The Frenz Experiment* I was irritated, because Mark had started to really push against me and cut me out – his aggressive passive-aggressiveness. The Adult Net was really shaking him up, although it was no threat to him, nor The Fall. But he was now stamping his authority everywhere, as a man and as a creator. Anything I would bring to the table would be refused: songs were rejected, and the good parts I would lay down, the underhooks and melodies, were wiped from the recordings.

'Carry Bag Man' is fine, and chugs along, but is a phoned-in effort from Mark, a song about how he likes to carry plastic bags. 'Get a Hotel' is just annoying. 'The Steak Place' is boring and conjures images of gross food, the kind of restaurant that might have photos of the food on their menu. The most annoying song I ever had to play on was 'Oswald Defence Lawyer'. I think it was the worst song we'd done since I'd joined the band. It was interminable, and when we played it live I watched the audience switch off. It makes me cringe today, just thinking about it. I was expected to really belt it out, but it just sounds irritating and grating: 'Oswald Defense Lawyer embraces the scruffed corpse of Mark Twain.' It was cool to name-check Twain, though.

The other records we'd done, *Perverted by Language*, and the three with John Leckie, have a timeless quality to them. *The Frenz Experiment* sounds tinny, with Steve buried in the mix, and very 1980s. There isn't one definitive Fall classic on the album. The cover was the first to be simply a band photo. We're all partially obscured by the enormous logo, or cropped out. Except Mark, who is grousing in full view above us, lording it over us.

Even with all the simmering tensions, we were still a powerful live band, though. During our world tour Michael Clark had been given a grant to produce a ballet to celebrate the three hundreth anniversary of William of Orange's ascent to the throne. We had never lost touch with Michael, and would always go clubbing with him in London – and once, we went to see him perform in Paris. He enlisted Mark and The Fall to compose an entire score for the ballet and perform live on stage, choreographed and integrated into the ballet itself. *I Am Curious, Orange* would be the realisation of all of the literary and performance aspirations Mark had hoped to achieve with *Hey! Luciani*.

We had to come up with an entire album's worth of material to score the piece – all the while playing shows on a nightly basis and spending the days on the road in the van. It was a completely different way of writing, because we were under pressure. We weren't just bringing whatever we had made up when inspired and presenting it to the group. We had a deadline, and there was a theme. We would frantically write in our hotel rooms, put it on a cassette and send it to Michael. He had to hear the songs to see if they spoke to him; if he could choreograph them. By now he knew the music of The Fall so well it was an integral part of him as a person, it was like his blood. He would know instantly if something would work.

The problem was dancers need exact beats to choreograph a dance. You cannot have changes in the tempo. Everything has to be regimented and locked in, and timed perfectly for the dancers. This wasn't just a free-for-all abstract modern dance piece. This was a proper ballet. And the songs were being road-tested during our concerts and would develop and change at soundchecks and performances. Sometimes we would perform a song for years before recording it. We had to learn to lock them down and take a step away.

Working under those constraints was challenging for The Fall – our method had always been spontaneous, and we worked almost on a psychic level. Whereas this was an exhaustive process that involved dealing with the postal service in various countries. But it was a new way to work, and pushed us as a band, and the resulting songs were leagues ahead of anything on *Frenz*. We'd record the songs as a companion album, *I Am Kurious, Oranj*. It wouldn't reach the commercial heights of *Frenz*, and neither did it get rapturous reviews. I think it is an overlooked gem, but I'm proud of it.

I sang snippets of the songs' lyrics and titles in 'Overture From "I Am Curious, Orange"'. This came about on the occasion Mark didn't show up at the studio. My vocals are deep and masculine because I was trying to imitate Mark. 'Van Plague?' is an often forgotten song, but I think it's one of Mark's most touching, a reflection on the origin of AIDS. He was beyond singing about his penchant for plastic shopping bags. I'm proud of it being one of our last joint efforts. The band remade 'Hip Priest' into the glam stomp of 'New Big Prinz'. One of my most endearing songs, 'Deadbeat Descendant', was part of the performance but not on the album. I don't know why. I think it was another power play from Mark, not wanting anything to outshine 'Prinz' and its 'He is not appreciated' chorus.

I wrote one tune that started off like a slow lament and built into a fast-paced punchy song. Mark turned it into 'Bad News Girl'. It was clearly about me; this wasn't some kind of riddle, he was putting our problems to the forefront. I knew it. I demanded, 'Is this song about me?' At first he told me it was about one of Michael's dancers, a very sweet, gentle, kind woman. We all loved her. We'd done a studio performance of 'Deadbeat Descendant' for television and she'd danced with us, in a leotard and furry boots. I was later told she was allegedly having an affair with Mark and would be taken on tour to dance with the band – all of his girl-friends, it seemed, would have to be connected to the band in some sense. I think the band knew he'd been cheating on me. I felt they must have known. I strongly suspect this was not the first time. It's a cliché, but when you're in a band there's something called 'code of the road'. When you're on the road anything is allowed. It almost gives you a hall pass, or carte blanche to have flings or do whatever you want to. I now believe Mark had been doing this throughout our marriage, and no one had dared to tell to me. I myself had turned a blind eye and kept silent about other band members' transgressions.

Finally, Mark admitted to me that I was 'Bad News Girl'. It was a real slap in the face. Humiliatingly, I would have to actually perform the song in the ballet on stage in Amsterdam, a five-day residency in Edinburgh and a two-week stint in London.

I was frantically strumming my Rickenbacker guitar, Whitey, on top of a gigantic spinning hamburger. Leigh Bowery, dressed as a massive can of Heinz baked beans, was one of the main spinners, and sometimes he would be so aggressive that I was scared I would fall off, vomit, or hit a wrong note. I was prone to motion sickness, both on winding roads and, it seemed, on spinning burgers.

I Am Curious, Orange was a sell-out hit at London's Sadler's Wells Theatre. No matter how fast that burger was going I never stopped smiling. It was a manic smile, really the grin of a woman losing her grip. It was a mask. My life was spiralling away a lot faster than that giant hamburger. I was thin and looked great in my custom David Holah and Stevie Stewart BodyMap leather bathing suit, white tights and ballet flats. It was all a mask. In reality I was depressed and controlling the only thing I could: my food. I'd allow myself to eat a little, but my daily ration was one teaspoon of Greek yoghurt with a single strawberry and a cup of tea, with a dash of non-fat milk. It was a facet of my life I had control over.

The designer Rifat Özbek came backstage and said, 'Honey, you're the burger queen.' The hamburger was Michael's idea. He said to me, 'I'm going to have you sitting on the giant hamburger playing guitar.' My guitar plugged straight into a radio pack, which I always used on stage. It was fantastic because I was free and cordless, although sometimes it would pick up minicab chatter, adding to the sonic texture. Each night I'd get wheeled out, and I felt so special on my hamburger. I would have to get hoisted atop it backstage. The texture of the burger was a combination of squishy and hard; the giant sesame seeds added extra grip. It was like a ride at a funfair, a surreal tilt-a-whirl.

I Am Curious, Orange was an emotionally schizophrenic time for me. It certainly was one of the high points of my career in The Fall; one of the most creative and interesting periods. We were mixing high art, ballet, history, rock music, surrealism, performance art and fashion. It brought acid house to the stage for the first time. It was the most grandiose thing we had done, and I don't know of anything that has bettered it since. Anyone in that audience was truly lucky. There are few surviving videos of it. Charles Atlas was there filming, and I hope some day a full performance will emerge.

It was the pinnacle of my creative world, but my life was simultaneously disintegrating every second. By now, although I didn't find out until later, Mark was well into a serious affair, and it was no longer a complete secret. Although I still didn't know for sure, he had already confessed to my dear friend Lisa Feder and sworn her to silence. When he looked at me, it was with venom and not love. He had totally gone off me.

The only love I felt at that point was from the gay men in the troupe, and the make-up and hair stylists. They were taking care of me. They caught me crying alone in my dressing room a couple of times but, for the most part, I just alluded to what was going on. I didn't let them know how bad it was. When Mark and I would interact, we were fighting like vicious barracudas. During the London performances, we officially separated after a particularly brutal argument. He went to live in one hotel and I stayed in another. We were coming to the theatre in different cars, from different places, and not even speaking. I just kept my mouth shut. 'The show must go on,' I repeated, over and over in my head.

David Holah and Leigh Bowery would help me put on my make-up every night before the performance. I would get dressed up in my little sexy costume and I'd go on stage. Inside, I'd be weeping. The hardest thing I had to do was to pretend that we were a happy couple. I was ashamed, embarrassed, frightened and angry all at once. At the end of the performances, Michael Clark would hold my hand and bring me out for the curtain call, and I would curtsy like a prima ballerina. My being singled out like this didn't cause consternation or jealousy in Mark. I don't think he ever watched from the sidelines. He just didn't care.

THE TRUTH

The early morning light was weak as it filtered through the dirty bedroom windows of our house. The sun seemed masked behind a veil of deceit. As I opened my eyes I heard a strange sound. Quiet sobbing. Mark's face was buried in the pillow; lying next to me, his thin body was shuddering with grief. I could tell he was trying not to wake me, but at the same time wanted me to wake up.

'You're crying,' I said. 'What's the matter? Why are you crying?'

'I'm leaving you,' he said.

'Leaving me? *Leaving me?* Where are you going?' I asked.

'I'm leaving you today.'

He managed to choke out those awful words, his sobs growing stronger as his resolve deepened.

'Where are you going?' I asked again. 'What do you mean, "leaving me"?' I remember actually laughing a little. Incredulous, I couldn't quite fathom the magnitude of his news.

He sat up and wiped his eyes. 'I'm leaving . . . *you.*'

At last I got it. Panic hit me hard in the stomach. Panic, then anger, then nausea all at once. I wanted to punch him in the face and vomit at the same time.

'You *can't* leave me!' I started to wail. I tried to grab him and cling to him, to physically stop him from leaving.

He wrenched out of my arms and rose from the bed to dress. His clothes had been laid out neatly the night before. He disappeared from our bedroom into the box room, the room in which we kept his microphone and lyric sheets, where we kept my spare guitars and the three-stringed violin we used on 'Hotel Blöedel'.

The dirty little protest room.

He retrieved an already-packed suitcase.

I heard a car horn beep outside.

Mark left the room and headed for the stairs, suitcase in hand. I flung myself at him. In my panic and desperation I wrapped myself around his legs. I tried to stop him. He dragged me down the stairs. I was screaming, crying and trying to reason with him; make him hear sense. Nothing worked. He was determined. This was premeditated.

I felt ashamed of myself at the loss of control over my emotions. I felt weak, ugly and undignified. I was a shrieking banshee. I couldn't think straight. I was in shock.

'They're here,' he said.

'Who's here? WHO'S HERE?' I screamed.

He opened the front door at the foot of the stairs. I released my arms from around his legs. I saw a car idling in the street. The getaway car. I thought I saw Simon Wolstencroft, our drummer, in the driver's seat behind the wheel, but I couldn't tell for sure. 'It can't be Simon,' I thought. 'He wouldn't do this to me.'

Mark got into the car with his suitcase and it drove off. I sat on the floor with my head on the stairs and sobbed. I was broken, bewildered, betrayed and abandoned.

I thought about killing myself the day he left me. To punish him.

Little did I know it then, but my anger is what saved me. Anger was the life raft that pulled me up from the pit of my desperation. It gave me a reason to get up, go on and fight for what I wanted in life. Depression gave way to grief. Grief gave way to anger. Anger gave way to resolve, and resolve gave way to hope. I lay in a heap on the floor of my house for what seemed like hours. I cried it out. I wallowed. As the initial shock wore off, something inside me began to stir. My survival instinct.

I needed to call my mom and Marvin, or a friend, but I felt so humiliated I could barely pick up the phone. The thought of telling Mom and Marvin was beyond awful. My worst fear was that my mom would say, 'I told you so. I knew your marriage would never last.'

In fact, she said the opposite. After a few hours, when I'd pulled myself as together as I could, and I knew she'd be awake in Chicago, I called her. I sobbed incoherently into the phone. After I'd finished the re-telling and re-living of the events of the morning, my mother calmly said these words to me. I will never forget them. They will stay with me for ever. They permeated through the darkest recesses of my agony and gave me hope. She said, 'This is the best thing that has ever happened to you.'

Having got the hardest call out of the way, I began to formulate a plan. This was done on gut instinct alone. I was still in a nightmare fog and everything seemed surreal and intangible. My first thought was to get out. Leave the house and get out of Manchester. I couldn't stay in the house filled with memories and the psychic stains of past and recent emotions that were held within the walls.

The next phone call I made was to Craig Leon and Cassell Webb. Craig and Cassell were the producers of The Adult Net. I had grown very close to them in the previous year, working on my album. They were like my musical parents, and also American. I felt safe with them. They had seen all my vulnerabilities as we worked together. I trusted them, and could be open with them; they were non-judgemental of me. Both of them had been in the music business for many years and had seen it all. They were unshockable. Craig and Cassell knew just what to do. Seemingly unsurprised, they calmly told me to pack a bag with my immediate needs and get on a plane. Cassell told me to fly to Heathrow and they would pick me up. She said I could stay with them at their house in the country, near Maidenhead, and they would help me to pick up the pieces of my life.

Craig also reminded me that I had enough money from my Adult Net recording deal and my publishing deal to rent or buy a nice flat. He reminded me that I didn't have to worry. I wasn't broke. Together they would help me find somewhere to live in London. I was beyond thankful for their kindness and friendship.

I packed my bag and called one of Mark's sisters to look after the cats, to feed them and pet them in our absence. I can't remember the conversation or what I said. Or even which sister I called. I just wanted the cats to be safe.

During the taxi ride to the airport, and on the flight, I fought hard to hold down my surging emotions. Every so often I began to weep uncontrollably. I hadn't yet started to piece together the whole story of Mark's departure. That was still to come. Each segment that I would uncover in the following weeks would open fresh wounds. I remember thinking I could have filled a swimming pool with all of my tears.

My memories of the days and nights spent at Craig and Cassell's country cottage are vague and gauzy, as if clawed back from the swirling delirium of a raging fever. I remember soft voices and long walks down an ancient dirt road, through the woods. I think it was called the Old London Road. Long ago, highwayman Dick Turpin was rumoured to have used it to lie in wait for rich folk travelling by carriage to and from London. The ground was sodden with sycamore leaves, the trees above barren and skeletal.

There was something about the country air that helped to focus my senses and pull me back, little by little, to something resembling the beginnings of equilibrium. I was starting to comprehend the reality of my situation. The worst time for me was always first thing in the morning. When I would wake up and remember it freshly, all over again.

He left me.

Like a zombie I struggled through the motions of barely living. If I could have slept all day I would have. The effort of getting up and getting dressed and brushing my hair and facing another day of pain was overwhelming. The most mundane tasks felt insurmountable. I kept thinking, 'This is what it feels like to have a broken heart.'

In reality, what I was feeling was depression.

When you lose your confidence the world becomes a very frightening place. I didn't know how to fend for myself because I'd never really had to. I'd gone from my mom and Marvin's house to Bennington College, and from there straight to marriage with Mark and life in The Fall. I went from child to rock star, and now I had been kicked to the kerb. I had no idea how to sign a cheque, let alone rent an apartment.

Craig and Cassell did the initial work on my psyche in the earliest, darkest days. They forced me out of the house to take walks, and distracted me with their stories. Mostly, they listened to me whinge, weep and vent.

After about five days at their house, we all drove to London to start hunting for a flat for me. Cassell suggested I move to an elegant neighbourhood and rent the nicest apartment I could afford. They obviously knew I was depressed, and at least if I had a place I felt good in, and was surrounded by beauty and an affluent lifestyle, I could start to rebuild my life. We headed for Holland Park in West London. Holland Park is a glamorous and wealthy part of London, leafy-green and criss-crossed with wide, imposing streets. It felt as far from Prestwich as you could get.

The first flat we saw was in the basement at 15 Royal Crescent, a semi-circular street made up of elegant Georgian townhouses designed by John Nash, who designed some of the most glorious iconic period architecture in London, including Regent Street. It might have been minuscule but it was a perfect pied-à-terre. The second I saw it my mind was made up. This was the flat for me. It was perfect.

It would be a few weeks before the apartment was ready for me to move in. It had to be spruced up a little and we needed to get the rental agreements in order. Craig and Cassell helped me deal with the landlady, who was a gentle, understanding woman.

Waiting for the apartment, I moved in with my manager, John Lennard, who was also managing The Fall. I felt I had outstayed my welcome at Craig and Cassell's house, so John graciously offered me a room at his house in Gospel Oak. On the one hand I was excited about moving into my own flat, but at the same time I expected the phone to ring and it to be Mark on the other end. I imagined Mark realising he'd made a dreadful mistake and asking me to come back. I remember sitting in John's house, jumping every time I heard the phone. I had told only Mom and Marvin, John, Cassell and Craig about the split. I had sworn everyone to secrecy. I felt overwhelming embarrassment at being left. I had no idea if I was still in The Fall. The last thing I wanted was for the music press to get hold of the story, or for people to start gossiping. I was already mortified. Plus, I hadn't heard from Mark, and I was clinging to the hope we would get back together.

A day or so after I moved into John's house, I decided to call Lisa Feder in New York. I needed to confide in my close friend. I knew she adored Mark and, even though I felt shame at having to tell her, I needed a friend, I needed a fresh pair of ears. I called Lisa, and through heaving sobs managed to squeak out the story. 'Why?' I kept saying. 'Why did he leave me? Where did he go? Why hasn't he called me?' I repeated this over and over, like a record stuck on its run-out groove. When I had finished, there was silence on the other end of the line. It wasn't a normal silence. It was a pregnant silence, suspended with tension.

Lisa took a breath. 'Brix,' she said. 'I have to tell you something. I've wanted to tell you for months, but I didn't dare. I couldn't tell you, because if I did, I knew you'd leave Mark.'

My heart thudded in my chest. My body stiffened. My hands tightened around the phone as I pushed the receiver closer to my ear. Her voice lowered and she spoke quietly and slowly and deliberately.

She said, 'Remember when you guys were last in New York on tour? After the show while you were doing interviews? Mark and

I went out for a drink. He confided in me. He told me he was having an affair with Saffron Prior [the daughter of one of Mark's friends, whom we had first met when she was just sixteen]. He told me it had been going on for six months. He swore me to secrecy. I'm sorry for not telling you. Please forgive me.'

Then a very strange thing happened. Some kind of psychic preservation instinct must have kicked in. It was as if my soul disengaged from my body. My spirit floated up somewhere near the ceiling. Clinically and calmly I remember observing my body fall to the floor. As I watched myself, I lay on the floor curled in the foetal position. Disconnected, I witnessed my body emit a low keening sound, a sound so painful and primal I can only liken it to that of a dying animal. It was the same method of dealing with pain as during the neck-bite incident at Bennington.

I felt so many conflicting emotions at once, I couldn't begin to separate them. I suppose betrayal (by everybody, including Lisa) had to be high up on the list. Rage was also near the top. The worst one, though, looking back, had to be fury . . . at myself. My gut instinct had tried to tell me months ago. As I dug back into my memory bank, I began to piece together incidents that had been clear red flags that he was being unfaithful. Like a detective I sifted back through time. What I came up with made me feel like a fool. I remember once actually asking Mark if he was having an affair. He laughed out loud. He told me I was paranoid. He told me to stop being insecure. I talked myself out of my paranoia, putting it down to anxiety and exhaustion. After all, I had been going flat out for over a year making two albums in between relentless touring.

Of course, I knew some women threw themselves at Mark. This came with the territory of being married to a rock star. But the list of red flags that I chose to ignore was staggering. With a mental sieve and mounting rage I raked through them all. I *was* a fool. I was the last one to know. Humiliation is a horrible way to feel, but the root of humiliation is humility. Humility, at this particular juncture of my life, was a leveller. I had been riding high for a long time, dining on my ego and a sense of omnipotence. Humility brought me down to the ground and forced me to confront my vulnerability. In that moment I learned empathy; in that moment I became a better person.

It transpired that Saffron Prior was only one in a series of Mark's infidelities. Only a few did I know about. I found out from Lisa that he had tried to get off with her, and also with one of my step-sisters, Leah.

When we were in New York after one of our gigs, staying at the Mayflower Hotel, Mark went for Lisa, right under my nose. I was conked out in bed on a sleeping pill and Mark snuck out of bed, crept into the next room in our suite. He'd had the audacity to crawl into bed with Lisa and her (then) girlfriend Gina. Once under the covers, Mark put his hands on Lisa, again and again. Lisa repeatedly removed them. She told me she had never said any-thing to Mark at the time, she just kept her thighs locked together and took his hands off her body until, presumably, Mark became bored or realised his attempts to seduce her were futile.

He'd also made a lustful, snogging pass at our long-time female sound engineer, which had left her shaken and in tears. As each transgression was revealed to me, I felt the cleaver sink ever deeper into my heart.

Those days I spent at John Lennard's house, waiting for my flat in Holland Park to be ready, were some of the darkest. I struggled to get out of bed at all. My weight plummeted as full-blown anorexia set in. Again, I forced myself to eat a spoonful of Greek yoghurt, three Cheerios and half a strawberry. I remember thinking, 'I wonder how thin I can get?' I thought if I got thin enough he'd want me back, or else he'd be sorry and rue the day he'd left me. It still wasn't clear if I was in The Fall or not. I hadn't spoken to Mark and my life was on hold.

My mother must have heard the despondency in my voice, or perhaps John had said something to her. Whatever the case, she flew to London to take care of me. After my mother assessed the situation, she began making plans and appointments. The first appointment was with my doctor, Marisa Viegas.

Dr Marisa immediately diagnosed that I was suffering from depression and prescribed Prozac and cognitive therapy. Next, my mother dragged me to an Al-Anon meeting. Al-Anon is a twelve-step group programme, like Alcoholics Anonymous or Narcotics Anonymous. But Al-Anon is a meeting for the families, friends and spouses of alcoholics and drug addicts. I went to only one meeting, but I learned that I was not alone. Not only was I not alone but the stories I heard from the people in the group were, in so many ways, the same as mine. I recognised Mark in every one of those stories.

The meeting set off changes in me that would go on for years. I started to understand the disease of addiction. I began to recognise the behaviour patterns that accompanied it. I was eventually able to stop blaming myself. I was able to stop feeling guilty, and I took my hands off the 'steering wheel of control'. I started divorce proceeding without talking to him. When I make up my mind to do something, I don't stop till it's done. I didn't want a bitter divorce, like my parents had had. I wanted it to be clean and non-confrontational: I wasn't going to take him to the cleaners. I wanted our union severed and the past put behind me. I asked for half the house, which we had bought together. I told him he could continue to live there. I didn't want it. In retrospect, I should have asked for royalties from the records we had made together.

I received my publishing royalties from John Fogarty at Minder Music, but from the day Mark left me I have never seen a penny from the records I made with The Fall.

THE TRUTH (PART 2)

I went over my memories with a fine-tooth comb. Over and over and over, OCD-style, I compiled a mental dossier. I traced it back to Clitheroe Castle, 16 June 1985. It was a balmy summer's day and we were playing an open-air festival in Lancashire, the backdrop of which was a crumbling castle. Mark and I were walking through the festival on the way to the backstage area. Occasionally someone would recognise us and say hello, or we'd see someone we knew. A couple came up to us and said hello to Mark. I hadn't seen or heard of them before. The man was tall with sandy-coloured hair; the woman was short with bushy dark hair. They had with them an awkward teenage girl, with dark blonde hair and a vaguely froggish face.

They seemed really excited to see Mark. They were somewhat nervous and star-struck. It became obvious to me that they hadn't seen him in years, but had been friendly with him a long time ago. They introduced us to their daughter, Saffron, and reminded Mark that he used to babysit her. 'Wow!' Mark said. 'You're all grown up.' Saffron was sixteen. I took very little notice of them. My mind was preoccupied with the show. I remember Saffron looking at Mark with adoration – she probably had a little crush on him. Honestly, it didn't faze me. I was used to it. It was one of many exchanges between fans and acquaintances on the day.

Over the next two years, these people began to slowly filter back into Mark's life. There was something about them that slightly irritated me. I didn't completely trust them somehow, and I showed it by keeping them at arm's length and erecting a frosty barrier around me. Mark began to rekindle his friendship with the man, whom I will call S. They would occasionally go out to the pub together in the evenings. Whenever Mark would come back from hanging out with S he would be blind drunk. This would infuriate me. He would come back so late that the dinner I had cooked was often ruined. Usually, I let it wash over me, with only a nasty remark, but once, after one too many times, I let it rip. I screamed at Mark, like a she-devil on crack, and had a go at S as well. To my fury, I could tell that S was also extremely intoxicated. He had been driving Mark around to and from the pub while drunk. But nothing changed: sometimes they would get home so late I was sure they had gotten into a car accident. I'd spend hours pacing the house, anxiety and panic building inside me. When they got home, I'd explode into a rage and let them both have it.

Around this time, Mark decided that he wanted to start a small record label up in Manchester. He decided to call it Cog Sinister. I remember suggesting the name. It was an amalgamation of Cogswell Cogs – the name of the company George Jetson worked for on the postmodern American cartoon *The Jetsons* – and *Bend Sinister*, our recent album.

When Mark set up Cog Sinister, he needed someone to run the small office he kept in the city centre, on a day-to-day basis. I suggested a girl named Karen, one of the receptionists at our record company, Beggars Banquet, as a competent person who could do the work, part-time. At least she would know the record business and be familiar with the paperwork and the specific music-related details that went along with it. Mark suggested Saffron Prior, the teenage daughter of his new best friend S. I was horrified. Something in my gut said no. It was my intuition, loud and clear.

I fought Mark hard on this. Making a point about how Saffron had no experience and she was just a kid. I told him he didn't need to do a favour for S. I railed and argued and made a case. It was no use. Mark's mind was made up.

This was the first sign something was up with them. He was just too determined to have her work for him. He had always listened to my advice before. I should have kept a closer watch and listened to my inner guidance. Instead, I accepted it, put on my blinkers and continued to trust. One morning, a few months later, Mark turned over in bed. His shirt was off and I noticed he had scratches all over his back. 'Mark, what happened?' I asked. 'You have scratches all over your back.'

'I fell on to a sprinkler,' he said. I imagined he'd been drunk and slipped on wet grass, falling awkwardly on to his back, scratching himself on sprinklers embedded in a lawn somewhere. I look back at this now and cringe. How could I have been so naive?

Another time, he came to bed and smelled like another woman. I'm not talking about bottled perfume, I'm talking scent of 'lady garden'. I noted this, but pushed it deep down into the recesses of my mind. I didn't want to think bad thoughts. I didn't want to live my life caught in a web of suspicion and paranoia. I admit I did have a jealous and possessive streak. Sometimes it would flare up, seemingly irrational. Now I know it was inner alarms going off.

I began to notice Mark behaving in a secretive manner. Previously, it seemed we had shared everything. He valued my opinion, and every detail of our band and our business was transparent and discussed. He would turn to me as a sounding board and run things past me at every opportunity. I know I served as his muse, helping to stimulate his creativity and dish out advice. Sometimes I'd be upstairs and the phone would ring. Mark would answer it downstairs, and speak on the extension in hushed tones. Whispered conversations I could not quite hear, even though I tried. When Mark would come back upstairs I'd question him about who was on the phone. He would make up some vague tale about a random, unimportant person.

I began to smell a rat. Yet still I remained deluded.

Around this time, I remember our sex life going downhill. It became a shadow of what it once was. When we did have sex it was mostly initiated by me. I began to feel Mark pull away from me both emotionally and physically.

My feelings about Mark were also starting to change. Sometimes I felt almost repulsed by him. His drinking and anger were making life very difficult and uncomfortable, both personally and within the band.

I began to fantasise, imagining him in years to come, a gutter drunk, spewing expletives. I had visions of him with Tourette's syndrome: mad, bitter and wizened like a prune, walking alone down streets, twitching and muttering to himself.

As things began to disintegrate between us, daydreams started making their way into my thoughts. I imagined myself leaving Mark and starting a new life. I knew, deep down, things were not right between us. Neither of us was happy. We both probably came to this realisation at the same time, in our own ways. Still, I clung on, hoping to right the ship, telling myself it was a phase, a bad patch. Every marriage went through this, it was normal.

In the autumn of 1988 I left Manchester for an extended time, to finish recording some more material for my album *The Honey Tangle*. We had been recording stuff all year in various studios. This time I was heading down to a studio called the Sol. Sol Studios was owned by Jimmy Page (one of the biggest musical inspirations in my life) and was a converted old mill house located on the banks of the Thames, near Cookham in Berkshire. It was breathtaking and isolated. A small tributary off the Thames meandered through the property. The tributary was home to a plethora of ducks and swans, which I became slightly obsessed by. Sometimes you go to a place which seems to have an abundance of natural energy. This was such a place. It felt to me as if it was built on a ley line or some other earthly yet otherworldly magnetic portal. It was one of those places where I felt all my senses were heightened. I became extremely focused and creative there. There was some sort of psychic energy in the atmosphere and location. I became a recluse while there and never wanted to leave the grounds. So much so that Craig and Cassell became worried. They too were attuned to the energy; in fact, I think every creative person could feel it. It was someplace special, but also a little scary.

I stayed in the wheelhouse of the old mill, which had been converted into bedrooms. Craig Gannon was staying next to me, in a room overlooking the weir. The water ran under his room and there was a glass window built into the brick, from which you could watch the stream. One morning, Craig woke up and stumbled into the kitchen looking exhausted. 'Why did you put the radio on last night?' he asked me. 'I couldn't get any sleep. I had to get up and turn it off.'

'I didn't put the radio on. Honestly, I don't know what you are talking about,' I told him.

Thinking no more about it, I went down to the studio, which was in the main farmhouse, and started getting on with my vocals and overdubs. When I wasn't recording I usually sat by the banks of the tributary and fed the swans. I seemed to have a weird connection with them. They were intense creatures, which had gone through a physical transformation, emerging fully grown into their beauty and grace – but under that surface was a fierce and swift power. A power, I heard, that could take down dogs or break your arm. I fed them bread crusts by hand and spoke to them endlessly. I observed them for hours on end.

The next morning, Craig emerged from his bedroom with a new tale. He had been woken up by an old man. He had woken to find an elderly man sitting on the foot of his bed! He asked me if I had seen the man; did I know who it was and if he had come into my room? I hadn't seen the man – I had slept soundly all night. This was worrying to me. I didn't want some old guy wandering into my room. I went to tell Craig and Cassell about it. Maybe they knew who the guy was, as they had worked at Sol before.

'Oooh,' Cassell said, 'it's just the ghost. This place is haunted. Can't you feel it? It's got super-intense energy, and that's why creative people are attracted to it.'

I was scared of ghosts back then due to experiencing hauntings in my mother's and Marvin's house in Ellis Avenue, Chicago. It would be years later that I would understand about other dimensions and the transference of energy. It would take me thirty years to conquer my fear of ghosts.

Back at the Sol, although frightened, all this didn't stop me from poking around the studio, trying to uncover mystical, magical things. After all, the place did belong to Jimmy Page, and he was associated with Aleister Crowley and Magick. Rumour was that the mill was also once owned by Mary Shelley, who wrote *Frankenstein*. I have no idea if that is true, but it added fuel to my mounting fascination with the place.

During my time at the mill, I would call Mark frequently. Very frequently. I had a nagging feeling about him, and an ugly seed of mistrust was growing inside me. I kept calling to check up on him and monitor his movements so I could relax and focus on my work. If I was worried, I would obsess and churn inside, unable to concentrate, creating scenarios of what he might be up to, in my mind. I begged Mark to come and visit while I was recording. Reluctantly he came for two days. While he was visiting, he too poked around. He seemed on edge, distant and almost prickly. He instantly knew the place was haunted, and worse. He told me he found pentagrams scratched into the earth and that in the morning when he woke up, the bathroom window had been caked in dead flies. Apparently that was some sort of sign to him. What it meant, I didn't know. Maybe it was just an excuse for him to leave early, cutting his visit short.

A few days after he left, I tried to call him late at night. It was after our recording session had ended and I was going to bed.

It was also after the pubs closed in Manchester so, anticipating Mark's normal routine, I concluded he should have been at home.

He wasn't.

I got twitchy.

I waited fifteen minutes and called again.

No answer.

I waited another fifteen minutes and called again.

No answer.

Then I became like a woman possessed. I called every fifteen minutes until four in the morning. That horrible obsessive feeling of anger and distrust began to ricochet through my entire being. This is such a destructive feeling to have. I hated myself, but I was incensed with Mark. All my instincts were screaming at me. Where the fuck was he? Why wasn't he answering my calls? If he was staying out late, why hadn't he used the phone to call me and let me know? Why didn't he call me to say goodnight, at least? Like normal. Either he was up to something or had had an accident – or worse, maybe he was dead? My mind churned with possibilities. I decided to make a surprise visit. Without telling anyone, at daybreak I called a taxi to take me to the train station. I figured I could get up to Manchester for around 8 or 9 in the morning and see for myself what was going on. If he wouldn't answer the phone to me, I was going deal with it in person.

I arrived at our house to find it empty. I sat on the floor and waited and waited. I made a few phone calls to some of his friends to see if they'd seen Mark or knew where he was. At this point I was oscillating between rage (that he had been out of communication) and the fear (that he was dead).

Finally, at around 2 p.m., Mark sauntered into the house. I reared up like a tsunami. 'Where the fuck have you been?' I shrieked. To say Mark was shocked would be an understatement, but he collected his composure fast. 'I got drunk last night and stayed over at Craig Scanlon's,' he said.

'What were you doing at Craig's?' I asked. 'You never go there.'

'I was just working on some songs,' he said, innocently.

I couldn't prove he was lying. I didn't believe what he was saying, but I didn't want to believe the alternative. We spent an uneasy few hours together. I watched his face and behaviour for any telltale signs. I could sense he was irritated with me for coming home. It was obvious that I didn't trust him, and was watching him like a bird of prey. I had to get back to the studio, which was costing thousands a day. But before I left, I made Mark promise to call me every night, without fail. I explained how freaked out I got when he went AWOL. He now knew that he was under the microscope. I thought this might make it a lot harder for him to play away, if, in fact, that was what he was doing. I wanted to scare him. To be honest, I felt mildly deflated at not having caught him cheating on me. I was so sure he had been.

Of course, I was mostly relieved. I still didn't know the truth and, until I had proof, I had to continue to trust him. I returned to my default setting of self-loathing, and chalked up all of this drama to my own paranoia.

I finished making *The Honey Tangle* and came home to Manchester. I spent the rest of the autumn travelling between Manchester and London where I would visit Phonogram/Fontana records to do press interviews, photo sessions and approve artwork for the upcoming album release.

One of the highlights was performing *I Am Curious, Orange* at the Edinburgh Festival. We were doing quite a few days there so, economically, it made sense to rent an apartment in the city centre. We took a grand apartment on Queen Street; a large, spacious Georgian flat with high ceilings. Although promising on the outside, inside it was worn and transient-looking. The decor was shabby and mismatched. It looked unloved, and it was obvious it was used as a rental flat and not lived in by the owners. The kitchen drawers were filled with odd cutlery; it felt like everyone who had ever stayed there had left a tinny fork behind or a cut-price spoon. I had a mental image of ugly people, sat shovelling takeaway curry from plastic boxes into their mouths, wrapping their greasy gobs around the metallic-tasting cutlery. Not even bothering to use the crockery – it looked like it had been picked up from a car boot sale. I can't remember ever eating in that flat the whole time we stayed there. Ugly patterned linen clashed with orange carpeting in the bedroom. I remember feeling that the bed was unclean; it smelled like other people's skin cells had sloughed off onto the sheets. Stained green scatter cushions littered a brown textured sofa in the living room. It was such a let-down after the outside of the building. I felt like the inside of the flat was also a reflection of what I was feeling inside.

Mark had insisted that Saffron come with us to Edinburgh . . . and stay with us in our flat.

I'd fought hard against this, knowing inside that it felt wrong to me and inappropriate. But Mark's argument was that he needed her there to do PA work for him, and there was a mountain of Cog Sinister work to do. Plus, he said, it would be nice for her to have a bit of a break from Manchester, a change of scenery.

I did not want to believe what was going on. The thought of it was so painful, I couldn't let myself believe it. I thought, mistakenly, that Mark would never be so brazen as to carry on an affair under the same roof, under my nose. Who would do that? When people have affairs they do it in secret. They do everything they can to put their partners off the scent. That way they can have their cake and eat it too.

Mark was using reverse psychology on me, and it worked, but my antennae were now twitching, and my senses were on high alert. I still couldn't prove anything. Mark was so convincing in his lies. My denial was deep-rooted, but that was about to change.

STRUGGLING TO BREAK THE SPELL

It took four months for me to heal just enough to begin to enjoy life after my break-up with Mark E. Smith. Of course, I was still lacerated inside, angry and vulnerable. It would take years for me to unravel and push through this. But after four months I began dating, eating and laughing again. My mother's friend, the painter Andrea Tana, suggested I go and see a friend of hers who was a Jungian therapist. Her name was Eva Loewe, and she was instrumental in helping me find my way through the pain and insecurity. Eva was very spiritual and poetic. She was also a master astrologer. Being in such a vulnerable state, I was looking for anything to help me find a way back to happiness.

Astrology seemed like science and spirituality mixed together. This wasn't some random column in a newspaper, making sweeping predictions about a star sign, this was my personal chart. My unique data was used, including the time, place and date of my birth.

At this point I was still technically in The Fall, and *The Honey Tangle* was due to be released soon. I'd finished the final bit of recording, and Craig had mixed the album. We were getting ready to film the videos for the singles 'Waking Up in the Sun', 'Take Me' and 'Where Were You (When I Needed You)'.

When Eva unveiled the information that was contained within my chart, I was not prepared for the interpretation; what she told me was not what I wanted to hear. Eva said that she had only ever seen a chart like mine once in her life. She explained where each planet was, and the moon and sun, at the time of my birth, and how the planetary placement affected my personality. All of the information seemed spot-on. Then she got to the bad part. There would be a massive disruption in my life path. Apparently I was already entering this phase of my chart. Perhaps the beginning of the disruption was the failure of my marriage? She went on to explain that the chart showed a complete breakdown of everything I thought was important to me in my life.

'How long will this "disruption period" – this brick wall – last?' I asked (thinking in my head three months).

'Eight to eleven years. In eight years' time,' Eva said, looking straight into my eyes, 'you should be through the worst of it and starting to rebuild again. This is a great chart . . . it's spectacular.'

It didn't sound spectacular to me. I hoped and prayed she had misinterpreted the first part.

Craig and Cassell had made it their personal mission to get me dating again. Someone once told me that to get over one man, you needed to sleep with another. So far, I hadn't even felt like talking to another man, let alone seeing one naked. Of course, that changed.

The Adult Net never had any permanent members. Instead, it had an ever-changing line-up of talented musicians. The first few singles, which were released on Beggars Banquet – 'Incense and Peppermints', 'Edie', 'White Nights (Stars Say Go)' and 'Waking Up in the Sun' – featured members of The Fall playing under pseudonyms. For most of the time The Adult Net existed, Simon Rogers was my partner in crime. I loved working with Simon because he was classically trained and brought a slick balance to my self-taught groove. He also had a great sense of humour and made me choke with laughter. Simon's Adult Net pseudonym was 'O. Kippling'. Karl Burns, who played the drums, chose the name 'Mask Aichman'; Craig Scanlon was called 'Silki Guth', after his then German girlfriend, and even Mark E. Smith made an appearance as 'Count Gunther Von Hoalingan'. Also present, playing guitar on 'Incense and Peppermints', was Phil Schofield (Marcia's ex-husband). This made up the original Adult Net. There was then a mid-period live version, which included The Smiths boys, Mike Joyce, Andy Rourke and Craig Gannon.

Craig Leon had also put together my new band, The Musicians, which included Craig Gannon and James Eller, who played bass in The The. Craig Leon even got the legendary Van Dyke Parks, producer and arranger of the Beach Boys, to do a string arrangement on a song I wrote called 'Sad'. I practically worshipped the Beach Boys, particularly Brian Wilson and his precarious genius. The connection between his mental health and his creativity was utterly fascinating to me.

When it came to a drummer, there was only one possible choice in Craig's mind. He got out his little black book of musicians and dialled a number. It belonged to Clem Burke, the drummer of Blondie. I had met Clem a few years before with Lisa, when we worked at Chicago Fest on Navy Pier, helping children make art on paper plates. It was in the summer after our first year at Bennington. We were fans, and dreamed of one day being rock stars. Meeting Clem, and Nigel Harrison, had been a big deal to us. Clem was an amazing drummer. He had immense power, which tore through me as I stood riveted to the floor in front of his drum kit. I could feel my vital organs vibrating.

Craig and Cassell arranged a night out for all of us. We were off to the Ivor Novello Awards and then the after-party at the VIP room in Limelight, a club in an old church on Shaftesbury Avenue. Clem knew everybody. Practically every rock star, every musician, came up to him and paid homage. 'What are you doing here?' they asked him.

'I'm here recording with Brix Smith and her band, The Adult Net,' he said.

My body smiled on the inside. I felt like I had arrived. In the taxi on the way to the Limelight club I sat next to Clem. I felt a strong electrical current charging between our bodies. I saw Craig look at Cassell with a knowing expression. I fancied Clem so much right then. Sexual tensions were building, and had been building all through the weeks of recording. I hoped I wasn't imagining it. I had been so hurt by Mark's infidelity I was insecure and thought that no man would fancy me again. I think every woman who has been cheated on feels this way at some point. My manager, John Lennard, told me he would need a bat to beat men away from me once they found out I was single. I hoped this was true, but feared it was only him trying to cheer me up.

At the Limelight I began to drink. I mixed white wine with champagne assuming, because they were the same colour, it was OK. I got very drunk very fast and lost my inhibitions. I flirted overtly with Clem, leaving him in no doubt as to what my intentions were.

We left the club and went back to my flat in Holland Park. We then proceeded to have a brief fling. Our union lasted a short period of time. I was not in love, and after the first thrill of hooking up wore off, we drifted apart and eventually lost touch.

I had taken the first step, as I struggled to break the spell of Mark. I began to date with a vengeance. It wasn't always smooth, but I still persevered in the hope of finding someone. I went out with some notable musicians, some famous, some not. Most dates were awkward and I never clicked with anybody.

I did, however, have a secret crush on my booking agent, Ian Flooks. Ian was the forbidden fruit. Dating one's agent has its own kind of thrill. I had a massive thing for Ian. He was extremely good-looking, charming and cultured. He was a big player in the music world, an über-agent, with a jaw-dropping roster of artists, including U2. Ian was a godsend to me. He took me to fancy restaurants and literally spoonfed me back to health. He loved aerobics and yoga, and dragged me to classes with him. He took me away for weekends to stunning hotels and treated me like a princess. Ian helped me to regain my self-esteem, while remaining extremely detached emotionally. No matter how much I wished and thought he was the man for me, Ian knew he wasn't.

I realised, quite rightly, I was way too fragile, and still almost certainly on the rebound.

As all this was going on, The Fall were recording their album which would end up being called *Extricate*. It was recorded in London, with my Adult Net producer (I felt marginally stabbed in the back) Craig Leon at the helm. I couldn't understand why Mark wanted to use Craig to produce The Fall's album. It was obvious I was very close to Craig and had been spending large amounts of time with him. Yes, he's a great producer, but I suspect Mark wanted to keep tabs on me.

Craig had taken it upon himself to educate me on fine wines and had bought me a 1982 bottle of Pétrus Pomerol to get my collection started. It was a present for finishing the Adult Net album. He told me to hold on to it and one day it would be worth a lot of money. On one of my trips to Manchester, before Mark and I broke up, I left the bottle of Pétrus in the kitchen. I put a note by the bottle saying 'Do not drink!' When I went back to collect some of my belongings, after we'd split, I looked everywhere for the bottle. I called Mark and asked him where he put it.

'Oh, that?' he said. 'I drank it.'

'*You drank it?*' I screamed. 'That was my present from Craig and Cassell!'

When I calmed down, I asked him if it tasted good. He said it tasted shit – it had been late at night, he was really drunk and there was nothing left in the house, so he drank it. He told me it tasted like grape juice. That was the inspiration for the Fall song 'The $500 Bottle of Wine'. The price of that bottle today is £6,900.

Unbelievably, I had not been sacked from the band. Every time the phone would ring I expected the 'sacking call'. I dreaded the idea of going into the studio and possibly running in to Saffron, who was still very much with Mark. Although I was starting to get over Mark, the thought of seeing Saffron was much more troubling. My anger at her was so intense, I didn't actually trust myself not to go psycho.

I wrote some songs for the album and I went to record my parts. I made sure Saffron wasn't around. I told them I wouldn't record if she was there.

It was hard. It was the first time I'd seen Mark since our split. I had a lump in my throat and sucked back tears. I missed him and our partnership. Part of me wanted to hug him and the other part wanted to kick him.

One day, I was whining to Ian about how much anxiety I felt about having to see Mark and continue to record with him. Ian convinced me to leave The Fall. He told me I had a real chance with The Adult Net, and that I shouldn't have a foot in both camps. He helped me to plan my exit. The Fall were due to fly to Germany to record a TV show. Ian suggested I simply not turn up to the airport. This way there would be no chance of a direct confrontation. Instead, when I was due to leave for the airport, Ian sent a car and driver to take me to a gorgeous country house hotel in Sussex. I spent five days, all expenses paid, in the lap of luxury. It didn't stop me from feeling bad inside, though. I felt unprofessional and guilty.

I hoped and prayed The Adult Net would take off. I could no longer rely on The Fall, for income or kudos.

One night, a few months later, there was a knock at the front door of my new apartment. I opened the door to find Mark E. Smith standing there. He was drunk and held a half-empty bottle of whiskey. He begged me to let him in, and was in a state. He told me he had made a mistake leaving me. I let him in and tried to calm him down. He asked if he could sleep over. He was emotional. I was torn. Part of me was happy he'd come to his senses and realised what he'd lost in leaving me. The other part of me was cold and shut down. After having experienced the attentions and kindness of other men, I was no longer attracted to him.

But still, I felt connected to him. That would never go away. He had been my soulmate. The songs we wrote together would forever be a testament to that. I allowed him to sleep over, in my bed. I made it patently clear he was not to touch me. As he lay next to me, I felt sad. The next morning, he left. It would be years before I ever saw him again.

HAIL 'THE CLASSICAL'

I began to embrace living in London, even though there were moments when I felt pangs of emptiness. I missed playing in The Fall, but mostly I missed the band members who had become like family. I certainly did not miss the rollercoaster of drama with Mark or my old life in Manchester, where I had always felt alien. The loneliness of living in Manchester was increasingly a distant memory. I had lots of friends in London, including Angela Dunn, who was a stunning model with the most glorious head of red hair. She was wild and feisty and had impeccable taste. We hit the club scene hard, Fred's in Soho being our haunt of choice. We spent many a night there drinking, dancing and generally causing mayhem. In London fewer people knew or cared who I was or what I did, or to whom I had been married. I had plenty of girlfriends with whom I hung out, gossiped and shopped. Another new friend was a woman named Pamela Esterson, who worked for Island Records and was making a documentary about West African music.

Pam was always going out to events and concerts. One night, she begged me to come with her to a classical concert at the Royal Festival Hall. I really didn't feel like going out that night, or listening to classical music. 'Please come,' Pam pleaded. 'It's my friend Nigel Kennedy playing,' she continued. 'He's given me two tickets and he'll kill me if I don't go. Plus, I think you'll really like him,' she said. 'I know he'll really like you. You're just his type.'

I knew who Nigel Kennedy was – a virtuoso violinist and a real character. He had spiky hair and spoke with a cockney accent and a faint lisp. He was eccentric and charming – a sort of cross between Wolfgang Amadeus Mozart and Keith Moon, although he was not everyone's cup of tea. Mark once referred to him as a 'dickhead' when we saw him on TV.

I had a choice: stay home and do nothing, or go out and maybe have some fun. Finally, I caved in.

By the time we got to the Festival Hall, the concert had started and we were shut out. Once a classical concert starts, they close the doors. We watched it on a fuzzy black-and-white TV from the bar. When it was over, we were expected to go backstage. Pam told me to out-and-out lie to Nigel. He could never know we had missed the concert and watched it from the bar. I told Pam I wouldn't lie. Instead, I'd say nothing.

Backstage at the Festival Hall was very different from backstage at a Fall gig. Fans, predominantly middle-aged women and girls – all dressed in muted, floral, Laura Ashley dresses – queued to get into Nigel's dressing room. Politely and patiently they held their autograph books and shifted from foot to foot in anticipation of meeting their idol.

Pam pushed her way past the Laura Ashley girls, and dragged me in with her. She grabbed two chairs at the back of the dressing room and we sat down. I looked at the floor.

Nigel was a ball of energy. He never stopped talking. He had a very nasty welt on the side of his neck where the violin rubbed. I tried not to look at it. He used the words 'monster' and 'animal' when addressing men, and all women were simply called 'baby'. The fans were marginally hysterical.

I sat in the corner sipping a glass of champagne, my blonde hair hanging down. I felt invisible. Evidently I was not. 'Who are you, baby?' Nigel asked. He had made a beeline straight for me. He grabbed my hand and pulled me up from the chair, staring straight into my eyes.

'I'm a friend of Pam's,' I said, coolly.

All of the sudden it was as if a giant searchlight had turned on me. Nigel focused all of his attention on the one person who wasn't pandering to him. The focus of his energy was powerful. He had charisma by the truckload. Still, I remained cool and detached. I observed Nigel as if he were an exotic creature in a zoo. He was charming. He was clever. He managed to engage me in a conversion and we began to banter. Then we came to the elephant in the room: 'What did you think of my gig?' Nigel was used to having people fawn and spew superlatives over him. All his life he had been special, gifted, extraordinary and revered. His ego was large and needed feeding. I recognised this and purposely held back.

'Actually, we missed the concert,' I said. 'We got here too late and didn't see you play.' This was a call to arms for Nigel. Now he knew if he wanted me, he would have to work for it. He was up for the challenge and I was enjoying the game.

He invited Pam and me back to the maestro's (the conductor of the gig's) house for champagne. Then, if we fancied it, on to his place in Hampstead for an all-night party/jam session with some of the 'cats', 'animals' and 'monsters' from the orchestra. 'What the hell?' I thought. If nothing else, it would be an experience.

The maestro's house was somewhere in Kensington. After about an hour, the party broke up. Nigel begged us to come on to his.

'I don't know,' I said, still playing it cool. Although I was lapping up the attention, I wanted to see how hard he would work. I was enjoying my power as a woman. That night I had a choice. And I made it.

Pam hailed a black cab. We drove to Hampstead in North London. The taxi deposited us at a discreet gate on the corner of Lyndhurst Road and Rosslyn Hill. We walked down a gravel path. 'The Annex' was situated in the lavish grounds of 'The Great House'. It was a separate dwelling out of which poured the sounds of laughter and music. The door was closed, but unlocked. We pushed it open and entered into the extraordinary world of Nigel Kennedy.

CHAOS AND DISCIPLINE

Never before had I seen such a tip. Nigel, it seemed, lived in absolute chaos. His small, single-storey bungalow was so untidy it was a work of art. People were drinking, laughing and smoking. There was a battered old upright piano in the front of the room. Nigel sat down to play. Other guests, who were obviously musicians, opened their respective cases and brought out their instruments: violins, violas and a cello. They all started to jam. Nigel was an unbelievable piano player. He started playing complex, left-brain jazz, and the others joined in. The party really kicked off. Pam and I sat on the floor and listened.

We drew an imaginary circle around us, six feet in diameter. Inside the circle, we counted as many items as we could. They were varied to say the least: an ashtray-full of fags, an overturned Heinz ketchup bottle, an empty, stained teapot, a cigarette butt (that had not made it to the ashtray), a ceramic jug in the shape of a fish, some boxer shorts, the *Sun* newspaper, a can of Coke (full-fat), a wadded-up tissue, a lump of hash, or was it mud?, one trainer, a plastic comb, a fork, matches, a receipt, a credit card, a dirty bowl, a lipstick, an earring, a broken violin bow, someone's phone number written on a matchbook, a sock, a pebble and a plastic spoon.

That was a microcosm of the whole place.

During an interlude in the music, Nigel came and sat down next to us on the floor. We picked up the conversation from where we had left it at the maestro's house. As the night wore on and the drink flowed, I became intrigued by this small, enchanting, elf-like dynamo. Still, I held my emotions at arm's length and remained cool. Part of me was playing a game, the other part was wary and protective of my delicate and precarious state. I was like a newly glued-together china cup.

In the early hours of the morning, Pam and I decided to make our exit. Nigel didn't want us to go. He had an appetite for fun and seemed like he was still on a high from his gig. He invited us to go to Birmingham to attend an upcoming Aston Villa football match. He said he would drive us up in his car and we could sit in the directors' box. He adored Aston Villa and was their honorary vice president. I had never been to a football match. Nor did I really care about football, but the invitation sounded fun and I said I'd think about it.

The next day Nigel called Pam to grill her for information about me.

I had told him I was a musician and in a band called The Fall. Unsurprisingly, he had never heard of us.

As it happened, I needn't have worried. Nigel was fascinated by the fact that I was in a band and longed to play the type of music I was playing. He wanted to be included in my world and hang out with the cool and edgy musicians who were my friends. He was obsessed with Jimi Hendrix, even going so far as to buy his scarves at a Christie's auction, wrap them around his head and drape them off his jacket when he played the violin.

Nigel was nothing but encouraging to me about my music. He never judged me and always wanted me to jam with him. After he first heard my new Adult Net album he worked up some violin arrangements for a few of my songs. That way we could play them together at parties or wherever. It was amazing playing with him – a real treat. Too bad my insecurities stopped me from enjoying the experience fully.

I thought about Nigel for the next couple of days. He was such an interesting character. I loved his free spirit, his boundless joy and enthusiasm. I was looking forward to spending more time with him.

Pam and I met up at Nigel's house a few days later, to go with him to the football match at Villa Park. We got into Nigel's car, which was a sight to behold: a BMW, which he had customised himself. He had spray-painted the car maroon and light blue, the colours of Aston Villa. By 'spray-painted', I mean graffitied. The inside of the car was as messy as his flat. It looked like it hadn't been cleaned out in years. As I climbed in the back, I pushed aside a rotting sandwich, a brown teapot, an old newspaper, some golf shoes and a jumper, to make enough room to sit down.

Nigel made no apologies for the state of the car. We bombed down the motorway listening to live sports reports on the radio. Nigel drove like a demon, with little or no regard for the speed limit. I began to see a pattern. Normal rules did not apply to Nigel.

Just before you reach Villa Park, you drive through a very working-class neighbourhood, made up of simple red-brick ter-raced houses. Nigel informed us that it was always his dream to buy three of these houses and knock them together so he could have one big house, near the entrance to the stadium. That way, he would have somewhere to stay and party on match days. His sitting room would look over his beloved football ground.

As we pulled in, footballers making their way to the dressing room walked past us in the directors' car park. Nigel knew all of them and greeted each of them as 'monster'. I had never met a footballer before. They were all amazing physical specimens, and the oozing of testosterone from their bodies was not lost on me. I remember meeting David Platt that day, whom Nigel called 'PlattyPus', and who would go on to captain England. The match itself seemed interminable to me. I kept looking at my watch. I hoped Villa would win, as I was worried about Nigel's mood if they did not. Thankfully they did, and Pam and I were deemed lucky charms by Nigel.

After the match we went to a reception with all the players, managers, wives and sponsors. Nigel got out his violin, which he took everywhere, and played an impromptu tune for the rapt crowd. We then returned to the car and drove the hour and a half back to London. It was a great day out and I enjoyed doing something new. One thing was for sure, he certainly got the most out of life. Every single moment of it.

SCRAPER

I found myself thinking about Nigel Kennedy a lot over the next few days. He must also have been thinking about me too, because he called and asked me out again. He invited me over to his house. We bought a picnic and grabbed some blankets and headed out to Hampstead Heath to spend a lovely English spring afternoon lying in the sun, talking and talking.

What became clear was that Nigel was like a child. He was totally in touch with the childlike wonder of the world. And soon I was seeing the world through his joyful eyes. He seemed free from most adult constraints and behaviour. If he didn't like a mouthful of food, he'd spit it out. If he wanted to play with mud, he'd smear it on his face, and if he didn't want to tidy his house or his car he simply wouldn't. Lying on the tartan wool blanket under the big British sky, looking up at the sycamore trees, Nigel softly took my hand and held it. I felt the first flutter of butterflies in my body. He then rolled over to me, and kissed me gently on the mouth. No tongues, no pushing, no earnestness. It was simply the sweetest kiss I'd ever had.

We began to spend more time together, mostly at his house. Nigel was extremely busy as his new album, *Vivaldi: The Four Seasons*, was about to be released. At the same time I was building up to the launch of the Adult Net album. Nigel's schedule was written in stone. He had concerts booked two years in advance, sometimes more. The life of a classical musician is very different to that of a rock musician.

While we had to rehearse before we went on tour, or before recording an album, Nigel had to practise for a minimum of two hours a day, sometimes for as much as five. Plus he had to memorise whole symphonies and concertos, as well as write cadenzas, orchestrations and arrangements. I realised that this level of perfectionism was so intense and rigid that he had no room for any other restrictions in his life – which is why he had none. All of his focus went on this; everything else could go to hell.

Nigel's violin was called 'Scraper'. He called it this as a joke, because he said violinists were scrape-scrape-scraping all day long. Scraper was a Stradivarius. Its real name was 'La Cathédrale'. There are very few Stradivari left in the world, and fewer still that are playable at a concert level. All Stradivari have names and histories. There is a huge book about them, which Nigel had, and I found captivating. Scraper was extremely old, dating from 1707, and had to be treated with utter respect. It was insured by Lloyd's of London for over £1,000,000 and was only allowed to be driven in the front seat of the car, not in the boot, which meant I had to share my seat with it. Its case was covered in the Aston Villa colours, naturally.

Scraper was only part-owned by Nigel. Nigel had patrons who were wealthy classical music lovers who had bought it for his use. I believe Nigel was paying them back slowly.

Nigel took me to meet his parents, who lived in a small cottage near Brighton at the foot of the South Downs. He had a very odd relationship with his mother. He had been sent to the Yehudi Menuhin School at the age of just six. Nigel's mother had realised she had an incredibly talented prodigy on her hands, and sought out the best education for him. Yehudi Menuhin took Nigel under his wing and brought him up and paid for his entire education. I feel that Nigel had some issues with his mother. Perhaps he felt that six was too young to be sent away, and resented her for that. Whatever the case, there was some tension between them. I remember one night, his mother, whom I liked very much, referred to us as 'a horrid little couple', which did not make me feel good.

Tension or not, horrid little couple or not, I loved visiting his parents, and staying in their charming cottage.

Nigel and I began to spend all our time together. We simply didn't want to be apart. This had become a pattern for me. It was all or nothing. When I was with a man, I became glued to him. I dropped my girlfriends for a time and neglected aspects of my personal life, and work. We were very happy and getting along well. I had embraced Nigel's childlike behaviour and now we were like two children.

The lease on my apartment in Holland Park was up for renewal. I hardly ever spent any time there since I'd met Nigel. We decided it made sense for me to move into his place on Rosslyn Hill. I was happy. Life was fun with Nigel. Yes, he had his peculiar quirks and demands, but at that point we were just having a blast. His messy apartment had grown on me; I was no longer as horrified by it. I vowed to keep it as clean as I could. I did a really bad job.

KITCHEN CRICKET

When Nigel released his version of Vivaldi's *Four Seasons* our life together changed. It shot to the top of both the classical and pop charts. Of course it was expected to do well in the classical charts, but when it hit the pop charts a whole new level of fame whipped its frenzied mane in Nigel's face and, by association, mine.

Nigel's manager was a gentleman called John Stanley. He was a total mastermind and a visionary. He saw the big picture of Nigel's career, and understood strategically how to transform him from a classical music star to a celebrity. John was instrumental in helping to demystify classical music in England. Historically there had always been a perceived snobbery and elitism attached to classical music. John helped Nigel to break that mould, and bring classical music to the masses in an inclusive and modern way.

We began to move in rarefied circles, with royalty and celebrities. Every night brought another high-profile event at which Nigel played. He was asked to entertain at prestigious charity functions like the Prince's Trust concert and the Royal Variety Show, and was invited to join 'The Magnificent Seven', part of the Duke of Edinburgh's Award scheme, fronted by seven British people who were, at the time, at the top of their game and considered icons in their respective fields. It was hoped these figureheads would help inspire the kids of Britain to aim high in their own lives. They represented the best of British, and included Gary Lineker, then captain of England's national football team.

One of the first Magnificent Seven get-togethers was at a breakfast at the Ritz Hotel in Piccadilly. I was beginning to find these events somewhat challenging. This wasn't my world, this was

Nigel's. I was still so insecure it was hard for me to stomach the feeling of invisibility. I knew, from previous experience, insecurity put men off and drove them away. Still, when Nigel would walk into a crowded room, turn his back on me and focus his attention on everybody else, I felt like a temporary, trophy girlfriend, super-fluous. I had allowed myself to feel this way.

At the Ritz breakfast, I noticed another lone woman. We met over a tray of profiteroles. Her name was Michelle, and she was married to Gary Lineker. Michelle was the sweetest, loveliest woman. She was petite, gorgeous, blonde and softly spoken. The energy around her felt angelic; the air seemed to tingle with light-ness and trilling bells when I stood in her presence. We started talking, and bonded right then and there. Both of us were there to support our famous partners, but Michelle did it with grace.

The four of us became friends. Since Nigel was so involved with Aston Villa, and Gary was playing for Tottenham and England, we spent huge amounts of time watching football and hanging out with the players. Once, we went to watch Gary play in the FA Cup at Wembley. We all sat in a special box and went psycho when they won. It was an unbelievable moment. That same night Gary and Michelle threw a small dinner party at their house in St John's Wood, just round the corner from Abbey Road Studios. Before the dinner, after more than one glass of celebratory champagne, I had asked Gary to show me how to play cricket. I wanted to see if it was like softball, and maybe I'd actually be good at it. For some reason we decided to practise inside the house. He tossed me the ball, I swung the bat and made contact. It seemed I was a good batsman and all my high-school softball practice came in handy. I wanted to impress Gary: he was, after all, a professional athlete, whom I had just seen win the biggest football match of the year. There was an almighty crash. The ball smashed into a shelf and decimated all Michelle and Gary's Royal Dalton porcelain figurines, an entire collection given to the couple by Gary's dad, Barry. I was so angry with myself, I crumpled into a cringeball. Michelle, unbelievably, took it in her stride and totally forgave me.

Other guests that night included the cricketer David Gower and his wife, Eric Idle from *Monty Python* and his wife. The celebratory dinner took place in the Linekers' large glass conservatory, which, thankfully, I managed NOT to destroy with the cricket bat. During the first course, the doorbell rang. 'Who could that be?' I thought to myself. I heard heavy footsteps coming down the stairs into the kitchen. In came two uniformed guards . . . carrying the FA Cup! Everybody freaked out. We all started screaming with joy. Gary had planned it, of course. We passed the Cup around and touched it. Nigel acted as if he was touching the face of Jesus. We played with the Cup, we held it up as if we had just won it ourselves. We put the lid of it on our heads and wore it as a hat. Then we filled it with bottles of Cristal champagne and drank from it, passing it round the table again and again. What a night.

Around this time, Princess Diana began to take a very personal interest in Nigel. He was invited to her birthday party – and so, by default, was I. We had met Diana and the Prince of Wales a few times. She was unbelievably charismatic, tall and statuesque. She towered over both me and Nigel. She flirted outrageously with Nigel in front of me. She invited him to the palace, to give private violin lessons to the young princes, William and Harry. My mind went wild when she extended her invitation to Nigel, for a 'home visit'. I read all kinds of things into it.

Prince Charles, who was by this point, in the public's perception at least, trailing in Diana's wake, was eternally gracious. When he spoke to me he looked me directly in the eyes. He had a way of effortlessly putting you at ease. His energy was calm and soothing. Although Diana was always polite and courteous to me, remembering my name and so forth, she remained coolly detached. I felt nervous around her and intimidated. We never had any deep, meaningful conversations. I felt like she merely tolerated me to get to Nigel – on whom she shined her magnetic light. I've rarely seen a woman turn it on the way she did.

Nigel was very charitable with his time. Whenever the royal family requested something, he was only too happy to help. We visited a few of the different palaces, for parties and dinners, and over that period met almost the entire family. One night, Nigel was invited by Prince Philip to play a classical recital in St James's Palace.

St James's Palace was very different in feel and atmosphere to Kensington, Buckingham or Windsor. For a palace, it felt strangely relaxed and inviting. The state rooms, like the one that Nigel played in, were opulent and dripping with history. Huge oil paintings hung on the walls in baroque frames, depicting historical scenes. Intricate carpets and the rich wood floor, glittering crystal chandeliers and rare tapestries created a textural, visual richness that was warm but not intimidating. I could imagine living there. It had good vibes.

The vibes got even better when Nigel started playing. The room was lavish yet intimate. Everything seemed to radiate with gold. It was spellbinding. There were fifty or so invited guests, all sitting in chairs for this private performance. I was totally transported. It felt as if I'd gone back in time. I closed my eyes and imagined the room as it must have been centuries ago – all the kings and queens and courtiers who had come before, enjoying similar experiences in this very chamber.

In the beginning, as Nigel's fame built, he wanted, or needed, me by his side at all times, which soon became difficult for me. I needed to concentrate on my own career, as I began to start the PR campaign leading up to the launch of *The Honey Tangle*. I was confused and conflicted about whether to prioritise my work or my love life. I felt I needed to shower Nigel with attention, and was getting dangerously used to the high life. Nigel was very generous, but he didn't like feeling taken advantage of, or lived off. I was very conscious of this. He insisted we go Dutch for most things. For the time being, I could still just about afford to pay my own way. Really, though, he was calling the shots, and it was his career that we were living off.

I started to notice a disturbing pattern. As our world began to revolve more and more around Nigel, and he grappled with the pressures of his new-found super-fame, it became increasingly important for him to control every aspect of his life, including me. Because of my own demons (which I had yet to conquer) of weakness and insecurity as a woman and as an artist, I allowed this to happen. At the same time, I understood Nigel's need to be in control, because at that level of fame everybody is out to take a piece of you.

Thankfully, I was still seeing my Jungian therapist, Eva Loewe. I had been visiting her once a week, in her home office in Hampstead, just down the road from mine and Nigel's place on Rosslyn Hill.

John Leckie, my old producer, lived a few houses down from Eva. Sometimes I'd pop in to visit him and his wife, Christine. These visits were a godsend for me; they kept me somewhat attached to my old life, and provided me with much-needed grounding.

Eva helped me to weed my mental garden. She had a great overview of everything, and seemed to understand the dynamics of mine and Nigel's relationship. One day, I went to her crying. I was due to go to New York to meet the American branch of my record company, which should have been an exciting proposition. It was my turn to shine, luxuriate in the attention of the record company and the press, and I was proud of my album, something I had been working towards since I'd been a teenager. But I was very worried about going off and leaving Nigel. I was fearful of giving him too much space. When I'd done that with Mark, he had cheated on me.

Eva gave me a metaphor to think about. She said, 'If you build a temple, it needs separate pillars on which to stand. Air needs to be able to circulate around those pillars. Then the temple will stand strong and last the test of time. If you put those pillars next to each other, without the space between them, the temple will topple and fall. You are building a temple of love. Your relationship is your temple. You must allow air to flow between the pillars.'

She also believed that Nigel was extremely childlike. She suspected that he had many unresolved issues from his formative years. Now, with his increasing fame and new-found power, he was acting out in a whole new way. She christened him 'The High-chair Tyrant'.

Eva was loving and gentle with me, and never critical. She gave me encouragement and helped me to begin to appreciate who I was as a person and to rediscover my confidence. She was one of those great teachers who come along once or twice in a lifetime, if you are lucky. 'When the student is ready, the teacher appears.'

I went off to New York to meet the American arm of Phonogram/ Fontana. I was wined and dined and undertook multiple interviews for both TV and press. It felt good to be the focus of attention again. I was excited about the future and looked forward to the release of my new single and the album.

One night, my record company took me to a Midtown restaurant for dinner. Another British act, The Lilac Time, was over, promoting their album; they had just been playing CBGBs. The lead singer, writer, multi-instrumentalist and mastermind of the band, Stephen Duffy, had had a few hits previously as a solo artist, when he'd performed under the name Stephen Tintin Duffy. He was from Birmingham and had been in the original line-up of Duran Duran. Stephen and I had never met before, but sitting opposite each other, we hit it off big time. He was handsome, smart, understated and had a dry, sarcastic wit. During the course of the conversation, Stephen mentioned that he was living in Malvern, near Worcester, which he made sound a magical place. I only knew the name because that was where Malvern water came from. He told me there were taps by the side of the road, next to the hills from which you could fill your bottle with gushing, fresh spring water.

I knew that Worcester was very near Birmingham. I explained that we went to Birmingham all the time to watch Aston Villa play.

I mentioned that my boyfriend was the honorary vice president of Villa, and invited Stephen to come to a game with us sometime. He said he'd love to. We finished dinner and went to our respective hotels. I didn't realise it then, but Stephen Duffy would become a very important person in my life.

At the tail end of my PR trip to NYC, Nigel flew out and joined me. He had a rented apartment in New York, on 69th and Broadway. We decided to spend a week or so there. Nigel had always kept a place in New York, since he had gone to school at Juilliard. He purposely took an apartment within walking distance of the Lincoln Center, which was where he played most often and was the hub for classical music. Nigel's apartment was in an old building, and the hallways and common areas smelled like boiled cabbage and old ladies. You could hear everything the neighbours were doing through the walls, which, at various times, could include: trumpet practice, opera-singing exercises, fighting in a foreign language (as well as in English), watching TV, and loud, banging sex. But still, it was an apartment in New York and, for a while, our filthy, tiny, roach-infested love nest.

Being in love did a lot to mask the conditions in which we lived. Much as I had done when I first moved to Manchester and saw Mark's flat, I was able to concentrate on the good things in my life. Although there were already 'red flags' beginning to wave at me, concerning mine and Nigel's relationship, love's rosy glow put the ugliness and early warning signs into soft focus.

We spent our days roaming around the city together, going to concerts and dropping in to visit some of Nigel's ex-classmates from Juilliard. These included the cellist Yo-Yo Ma, who was already by then a classical legend. He was lovely, with a great sense of humour. His apartment was in a modern tower block. The interior of his apartment had white décor, and was scrupulously clean.

We arrived back in London in time for the release of my first single, 'Take Me', on Phonogram. I remember eagerly awaiting news of the midweek chart position. I was hopeful that, with the power of a major label behind me, the single would enter at a strong position and crack the charts. The midweek position was middling, just outside the top 40. I prayed for it to go up by Sunday, when the chart was announced.

I trusted and believed that Phonogram would know how to make that happen, to pull all the corporate strings possible to secure a hit. Sadly, this was not the case.

Although the midweek was hopeful, the single dropped on Saturday and failed to crack the top 50. I was gutted. I pinned my hopes on the second single, and vowed to work even harder promoting it. Inside, I worried that I had let myself get distracted from my work and music by my focus on Nigel and our relationship. I had taken my eye off the ball. A small voice in the back of my mind warned me that, perhaps, I was not a priority for Phonogram, and they hadn't put their full resources and power behind me. 'Maybe I should have stayed on Beggars Banquet?' I fretted. Maybe my music was better suited to an indie label? Somewhere inside, I wondered if Mark E. Smith was monitoring my single's progress and was secretly happy to see me fail to chart.

Then a new thought popped up. What if I failed completely? What if The Adult Net was a flop? What would Nigel think of me then? Would he dump me?

The build-up of anxiety started very slowly. It went unchecked and ignored. I swallowed my fears and pushed them away. I did not deal with them. I bottled them. I did not turn them around, from negative to positive. The anxiety was a signal from my subconscious; a signal that something was fundamentally wrong. The bad thoughts crept in, permeating my waking hours, breeding with each other . . . multiplying. The build-up of anxiety continued for two years. Until one catastrophic night I was felled, quite literally, by the weight of it all.

HEAD FOR THE HILLS

As we left the motorway and hit the country roads, my eyes widened with every mile. We were heading to Stephen Duffy's house to spend the night. It was beautiful, heart-stoppingly beautiful. As we began to drive up into the hills, a strange sense of calm came over me. The main town of Malvern is largely Victorian, built on the steep roads leading up to the hills. The hills themselves are undulating and glorious. The views are spectacular. Fresh mineral-water springs run underground, and the healing water is plentiful. There is an energy coming from the earth that I felt very powerfully, like the energy I felt at Bennington College, or Stonehenge.

I didn't know it then, but Malvern has always been a magnet for creatives, travellers and spiritual people. All types of healers – practising every type of alternative therapy – psychics, artists, weird wizard types and musicians make their home in the area. Edward Elgar is buried there. Nigel loved it, especially for that reason, as one of his most critically acclaimed recordings was his version of Elgar's violin concerto. Both Nigel and I fell in love with the place, and over the course of our dinner we decided to move there. The increasing pressures of Nigel's fame were beginning to feel claustrophobic in London. It was like living in a goldfish bowl. Malvern was a place where Nigel could unwind and ground himself. It was close to Villa Park and we could get into London easily if need be. I felt like I could be very creative in Malvern, and it would be an inspirational place for me to continue writing songs. We would, of course, keep the annex on Rosslyn Hill as our London base. After dinner we all decided to take a walk up the road, past the houses and into the hills proper. As we walked up Old Hollow, about five minutes up the road from Stephen and his girlfriend Kate's home, we passed a house with a 'for sale' sign.

Moon Sun house was high up on the hillside, and had a spectacular view. It was Victorian but had been developed and modernised. In fact, it wasn't yet completed, as building materials were evident. We decided to try to get inside to have a look. Unbelievably, the back door was open. It was a sign.

That night we stayed over at Stephen and Kate's. When we woke up the next morning, we back went to Moon Sun house again, just to make sure we still loved it. Nigel had his assistant call to make an offer. We didn't use Nigel's name at first, because we were worried that the vendor might jack up the price.

The offer was accepted, and we set about finishing the house to our taste. In a few short months, we were ready to move in, just in time for the bluebell season. Our view from the front porch overlooked the Old Hollow woods, the sight of an ancient witches' coven, now carpeted by nature in mesmeric lavender-blue flowers that brought to mind the otherworldliness of a fairy glen.

We began to spend 75 per cent of our time in Malvern, only going back to London for work commitments and my therapy sessions with Eva. Nigel still had a packed concert schedule and the *Four Seasons* album continued to sell, remaining high in the classical charts. We based ourselves at Moon Sun house and set off to all Nigel's gigs together in his graffiti-covered BMW.

My second and third Adult Net singles came out and faded away as quickly as the first, failing to make a significant dent in the charts. Even though the reviews had been favourable, and much was written about me in the press, the singles failed to live up to the hype. I was becoming increasingly depressed as I felt my dream slipping away. I consoled myself with the fact that I still had the album to come, and I hoped the fans were saving themselves for that.

As my career started slipping, Nigel's continued to soar. The balance in our relationship began to seriously shift. I felt hollow inside, and crippling self-doubts about my musicianship and songwriting skills were plaguing me, blocking me from being creative, undermining my every thought. Nigel still pushed me to play. I watched and listened to him practise for hours, every day. I could barely look at my guitars any more, let alone play them.

My album was due to be released in America. The record company wanted me to go on a promo tour there, and do press and radio interviews across the country. The only problem was that Nigel was due to tour America at the same time and had already asked me to go with him. He suggested that I got the record company to schedule my interviews in the cities that he was playing in. I decided it would be beneficial to me and our relationship to keep Nigel happy. I knew it was a compromise, but it would prove to him that I was putting his needs first. When I informed the record company of our plan they were not thrilled. They had their own plans for me. To their credit, though, they got their heads around it and created a schedule. Everything seemed all right. 'Crisis averted,' I thought. I thought wrong.

Nigel's first concert was in South Dakota. It had been in his schedule for two years, before *The Four Seasons* was even released. EMI, his record company, needed him to do an important TV show in London the day before. This made getting to Dakota in time almost impossible. The only way to do it was for us to fly to Paris after the London show then take Concorde to New York. From New York we could jump on a private charter to South Dakota. We would land just in time for Nigel to make it to the concert hall.

Dakota was very straight. The people who organised the concert, the patrons of the orchestra, were conservative and snobby. They treated Nigel like the second coming: the rare English eccentric musical genius. They indulged him, and us. We behaved badly. After the concert we were invited to a large reception at the mansion of one of the patrons. Nigel insisted I sit on his lap at the table, throughout the entire dinner. At these events people liked to separate us, so the heavy hitters could spend time with Nigel. I was usually shunted to the far end of the table with less important people. We always moved the place-cards around to suit us. I actually loved Nigel for this. It made me feel wanted and adored. When dessert was served it was profiteroles and chocolate sauce. We asked for two bowls of just the chocolate sauce and ate them with a spoon, like soup.

By now, I was getting used to hanging out with classical musicians – orchestra members. I was shocked to discover they were wild. On first appearance they might look straight and proper, but after spending time with them I observed another side. They loved to let their hair down and party like animals. By 'party' I mean drink like fish, snort coke, smoke pot, play wild games and shag each other. They looked like librarians but behaved as badly as any rock star I'd come across.

Sweeping generalisations were made about musicians depending on what instrument they played. For instance, everyone was really down on viola players. They were joked about mercilessly. All the male musicians made lascivious cracks about the girls who played flute. It was something about *embouchure* and the 'fitness' of their mouths.

By the time I got back to England, *The Honey Tangle* had been released and had failed to make a significant mark on the charts. My press tour in the States had been a damp squib too. I wanted to blame the record company, but I knew inside I had fucked it up. It had been a poor choice on my part to put my relationship with Nigel ahead of my own career. Nigel did not make me do this. I had made the choice. I'd blown it, big time.

I retreated to Malvern, licking my wounds. Stephen Duffy rallied to my side. He had known success and he had known failure. He helped me begin the writing process again. It seemed that Phonogram, although disappointed with the performance of my records, still wanted more.

One day Stephen arrived with a bizarre discovery. Close to our houses, isolated in a remote section of Malvern woodland, was a retreat. It was a place of spiritual healing for mind, body and soul called Runnings Park. It was a centre for all types of alternative therapy, including meditation, yoga, massage and colonic hydrotherapy. It had, Stephen discovered, a flotation tank, a sensory deprivation chamber. We had heard that when you float in water heated to body temperature in the dark your mind, deprived of stimulus, unleashes its own torrent of psychedelic visions. It was said that this experience was similar to tripping on acid or peyote, and was thought to be highly stimulating for the psyche – a way to unblock creativity. At that point, unable to write music, I was willing to try anything.

We all took a drive to Runnings Park, where the owner showed us around. It was an oasis of calm. There was a Japanese garden in the middle of the grounds, in front of the main building, with a pond and a meditation hut. We were given a tour of the facilities, but what we really wanted to see was the tank.

It wasn't a tank at all. It was much better. The room looked like a small hut. It was big enough for one person to lie down and spread out their arms and legs like a starfish. I was scared, fearful of what might be unleashed from the depths of my psyche. Stephen went first. He loved it. He said he'd never been so relaxed, and that he felt reborn. I couldn't wait. I floated in the dark, listening to the classical music coming from the underwater speakers. At first my body hurt. All the stresses I had been carrying around with me began to unwind as my body felt no gravity. Stimulated by the music, I began to see intense colours. I slipped into a deeply relaxed state of Delta brainwaves, and then went deeper. The next thing I noticed was the music getting louder under the water. I had been completely out of it for a whole hour. They had to turn the music up loud to wake me up.

I felt elated afterwards. My body felt young and flexible. I felt like my mind had purged itself of layers of unneeded debris.

Of course, we all became infatuated with the tank. I went up to Runnings Park whenever I could. I joined groups and went to lectures there. I became besotted by crystals and the power of stones. I carried my favourite stones with me and I talked to them during Nigel's absences, which were getting more and more frequent. I started to go to spiritual workshops, with healers and psychics. Even so, I was finding it nearly impossible to write anything.

Nigel's nasty, angry sore on the side of his neck was giving him trouble. It was caused by the constant rubbing of the chinrest, and a bad reaction to the shellac or lacquer used on the wood of the violin. This dreadful wound had built up over Nigel's lifetime of playing and was now so inflamed and painful it had to be excised.

It was not pretty to look at either. I tried not to kiss him on that side, as it was truly a passion killer. Sometimes a crust or scabbing would build up on it. It was always red and bulbous, and it made my stomach clench. The doctors decided they needed to remove it, and Nigel was forced to clear his schedule. He was told to take three months off playing, the longest break of his life.

The operation was complicated. Nigel suffered from keloid scarring. He told us, terrifyingly, he woke up in the middle of the operation and overheard the doctors saying how shocked they were at depth of the wound. They'd said, 'We've got most of it, we might as well take it all.' The operation turned out to be much more serious than initially thought. We were surprised Nigel had any neck left at all. Nigel insisted the doctors save the massive cyst of keloid scarring they removed that day. He brought it home in a jar and kept it on a shelf in the music room. I kept thinking, 'Eleanor Rigby'.

Having nothing to do sent Nigel off the rails. The devil makes work for idle hands, so to speak. Nigel let his inner child run wild, unchecked. Then came three months of going crazy in the country. I had always been great at baking cookies and brownies, American-style. Growing up in California, in high school I had perfected the art of hash brownies and chocolate-chip pot cookies. I remember eating brownies for breakfast and nibbling on them all day. We had three-day-long parties in Moon Sun house. Musicians would come from all over and jam for hours, fall asleep on our floor then wake up and jam again – all fuelled on my hash brownies, of course. I kept them in an old metal coffee container from America, and everybody helped themselves at will. Nigel, Stephen, Kate and I would take long walks up to the hills, off our heads. Sometimes I would ride Lucky, my white pony that Nigel had bought me, and imagine she was a unicorn, I was a maiden and we were all on some medieval pilgrimage.

One of Nigel's favourite pastimes was a game he loved to play in the car while driving. He called it 'free-wheeling'. At the top of a long, steep road, he would take the car out of gear and pull his feet away from the pedals. Not only would he take his foot away from the brake, but he'd take his hands from the steering wheel too. He'd reach to the sky, as if on a rollercoaster. The car would then pick up speed and 'free-wheel' down the hill, gathering huge momentum. It was forbidden to put your foot on the brake. I absolutely hated 'free-wheeling'. I was terrified that Nigel would lose control completely, and we'd crash into a tree or, worse still, into another car with people in it. I tried to keep quiet, and stifle my screams. My white-knuckled fear only egged Nigel on more.

One night, while driving home in the darkness through the Malvern Hills, Nigel decided to take the game one step further. He drove off the road and on to the Malverns proper. He wanted to 'off-road' and attempt to 'roll' the car down the hills sideways, stuntman-style, with all of us in it! We screamed and clutched the seats for support. Nigel gave the car gas, and tried to tip it over, to unbalance it and get it to roll. He attempted it from every angle: he drove over rocks, aimed the car sideways on the steepest part of the hill, zigzagged to try to get it to tumble. Thankfully BMW had manufactured a well-grounded car with a low wheel base, which hugged the ground, like an octopus sucker.

Eventually, Nigel's neck healed. He was grumpy when he started playing again, and still in pain, but he persevered and went back to work. He started spending more and more time away again. I couldn't face going on the road with him and made up excuses to stay in Malvern. The truth was I was slipping into depression. I slept all hours and watched endless amounts of TV. I took Valium in the day. I was also lonely, and isolating myself was doing me no good.

Stephen and Kate tried to pull me out of my hermitage. Whenever Stephen called, I'd tell him the same thing: 'I'm taking Valium and going back to bed.' But I did have one thing I was looking forward to: a vacation. The year was 1990, and it was the summer of the World Cup, Italia '90.

One night, over at the Linekers' house, Nigel had discovered that the England team had a rule that none of the footballers were allowed to bring their wives to major tournaments. Bobby Robson, the manager of the national team, decreed that wives were a distraction. If the wives wanted to travel to Italy, they'd have to make their own arrangements. Immediately, Nigel decided that we would take Michelle Lineker with us, and the three of us would rent a villa in Sardinia, where the England team were to be based. We decided to go for five weeks and see what happened. If England stayed in the World Cup, we would stay too.

ITALIA '90

Nigel, Michelle Lineker and I arrived in Rome a week or so before the first game of Italia '90. We checked into the Cavalieri Hilton, which was a gorgeous hotel on a hill overlooking the city.

Our hotel was also the home base for the FIFA officials. They swarmed the bars and the pool areas, like uniformed politicians, drunk on their own cocktail of power and corruption. They were unfriendly and arrogant. They moved in packs, and only socialised with each other. We observed them from a distance, avoiding their unpleasant energy. (When the recent allegations of their dirty dealings came to light, I was not surprised in the least.)

We wandered around Rome for a few days, taking in World Cup fever, until our villa was ready in Sardinia. The England team were stationed near the town of Cagliari. Nigel had picked out our villa from photos and a description his assistant had provided for him. It was old, but newly rebuilt, especially for the World Cup. When we finally arrived we stood before it in silence. Dumbfounded, we looked at each other, and then Nigel went mental.

The villa wasn't finished. It wasn't even habitable. There was no running water; it was basically a building site. Small, dirty, half-dressed children ran around an open septic tank, hitting each other with fly swatters. The property's manager, who was there to greet us, got an earful. I think Nigel was embarrassed, in front of Michelle. He wanted it to be especially nice for her; after all, her husband was the captain of England. We got back in the car, and the property manager drove us to a nearby five-star resort, the Forte Village, to see if there were any rooms still available.

Thankfully, they could accommodate us. Nigel and I got a room – a small, dark cabin, painted white to disguise its bunker-like atmosphere. Once the hotel managers realised who Michelle was they put her in her own private villa, the size of a two-bedroom house. It was painted soft Italian sun-bleached pink, and had its own garden and patio. We checked in for a five-week stay and put the unfinished villa fiasco behind us.

Forte Village turned out to be the base camp for every journalist, sports reporter, ITV crew member and high-profile British football manager and club owner present in Italy. Everyone knew Nigel and his close association with Aston Villa, and Michelle was a super-VIP, loved by everyone who met her. It was a very friendly crowd, and soon we were included in all of the events and get-togethers. One of the producers from ITV Sport had the great idea of filming Nigel entertaining the England team, serenading them with his violin. This would take place at their secret training camp, where they were stationed during the group stage of the tournament. Nigel insisted that I accompany him on guitar. They wanted us to do the performance for the next episode of the *Saint and Greavsie* show. In return for the performance they promised to pay for our entire stay at the hotel – and to sort us out with press and VIP accreditation for all the England matches. We would be going to every match, courtesy of ITV. Nobody but nobody was allowed into the England camp.

My live chops were not up to scratch. I hadn't been gigging since I'd left The Fall two years previously. The thought of playing with Nigel in front of the whole England team, live on TV, before millions of viewers, filled me with dread. The pressure – just the mere thought of doing it – gave me hot flames of palpitation and cold clammy sweats all at once. One of the big bosses at ITV came to get us in our room for a meeting about the performance, and saw where we were staying in the hotel. 'Is this your room?' he asked, horrified by our small stone cave. He marched us to reception and demanded we be rehoused in a VIP villa, right next door to Michelle's.

Now we too had a pink Mediterranean casita with our own private garden, situated in the large area of parkland. I locked myself in the villa all day, practising my guitar over and over again, until my arms and fingers throbbed with pain.

Over the previous months, I had been getting sharp pains in my left forearm and left hand. This happened when I played – and the throbbing continued long afterwards, sometimes becoming an unbearably sharp pain in my hand and fingers. At its worst it felt like I was being stabbed by ice picks. It hurt all day, on and off, and sometimes at night. Often I'd lie awake, unable to sleep from the pain. I knew something was very wrong. I assumed at first that I was practising too hard and my hand was stressed.

If only I had known about positive thinking. How music was a connection. A vibration.

If only I had known how to choose a better thought, how to turn around the scenario in my head and how to relax into the moment. With positive thinking and visualisation I could have created a successful scenario of the outcome. I could have given myself relief from these negative, uncomfortable thoughts. I wish I had understood that the differences in the musicianship of Nigel and myself were the very thing that would make our performance special and interesting, that our unique set of skills coming together would form something noteworthy in its own way. Sadly, I crumbled under a mountain of negative thought patterns and insecurities of my own making. I hobbled myself. Because of this, I was unable to enjoy the anticipation of the once-in-a-lifetime moment. Instead, I turned it into mental torture for myself.

The day of the performance soon arrived. Nigel had managed to persuade the powers-that-be to include Michelle in the party. It was very special for her, as she and Gary were kept apart for most of the World Cup. I think Nigel had to get special permission from Bobby Robson. We were taken by car to the compound. The entire team and all their crew were waiting for us in a room and greeted us warmly with clapping and cheers. My heart was beating so fast I could barely breathe, let alone take in being in the England team camp. Nigel, of course, was in his element.

The cameras were set up, and a link was established with ITV back in London. Nigel and I stood in front of the players and played two songs. One was something Nigel wrote called 'Melody in the Wind'. The other song was 'August', off my Adult Net album.

In the end, of course, I needn't have worried. The players loved it. Nigel, as always, was a consummate professional. He made it easy for me in the end. He's a world-class musician, who calibrates his performance to the circumstances in every nanosecond. Nothing throws him, and it was gracious of him to include me in the performance and nurture me through my insecurities.

After the performance I could breathe again. The England team had laid on a massive sit-down lunch for all of us. Michelle got to sit with Gary. Nigel and I were seated at a different table. I was seated next to Gazza, who was great company, cracking jokes continuously throughout lunch. When the waiter came to take drink orders, I ordered a vodka without thinking. I forgot the players weren't allowed alcohol. When my vodka arrived, Gazza eyed it like a dehydrated dog on a dirt road in India. I could see he was desperate for it, so I let him have some. He drank the small bottle straight, in one gulp. I ordered another. By the end of lunch we'd bonded. The whole team was in great spirits. I particularly liked John Barnes, who was a handsome beast, and as smooth as they come.

After the lunch my arm was aching badly and I was holding it and massaging it without even realising. One of the players noticed and asked what was wrong. I told him it hurt from playing, and he suggested I have a word with the England team doctor. I was introduced to the doctor, who began rubbing and manipulating my arm and fingers. 'Do you hear that clicking?' he asked, as he dug his fingers into the web of my hand.

'Yes,' I said. 'I've noticed that before.'

'You have a form of tendinitis,' he informed me. 'Carpal tunnel syndrome, which is a result of overuse.'

He gave me some treatment. And put my arm in a splint. I was told to rest it completely. No opening car doors, no lifting bags. Nothing. My first thought was, 'Good. Now I don't have to play any more.'

I should have paid attention to that thought. Why I was having it? What were my body and mind telling me? I was not listening to my gut instincts, and consequently my body was now physically manifesting what was going on in my subconscious mind.

The first England match was a few days later, on 11 June. It was England versus the Republic of Ireland. I can't begin to explain how excited we were. The build-up to this match was a long time coming. We were invited on to the press coach and set off for the stadium. Nine minutes in and Michelle, Nigel and I were all going bonkers as Gary scored the opening goal. At some point during the first half Gary sat down on the pitch and looked like he was in pain. Michelle gripped my hand. This wasn't normal. We hoped he was OK. He had recently suffered a nasty injury to, of all things, his big toe. The nail had been rancid and festering and was threatening to come off. A few minutes later he was down again. He looked to us like he was squatting on the ground, and was unable to get up. Play carried on, the other players running around him. Eventually he was taken off and a sub was brought on. We would have to wait until the end of the match to find out if he was OK.

It looked like Gary had scored the winning goal. Ireland had not scored, but played well. Then, in the seventy-third minute, Kevin Sheedy scored an equaliser and the match finished 1–1, a draw. We made our way down to the press room for the after-match conference. We couldn't wait to see the players and congratulate them. Gary was nowhere to be seen. We ran into Jim Rosenthal, who was presenting the TV coverage for ITV, and he told us Gary was poorly and had a bit of a 'tummy ache'. 'Thank God it wasn't the dreaded toe,' I thought.

The team then had a five-day break before their next match. They had to train almost every day. Sometimes we were invited to the training ground early in the morning to watch their preparation. One day, Bobby Robson gave them a day off and Gary was allowed to come to the hotel to spend it with Michelle. He brought John Barnes and Gazza along with him.

Nigel and I were very friendly with 'Deadly' Doug Ellis, the millionaire chairman of Aston Villa, and his German wife, Heidi. Doug, who Nigel called 'Deadly' to his face, had previously invited us on holiday to their home in Palma. We had forged a bond on that holiday and I was happy to see him at the World Cup. Also there were 'Big' Ron Atkinson and his wife, Maggie. He had managed both Aston Villa and Manchester United. He was a huge character. Everybody called him 'Big', never just 'Ron'. Although people were nasty about Deadly Doug, I found him grandfatherly and enjoyed his company. One of Deadly and Big's football cohorts was the chairman of Tranmere Rovers, who was also there and had moored his yacht off the beach at Forte Village. He invited all of us, players included, on to his yacht for a day of partying. Gary, Michelle, Nigel and I swam out to the yacht and climbed aboard. Gazza, John Barnes and some assorted football bigwigs were already there, getting stuck in. Michelle and I were the only women, apart from the most gorgeous Swedish waitress, who was part of the ship's crew. Gazza was already cosying up to the waitress. We spent the whole day in the searing Italian sunshine drinking endless bottles of champagne and browning our bodies. At some point in the afternoon, the man who owned the yacht fired up the on-deck barbecue, and we ate hamburgers and sausages.

Michelle, Gary and I decided to take a swim back to the hotel beach. When we got near the shore we started playing around in the waves and chatting. I asked Gary what had happened on the pitch during the Ireland match. Was he OK? Why did they substitute him? Gary then launched into a detailed explanation of what happened. It had nothing to do with his injured toe, which had by now lost its nail. The toenail had been saved by Gary, and given to Nigel. Who I imagined would take it home, to our house in Malvern, and deposit it in the 'scar-jar'. There it would commingle with the recently excised chunk of Nigel's neck. On full view, sitting in pride of place on our mantelpiece in the music room.

Standing in the lapping emerald water, on the shores of Forte Village beach with a completely straight face, Gary imparted to us what had happened during the match.

He had indeed had a 'tummy ache'. He told us, before the match he had a 'turtle head on deck'. His guts were groaning, and he felt 'wind' building up in his intestines. He decided to fart, to try to relieve some of the pressure. It was worse than he thought. When he farted, he followed through, and a huge pile of semi-liquid diarrhoea squelched into his shorts. He didn't know what to do. Poo was dripping down his legs, like hot mud. So he sat on the ground, and dragged his ass along the pitch, like a dog, trying to wipe himself.

This did little good as his shorts were fully loaded. They were filled to the brim with messy cack. He continued to scoot along the ground, leaving a trail of poo in his wake. When that technique failed to empty his shorts, he had no choice but to sit down on the pitch, and use his hands, like a shovel, to 'scoop the poop' out of the leg-holes of his shorts, wiping the excess excrement on the grass. The other players were gagging at the stench, and ran around him, avoiding the stinking-shit-slicked part of the pitch for fear of slipping in it. Bobby Robson decided to take Gary out of his misery, and substituted him, allowing him to get to the privacy of a toilet.

As Gary told us the story we were retching with laughter. We were doubled over and gasping for air between heaves. We laughed so hard, we peed in the sea. In all my life, this was the funniest story I'd ever heard. It was so excruciatingly embarrassing and everyone's nightmare. To his credit, Gary totally saw the humour in it. Gary's father taped every match on video cassette. When we got back to England after the World Cup, we located the 'poo tape' and watched it together again and again. Gary did a running commentary for us. We howled with laughter.

The England team were on fire during Italia '90. They continued to play well and progressed through to the semi-finals. The semi-final was between England and their old rivals West Germany. The stakes had never been so high. All along the way, Nigel and I had been carrying our special crystals with us into the grounds for luck. We had four different crystals, of varying sizes. As we entered the stadium in Turin, we were searched and they took our crystals off us; they were worried we might use them as weapons. The match was riveting and extraordinary. Both teams played their hearts out and the final score at the end of 90 minutes was 1–1. At one point Gazza had been booked and started sobbing, as he knew he was out of any final. Gary looked after him, mouthing to Bobby Robson that he was not all right, so to watch him. Then there was extra time, which went to a penalty shootout. When it was Gary's turn to take the penalty I thought I was going to throw up. Gary scored, but, of course, sadly Stuart 'Psycho' Pearce's penalty was saved by the German goalkeeper. All of us were shocked by the defeat in the final moments. The bottom seemed to drop out of the earth. Everybody's World Cup dream had ended. We were crushed. The players' hearts were broken. Michelle, Nigel and I sat hunched in our seats in the stadium, tears rolling down our faces. Steve Cram wept along with us, united in misery. We were so depressed, Nigel refused to go to Bari for the third-place play-offs between England and Italy. 'What's the point?' he said. We took a plane home the next day and headed to Malvern to lick our wounds and recover our addled wits.

DONOVAN AND THE BEGINNING OF THE END

Once the World Cup was over, and we were back in the UK, it was time to come to terms with what was going on in my career. The Adult Net album and all of the singles, though well received, had failed to make a significant mark commercially. It was time for me to galvanise myself and start to think about how to move forward. I desperately needed new material. Phonogram/Fontana were keen to hear new songs and ideas. I was having complete writer's block, plus my arm was in agony due to the tendinitis – I could barely grip my guitar by this point.

Stephen Duffy came to the rescue. He suggested that I do a cover version of something I loved. Immediately I thought of doing a Donovan song. Since high school in Chicago, where I had listened to *Sunshine Superman* obsessively, Donovan's music had always resonated with me. I turned to it time and time again over the years. It was simple, folky and psychedelic. Something about it calmed me. I never tired of it. I began re-listening to all my old Donovan records and, bingo, a song popped out at me. 'Hurdy Gurdy Man' seemed to me like the perfect Adult Net cover, much like 'Incense and Peppermints' had been. It had the same vibe.

Stephen set about creating a backing track for it. He decided to use looped drums for the rhythm section. At that time looped drums were all the rage, and it took the song forward and made it even cooler. There is a cracking guitar solo on 'Hurdy Gurdy Man', which Nigel suggested he'd play electric violin on. Electric violin usually makes me cringe, but I figured with distortion pedals and effects, if we treated it like a guitar, we could make it sound fabulous. Nigel was such a big star at that point that I assumed having him on my record might bring The Adult Net to the attention of a wider audience. I also assumed the record company would be thrilled to have the number-one classical artist playing on my track. I figured this would be a PR coup.

John Leckie seemed like the logical producer for the project, plus I adored being around his soothing energy. We got John to come up to Malvern and hang out, so we could brainstorm and plan. Stephen was taking me in a slightly new musical direction. What we were creating felt fresh. It was important that I now moved on, grew musically from what I had been doing with The Fall and the early Adult Net. The Adult Net had been all about very pure poppy tunes with a psychedelic feel. That sound needed to be toughened up a little and given an edge. I was beginning to get excited about making music again. I felt hope about the future, instead of constant anxiety.

One day while looking through *Vogue* magazine I came across an article about Valentino. In the article he was surrounded by his dogs. They were the same dogs I had seen a gentleman walking with in Kensington, on my first trip to London, with Mom and Marvin in 1981. I ran to Nigel, magazine flapping in my hand. 'Look, Nigel, look. These are the dogs I love!' I shrieked.

'They're pugs, Brixie.'

'I love them, I love them, I love them,' I ranted.

We did a little research, and decided to get a pug. We drove down to Southampton to meet Nigel and Terry of Tidemill Pugs. A new litter had been born a few weeks earlier. We spent time with the adult pugs – they ran riot in the house. They were hilarious. One kept jumping on the sofa and on to the coffee table to get to a bowl of cheese balls. He snatched the cheese balls at lightning speed, jumped down from the coffee table and faced the wall, while crunching greedily and snorting like a pig. I fell in love. Nigel insisted we get a male pug. We were taken to see the litter and I melted. I'd never in my life seen anything as cute as a baby pug. We picked out our boy. And over the next six weeks visited him once.

Nigel thought of the name 'Satchmo' for him, after Louis Armstrong. We brought Satchmo home to Malvern, and I loved him so much I wanted to sleep with him in his dog bed at night. Nigel refused to let him sleep in our bedroom, never mind our bed.

I went into Rak Studios with Stephen and John Leckie to record 'Hurdy Gurdy Man' and 'We Can Change the World'. During the recording we were joined by a musician named Jonathan Male. He was in a band called Soul Family Sensation and later joined Republica. We called Jonathan 'The Vibe'. Although Jonathan didn't play on the tracks, we loved having him in the studio to create and maintain a vibe. He was the vibe master.

Everything was going well, and we were thrilled with the way 'Hurdy Gurdy Man' was sounding.

But when it came time for Nigel to do his electric violin solo, we hit a snag. Nigel hated the drum loops. He said he wanted to play to live drumming. He insisted we get a drummer in to replace the loops. We brought in Michael Giri, who was the drummer in The Lilac Time. I was ecstatic to have Michael in the studio. Michael was nicknamed 'Spacer' by Nigel and Stephen because he was always spaced-out and super-chilled. He also was obsessed with outer space and aliens, different worlds and dimensions.

What no one knew was that I was having a platonic love affair with Spacer. Spacer and I had a deep soul connection. When we first met, I heard a celestial orchestra. Unbeknownst to every-body, and especially to Nigel, we had been seeing each other every snatched moment we could get. We spent days lying in the grass at Hyde Park, holding hands and making daisy-chain collars for Satchmo. We walked the streets of Notting Hill, arms entwined. We never had sex. I was too scared of what Nigel would do if he found out. Plus, our relationship actually transcended sex. It was uncomplicated. It was so pure. It felt to me very different from what I had with Nigel. It was easy and blissful to be with Spacer. We didn't even need to talk. We communicated energetically. It was a beautiful love and it helped me to see a perspective on love I had previously not experienced.

Nigel played his violin all the way through the track. It added great atmosphere and a different texture to anything I'd ever done before. His solo was sublime. It was mind-bendingly psychedelic. It was (and remains) simply the best electric violin solo I had ever heard. It gave me chills, and blew us away.

Donovan asked to meet us and we arranged a dinner at 192 in Notting Hill. Stephen, Jonathan, Nigel, and a great friend and musician, Nick Laird-Clowes (from the band The Dream Academy, who was also at the dinner), were all nervous to meet Donovan. Nick Laird-Clowes was physically vibrating with delicious anticipation. Then the man of the hour walked in – Donovan, trailing in the wake of Linda Lawrence, his wife and muse. Of course, I instantly loved them both. How could I not? They were fascinating and hilarious and weird – spiritual, warm and wise. Donovan wore a vintage silk kimono over his shirt and trousers. We got to ask them every question we had ever wondered about to do with his music and the meanings of his songs. He was more than happy to answer us in depth, dropping names everywhere, of the great, the good and the superstars of music. We asked him about the now infamous and legendary trip he took with the Beatles, Mia Farrow and some of the Beach Boys to Rishikesh in India to meet the Maharishi Mahesh Yogi, and learn about transcendental meditation. During his three-month stay in Rishikesh, Donovan, inspired by the sounds he heard, wrote 'Hurdy Gurdy Man'. Linda told us in depth about her relationship with Brian Jones of the Rolling Stones. He had always been a fascination for me. He was wild and beautiful, and his death was such a mystery. Linda and Brian Jones had a son, named Julian. Linda told me Brian Jones had a few sons, all named Julian.

We became very close to Don and Linda. I grew to think of Linda as my rock and roll mom.

Shortly after recording 'Hurdy Gurdy Man', Nigel was asked to appear on *The Late Late Show* hosted by Gay Byrne, in Ireland. Nigel thought it would be a great place to debut the song, and invited Don and me to join him, and perform 'Hurdy Gurdy Man' live. I wasn't as fearful about this performance as I was when I played with Nigel for the England team at the World Cup. This time, Don would be singing with us, and we would have a backing band. It was less scary than doing it unplugged, acoustically. I didn't feel so exposed. Plus tendinitis meant I couldn't physically play guitar without agonising pain, which took some of the pressure off my nerves. This way, I could just sing, relying on Don, Nigel and the band to get the music right.

I couldn't believe this was really happening. I would be playing live on TV, duetting with Donovan and playing with Nigel. This was a big deal. Nigel and I flew to Dublin together. Donovan and Linda lived in Dublin, so we met up with him in the studios of RTE. Together the three of us rehearsed with the Dublin Blues Band, who were our backing band on the day. The show was filmed in Ireland but broadcast internationally. It had a huge audience.

Back in Malvern, Nigel and I continued hanging out with Stephen and Kate. I rode Lucky every day, and Satchmo was always at my side. Everything seemed normal on the surface, but strains were beginning to appear in mine and Nigel's relationship. Nigel was by now calling all the major shots in our life. The power base had well and truly shifted. His career trumped mine. I sucked it up and clung on to him. He had the money and the fame.

Even though his neck was still healing (it had taken longer than expected), he was doing sporadic gigs and loads of appearances. As his career was soaring, I became more diminished as a person. Women pushed me out of the way to get to Nigel in the supermarket. I felt invisible.

John Leckie had finished mixing 'Hurdy Gurdy Man'. He sent it over for us to hear. To me it sounded great. I loved it. Nigel had an issue with the sound and volume level of his violin. He was unhappy and demanded mix approval.

'I can't give you mix approval,' I said, trying to stick up for myself. 'That's for Phonogram to decide. They're the record company.'

A massive argument ensued. Nigel forbade me to use his violins on the track unless Phonogram gave him final mix approval. He said he was going to get his lawyers to sort out a contract with Phonogram, and demanded that, if they wanted him on the single, they would have to agree to his terms. I was too weak to fight him. I thought so little of myself at that point, I believed Nigel knew best. And part of me understood why he wanted approval – music was his entire life. I had allowed my personal relationship and my music to become irrevocably mixed up again. Hadn't I learned anything from my dealings with Mark E. Smith?

A day or so later the phone rang. It was the head of A&R for Phonogram. 'Brix,' he said, 'this is your record, not your boy-friend's. We signed you as an artist, not him. We don't care about Nigel Kennedy. We will not give in to his demands and, frankly, we don't want to deal with this any more. Your album and singles have not done as well as we hoped, and now with this extra aggra-vation it's not worth it for us. I'm sorry, but we are dropping you.' I put down the phone and cried. At the time, I blamed Nigel's hard line with the record company for getting dropped. Now, I suspect they used him as a convenient excuse to cut their losses.

IDENTITY CRISIS

I now had no job, no purpose, no band, no record deal, no inspiration, and no hope. My self-esteem was flat-lining.

In Malvern, I lay in bed all day, only getting up to let Satchmo out to pee. I was unable to go out, or motivate myself to do anything. I struggled to eat. I took pills every night to sleep. Sleeping was the worst. My mind churned anxious fragments of my life over and over. Each time I replayed the record company's words in my head – 'we're dropping you' – my emotions plummeted ever further downward, toward the basement of emotional hell.

Nigel was busy being Nigel. He bounced between Malvern, London and various concert dates. He was spending more time away from me. I was not great company. Mostly, I was on my own, with Satchmo. I hired a groom to look after Lucky. I couldn't even get it together to go down the hill to her stable.

One night, when Nigel was back in Malvern, we decided to go out to one of our favourite local restaurants for dinner. Planters was a Sri Lankan restaurant owned by a lovely husband and wife team. The food was delicious. The speciality of the house, cashew curry, was my favourite. Again, though, going out to a restaurant with Nigel was like being in a fishbowl. Everybody would stare at us and whisper as we walked through the room. It was impossible to be anonymous and relaxed. Even though he was the famous one, I felt like I was being judged. Paparazzi were now hiding in the bushes in both London and Malvern. We were forced to erect a nine-foot wooden fence and gate around Moon Sun house to protect our privacy. To make matters worse, Nigel was paranoid that the photographers might catch me off guard. His worst fear was that they would take a picture of me sunbathing topless (something I never did). He told me if they caught me topless, he would leave me. Now I was paranoid about walking outside my front door, paranoid I'd somehow be photographed, unknowingly, in a compromising situation, which made me paranoid I'd lose my only remaining lifeline.

During the meal that night Nigel informed me that he was going to tour Australia again. We had gone together to Australia before, and on our previous trip had caused havoc there. Well, Nigel had caused havoc, and I was a guilty by association. On arriving in Melbourne we had been taken to a fancy hotel, the venue for Nigel to play to assorted record company executives and local bigwigs. There was a random sculpture on a table in one of the reception rooms of the hotel. It was a figurine of some sort. As we passed the table, Nigel stopped to pick up the sculpture. He looked at it for a moment and then declared it too ugly to exist (or some words to that effect). Staring at everyone in the room, he let it slip from his grasp . . . It crashed to the ground and smashed into hundreds of pieces. 'That's better,' he said, to a room full of horrified people. In fact, we were shocked to learn that it was some major piece of art made by a beloved Aussie artist, and Nigel was billed £13,000 for damages. It was also a PR disaster for him. John Stanley had to work overtime to keep it from being plastered over the newspapers.

But now, as I had nothing else going on in my life and nothing particular to look forward to, going to Australia would be a welcome diversion. 'When do we leave?' I asked.

It was then Nigel informed me that 'we' would not be going. Only he was. Up until then, wherever he went, I went too. He made up some excuses about needing space, but by then I could not hear him. My heart was pounding so loudly and so fast it drowned out his words. All at once the room began to spin. My hands were slick with sweat. My vision became fragmented. A sea of black spots, dancing before my eyes, disconnected me from reality. The spots filled my vision. Heat flooded my body, from my feet to my face. The room grew dark. Then I began to feel my consciousness slip away. The curtains were closing. I couldn't breathe. I pushed myself up from the table, desperate for air. I didn't know what was wrong. All I could think about was getting outside and getting air. I headed for the restaurant door.

The next thing I remember was lying on the pavement. People swam in and out of my vision. Nigel crouched over me. The husband and wife, owners of the restaurant, were patting me on my back. They pulled me up to sit on the kerb. Someone gave me a sip of water.

'What happened?' I asked.

'You fainted, Brixie,' Nigel said.

I tried to rationalise it away. Perhaps the cashew curry was too hot? I hoped it would never happen again. Unfortunately it did.

A few weeks later we were in a Cajun restaurant in Hampstead. We were having an unpleasant conversation about our relationship. I could feel Nigel disconnecting himself from me ever so slowly, untying the knots that bound us together. At some point during the conversation my vision began to fragment. The disorienting spots danced before my eyes and my heart began to pound again. This time it didn't catch me by surprise; I knew the feeling. 'I'm going to faint,' I said. Nigel had me bend over, put my head between my legs and breathe deeply. It seemed to help a bit, but this time I thought I might throw up. 'Please take me home,' I asked. Holding me round the waist, Nigel helped me stagger to the door.

I went to see a doctor, who informed me that I was experiencing severe panic and anxiety attacks, and that I was clinically depressed. She recommended I go back on Prozac, which I had stopped taking soon after I met Nigel. I was relieved that my problems were mental and not physical. Still, I needed to address what was causing them.

I went to see my shrink, Eva Loewe. She diagnosed me as having a classic case of identity crisis. I no longer knew who I was or what my purpose in life was. Everything I had used to define myself – my music, my marriage, my relationships, my record deal – was now gone, or in flux. It was vital for me to figure out who I was. I needed to stop defining myself by my associations and relationships with other people. I needed to find a mechanism to learn how to resolve my own problems, to cope with life's dualities.

Eva begged me to treat the identity crisis with cognitive therapy and to avoid taking antidepressants at all costs. I was not yet ready to face the pain. I had a long way to go before I could do that. I chose to take antidepressants. It was the easy route. It gave me superficial relief. Almost instantly. Antidepressants buffered me against the harsh realities. They masked the symptoms. They prevented me from getting to the kernel of the pain and therefore finding the cure. In an impervious, medicated membrane I trundled along, my life unravelling, continuing its trajectory downwards.

The signs had been there for a long time – for ever, in fact. I had chosen to ignore them. I pushed them away and buried them. My gut instinct and my spirit guides (who I would discover later) had been trying to tell me, to show me, to warn me. When I failed to heed those warnings my body became a physical manifestation of the emotional pain that I could no longer deny. The tendinitis, the fainting, the depression were all clear signs I had ignored at my peril. Until I was felled.

MOUSE-HOLE

Everybody has a bucket list of some sort, and so did I. Up to that point in my life I had been to every single Disneyland on the planet except one. The big one. Disney World, Florida. Nigel decided to make my dream come true. He hoped it would cheer me up, and snap me out of my depression. I set about planning our dream holiday. It was actually due to be a working holiday for Nigel. He was writing a book, dictating his life story over the phone to someone in England. These interview sessions could be done anywhere. All that was needed was a phone. Nigel decided that in the morning he could spend several hours on the phone, and one or two hours practising violin, while I toured the theme park on my own. Then we would meet up for lunch, play golf all afternoon (which is what he loved to do) and have dinner in the park in the evening. It sounded perfect to me.

We decided to stay in the Disney resort village. This was a sub-urban-like community on Disney property, made up of A-frame houses big enough for a family of six. It was built around a man-made lake, home to ducks. We had this massive house and garden, stocked with all things Mickey Mouse: Mickey soap, Mickey sheets, Mickey shampoo . . . even a Mickey can opener. Everything was themed. We also had our own little electric golf cart, which, to charge up, we plugged into the socket outside the house.

Having been to Disneyland LA hundreds of times, I knew the lay of the land, as it were. The Florida park was much bigger. It had new and different theme parks attached to it besides the Magic Kingdom. I had bought every insider's guidebook and planned out my visit meticulously. I knew all the attractions I wanted to see, and every restaurant I wanted to eat in.

I was grateful to Nigel. We had flown over business class and no expense was spared. As an extra surprise, Nigel decided to fly out my best friend Lisa from New York. He thought it would cheer me up to have my girlfriend there, and Lisa and I could tour the theme parks together in the mornings, while he wrote and practised. For the first four days Nigel and I would be on our own, and then Lisa would join us.

Because there were so many rules at Disney World, it was natural for Nigel and me to want to break them. The first rule we broke was taking the electric golf cart off Disney property. We wanted groceries, fancied having a barbecue, and needed to stock up. Instead of getting a taxi, or one of the plethora of shuttle buses available, we drove our golf cart to the supermarket. At 10 mph we trundled down the wide, traffic-clogged city streets of Orlando. People honked and jeered and gave us the finger as we made our way painstakingly slowly to the market, holding up queues of rush-hour traffic. We bought so much food we couldn't fit it into the golf cart, so we tied sirloin steaks to the roof of the cart, Fred Flintstone-style. We made it back to the resort safely, but must have been spotted. Upon entering the house we received a phone call from the park, informing us we had broken the rules. They threatened to take our golf cart away. We pleaded ignorance. We claimed we thought Disney owned the whole town. It was, after all, called Disney World.

The next morning, Nigel woke up early to practise and write. I hit the park hard, and decided to start with the Epcot Center. I had read so much about it over the years and remembered watching *The Wonderful World of Disney* on TV as a child. I remember seeing Walt himself unveil the plans for the Experimental Prototype Community of Tomorrow – Epcot.

Epcot was a mini-world. It's an amalgamation of two different realms. The premise of the park is to 'celebrate the human spirit'. Future World celebrates technological innovations, while World Showcase is all about different cultures around the world. It boasts eleven sponsored pavilions from multiple countries. Japan, Morocco, Canada, the USA, France, Germany, China, Norway, the United Kingdom and, my favourite, Mexico . . . each pavilion is like a walk-in installation in which you experience the unique culture and flavours of a particular country. Some countries had rides to go along with the restaurants. I had read that the Mexican pavilion had the most romantic restaurant at Epcot. Five stars for romantic ambience. I decided to check it out.

It was pure Disney. I stepped off the sun-soaked, baking hot Florida pavement into Guadalajara at night. It was utterly romantic. A mariachi band in full swing played from the second-floor balcony of an 'artistically aged' casita. Diners ate food under fake starlight and plastic trees. The branches were adorned with colourful lanterns, which fluttered delightfully in the mechanically contrived breeze. I could smell the wafting synthetic scent of night-blooming orange blossoms, commingling with tacos. I was determined to try to reignite the romance in mine and Nigel's life so I booked a table for two for that evening. I was so excited to show Nigel 'Mexico', I took him by the hand and led him through Epcot to the pavilion. I made him close his eyes and open them when we were inside the restaurant, to heighten his experience of stepping from daylight into night. It was like walking on to a movie set, an immersive, romantic fairytale.

The evening started well enough. Nigel seemed to like the restaurant. We made small talk. We talked about his book and golf. I gushed about what a great time I was having, and the wonderful things I saw at Epcot. We ordered dinner. Two courses each. Guacamole and tortilla chips and quesadillas to share, and then two large Mexican tasting plates each, with tacos, burritos and chile rellenos.

One of the side effects of Prozac is the loss of appetite. As the Prozac kicked into my system, my appetite diminished. Ordinarily this would have been a great thing. I've always struggled with my weight and felt fat most of my life, even though I wasn't. This night, however, my loss of appetite was my undoing. I had forgotten all about American-size portions. They are huge. One starter is usually enough for a whole meal. I ate as much as I could of the starter. When the main course arrived I was already uncomfortably full. I picked around my plate. I tasted everything and put my fork down. I watched Nigel eating his dinner. He had a particular quirk when he ate. He revolved his plate in a circle with his hands, turning it round and round, inch by inch, to line up particular food on the dish in front of him. He always did this. It was marginally irritating, but tolerable.

The waiter approached our table dressed in Mexican attire and a sombrero. America is a country that prides itself on its service industry. The waiters and waitresses are always polite and attentive. When you are finished eating, they remove the plate quickly. It's normal. It's considered bad service to leave finished plates of food on the table. 'Are you finished, señorita?' he asked me. 'Yes,' I said. 'It was delicious, thank you.' With that the waiter whisked away my plate, doing his job.

Nigel looked up from his plate. It still had a few bites of food on it. He stared at me. His mouth was tight and pinched.

'What's the matter, Nigel?' I asked, in a small babyish voice.

He didn't say anything, but I knew that our romantic evening was ruined for him. I wasn't thinking of Nigel. I should have put the evening first. I had to fix it.

'I'm so sorry,' I said. 'What can I do to make it up to you? I'll do anything. It was because of the Prozac. I wasn't hungry. My appetite . . . it's . . . gone. Please understand, please understand.'

Silence (the sound of recorded crickets).

Back at the Disney World house we went to sleep. Nigel barely spoke to me. As we lay in the bed, our backs turned to each other, facing opposite walls, I felt a new emotion growing in my belly.

The emotion was anger. Anger was actually a positive emotion, because it was the catalyst for self-preservation. My anger was the first sign of a call to arms for myself. For the first time, as I lay there, unable to sleep, I allowed myself to imagine my life without Nigel. The next morning he left the house early, to get in a quick round of golf, before it got too hot. I was still shaky, the spectre of last night's argument hanging over me.

He returned a couple of hours later to dictate his book over the phone, so I decided to head out to the Magic Kingdom park. There was a new land that I had never seen before. It was called Mickey's Birthday Land, and featured a 'backstage area' where you could wait in a queue to meet Mickey. 'What the hell?' I thought. I wanted to see every nook and cranny of this place. As I entered Mickey's Birthday Land I saw that a long queue had already formed. I was actually not that bothered about meeting Mickey. I just wanted to know what happened backstage, what it looked like. Basically, I was ticking a box. This was one attraction I'd never seen. I was determined to see everything.

Finally, it was time to go in. I was the last of the line of twelve in my group to enter. We entered a fake backstage area, which looked like a dressing room in a theatre. Mickey Mouse, ebullient as ever, stood by the mirror and greeted and hugged his new group of visitors. He signed autographs and mimed kisses. He never spoke, of course. Hand gestures and mime were his only form of communication. I hung back, taking in the scene, trying to stay invisible.

After all the families in my group were done meeting Mickey, I tried to sneak out discreetly. Suddenly, I felt a hand on my shoulder. I turned around to find Mickey looking at me with massive eyes. He was opening up his arms as if saying, 'What are you doing here?' A surge of embarrassment went through my body. Mickey was singling me out.

'Oh, Mickey,' I said. 'I've never been to Mickey's Birthday Land before, and I just wanted to come and see what it was all about. It's

been a pleasure to meet you . . . Thanks for having me . . . Bye,' I
stammered, trying to escape.

Mickey threw his arms around me and pulled me back into the
fake dressing room. He looked at me and made moony eyes at me.
'Is Mickey flirting with me?' I thought to myself. Or was he just
doing his job, indentifying me as a lonely woman? Mickey then
covered his mouth with both hands and blew kisses at me. He was
flirting with me! Or was he? 'What the *hell* is going on?' I thought
to myself.

Mickey then gestured that he would give me his autograph.

'No, thank you,' I said. 'I just wanted to meet you, and see what
backstage looked like.' Mickey reached for a brochure – it was
a timetable of shows. He grabbed his pen and scribbled, 'Have
you seen my show?' 'No, I haven't,' I replied. He scribbled, 'Please
come!' He continued scribbling: 'I'm doing a few shows tomorrow.
Here they are.' He then circled the shows and times he was performing, and, I swear, begged me to come. He then wrapped his
arms around me and hugged me. The hug was a little too tight and
urgent, or so it seemed. 'What the fuck is happening?' I thought
to myself. I must be losing my mind. Perhaps the fight with Nigel
had made me feel starved of affection? 'I'm reading way too much
into this. I must be so lonely,' I reasoned. Even so, as I finally left
the backstage area, delusional or not, the thought and feeling of
Mickey flirting with me had lifted my spirits.

The next day my friend Lisa arrived from New York. She
brought her sunny disposition and a bag of pot. I was grateful to
have Lisa with us. She could act as a buffer between Nigel and me.
Lisa and I walked to the Magic Kingdom the next morning. I told
her about the bizarre incident with Mickey. I had the programme
of shows that Mickey had given me in my bag. I showed Lisa.
'We have to go!' she said. 'Something's going to happen, I know
it.' We checked the times of the show and there was one at noon.
That would give us enough time to see the show then get back in

the afternoon to play golf with Nigel, who'd booked a particular tee-off time for which we daren't be late. We raced to Mickey's Birthday Land, where the theatre was located, and prepared to wait in line.

As the doors opened, Lisa let go of my hand and determinedly wove her way to the front of the queue and entered the theatre. Using her well-honed, New York, cut-the-line-to-get-into-club skills, she rushed inside and nabbed us two seats, front row centre. We then watched a show of Disney characters singing and dancing to Disney classic songs. Mickey made a brief appearance here and there. If Mickey noticed me in the audience, he didn't show it.

I figured, maybe today it was a different Mickey for some reason. There must be more than one Mickey Mouse at Disney World. Maybe yesterday's Mickey was poorly or twisted his ankle, and this one was a replacement Mickey? Maybe it had all been my imagination, after all. Whatever the case, I have to admit to feeling a little bit disappointed. I had been feeling so shit about myself that even a brief, imagined flirtation with Mickey Mouse had made me feel special.

As the performance ended and the cast of characters were taking their curtain call, Mickey clocked me in the audience. Walking to the front of the stage, he pointed to me. He blew me a kiss and covered his beating heart (presumably pounding with love) with his hands. He gesticulated for me to sit in my seat and remain there. I assumed he meant for me to wait for him. I could feel my grip on reality starting to slip. The entire audience turned to stare at me. 'Who is this woman?' I heard five hundred people think at once.

The lights went down, and the theatre emptied. Lisa turned to me, grabbed my arm and said, 'Oh my god, Brixton, you are going to fuck Mickey!'

I thought about it for a second. I rotated in my seat to look Lisa in the eyes. 'I would fuck Mickey,' I said. 'But only if he keeps his

head on. I don't want to know what's under that suit . . . I'll do it,'
I said, 'only if he unzips his pants, sticks his dick out, and keeps
his head on.'

Before we had time to discuss the matter further, Mickey
appeared with a flourish from between the parted, velvet stage curtains. One of his arms was hiding something behind his back. He
rushed forward to the front of the stage where we were sitting and
thrust a stuffed toy into my hands. It was a baby Mickey. Pinned
to its chest was a handwritten note.

Go next door to the white tent, and wait . . .
Just wait for me.
Love, Mickey.

'OK,' I said. 'I'll go next door and wait for you.'
With that he turned and left the stage. I was getting nervous.
What had I gotten myself into? Why was I even considering having sex with Mickey Mouse? It dawned on me that I had probably
read way too much into this and that Mickey had seen my pain
and was doing nothing more than making it his mission to cheer
me up. The whole scenario was so bizarre I decided to let it just
play out. At least the episode had done one thing. It had made
me forget about Nigel and my own mounting misery. Now I was
caught up in a new drama and, as odd as it may sound, it felt good
to take the focus off my old problems.

Lisa and I went next door. There was a permanent white tent
next to the theatre. It was huge like a circus tent and had souvenir
shops and drink kiosks as well as benches to sit on and rest. We sat
down on a tropically themed sofa next to a fake palm tree.

'What do you think is going to happen, Lisa?' I asked.

'Brixton, this is the most bizarre and hilarious thing ever!'

'Why do you think Mickey likes me?' I asked.

'It's because you are like a human cartoon character,' she said.

'What do you mean, Lisa?'

'Your personality, it's larger than life. You're special, and Mickey can see it.'

We sat there for what seemed like twenty minutes. With every minute, I felt more awkward and wondered what the hell was going to happen. I considered leaving and standing Mickey up. I had promised to wait, though, and I was so curious as to the outcome. I clutched my baby Mickey toy and waited.

Finally, a woman walked over to us and introduced herself as Mickey's assistant. She apologised profusely for Mickey's absence. She explained that Mickey had gotten delayed. He was now between shows in the canteen, cramming down his lunch before the next show. He was apparently eating a 'cheese pizza'. She said Mickey would like to call me and take me out in the real world. I wondered if the date would be sans suit. If so I'd freak. Not in a good way. She then took out a 'Mickey' notepad from her bag and tore off two sheets of paper. She used a Mickey pen and scribbled down my phone number on one and contact details for Mickey on the other. I asked her to thank Mickey and said goodbye.

Lisa and I left, and headed back to the Disney house. We rushed to make it on time for Nigel's tee-off, at the golf course. Waiting for Mickey had put us under time pressure. I was relieved that nothing had happened with Mickey, but I was also felt a little deflated.

When we got back to the house to meet Nigel, I found him fed up and in a fractious mood. He had lost an earring and had been looking for it all morning. He decided he now didn't fancy playing golf. He asked me instead to go out and buy him a new earring. I wanted to tell him about Mickey (obviously not the whole story, but the family version).

'I'm sick of Mickey,' he said, and grabbed the toy from my hands. He kicked it across the room and stamped on it. I rescued my toy and seethed inside. I was rapidly going off Nigel.

Lisa and I boarded the shuttle bus to take us to the village shopping centre. I had called the concierge, and discovered that that was where the jewellery shop was located. All the way over there, we talked about how weird the whole incident with Mickey was. When we got to the shopping centre, the first thing we saw was a restaurant called Chef Mickey's. Standing outside the restaurant was Chef Mickey himself. This time Mickey Mouse was dressed in chef's whites and an apron. 'There is no way this Mickey could be the same Mickey,' I thought. No sooner had we got off the bus, it seemed Chef Mickey clocked me. He ran over to us and threw his arms around me. I was flabbergasted. 'Why is this happening to me? What the hell is going on?'

'What the fuck, Brixton?' Lisa said. 'It can't be the same Mickey! How does it know you?'

We extricated ourselves from Chef Mickey, located the jewellery store and went inside. I found a replacement earring for Nigel. Unable to help myself, I leaned over the counter to the sales assistant and whispered, 'Do you know who is in that Mickey suit out there?'

'Yes,' the sales assistant said. 'It's a black woman.'

She went on to explain that there were 250 Mickey Mouses at Disney World, and 248 of them were women.

Lisa and I then boarded the bus back to the house. While on the bus I had an idea. From my bag, I took out the original show schedule that Mickey had written on. Then I took out the note that was pinned to baby Mickey, and the note with Mickey's number on it, written down by his female assistant. I compared them all. They were all written in the same handwriting.

Our vacation ended, and it was time to go back home to England. By the time we left Disney World, my feelings towards Nigel had soured. At last, I began to imagine a different life. Daydreams and fantasies were making their way into my thoughts. I wasn't completely conscious yet, but I was awakening, for sure. The end came very rapidly. The writing was on the wall.

I spent a month on my own in Malvern with Satchmo and Lucky, while Nigel toured Australia. Our phone calls were fraught with tension. I began to go to spiritual meetings every day I could and seek the guidance of psychics and healers, as well as talking to Eva on the phone at every opportunity. I wanted someone to tell me what to do. I wanted someone to make the decision for me.

In reality, I knew what to do. I felt what was right. The thoughts I had about my life without Nigel felt better than the ones I had if I stayed with him.

During the time that Nigel was in Australia, I received some bad news, which threw me. In fact, I felt as if I were being thrown under a bus. My accountant from Manchester, Joe Cohen, had rung me and asked me where my money was.

'What do you mean?' I said. 'It's in the bank. I should still have some money left from my Adult Net publishing and record deals.'

Although I had spent quite a lot of money while I was with Nigel, I still had my life savings put away. I hadn't touched them, or looked at them. They were a safety net.

'It's all gone,' the accountant said.

'All of it?' I asked, stunned.

'All of it.'

'Where did it go, Joe?' I asked.

'Well, I've been on the phone to the bank and managed to find out that it was withdrawn by someone who had access to your account.'

I freaked out. The money had gone, but I hadn't spent it.

We did eventually track it down, and some of my savings were returned, but by then my life was unravelling at an alarming pace. It was all I could do to keep my head above water. A week or so after the money incident, a car and driver arrived at Moon Sun house in the morning to collect me and drive me to Heathrow to meet Nigel. He was on his way back from Australia. Our tense, transcontinental phone calls had left me anxious. Still, I hoped that the time apart had somehow healed us. I brought Satchmo with me for the journey. He was a sweet dog and gave me comfort.

Satchmo and I waited for Nigel in the arrivals terminal. Out of the blue a man came up and wanted to pet my dog. To my surprise, it was Tom Jones. He chatted to me and it took my mind off my momentary nervousness. Finally, Nigel arrived. He seemed happy to see us. I was eager to get back to Malvern to spend some time together. I was really going to try harder with Nigel, I told myself.

Nigel wasn't ready to go back to Malvern yet. He had other ideas. He decided we needed to go to Fortnum & Mason's to pick up a huge hamper for his A&R man, who had been ill with tuberculosis.

On the way back from the A&R man's house Nigel and I began to snap at each other. The mounting months of tension could no longer be held back. We had an altercation. We were both to blame, but I came off worse. It was over. I knew it. We both knew it.

PART THREE
THE RISE

Killing it with Brix and the Extricated

WAKING UP IN THE SUN

The heat was making me feel sensual.

The heat from the sand, the temperature of the air, my pulse, my desires. The sand formed a hot seal against my stomach. I ground my pelvis into the sand.

It felt good to be alive. I turned my head to the side, and lay it against my towel. The rhythm of the ocean took my body out of motion. I closed my eyes. How lucky I felt, to be here. I watched a pair of long, slim, tan muscular legs pass two feet from my face. The striding movement stirred the air, and a waft of coconut oil and Tahitian tiaré flowers momentarily intoxicated me. Without thinking, I dug my palms into the sand and scooped up a handful. I watched the grains slowly slip through my fingers, like hourglass sand. And I thought, 'What if all these grains of sand represent all the people on earth? No . . . it's much more than that: all the grains of sand on the beach must be equal to all the people on the earth.' In my hands, I imagined I held all their collective thoughts and beliefs, their dreams and fears. 'How do people find each other in this overwhelming chaos of sandy haphazardness?' I wondered. So many souls in layers and depths: all the colours of earth, and never a same shape. 'Is it a crapshoot? Or is it pre-determined?' Where was my soulmate in this sand? How would I ever find him or her? Or they find me?

We are bouncing molecules. Repelled, propelled; all of us particles in a shaken jar. When our sticky particles connect, that's it. Until it isn't. Until our stick becomes slick, and we drift apart on separate cushions of currents.

A tiny, clear crab pulled my focus from my thoughts. Its body was see-through, and I could see its inner workings through its shell. Its eyes were on stalks and comical, like periscopes. Both eyes worked independently of each other. It scanned the horizon for danger and, sensing a clear path, made a dash for a nearby centimetre-high sand hill. It was funny the way it scuttled, sideways and paranoid. Its route was ridiculous. It chose to go the most indirect way possible. It moved neither forward nor straight. It disappeared into the sand and vanished; its camouflage so perfect its existence might have been doubted. It found its hole in the end. Wasn't it all about finding your hole?

I sat up and looked to the horizon where the two blues blurred, the sea and the sky; where two bands of vibrating colour met and created a third. The third was an illusion. But the illusion was the focus. The horizon was never-ending, always in the distance and never getting closer; a destination that could never be reached. A lone gull cut across my vista, its wings stretched out and powerful. It used the rising blasts of shimmering heat vapours to its advantage. It circled then called out. Pointing its body to the sea, it closed its wings, and dived. Birds are such different creatures from us. They are bird-bone light. I used to underestimate their prehistoric minds, thinking them simpler than a human. But, in fact, they are more perfect in their makeup. Birds only have one hole, from which they urinate, defecate and procreate. A 'hole' is a crude word. A place we fall into. A grave or a trap. An 'opening' is a better word – a place for beginnings; for birth; for hope. From an opening, we can create.

My back began to tingle with the familiar feeling of sunburn. I only noticed it when it was too late, when the damage was already done. It was a sweet pain. I love the feeling of someone's fingertips tracing minute patterns on the sun-sensitive skin on my back. Barley touching me; delicious pleasure; shivering pleasure. The sun was low now, but the heat was still narcotic. I turned and lay on my back to protect it from any more rays. I put my towel over my face and thought again about holes and emptiness. I remembered when I was a child, having the strangest feeling come over me. The feeling

would surge through my body after meals, and only when I was with
my family – my father's side of the family, to be exact: Grandma,
Grandpa, Aunt Susie and Fred, my cousins, and Karina and Jon. It
would happen after a big meal, like Thanksgiving. After I'd finish
eating, and was surrounded by my family, I'd feel a dull emptiness
rising up from the depths of my body. It flooded upwards, like a
bath filling with water. The airy space in my body was replaced by
the density of the feeling. I was light-headed and heavy all at once.
This feeling was akin to profound loneliness; a singularity of heart-
breaking sadness. It was so overwhelming, I could not speak. I could
not articulate it to another person. I felt marginally ashamed by it,
like there was something broken in me. The feeling separated me from
the din and pomp going on around me. It focused my thoughts . . .

I'm alone.

I'm empty.

I'm alone.

I can only describe the feeling as similar to that of the tail-end of
an orgasm; an orgasm that has been taken too far . . . for too long,
where the dissolution of the pleasure merges with the sadness of the
loss of connection. The pleasure cliff, over which we are not meant
to be pushed. The seam between dualities. Where the now is lost to
the ether. The grey area, the horizon; the place of nothingness. Is this
the place we pass through as our spirit leaves our body? When our
physical energy breaks the bonds of bony confinement, and joins the
non-physical? The vast universe of collective consciousness?

Yes . . . this place was the threshold. This was the place where feeling
and being met. I had been shown the answer as a child. It's only ever
about connecting the dots.

FULL CIRCLE

Here in LA, the sun had a starring role. The temperature outside was a perfect 80 degrees. Inside the car it was freezing. The air conditioning was cranked up to arctic. I held Satchmo close to my chest for warmth, for comfort. I clung to him. We were in this together now, just the two of us. I watched the familiar sights of LA blur across my vision, through the window of my uncle Fred's car. Each landmark along the way brought back echoes. I saw the roadside café with the giant brown doughnut on top of it, where all the cops ate breakfast. I saw the strange, prehistoric-looking oil derrick, which had been an endless source of fascination to me as a child. Relentlessly, it burrowed its nose into the hard, unyielding earth. Day and night, year after year, it was persistent in its futility. We passed the ice-skating rink I had begged my mother to take me to. I took in the seediness and the desperation of the iconic strip club near the airport, with its faded plastic billboard, now missing some letters, reading Girls G ls Gir s xxx. I craned my neck to catch a fleeting glimpse of the restaurant with the surrealist lobster doorway. I watched it disappear behind me as my uncle drove on, towards Brentwood, the up-market West LA enclave where I would be staying with him and my aunt, until I got my bearings. I arrived in LA with my pug, my suitcase and nothing else.

After my split with Nigel I felt I could no longer stay in England. It was so public. I couldn't face the scrutiny and the shame. I felt like a failure in every way. When I thought about it, I realised I'd rather be in LA. If you're going to be depressed, why not do it where the weather is warm and the sun shines. I wanted to go home.

In the end, Nigel was generous to me. He did good by me. He told me he would pay my rent for a year, and give me a bit of cash to get started. He also agreed to let me take Satchmo. So Satchmo and I flew first to Chicago. I needed my mom. At twenty-eight years old, I was moving back in with Mom and Marvin. I sobbed every day. My mom held me in her arms and comforted me. She and Marvin helped me to start picking up the pieces of my shattered life and broken dreams. Eight years before, I had left this very house, with high hopes for the future. I was convinced I would make it as a musician and never look back. I was blissfully in love and embarked on a thrilling adventure. Now, nearly a decade on – and what seemed like an entire lifetime ago – everything had come full circle. I had had it all, and I had lost it all.

One night, while asleep in my old teenage bedroom – still with posters of Andy Warhol and Robert Plant on the walls – I was awakened by Satchmo tossing and turning. His little paws were scrabbling in his sleep. I woke him and soothed him. I imagined he was having a bad dream. The move and the upset in my life must have affected him adversely; not to mention the long plane journey. He was still a puppy, barely five months old. The next night he had the dream again, but this time it was worse. He foamed at the mouth and lost control of his bladder. I took him to the vet in the morning and they explained that Satchmo had had a seizure. He was diagnosed as epileptic. I was beside myself. They put him on phenobarbital, which kept him fairly doped up. Just like me on Prozac. I feared my dog was a manifestation of my own emotional trouble.

Before I had left England, while I was still with Nigel, I had gone for a big job on TV, for the show *The Word*. It was to replace the presenter Amanda de Cadenet. I thought it would be the perfect job for me. I was a natural on television, having done loads of it with The Fall.

When I went to the audition I was fairly confident I'd get the job. In fact, I was told I had it. But, the day before shooting was to begin, I got a phone call and was informed the producer had changed his mind. They had gone with someone else. It turned out to be another cute, smart and sassy American, Katie Puckrik. Katie and I were actually friends. We had met during the ballet *I Am Curious, Orange*. She was one of the dancers in Michael Clark's company. I was happy for Katie. But I was also gutted. I had seen the opportunity as a way to reinvent myself. What it did, though, was whet my appetite for acting and TV presenting. This was something I had never been able to devote much time to, but I had always wanted to. Watching my mother excel in TV production and news reporting, and running the film commission for the state of Illinois, and having spent many childhood years on film sets, soundstages and news rooms, I felt very much at home and energised by it. I actually felt 'bred for it'. That was one of the reasons I decided to go to LA.

My body seemed to crave the caress of the temperature on my skin; the vibration of the light and the colours, flickering on my visual cortex, soothed my aching eyes and diffused the ugliness of reality, softening the edges. The smell of LA was perhaps one of the most powerful stimuli for me. I closed my eyes and inhaled deeply. Night-blooming flowers . . . coconut-oil sweat . . . hot, freshly laid tarmac . . . salty sea spray . . . and two-day-old patchouli on unwashed, oversexed skin. I had never written a love song for a man, but I had written many songs inspired by the city, including two out-and-out love songs: 'LA' (for The Fall), and 'Waking Up in the Sun' (for The Adult Net).

I ended up staying with my mom and Marvin in Chicago for a month, before I made my final move to LA. With nowhere in LA to stay, I asked Aunt Susie and Uncle Fred if Satchmo and I could live with them until I got on my feet. Aunt Susie is one of the most positive human beings I know. She is a mini-dynamo of a woman. She's just under five feet tall and blonde. She definitely has the 'elf gene'. She also has great taste in everything. Her and Uncle Fred's house in Brentwood was the same house they had had since I was a child, so it was very familiar to me and held many fond memories.

This was only the second time in my life I had looked for my own apartment. Now Aunt Susie and Uncle Fred were helping me. I had spent my whole adult life in the UK, and had no bank account or credit rating in the states. Without either of those things, it's very difficult to do anything, and impossible to rent an apartment. Uncle Fred helped me to set up a bank account. I deposited the money that Nigel had given me. I was still extremely depressed and very sensitive to my surroundings. I decided that, as I was in LA, I would try to live as close to the sea as possible. The problem was the closer to the sea you got, the more expensive the properties were. I didn't really have enough money to live alone in even a modest apartment. I needed to have a roommate to cut the costs. But the idea of having a roommate was unthinkable. I couldn't take anyone else and their needs and quirks at that point of my life. I had never lived with a stranger, and I wasn't about to start.

I had a brilliant idea. It was inspired and, although it was partially selfish, it turned out to be the right call for everybody involved. The one person I had lived with multiple times and had gotten along with and thrived with was Lisa Feder. I wondered how she would feel about relocating to California to live with me and Satchmo by the beach. She was an art director now, who worked on commercials and interiors, as well as still doing some fine art. Maybe she was ready for a change, an adventure? She had been living in New York since Bennington, and dating a college friend, Gigi, on and off. They had recently broken up. I called Lisa, put the proposition to her, and she was totally up for it. I scoured the for-rent ads in the *LA Times*, and with Uncle Fred at the helm set off to look at the possibilities.

We found a very simple two-bedroom apartment in Marina del Rey, on the border of Venice. It was on (the appropriately named)

Voyage Street. I could just about hear the ocean from the window. My mom came to stay and she arranged a lunch with her dear friend Tammy Hoffs, a talented film director, and her daughter, my old friend, the musician Susanna Hoffs. Although Susanna and I had been in sporadic contact over the years, she had been touring and recording with The Bangles practically non-stop. I'd been doing the same with The Fall, and when we were in the same town at the same time we'd make a concerted effort to hang out, and, if we could, we'd arrange sleepovers, girly pyjama parties, and cram in the hours to maximise our catch-up time.

I had been shy, and reluctant to contact Susanna when I first arrived back in LA. I felt ashamed by my failure. Sue had conquered the world, with number-one records and albums in practically every country, while I, who had been in one of the most influential and artistically credible bands, had blown it. Now I had nothing to show for all my work, and had come back to LA with my tail between my legs.

At the time there was a hugely popular song on the radio. It was called 'Loser' by Beck. 'I'm a loser, baby, so why don't you kill me?'

'How apt,' I thought.

VOYAGE STREET

It occurred to me, as I was lying in bed in my rented apartment on Voyage Street, that Eva had been right. The astrological predictions she had inferred from the information contained in my chart had been spookily correct. I had lost everything in my life that I considered defining of me: my husband, then my boyfriend, then my job, home, money, inspiration and, finally, my identity. Of course, I had an identity, but I no longer knew what my purpose was. All my life I'd had a clear vision of what I wanted to do. Now I was humbled, levelled. I was floundering, searching, and bordering on desperate. Eva had warned me, 'Don't try to fight it. Take the path that opens up in front of you. If you hit a brick wall, change tack.' I was trying to do that, but the problem was I didn't know where the path began.

Since I had nothing to do each day, I thought it was important to give myself a routine. I decided to write a book about my experiences. It was called *100 Days at the Beach*. It didn't amount to much. It was an observational exercise, really, about the people I saw each day and how I imagined their lives to be. Each morning, I woke up and wrote for about an hour. Then Satchmo and I would walk down to Venice Beach, eat blueberry and chocolate-chip pancakes on the boardwalk, and walk back home again. In the afternoon, I'd sit on the beach, stare at the world and people-watch. The colour of the ocean, merging with the sky, the shimmering heat coming off the sand in undulating vapours, the repetitive rhythm of the pounding of the sea. Little by little this new environment was beginning to heal me. Although leaving England and severing my ties was abrupt and dramatic, it was beginning to feel like the right choice.

Still, I was hideously lonely. At night I'd break down and ring Nigel. I couldn't stop myself. I hated myself for my weakness. Susanna, realising I was struggling and lonely, decided to make it her mission to get me back on my feet. Taking control of my situation, this petite livewire of a woman changed the course of my life with her friendship. Each day, Susanna invited me out to lunch. Which was a clever move on her part, as it gave me a focus for the day and broke up the solitude in my life.

One night while at dinner with the Hoffs, I admitted that I would really like to do some acting. Susanna had done lots of acting and she'd even starred in a movie. Her mom, Tammy, was, of course, a writer and director, and Sue and Tammy had an idea: they knew a woman named Marilyn Fox, who was a much-respected acting teacher in LA. Everybody who acts in LA goes to class at one time or another: it's great to hone your skills and keep your chops up between jobs. There are multiple teachers and theatre programmes around the city, but some teachers are very special and their reputations precede them. To get into their classes is almost impossible unless you know somebody and come highly recommended. And you are still expected to audition. Susanna was convinced Marilyn Fox was the right teacher for me. She called up Marilyn herself and arranged an audition for me. In a week's time I would audition for Marilyn Fox and Gar Campbell of the Pacific Resident Theatre Ensemble.

I was nervous before my audition. What did I really know about acting? The darkened theatre was small and intimate. About thirty people sat in the tiered seats, arranged in a semi-circle around the stage. The audience was made up of a wide age range of people. Everyone seemed to know each other. Every so often, a latecomer would arrive and they would be greeted by name. I realised this was the class. I sat silently in my seat, observing. I hoped I would not be called up to the stage in front of everyone for my audition.

Before the class began there was a lot of chit-chat about who was working on what shows and what auditions they'd been to this week. One or two of the students looked familiar from television shows. I felt intimidated, but also intrigued. The class started and Marilyn introduced me by name: 'This is Brix, and she is sitting in tonight.' Marilyn was about forty-five years old with wild, frizzy blonde hair. She was witchy and compelling. When she delivered lines, or acted out a scene, her entire face would transform and morph into the character. Gar, her partner, was about fifty-five. He looked like a man I might have seen at a roadside truck stop while on tour, crossing the country during my Fall days. I could imagine him sitting at the counter, his stare menacing, his eyes dark and pain-filled, drinking a black cup of coffee, his slow Southern drawl hiding a violent past. He had a white goatee and a dangerous edge. He could have easily played a death-row inmate. He only ever called me 'darlin'. While Marilyn was warm and nurturing, Gar's praises were few and far between. When he singled you out, you felt special. Marilyn seemed to defer to Gar. I knew that he was 'a brilliant actor' from the brief flashes I had seen in our class. But I suspected that he too may have had his demons.

Finally, Marilyn invited me on to the stage. My heart beat fast. I realised I was nervous. I had to improvise a scene with another actor in the class. Marilyn gave us a situation and a motivation. We were both in a lift. By the end of the journey, by the time the elevator doors opened, I needed to get the guy to take me for a drink. Little did I know that later on in life, I would be in this exact situation, with very, very profound consequences.

We played out our scene. The actor I worked with was very calm, natural and funny. The adrenaline and the nerves energised me, made me feel alive. I forgot how much I missed the feeling of performing. Being on stage, whether it was playing music for thousands of people, or saying lines in front of a class of thirty, felt fantastic.

Marilyn and Gar invited me to join their class. The class would meet three nights a week. At some point during the year, the students would prepare scenes to perform. The Pacific Resident Theatre Ensemble would put on a showcase for all the casting agents in the city. The main goal for all of the new actors was to secure an agent.

I called my mother and Marvin and discussed my financial situation. They said they would be happy to pay for my shrink and any medical bills, but I would have to get a job to supplement my income and pay for anything else. I knew I could always work in a shop and sell clothes. But shop hours were long and took up most of the day. I needed to be free in the day to attend auditions, which took place all over town. I needed a job that was flexible. I worried that no one would hire me. It's not like I had any kind of a CV. I'd never had a CV in my life. If I did it, what would it have said?

Career:
1981: graduated high school
1980–81: worked in Fiorucci
1982: dropped out of college
1983–88: rock star
1988–91: famous person's girlfriend

Skills:
Playing guitar and songwriting
Horse riding and driving a car

Susanna came up with the solution. We were sitting in À Vôtre Santé, the gourmet health food restaurant we loved on San Vicente, having lunch. As we drank our carrot juice and chowed down on hijiki salad, Susanna looked at the placemat on the table and saw an announcement. 'À Vôtre Santé, opening soon, in Santa Monica.'

'Brix, you could be a waitress! It's perfect. You could work at the new À Vôtre Santé. I bet they are looking for staff now. You should ask; you should apply. How hard can it be?' she wondered. 'Everyone does it here to make money between acting jobs. It's totally normal. Practically every waiter is an out-of-work actor. You're smart, you can do anything, just act like you've done it before. I'll help you fill out your application and we can make up fake restaurants you worked in, in England. They'll never know the difference.'

True to her word, Sue did help me fill out the application, and we did make up fake restaurants references – and I did get the job.

This was a very special restaurant that catered to the fussiest, most finicky Californian eaters. Everyone was allergic to something or intolerant to this or that. The clientele were mostly actors, models and moguls. We were expected to memorise every detail of the menu, and all of the ingredients. We also served wine, so we needed to know about that too – where it was grown, the type of grape used, and the perfect adjectives to create a mouthwatering description of the flavour. In order to secure the job, we had to take a written exam and know the sourcing details, makeup, and health benefits of each dish and ingredient.

People were rude. One day, I was serving a large table of eight. They were all men and they were all assholes. I could tell that before I even started speaking to them. They had already been drinking. Showing off and humiliating the waitress was sport for them. I started to take their order and began to describe the daily specials.

'Excuse me, miss,' one of the men interrupted. 'Do you have any pussy on the menu?'

I felt my face turning beet-red. The entire table erupted into laughter. I stood there and looked at them. I cocked my eyebrow and said, 'I'm afraid we are out of pussy today, but we have a lovely fresh salmon. Perhaps some nice fish might satisfy you?'

They were shocked at my quick and vulgar comeback. After that, I had no more trouble from them.

My favourite moment waitressing was filling an order for Burt Bacharach. He was one of my all-time songwriting heroes. He ordered a takeaway one night when I was working in the Venice branch of À Vôtre Santé. I remember him ordering a soup and a very low-calorie superfood salad for dinner. He came in to collect the order himself. He handed me his credit card and it said Burt F. Bacharach. I'm not often star-struck, but this time I was. He was so handsome, and in great shape for his age.

When I would meet people and they asked me what I did, I now described myself as an actress who was waiting tables. I never referred to myself as a musician, and never ever told anyone I had been in The Fall. In my mind I had given up music. No one who worked at the restaurant with me knew my story.

My tendinitis was finally gone, but my left arm had withered considerably. I had been forced to stop playing guitar physically, but really the whole thing was mental, I'm sure of it. I tried to put my past behind me, by not thinking or speaking about it. Just like all the painful things that had happened in my life, I shut it down and denied it. This process of denial worked for me until the inevitable happened.

I was recognised.

One afternoon, I approached a table where a few guys were seated. I took out my tablet to take their order. My ears pricked up when I heard their accents – Mancunian. I glanced up and looked at them. To my mortification, I realised I knew them. It was the band James. I was fairly certain James had supported The Fall once or twice. I prayed they wouldn't recognise me. From being a headlining act to serving gluten-free pancakes and waiting tables was a big drop in anyone's eyes. I couldn't bear to see the look of pity when the James boys put two and two together. I didn't have to wait long. One of them looked at me, and I watched the slow-motion wave of recognition cross his features. Before he could stop himself he blurted out, 'Hey! Weren't you Brix Smith?'

I felt like I'd been smacked in the face. I wanted to rip off my apron and run out of the restaurant. Instead, I swallowed my embarrassment and responded in the best way I could. 'I still am Brix Smith,' I said.

'What are you doing here?' they asked. 'Why are you a waitress?'

'I've come to LA to do acting,' I said. 'I'm working here to support myself.'

I tried to put a glamorous spin on it by throwing in the acting but, in reality, I wasn't fooling anyone. It was all very awkward and unpleasant. The James boys were nice enough, but my own feelings about myself and my perception of who I was – who I had become and where I was going – had to be addressed. When I went home that night the whole uncomfortable scene kept playing out in my head, over and over again. I squirmed, thinking of it. Why did James seeing me working as a waitress upset me so much? Why was I denying who I was? I was a musician, a songwriter, a singer. I had been in an important, influential band. I had made multiple albums and I wasn't yet thirty. Somehow, I had allowed myself to be broken.

As awful as that moment with James was, it was also pivotal for me. For in that moment I hit my rock bottom. I was forced to accept myself, and make peace with where I was in my life.

LIVING IN A GARAGE

It was wonderful having Lisa around, even though we actually didn't spent much time together. Her boss, Nord, kept her very busy, running all over the city doing strange tasks. Lisa and I began to rekindle some relationships with old friends from Bennington who were living in LA. One of them was my old boyfriend, Brian Peeper, who was now an artist. Lisa and I discovered he was 'free' and in town when we saw his exhibition advertised in the *LA Reader*.

We were also back in touch with Claus Castenskiold. Claus and I talked on the phone quite often. One night, he let slip that he had a crush on Lisa. He thought he had no chance, as Lisa had been in a lesbian relationship for a long time. I knew Lisa was bisexual and, in fact, had always secretly fancied Claus. Very gently, I eased them together. Obviously they both had feelings for each other that had been percolating for years. They started dating. Very soon they became a couple.

I, on the other hand, had not moved forward with my relationships with men. Susanna and I spent endless hours pondering the subject. Sue, who was also single, took it upon herself to fix me up. I went on all kinds of dates, including one with Sue's little brother Jesse, and one with her cousin Jason, who worked with Steven Spielberg. Although I tried dating out of my comfort zone, I was always attracted to the same type of men. Crazy, brilliant, charismatic oddballs; angry, dangerous and compelling, who were – you guessed it – just like my biological father.

I had a developed a definite pattern with men, and it needed to be broken. One way to break the pattern was to confront it at its source. I wanted to try to repair my relationship with my father. I started by reaching out to him with a phone call. It was hard and there was still anger and distance on both sides, but we at least we were talking.

By now my father had left LA and was living up in Big Bear, in a cabin in the mountains. He lived in an isolated and rustic house made completely of logs. It reminded me of the shack the Unabomber lived in. It was at this point my father had the three big Rhodesian ridgebacks with African names. He lived with wife number four, or was it five? Both of whom were lovely women. We saw each other at first with the safety of family members around us, usually on traditional family occasions at my grandparents' or Aunt Susie and Uncle Fred's.

My family is American. My grandfather was born in Russia, but his children were born in America. Although we have distant European ethnicity in our family, to my knowledge we do not have any Scottish blood running through our veins. For some unknown reason – while I had been away living in the UK and we had not been in contact – my father had fallen in love with Scotland and had decided to fully embrace Scottish culture. He now spoke with a Scottish accent. He wore kilts to all family occasions. If you asked him which clan he came from, he would have probably replied 'McAsshole'.

Nigel and I were now on very friendly terms. We spoke often on the phone and had arranged for him to come and visit me and Satchmo in LA. We decided to take a holiday together. I could tell that Nigel had moved on with his romantic life and was seeing someone else. But I could also tell that he really still cared about me. For once in my life I did not feel jealous. I realised that Nigel and I were meant to be friends, and we remain so to this day.

I was sitting in my living room one day in my apartment on Voyage Street when I heard a knock at my door. Thinking it was my upstairs neighbour with Tourette's syndrome, who quite often had meltdowns, I flung open the door without thinking. I was shocked to find a camera shoved in my face. Behind the photographer stood a journalist. I was being doorstepped! They were from a British tabloid. They wanted me to dish the dirt on Nigel, specifically on details of his alleged drug use. As far as I know, Nigel's never taken anything harder than pot. They offered me $10,000. I slammed the door in their faces and called my lawyer – my longtime lawyer and dear friend, Candice Hanson, a Canadian woman.

Candice is also a role model of sorts. She is one of the most powerful and respected entertainment attorneys in America. She has looked after me in every aspect of my various careers since I joined The Fall in 1983. Candice made sure I was never bothered again by the tabloid.

My phone call to Candice got us talking again. I hadn't spoken to her since Nigel and I had broken up. I was ashamed that, yet again, another relationship had gone down in flames. I knew Candice (whom I called Auntie Candy) would be upset that I had lost my record contract. I think I was even more embarrassed to tell her that, as she was the one who had done the deal in the first place.

Candice Hanson was not about to let me give up music. She listened to my tales of woe and then stepped in to help me. First of all, she hooked me up with a Hollywood acting agent named Hilary. She convinced Hilary to take me on. This was a big deal. Now I could go on auditions for everything. Candice invited me to parties and dinners with all the important musicians and record company bigwigs. She also put me in the room with other songwriters, hoping against hope, something would spark. It would take a long time before I picked up a guitar again, but at least I was talking about music.

Susanna Hoffs decided to sell her car. She sold it to me for an amazing price. I loved Sue's car. It was a white BMW 3 Series. It had a car phone built in, which was my first mobile phone. Now I had a clean, white girly car to drive around town in to get to my auditions. I also used the car for emergency runs to the vet in

West LA. These trips were becoming all too common: Satchmo was really struggling with seizures now, and his blood had to be monitored constantly for the correct levels of phenobarbital. Each seizure was growing longer in length, and more violent.

One day, while out walking Satchmo, I passed a palm tree in front of my apartment on Voyage Street. I was on my way to the beach, walking down the pedestrian sidewalk. The palm tree caught my eye. Inexplicably, there was a large piece of paper taped around the trunk of the palm tree, which was actually a note. What caught my eye next was my name. In kidnapper-cut-out-collage-style letters someone had left me a message. It read:

Brix Smith
I am watching you
I am waiting for you
I know what you are doing

'What the fuck?' I thought. Maybe Lisa had done it, as some kind of a jokey art piece? Maybe she'd smoked some pot, and thought it would be really funny to tape a message to me on the tree, and see how long it took me to find it?

For the moment, I ignored the message and left it there. When Lisa got home I asked her about it. She looked at me with a totally blank expression. She had no idea what I was talking about. I went back outside and ripped the message off the tree. The next day there was a new one in its place. It said:

Brix Smith
I will have you
I am here

I freaked out. As I drove to and from work, and to and from acting class, I began to notice something disturbing. I was sure

I was being followed. Each time I looked in my mirrors, I saw a man on a motorcycle, dressed head to toe in black leathers and wearing a shiny black helmet, with a tinted visor. I could not see his face.

Lisa and I kept the shades down in the apartment. We bolted the doors. We switched off the lights and lived in darkness. We slept with kitchen knives under our pillows. I racked my brains but I couldn't figure out who it was. In the past, there had been some obsessive Fall fans. Guys had waited for me on the doorstep of my house with Mark. I had received a few creepy letters over the years. In one letter a man professed his love for me and demanded I divorce Mark. That was a little disturbing, but nothing as serious as this.

One night, I heard some glass smash. I was terrified it was the big plate-glass window in our living room. Lisa and I, with Satchmo in my arms, crept into the darkened room, to find everything as it should be. With a sigh of relief we got back into bed. In the morning, I went out to my car, which was parked in the garage, in the alley behind the apartment. My windshield had been shattered. It looked like someone had taken a sledgehammer to it. Small chunks of thick glass lay scattered on the garage floor. Reflections of sunlight bounced off their sharp edges, backscattering the walls and ceiling. Angry rays decorated the garage as if dappled by a mirror ball. I swept up the broken glass on the ground. I used a jacket to dust the remnants of the glass off the front seat of my car. Nothing had been stolen from the car.

I took the car in for repair during the day, and that night I slept well – albeit with the kitchen knife still under my pillow. I was not awakened by any breaking glass or scary noises. I got dressed for work in the morning as usual, and went out to the car. When I got there I stopped short. Taped to the front windshield was a large cartoon. It had been carefully cut out from a newspaper. The cartoon was a drawing of cars parked in a parking lot at a car dealership. In the cartoon every single car alarm was ringing. The car salesman had his hands over his ears. The caption said something about the sensitivity of the alarms.

Now I got very scared indeed. This meant the stalker had been close to me when I had spoken to the BMW mechanics about how the car alarm needed repairing. I was definitely being followed, and he wanted me to know it. I went inside and called the police. They told me to get out of the house and stay with someone else for a while, if I could. They sent in a task force of special police, who dealt only with incidents of stalking.

Because LA is full of famous actors and actresses, stalking is rife; crazy obsessive nut jobs are two a penny. The police gave me a pamphlet explaining how I now needed to live my life: blinds permanently drawn, lights switched off, doors bolted. No walking around at night. I was to be accompanied by someone wherever possible. They also suggested I borrow a scary dog and get myself a boyfriend. Alternatively, they recommended I invite a strong, fit man to come and stay with me. They told me to be vigilant. They explained they would not station a guard outside my apartment since I had not been physically harmed. They suggested, if I could afford to do so, that I hire a private bodyguard.

I decided to stay with my aunt and uncle for a while. Lisa went off to stay with Claus. I also spoke to my father about the stalker. After all, he was a shrink and was used to dealing with extremely crazy people. He had by now left, or lost (I'm not sure which) his private practice in Beverly Hills. He had a new job. He had become the chief of staff at Patton State Hospital for the criminally insane. Talk about a monkey running the zoo. He did have some advice for me about how stalkers' minds work, though. 'Be careful,' he warned me – with those kinds of people anything was possible, and the slightest thing might set them off. 'Great,' I thought.

A few weeks later an old friend of mine, Lisa's and Claus's from Bennington had a dinner party. Jill Goldman was a film writer and a producer. She invited all of us to her house in Hollywood for supper. Unbeknownst to me, this dinner was to try to fix me up with a friend of hers. She thought we would be a great couple and hit it off. His name was X, let's say, and he was an actor. When we got to Jill's Spanish-Mediterranean-style house, we were served margaritas and started hanging out in her backyard. I remember sitting with Claus, who told me how happy he and Lisa were. He also told me he was going to train to be a pharmacist. We laughed. He had always loved drugs. Now, whenever I'd think of the song 'Mr Pharmacist' by The Fall, I think of Claus. I figured he'd definitely have his hand in the pill jar.

At the table, Jill introduced me to everyone. I noticed a terrifying-looking man. He was bald and bespectacled . . . he looked like a felonious intellectual. He was *huge*, like a gladiator, and covered in tattoos. This was X, my supposed fix-up.

X was incredibly intelligent. Of course, this piqued my interest a little. When the conversation turned to my stalker, X volunteered to be my bodyguard and sleep at my house for a few nights. X also told me he had two enormous bull mastiffs. I couldn't believe that the universe delivered to me exactly what I needed, when I needed it. X was an ex-con. He had done hard time for armed robbery. He had held up Maxfield's boutique with a machine gun. X was also an ex-junkie. These days X was addicted to the gym. He was a bodybuilder and trained at World Gym, owned by Arnold Schwarzenegger. X's training partner was an ex-Mr Universe.

Jill was right, there was something sexy about X. He was smart and dangerous. I felt protected by him, for sure. X decided that I needed to start working out, and he took on the job of training me. Each morning at 8 a.m., five days a week, X and I would hit the gym for an hour and half. He and his ex-Mr Universe partner made me their special project.

After about six to eight weeks of training, I had a new body. I was hard, lean-cut and strong. All my clothes hung off me. I also had more energy, even though I needed an hour nap every morning after getting back from training and finishing breakfast. Men looked at me again in the way they once had. I was getting my mojo back.

After X began staying with me, we started sleeping together. X was not just huge in body, he was freakishly and painfully endowed. I did find X sexy in a dangerous way, but I knew it was a temporary arrangement. One day I caught X with some syringes. I thought he might have been using again. It wasn't heroin, it was steroids. X had a very bad temper, which was erratic, and getting worse.

One night, Candice Hanson had a party at her house above Sunset Plaza for the band U2 and their beloved manager, Paul McGuinness. At the party was my old agent and lover, Ian Flooks. I was thrilled to see Ian again. I had always held a torch for him. He had helped me get through my break-up with Mark. He had fed me by hand to help me get over my anorexia. As I hung out and talked to Ian, I noticed X getting very agitated. When it was time to go, I drove X and myself home in my white BMW.

We had an almighty fight. He screamed so loudly, my car windows rattled. I had been looking for an excuse to extricate myself from my relationship with X. I told him it was over. When I told Susanna, she was thrilled. She had been trying to convince me to break up with X for ages. One good thing came out of my romance with X: ever since he had been staying at my house, the stalker had backed off and disappeared. I never found out who it was.

Shortly after I broke it off with X, Lisa came to me with sad eyes. She felt terrible telling me, but she had decided to move in with Claus. She was sorry to leave me on my own, in the lurch, with bills to pay. She knew I could no longer afford to stay in the Voyage Street apartment by myself. I was happy for her, but it meant I now needed to find somewhere else to live. So I moved into a garage. I moved into Susanna Hoffs' old garage, to be exact.

MY MAGIC BULLET, THE THOUGHT PROCESS
THAT CHANGED MY LIFE

I believe that places can have good energy and bad energy. This can be for a multitude of reasons. One of those reasons, I believe, comes from psychic staining: trace imprints of emotions and events that have occurred historically in a place. It's as if the walls and floor absorb the energy, then hold on to it, contain it, and vibrate it back out at the same frequency as the original energy, repeating the historical pattern.

Susanna Hoffs' old garage was that sort of a place. At first, the thought of living in a garage seemed grim to me. I imagined people asking me where I lived. 'Hey, Brix, do you live in a house or an apartment?' 'Actually, I live in a garage.'

I imagined power tools and oil stains. I had visions of a hard, filthy mattress, trussed up in Ralph Lauren sheets my mom had bought me. I imagined Satchmo lying on a cold, hard cement floor, and rain leaking through the uninsulated roof. I was grateful to have somewhere to live, but a garage sounded so unappealing.

'I can't believe you lived in a garage, Sue,' I said to Susanna.

'Brix, I *loved* living in that garage,' she said. 'It's special. I didn't want to move out. I was living there while we recorded "Walk Like an Egyptian". It's magic, you'll see. You'll love it.' She was right. It was special. From the minute I entered the garage I could feel it. Sue's mom and dad had converted the garage to be 'liveable'. It was like a mini-house. It was one room, with a separate bathroom and shower, but it was adorable; perfect. I felt safe there.

Almost from the second I moved into the garage my life began to improve, by tiny increments. At the same time, I also became aware of a very empowering thought. I looked at my situation in a positive light. I saw the good, instead of focusing on the bad. I was happy for what I did have and not miserable for what I did not have. At that moment, part of the old me returned. My positivity.

All we really have is now. Now, we can control by choosing our thoughts. We can choose how we feel, in every second. If we choose a good thought, we feel good. If we choose a bad thought, we feel bad. It's that simple.

Instinctively, this was the natural way I operated. When bad stuff would happen in my life, it would block out the naturally good. Sometimes I'd obsess on the bad stuff, and my life would become harder. When I learned to turn these thoughts around, when I accepted the duality of life and stopped trying to fight it, my life became easier again. When my life became easier, and the resistant, negative thought-blocks began to disintegrate, I could see the light at the end of the tunnel, and begin to focus on the good.

I was never able to put this into words myself. At first, I didn't understand what I was actually doing. It wasn't until I discovered the work of Abraham Hicks that everything fell into place for me. Abraham Hicks, in the book *Ask and It is Given*, helped crystallise the thoughts and make sense of the inner, instinctive knowledge I already possessed; this was the book that helped me to make sense out of a life that seemed connected by strands of chaos.

I am not a preacher. Far from it. But this way of thinking, which felt very natural to me, helped me to turn around my life. Everybody needs a belief system of some sort. If you are lucky, you find something that resonates with you; something that can give you hope in your lowest moments. Maybe it's God, maybe it's meditation, maybe it's being in the silence of nature, or music, or therapy? Everybody is different. But for me this worked. This way of thinking was my magic bullet. The thoughts and teachings of Abraham echoed what I knew, and felt instinctively.

EARTHQUAKE

Marilyn Fox, my acting teacher, took me aside one night. She sat me down and looked me straight in the eye. 'I have seen many students come and go over the years. I have seen all kinds of talents. I want to tell you, you are very special. There is something about you that is compelling to behold. You are engaging and loveable. You are hilariously funny yet unbelievably vulnerable, all at the same time. This is an irresistible combination.'

Marilyn's words were just what I needed to hear. I learned, at the core of great acting, is truth. You actually need to know your truth and be able to tap into it, to make any character you are attempting to portray believable. Very slowly in acting class I was able to peel back the onion-like layers of my mask – the falseness, the disguises, the safety nets and protective fields I'd erected around myself, over my lifetime.

I began to get auditions through my new agent, Hilary. They were for everything under the sun: commercials, soap operas, the lead in *Tank Girl*, a Winona Ryder film called *Reality Bites*. I auditioned three times for a role in a Sean Penn–Jack Nicholson film. I kept getting call-backs. They changed my character to a Russian at one point and called me back in to read with Sean Penn, in a Russian accent.

Sean Penn was the sexiest man I have ever been in the same room with. He had so much charisma. I totally got why Madonna went nuts over him. I nearly pulled down my pants in the audition. In the end, the role I would have played was cut from the script.

I noticed that, as I developed as a performer, the more relaxed and honest I felt on stage, the more the audience would laugh and connect with me. I had always been ashamed of showing my vulnerability. I thought of it as a weakness. Because of this fear of people discovering my weaknesses, I had actually been unable to communicate my feelings honestly, in any of my relationships. Acting class was teaching me more than acting. It was teaching me how to love myself, and how perceived weaknesses could actually turn to strengths.

I did start to book some jobs. I played a nurse on *The Young and the Restless*. My character had only a few lines. I had to tend to the needs of a man dying of AIDS. My scene was shot on a hospital set, filmed on one of the soundstages at CBS Television City, where, of course, my mother had worked as a producer on *Sixty Minutes* and the very place of my after-school education in television at the hands of Sonny and Cher. To me this was like coming home. It felt like I'd made it. I loved walking into the canteen in my white nurse's costume. All the stagehands asked if I would take their temperature.

Every so often, Marilyn would direct a play for the Pacific Resident Theatre Ensemble. There were company players, who were all serious, working character actors, and the play would be largely cast with them – but Marilyn and Gar's students were also encouraged to audition. The play that particular year was called *Ondine*, written by Jean Giraudoux in 1938 (Audrey Hepburn famously played the lead on Broadway in 1954). It was about a water-sprite who falls in love with a human. Marilyn's version was a musical. I auditioned and was cast as one of the water nymphs. All the water nymphs were sexy. We wore fishnet body stockings that were dyed greenish-blue and sparkled like sea jewels. We hung above the audience in twisted, fake trees and writhed seductively on the branches as we sang our haunting laments. Fishnet, as a material, is of course see-through. We wore flesh-coloured thongs to preserve our modesty, but our breasts were totally on show. Basically, I was topless in public, writhing on a tree branch.

Being in *Ondine* was extremely important for me and my recovery, for two reasons. Firstly, I was working, creating and performing with a group of people again in public. And, secondly, I was using my voice to sing for the first time since I had lost my record deal.

The play got rave reviews. Every show for the whole run was sold out. I had such a great time doing it. I loved every minute. Each day I took Satchmo with me to the theatre and he would wait in the large communal dressing room for me to finish the show.

Susanna Hoffs had a terrific work ethic. At that time she was on hiatus from The Bangles. The band had decided to take a break and do some solo stuff. Susanna had a solo deal for herself, much like I had had with The Adult Net. I had been lucky to have such a great songwriting partner in Mark E. Smith. As well as writing with the other Bangles, Susanna had always worked with some of the best writers in the business.

We hung out almost every single day. We were best friends now, and almost inseparable. I would watch as a stream of respected and interesting songwriters came to Sue's house, daily, to write with her. I realised that that was how people did it over here. I had been so used to working on my own, and then presenting the finished music to Mark. Seeing Susanna doing her songwriting sessions got me thinking: 'Maybe I should try it again? What do I have to lose?'

I called my lawyer, Candice Hanson, and asked her advice. Candice put me in touch with a beloved figure in the LA music scene, Marc Geiger, a talent agent and music executive who had co-founded Lollapalooza. Marc immediately hooked me up with all the cool writers in town, and specifically any Brit writers who were visiting.

Initially, these sessions were so difficult for me. I didn't think I could play guitar any more, and I had lost so much confidence I was afraid the other writers would think I was talentless. I was focused on what they thought about me. I was worried about being judged. It was hard to let go and be creative and free, because I didn't feel safe. My own old insecurities were blocking any clear channel of inspiration. Not for one moment did I stop and question how I felt about my writing partner, or even if I liked their writing style.

Before I started songwriting with anybody new, I was visited by an old friend, Stephen Duffy. We hung out together in LA for a few days and then planned a trip to the Wine Country. We would head to Sonoma in Northern California, where my stepmother Maggie was now married to Peter Haywood, a vintner who owned Haywood Winery. They lived on a gorgeous ranch, set deep within their own vineyards. The perfect place to write songs.

The day before we were going to leave, there was a massive earthquake early in the morning. Stephen and I were awakened from our sleep. Stunned, as if cracked on the head by the hammer of the gods, we both ran out of the house at the same time. Somehow Stephen had managed to get his shoes on. He was so English and proper that way. I came out in a T-shirt and knickers, carrying Satchmo. We stood on the pavement outside the garage, in an attempt to stay away from electrical power lines or falling debris. The ground rolled underneath us; the sounds I heard and felt were deep and sonorous. We were so disoriented we both felt nauseous. I've never heard such a soul-affecting sound in all my life. I can only describe it as earth-carnal. We packed up my white BMW with all our gear and headed for Sonoma with Satchmo.

We spent four idyllic days there. Maggie and Peter had two fabulous log houses. They were both built by hand, by Peter. Stephen and I had one to ourselves. The log houses faced a large, tranquil pond. A wooden deck, with Adirondack chairs, stretched out before the log cabins, from which you could dive into the shimmering silver forest-green water. Stephen and I wrote a bunch of songs up at the ranch. The best one was called 'Cool Your Jets'. It was an ode to Peter Fonda during his *Easy Rider* period.

When I got back to LA, I started writing with other people. All of them came highly recommended. Most sessions I could tell would never go anywhere, as I had no creative chemistry with the other writers. One person I did get on well with creatively, though, was Marty Willson-Piper from the band The Church. Marty was a Marc Geiger contact. He was a great guitar player, which made it easy for me to play as little or as much as I felt like. We hung out a lot and wrote an album together. That album turned out to be *Neurotica*. It would be a few years later, though, when we were at last able to record it. By then it seemed like a lifetime had passed.

Writing songs with Marty Willson-Piper and Stephen Duffy had put me back in the musical saddle. Unbeknownst to me then, I was about to get back on the horse. A few months later, I'd quit my job at the restaurant to be back on tour. In my wildest dreams, I couldn't have imagined where I would be playing and with whom.

MAKING MUSIC AND MAKING PEACE

The humidity in the air was so high it felt like I was being hit with a wrecking ball. I had never realised that Washington DC was technically in the South. As I walked out of the door of the hotel, I thought to myself that hot, sticky Southern summers were something I'd only previously read about in novels. Now here I was, experiencing it. As unpleasant as the barometric pressure was, absolutely nothing could dampen my spirits. The door to the van slid open, and I climbed inside, followed by Susanna. I sat back in my seat, and luxuriated in the arctic air blasting from the climate control. 'It's so hot, I can barely think straight,' I said to Susanna. 'I know,' she replied, 'this weather is insane.' Then she turned and looked me in the eye. 'Can you believe this is really happening, Brix?' she asked me. 'We are about to play on the steps of the Capitol building . . . with Crosby, Stills & Nash . . . for the vice president of the USA!' Our performance was broadcast live on C-Span across the nation.

Backstage, which was actually a public room in the Capitol building, we rehearsed with Stills and Nash. Graham Nash had been a Holly, one of Manchester's finest musical sons. I was so nervous and so hot due to the humidity, it's a wonder I didn't puke. We followed the musical legends out the door and waited by the side of the steps. Al Gore introduced us over the microphone. A few hundred people were gathered. 'Oh my God, Brix, Al Gore just said my name!' Susanna whispered into my ear. Both of us were pinching ourselves. We sang harmonies with CSN, a dream come true, backing them up on their song 'Teach Your Children'. We had both grown up listening to their albums, and had been hugely inspired by them. It was truly an honour. I couldn't actually believe it. So much had happened to me in such a short space of time, my head was spinning. Things had begun to move very fast indeed, and had picked up momentum practically as soon as Susanna had convinced me to pick up my bass again. Everything seemed to be falling into place. The wrongs in my life began to effortlessly right themselves. I had no idea where any of this would end up, or what I'd eventually be doing with my music. All I knew was that it felt fantastic to be playing again.

A few months previously, Susanna and I had been at lunch. Sue asked me if I would consider playing again. She told me that she wanted to do an acoustic solo tour, playing in small venues and folk clubs. She asked me if I wanted to play bass for her. I only had to think for a second before I said yes. I had a few of my guitars with me in LA. I had sent for them: both my Rickenbackers, Whitey and Blacky, and my pink paisley Telecaster and my beloved solid-body cherry-red Gretsch, which I had been happily reunited with after stumbling across it hanging on a wall in a guitar shop on Denmark Street. But I did not have a bass. I hadn't played bass in years.

Sue and I went shopping to Guitar Center and Sue bought me a small white Fender bass for the tour. We began to rehearse with a guitar player Susanna knew, named Bill Bonk. It would be the three of us on stage, no drummer. We would all be playing, and singing harmonies. We would do a set made up of a mixture of Susanna's solo material and a few cover versions The Bangles had previously done. Songs like 'September Gurls' by Big Star, and 'Hazy Shade of Winter', originally written and performed by Simon and Garfunkel. The Bangles' version was featured on the soundtrack of the film *Less Than Zero*. The original book of *Less Than Zero* had, of course, been written by my old friend (and Bennington alumnus) Bret Easton Ellis. I love it when seemingly random things connect, and fall into place.

We also did acoustic versions of Bangles songs. I particularly loved singing the harmonies on 'Eternal Flame' and 'Walk Like an Egyptian'. Singing with Susanna was sublime. Her voice is so pure and her spirit so lovely. The acoustic tour I did with Sue enabled me to thankfully quit my job at À Vôtre Santé. I was also getting sporadic acting work, enough to make ends meet.

During this time, I had not paid attention to what was happening with The Fall musically. I had heard that Mark had married Saffron Prior. I did not listen to any Fall records, including those on which I'd played. I couldn't do it. It was too painful. Memories of me and Mark, good and bad, would come flooding back. I wanted to shut all of it out, so I could continue to move forward with my life. Sometimes, though, it's important to face your fears head on. In order to move forward you must close the door behind you. When you shine the light on a monster, quite often you find it is nothing more than a paper tiger. It happened that Susanna was doing some songwriting with a talented singer-songwriter named Freedy Johnston, known a 'songwriters' songwriter'. He was named 'songwriter of the year' by *Rolling Stone* magazine. One day while Freedy was working at Susanna's, we were introduced. It turned out that he was, unexpectedly, a major Fall fan.

We began to spend time together. I adored Freedy and his music. His albums *Can You Fly* and *This Perfect World* came to be among my favourites. Freedy had lots of questions for me about specific Fall songs, particularly those I had written. He was a sensitive guy and noticed I disliked talking about my time in The Fall, and would become visibly uncomfortable when doing so. Still, he kept asking me, probing me, seemingly unable to help himself. Sometimes he'd ask me about songs I couldn't even remember. My mind had so successfully shut them out, as if to block the pain. 'Don't you realise how important those songs were?' he'd ask me, in his soft Kansas accent. 'Do you not understand the magnitude of what you guys created?' he'd implore me. 'Come on, let's listen to them together. I want to listen to them with you,' he urged. 'No way,' I said. 'I don't even own any of my records any more. I can't listen to The Fall. It makes me too sad.'

'You don't own any of your records?' he asked, shocked. 'That's it. Get in the car!' he ordered. And with that, Freedy Johnston drove us to Tower Records, where he then proceeded to purchase every Fall record he could get his hands on. We sat down together in my garage-cum-home and proceeded to have a binge listening session, a Fall marathon.

As I listened, he held my hand, and I cried for what I had lost. I allowed myself the honour of missing the songs, people and experiences I had once had held dear. Enough time had passed that when I listened to some of the classic Fall songs I had written with Mark – such as 'LA', '2x4', 'US 80s–90s' and 'Cruiser's Creek' – I could hear just how brilliant they were. Finally, I grasped what an important and intuitive songwriting partnership Mark and I had had. Without thinking about it, I grabbed the phone and dialled Manchester. I knew the number by heart, as it had been mine once. Mark was still living in the same house we had bought together in Prestwich. He was, of course, shocked to hear from me. At first he was sly and distrustful of my motives. I poured my heart out over the phone. I told him I'd forgiven him for cheating on me. Unable to stop myself, speaking without any kind of a filter whatsoever, I blurted out, 'I'd happily work with you again. Any time, any place, just give me the word.' By the end of the conversation, I could tell Mark was really touched by my call. He had warmed to me, and was appreciative of my words. I could also tell that he missed me.

ONE DAY IN HOLE

Susanna was managed by Gold Mountain Entertainment, who also managed Courtney Love. Hole's bass player, Kristen Pfaff, had recently OD'd. Courtney found out through Gold Mountain that I was living in LA and working with Susanna. I answered the phone one day, while sitting in my Magic Garage, to find Courtney Love on the other end. She spoke faster than a rapid-fire machine gun. I couldn't get a word in edgeways. She was the best saleswoman I've ever heard in my life. She invited me to audition for Hole. She flew me up to Seattle for a trial. I had listened to the songs on *Live Through This* and learned the bass lines. I loved the album. It was powerful, raw and girl-grungeful. Eric Erlandson, the guitar player, who was then dating Drew Barrymore (it was Drew this, Drew that) picked me up in his love-truck hippy van and drove me to the rehearsal room. I went into the room and started playing with them and bashing out the songs. Courtney, true to form and reputation, was three hours late for the rehearsal. When she came in, we rocked out with her. It sounded great to me. She had recently had a boob job, so she rehearsed in a bra. She was proud of her new breasts. I admired her freedom. I'd never rehearsed in my lingerie, and could not imagine doing so. Afterwards, we went back to her house and I stayed the night.

This was the famous house in which Kurt Cobain died. He had taken his own life only six months previously. The world was still reeling and mourning his untimely passing. I know I was. It wasn't creepy going in there, but there was a heaviness. The walls and the fabric of the house felt psychically stained to me. How could they not? The occupants of the house, Courtney, her baby daughter

Frances Bean, the two female nannies and the male PA, were all
still traumatised. There had been drugs, death and emotional turmoil in this house, and I could palpably feel it. I remember the
house being a place where sunlight couldn't penetrate.

Courtney put me up in a room called the Mozart Room. Lying
on the bed was a cream silk Christian Dior nightgown, which I
still wear to this day. I thought, 'Not only does she have great taste,
but she knows how to treat guests.' Laying out nightwear for me
was an elegant touch. I felt special and pampered.

But as I went to sleep, I had a sixth sense that something was
wrong. A bad feeling. Something was burning. I got up, out of bed
and rushed to Courtney's room and pushed open the door to the
master bedroom. In her room, she had a selection of candles and
incense burning. Two sticks of incense had fallen over and caught
fire. The carpet was aflame and I caught it just in time. Had I been
five minutes later I dread to think what would have happened.
I put out the fire by smothering it with a blanket and stamping
on it. Courtney was in bed, slumped over her computer. She was
limp and noodle-like. I glanced at her open computer. I fleetingly
clocked that she had been mid-conversation with Billy Corgan, of
The Smashing Pumpkins.

She said, 'Get into bed, sleep on Kurt's side.' So I did. It was
really weird, but I felt honoured to be asked to sleep there, in her
bed, on his side. Courtney was warm and kind. I feel she's often
misunderstood. She is a complex person, as we all are. At times she
has been her own worst enemy, but when you get down to it there
is kindness and warmth to her, that is not often talked about.

Courtney turned me on to Rohypnol. I had actually already
been prescribed Rohypnol by my doctor, to help me sleep. But
when I took the tablets they just knocked me out, and I couldn't
really see what was so appealing about them. Courtney enlight-
ened me. She showed me a new way to take Rohypnol. She
taught me to take only a half, so you do have a memory (only

just). This, however, would get me into some trouble in the coming year.

The next day when I woke up, to my surprise I found Everett True, a journalist from *Melody Maker*, living in Courtney's basement. Courtney had her own personal journalist/PR machine going on. 'She's so smart,' I thought. Everett was churning out stories for Courtney and managing her press profile. It would take less than a week before my picture was on the front of the *Melody Maker*. 'Brix Smith rumoured to join Hole.'

While at Courtney's that morning, I checked my answerphone in LA. There was a message from my gynaecologist. 'This could not be good,' I thought. He said I'd had a dodgy Pap smear, and they were worried about something they'd found. I needed a biopsy ASAP. I got really upset. Courtney could sense something was wrong. I confided in her. Her reaction made me respect her as a woman. I will always be grateful for how she handled me and my difficult, embarrassing situation. She said, 'It's the worst thing when something goes wrong with your vagina. It's so scary and horrible.' She was so empathetic, and I was so traumatised.

I flew back to LA and had the treatment I needed. It was hideous. It was some kind of small, cancerous growth that had to be removed. And I was really worried about what my vagina would look like. I asked my gynaecologist if I was going to be maimed, and he said to me, 'Honey, women have babies, and when babies come out of their vaginas their vaginas look like hamburger meat, but they all heal. And they're all fine.' So I felt better.

After the general anaesthetic, I needed someone to pick me up from the hospital and take me home. Susanna, who would've been my first choice, was by now married and pregnant with her first child, and wasn't free. None of my other friends were free either, so I had no choice but to reluctantly call my father. My father had always been good in a crisis, plus he was a doctor. He was actually very kind to me, and sympathetic. I was high on morphine from the operation and nauseous. As I rode home, in the cab of his pick-up truck, I vomited repeatedly into a plastic bag. As we drove, I held a large ice pack firmly between my legs. When I got home, after the morphine had worn off, I checked my phone messages again, hoping to find one from Courtney confirming my place as the new bass player in Hole. There was no message from Courtney but, to my absolute shock, there was one from Mark E. Smith. 'Please come back. We need you back in the band to kick ass. We will put you up in hotel suites, and fly you back and forth to LA. We just need you to come back.'

Now I had a decision to make. Do I go with Courtney Love, if she asked me, and join Hole? Or go back to Mark, not as his wife, but as the guitarist and the songwriter in my own right? I wouldn't have to endure the stigma of being 'the wife' any more, I'd be coming back as me.

In the end, I came to the conclusion that The Fall were the real deal. If it weren't for The Fall, there would be no Hole. There would be no Nirvana. They were so influential, and they were one of Kurt Cobain's favourite bands. There is that famous story about how he climbed on The Fall's tour bus in LA and wouldn't get off because he wanted to come with us, he wanted to join The Fall. Nirvana's first European tour was a double-header with Tad. They were touring Germany at the same time as we were. One night we were playing at the same venue, albeit on different stages. When Marcia and I saw them in their dressing room, we realised they had nothing to eat. They had no rider that we could see. They looked like they were starving. Our mothering instincts kicked in. Our band were too drunk and fucked up to be tempted by food. Marcia and I grabbed a tray of sandwiches from our rider and some beers. We took them down to Nirvana's dressing room and announced, 'Room service.' They were so cute and bedraggled and waif-like, but they made one hell of a racket when they played.

The call from Courtney never came. She had decided to go with Melissa Auf der Maur instead. Melissa had been championed by Billy Corgan, who Courtney was rumoured to be fucking at the time. But it didn't actually matter to me. I had already made my choice. When it came down to it, there was really only ever one choice. I would re-join The Fall. Having lived through it once, I would be going back into it again with my eyes wide open and the blinkers off. I was a whole lot wiser and a whole lot stronger. I had lived a life in between. I had loved again, and lost again. I had broken down, and climbed back up. I had grown up.

But I was not prepared for the state in which I found the band. The Fall were not as I had left them. They were not happy campers. Their ship was sinking ('Mark'll Sink Us' – life imitating art) and it was down to me to keep us afloat . . .

1995

I flew to London and then changed planes to Manchester. I was nervous yet elated. I took a taxi to Prestwich. It felt weird giving the taxi driver my old address. I wondered why Mark still lived there. It had been important to me to start afresh, to make a clean break and escape the memories and the trauma held within those walls. When I arrived at the house it felt like déjà vu; the street even smelled the same. Mark greeted me at the front door. He seemed genuinely happy to see me. He looked worn out, like the intervening years had been rough. I could tell when he looked at me he was thinking the same thing. He mumbled something in his underhanded sarcastic way about everybody getting old. As I stepped inside the front door, I was faced with the staircase. I remembered clinging to Mark's legs at the bottom of those stairs begging him not to leave me. Now I was back. He'd asked me back, but I was here on my own terms.

I walked into the living room and I was stunned. It was exactly as I'd left it. Mark had not changed one thing. Saffron had not changed one thing. They hadn't even repainted. The walls were still the dark grey-blue colour I had custom-mixed. They couldn't even get a new sofa. The house was frozen in time – in 1989. But to add to this *Twilight Zone*-like setting was the immense change in Mark that became apparent the more I looked at him.

During the five years I had been gone, there had been a deterioration in Mark, both physically and mentally. He looked like a different person. He had aged decades. He looked like a slowly wizening apple puppet. I too looked different. I had grown my hair really long, and I had lost loads of weight. I was on the verge of anorexia, controlling myself with food. I was under-eating and over-exercising. I'd cut out any fats from my diet. We had an awkward but warm conversation. Mark called Steve and told him to gather the lads and come around to his house. They, of course, had not been forewarned that I was re-joining the group, and had not heard from me since I'd gone.

It was essentially the same line-up as when I'd left. Craig Scanlon and Steve Hanley were still there, as was Simon Wolstencroft. Karl Burns was back too, and I was honestly ecstatic to see him again. It had been almost ten years. I was so happy to play with Karl again. He had been through a lot – had had a child, and more ups and downs – and he had matured. He was grateful to be back and he was behaving himself. He wasn't a psycho. The big difference was that Marcia had been sacked in 1990. She would cringe at this, but Mark quite fancied her and was weirdly possessive of her. I think he wanted to have her, but she wouldn't succumb to it in any way. When she started a fleeting relationship with my replacement, Martin Bramah (back for a second stint, at my suggestion), Mark ditched the both of them in Australia in the middle of a tour. He didn't outright fire them, of course. The band simply went on to Japan and left them on another continent. Mark couldn't stand that she was with Bramah, that someone from the original Fall, who thought himself as an equal and not a soldier, had created this faction with a woman whom he couldn't control. Their union threatened the power dynamic in the band, and it had to be excised. (Marcia would go on to medical school and become a successful doctor specialising in pain management, so don't worry about her. We are still dear friends to this day.)

In her place was a new keyboardist, Dave Bush. He was a talented musician and gave the band a modern, techno-sounding edge, adding samples to the mix and a genuine foot in the realm of club (instead of pub) culture. I'd missed out on the Haçienda's metamorphosis from rock club to acid-house haven. Bush was a

pleasant foil to the dourness. Besides adding my guitar, I felt that
what the band really needed was an injection of positivity, because
they were clearly miserable. They were all depressed and seemed
tarnished. I joined this rather bloated line-up, making us seven
members on stage.

I hadn't listened to any of the albums they had made during
my hiatus. I vaguely knew that they had done a cover of the disco
tune 'Lost in Music', which I thought was an odd and interesting choice. Before Marcia and Bramah were axed, the band had
made an album, *Extricate*, in 1990. It is genius – the first time I
listened to it was in 2015. Mark denied it in various interviews,
but the opening track 'Sing Harpy!' is so clearly about me, and
doesn't disguise my narrative at all. In it he sings, 'Thin white
skeleton/Just too good in bed.' It's a complete diss track, but I
love the song, and at least he calls me skinny and a good lay. Too
bad we didn't play it when I re-joined. I'd later find out that there
were many more songs clearly about me. But at the time I was
pleasantly oblivious.

Well, I had my suspicions, but I didn't want to think about it or
really delve into it. Mark had been angry and hurt; it was the end
of the marriage. He had every right to explore and deal with that
with his creativity. But I made a point not to listen to the songs
at that time – I didn't want to let any kind of negativity into my
system. That said, multiple people (including fans) would ask me
about these songs, so I finally brought it up with Mark. He lied
and said they were about Saffron, and I just accepted that because
I didn't want to believe that there was a series of anti-Brix songs to
go along with the Nazi tunes and speed anthems.

Saffron and Mark had divorced and she was long gone by then.
Mark's new girlfriend, Lucy Rimmer, was also the band's tour
manager. I get along with pretty much anybody. I accepted Lucy.
If she made Mark happy, that was fine. I obviously didn't want to
have anything to do with Mark on a personal level. Lucy was nice

enough: a loud, strong Northern woman. She spoke her mind and she had a personality.

We immediately set out on a tour of the UK that August, supporting their tepid *Middle Class Revolt* LP. Two songs were clearly about me, and we didn't play them. It went downhill somewhere in the middle of the British tour. Mark had been on his best behaviour early on. He was polite, and nice to me. He was relieved to have me back. He looked to me as a saviour who was going to pull the band up to where it should have been. By now they were playing in markedly smaller venues, so there was less money. The quality of the music was also down. They had made two great records, *Extricate* and *The Infotainment Scan*, and three artistic flops, *Code: Selfish*, *Shift-Work* and, worst of all, *Middle Class Revolt*. We were touring the nadir of the canon. There was a smattering of good songs, but not much else. By this point I had some demos accumulated, and one song was called 'Star'. In it I sing,

> You say that you're a star but I don't give a fuck
> I watch your head expanding as you're running out of luck
> I feel empty
> Cause baby you suck me
> I feel empty
> Cause baby you suck me clean
> Go feast on someone else
> Cause charity ain't my scene
> I feel nothing
> Cause it's nothing you make me feel
> Go shine on someone else
> Cause your act has lost all its appeal

Mark loved it and we merged it into the middle of their glitter stomp 'Glam-Racket', and it became a set-list mainstay. We recorded it for a Peel session. It was like a victory to me playing it nightly, because the lyrics were such an obvious swipe at Mark and even allude to the old Fall song 'The Man Whose Head Expanded'. Mark was so self-obsessed, he would never think that someone in his band was writing a song about him. After years of him viciously singing about me, I finally let him have it. It was subtle revenge for 'Bad News Girl'.

During the tour it was evident that Craig had lost his passion. He was always aloof, but now he seemed beaten down. Mark began to focus his fury on Craig and tormented him. Mark had his shit list, and everybody took turns being on it. He would berate and torture that person for the entire tour. He would turn against them. I had never before been on that list. I'd been immune to it when I was the wife. He started to really not like me around this time, because I started to stand up to him and tell him what was what. Mark behaved normally for maybe the first two weeks, and then his mask began to slip. He was now drinking so heavily that quite often he was belligerent before a show, if he was even awake. He would often pass out.

The following month's American tour was absolute misery. The first date was in Rhode Island. As we were about to go on stage, I had a terrible knot in my back and shoulder from holding the guitar and the tension of being around Mark. I said, 'I have such a bad backache.' Mark looked at me with these big blue, kind eyes, and said, 'Oh, here, let me help you. I can fix it. Turn around.' I turned around, and he hauled back and punched me between the shoulder blades. I looked at him, shocked and winded. My eyes must have shone black like the devil's. I said to him, 'If you ever touch me again, I will cut your dick with scissors! Snip.' It was right at the time when Lorena Bobbitt had cut off John Bobbitt's penis, so cutting off cocks was on my mind.

For the final songs, Mark just left the stage. We did one song as an instrumental, and I sang 'Glam-Racket'. This would become a habit. Sometimes he would snarl in my ear, 'Sing the fucking song', and then scurry off, mid-show. But mostly he would just disappear without saying anything and leave us on stage to go to the back to drink and do drugs.

I didn't know the words to the songs we were playing. Mark changed the lyrics constantly, and who could understand him anyway? Our set-list, which Mark, of course, wrote, was made up of songs the band had done during my absence. I knew a few scattered words here and there, and had to carry the show. The audience knew I didn't know the words. I was so angry at being dumped up there on stage.

Mark never used to do that. He was very professional. The Fall was a touring war horse. If fifteen people showed up, they would get a full-on show. The Fall started in the seventies, when spitting and a volley of beer cans was de rigueur. They would surmount any obstacle to play. But now Mark would fuck off if somebody threw something at him, or pissed him off. He would just get in a huff and walk off, like a pussy. It became an excuse. He just went backstage and drank. He just couldn't do it any more, and left me to carry the can. Usually, before he left, he would mess with all of the settings on our amplifiers, so it would all just sound like shit. Stereolab supported us for some of the shows. Most of our opening bands would go on to be bigger than The Fall.

Mark was so fucked up by the end of the tour that I called Matador, the American label they were on at the time, and asked them if they could make some kind of intervention, or book him into rehab, because I thought he was going to die. Everything was falling apart. He needed help. They felt bad for me, but they didn't organise anything. He wouldn't have let them do anything anyway.

While I was in the UK I would base myself in London, and travel to Manchester for rehearsals. Nigel Kennedy had been kind enough to let me use the annex, our old flat in Hampstead, whenever I needed it. He was on tour and not around, so I had the place to myself. I was enjoying being single again. It was a fairly wild period for me. After having been tied down to Mark for years, I could now partake in the adorations of my male fans. I was a hot-blooded single woman – a 'guitar goddess' determined to make up for lost time and opportunities.

Having been told by Courtney that if you take half a Rohypnol and go out, you feel super-relaxed and sexy, it became my drug of choice. I felt zero inhibitions. I wasn't shy. In fact, I was down-right free.

Normally, I find it difficult to approach a man I fancy, flirt, or try to pick somebody up. On half a Rohypnol, I had no such issues. Late at night, after I'd finished working and writing, I'd hit the London clubs. Not only was I brazen enough to go out by myself, but when I got to the clubs, I'd 'hold court'. I'd sit in a spot in the club, and survey the scene. I must have been giving off strong sexual vibes, because I was always besieged by both men and women. I would cast my net into the dark underbelly of London nightlife, and then pick and choose from the delights I'd snare. In hindsight, the reason I loved Rohypnol so much was that it freed up inhibitions about sex that I had been harbouring since my rape at the age of nineteen. I realise now I was taking the date-rape drug to get over the date rape.

One night, I was in the Atlantic Bar and Grill, which was under the Titanic restaurant, owned by chef Marco Pierre White. As I sat in a big comfortable chair, I scanned the room. Amidst the cacophony of swirling faces and blurred bodies, I saw what appeared to be a vision of Lord Byron. I saw a man so gorgeous he was like an apparition from another century. I sucked in my breath and wondered if the drugs were playing tricks with my eyes. I stared. I radiated. I silently called to him with my mind. 'Turn round, turn round.' It was like he intuitively heard my thought vibrations, because he did turn round, and our eyes locked.

As he moved towards me, all 6 foot 3 inches of him, I took in his look in its entirety. He was dressed in a bespoke Savile Row suit that looked as if it were from the Victorian or Edwardian era. The jacket was long, like a frock coat, and faintly chalk-striped. The lapels were trimmed in charcoal velvet. His shirt was made of a fine cream-coloured cotton and was collarless, but around his neck was some sort of stock-like scarf with a ruffled detail, also in cream. His shoes were dark chocolate and handmade. I looked at this glorious creature from head to toe, and up again to his eyes. Lock and load. I could smell him. Ginger, pepper and ylang-ylang. His hair was long, just past his shoulders, with dark curls free-falling and framing his aristocratic features. His eyes were blue and big and sparkling.

'Who are you?' I sighed.

His voice was deep and resonant. I felt its timbre hit me in the gut. 'Murray,' he said. Murray? I didn't expect that. The only Murrays I knew were old Jewish men.

'Murray what?' I asked him.

'Murray Lachlan Young,' he replied.

He had the look of a young Jimmy Page at the height of his Zeppelin sexiness.

'I'm a poet,' he said.

I just about crumbled. My inner monologue was, 'I will have you. You are mine. Game over.'

We were drawn to each other by a force so strong it could have created a world. We began a beautiful love affair. Murray was easy and sexy and kind. He was stunning, creative and smart. He was younger than me, and that was a first. We were very decadent together. We partied a lot, made amazing love, and sauntered around London like a golden couple.

Because of his addictions, or his personality disorder, or whatever it was, Mark was terrified of being alone. He needed someone to look after him. As far as I know, he never lived alone for an extended period of time since the day he met me. And because he never stayed home and was always on tour, he needed a girlfriend who was affiliated to the band. Unfortunately for them these girls probably didn't get to know the Mark I knew – by that point he was so fucked up that even he didn't know who he was.

We recorded *Cerebral Caustic* in London at the end of 1994. The Fall is a band with so many albums (well over thirty) that they have a canon. My great comeback record is considered by many to be the worst of all of them. I have a hard time remembering anything that is on it, or the recording of it. I don't know if I blocked it out.

I had songs I had written in LA, such as 'Shiny Things', eventually to become 'Bonkers in Phoenix', and 'Feeling Numb'. I thought 'Shiny Things' was maybe one of the best things I'd ever written. I didn't even understand exactly what it was about – but it was extremely personal. When I look back at it now, it was my inner child speaking. It was about not using the superficiality of outside influences to boost your self-esteem; but that all your strength and good feelings come from within you, are not false, from the outside, like clothes or jewellery. Superficiality is never going to make you happy. Happiness comes from the inside. It was a really special song. When I wrote it, I dug down really fucking deep.

When we went about recording it, it was all really good. Craig played this gorgeous, subtle soundscape counter-melody – melancholy pastures of sound – and I sang my part. I was expecting it to be another 'Hotel Blöedel', for Mark to come in and add his magic, make it a great duet.

Mark obliterated the song, in my opinion. He put the most ugly, vile noises on it, and drowned out any of the delicacy, and sped up my voice so I sounded like a cartoon demon – *Alvin and the Chipmunks* on crack. He wiped off Craig's guitar. It was re-titled 'Bonkers in Phoenix'. Mark says it was meant it to be an experimental exercise of wandering between bands playing simultaneously at a festival (at that time the Phoenix Festival was a major draw), but I think he just wanted to destroy something that was special to me. Of course, this is all subjective. I have heard that this track is among the comedian Stewart Lee's favourite Fall songs.

That song and its demise embodied our deteriorating relationship (once again). I remember fighting with Mark: 'What did you do to that song? How could you do that?' It was like he could not let the beauty of it exist. He had to destroy it and make it ugly.

You could hear traces of the original in the recording, though. And for years afterwards, random people would ask me about it and want to know how they could get a clean version. People said that they could tell there was something magical buried within it. I would apologise and say I didn't remember what song they were talking about. I wasn't trying to sidestep the question; I had self-imposed amnesia. I honestly had no clue what they were talking about, and it wasn't until 2015 that I went back and listened to the song and discovered it. I hadn't thought about it since recording it in 1994. I wouldn't let myself.

The explosion of Britpop was underway. It was infuriating because I felt that the songs I was writing could have fitted into the genre, but The Fall were being forgotten in all the hoopla of Oasis and Blur. All of those bands were Fall-inspired, and some were very vocal about it. It was frustrating because I thought that we could have been a little more commercially savvy, done poppier things, and given them a run for their money. But Mark had to be obstinate, which is one his best traits and why he is such an aberration. Instead, we had to make vile ugliness.

Cerebral Caustic could have been a great record, if Mark had been stable. We demoed the songs; there was such potential in songs like 'Rainmaster'. We only played it once live, I think. Because we all liked it so much Mark wouldn't put it on the setlist. He wanted me back to pick up the slack on stage when he didn't feel like singing or was too drunk to sing, but in the studio he would revert to despotism.

During my first stint in the band, Mark and I collaborated on almost everything. I knew what the album art was going to be like; I'd contribute and give suggestions. We would always go together to the mastering of a record. We knew what the running order would be. We would put secret notes in the run-out groove, carved into it. We would sometimes carve backwards samples on to the tracks of the master, so that if you played it backwards, like a Beatles record, you could hear things being said. I knew everything that was going to happen.

But I was no longer the co-pilot and wife. My input was mini-mised. Mark needed to completely mastermind everything, and he wasn't asking anyone's opinion. Not only that, if someone had an opinion or a strong feeling, he'd destroy it purposefully.

When I saw the cover art for *Cerebral Caustic* I was horrified. If that LP isn't the worst Fall album, it definitely has the worst cover art – a screaming skull with a clown nose. When I see it now, the skull clown is Mark. It's prophetic. He looks like a fucking skull, and he acts like a fucking clown. It's him. It's life imitating art, and art imitating life.

As per mine and Mark's agreement, I was still living in LA but flying to England to work with The Fall when they needed me. In January 1995 I came over to the UK for the release and promotion of *Cerebral Caustic* and to play some shows, which were becoming known for being shambolic. Come see the band that fights on stage, and see how wasted the singer is. Mark and I did a promo interview for the record company to distribute to radio stations. I was a Stepford wife, positive and chipper.

I arrived at a rehearsal in Manchester, and Dave Bush wasn't there. He had been sacked, but no one had told me. I was disap-pointed. I felt that Dave was a real friend in the band, not just a co-worker, and had been a steadying influence both personally and musically. I later found out he got fired via letter. In his place in the rehearsal room was Julia Nagle.

Mark and I had met Julia years before, cursorily, in a recording studio where she'd worked with her ex-husband, who was an engineer. She had apparently been after a job in The Fall for ever, and had been writing letters to Mark. She was a keyboard player who owned a guitar. Every opportunity she would get, she would get that guitar around her body and I would be like, 'Get it off. Get that guitar off.' I didn't rate her as a musician, but her keyboard playing improved and would come to define the sound of a later era of the band. I tolerated her because Mark wanted her around. I hated it when he told her to play guitar, but she was a nice enough girl.

She and Mark started having an affair, and that caused a schism in the band with Lucy Rimmer, whom he was still sleeping with. It was a dramatic triangle that I would be dragged into because Lucy was doing the hotel bookings, and would always put me in a room with Julia, so Mark couldn't get at her, even though it was distinctly stipulated upon my re-joining the band that I would require my own room on tour. So throughout the constant musical chairs of hotel-room changes we often ended up bunkmates. I was the pawn in Mark's fucked-up love life. One would think the strife and chaos caused by everyone he dates having to be directly involved in the band would be a burden to Mark. But no, he was a pig in shit, surrounded by women whom he was or had been intimate with – and they were all fighting, mostly for him. I removed myself from the drama as much as I could. I just wanted my own room.

Despite the bizarre love triangle, extreme drug abuse, strife, constant fighting and erratic performances, the shows were sometimes revelatory, especially when Mark was on point and you could really feel us all gelling. What is most memorable for me about that tour, though, was the fact it was the last time I ever played with Craig Scanlon. He was enormously important to the band, and for years Mark treated him like rubbish. Craig was quiet and shy, yet strong, and could take it. But he reached a point where Mark finally broke him. His passion for music and spirit were broken. You could see it in his eyes. When I was out of town either Mark fired Craig, or Craig quit, or it was a combination thereof. Nobody explained it to me, and we couldn't stop to mourn.

On 13 March 1995, a Monday night, my stepfather Marvin was in London doing a speaking engagement. He took me out to dinner at Bibendum, a fancy restaurant above the Conran Shop in Brompton Cross. After dinner, on the way back to his hotel in Knightsbridge, Marvin dropped me at the tube station on the corner of Knightsbridge and Sloane Street, across from the department store Harvey Nichols. As I stood outside the tube station I watched people going into the department store at night. 'It must be a party,' I thought to myself. 'How cool to have a party after hours in Harvey Nichols.' I decided to crash the party. I had never been to a private party in a department store after closing. I was compelled to go. I crossed the street and entered the building, following some other people, and trying to look like I belonged.

I was wearing a skin-tight forest-green Azzedine Alaïa dress, with bare legs and biker boots. My hair was long at that point, and deep copper-red, tinged with strawberry blonde. It was tousled and beachy. I wore no make-up. I looked around the foyer, and saw an elevator. The doors opened and three gentlemen got in. I followed them. The doors closed. I observed the men in the elevator. I instantly surmised they all knew each other. They were immaculately dressed and perfectly groomed. They looked pristine, in a wealthy, tasteful, way. The first looked like an effeminate businessman. He was tall and tanned, as if he'd spent three months on a yacht in Spain. He carried a man bag. The second was small, bespectacled and had a beard. He looked like a Jewish accountant. The third man was of medium height, in great shape and the best dressed of them all. He was wearing a navy blue suit, and looked powerful. He had strawberry-blond hair, blue eyes and a handsome face. He had an easy manner and an air of confidence. He reminded me of Robert Redford. He also looked vaguely familiar.

As the doors to the elevator closed, I turned to the men and said, 'I have no tickets to this party. I'm gate-crashing it. I'm just warning you so there won't be any embarrassment when we get there.' The men looked faintly puzzled, and then the man who looked like Robert Redford said to me, 'It's not a party. It's a bar. Can we buy you a glass of champagne?'

We arrived at the bar, which I found out was called the Fifth Floor. It was filled with men very similar to the three I met in the lift. The women were glamorous – all long legs and short dresses, with Knightsbridge blow-dries. We sat at a round table. Robert Redford went to the bar and ordered a bottle of champagne while the others sat down at the table with me. He came back and took the seat next to me. 'What do you do?' he asked me.

'I'm a musician,' I said. 'I'm in a band. I play guitar.'

'What band?' he asked.

'I doubt you've ever heard of it,' I said. 'It's called The Fall.'

Of course he'd never heard of us. This happened to me a lot.

'What are you doing here?' the man asked me. Hearing my American accent he assumed I was just visiting.

'I'm here making a live album,' I told him. He asked me where I was staying and I explained that my ex-boyfriend was Nigel Kennedy and that we'd had a flat together in Hampstead where I still stayed when I came over. Now Nigel Kennedy he'd heard of. This piqued his attention.

I had no such thoughts about him. He was lovely, yes, but I was all about Murray Lachlan Young. I was off the market, so to speak. Then I asked the man about what he did.

He worked in men's fashion (which should have been obvious by the way he was dressed. It was sheer perfection). He told me he owned the clothing chain Woodhouse. 'I bought my first husband an Armani suit from Woodhouse in Manchester!' I said. I remembered that the suit I insisted Mark buy years ago had cost £700 – and this guy had shops full of them.

He told me he was newly separated from his wife of twenty years. We then talked about divorce. I gave him a few pointers I had learned from my round in the marital battlefield. I sympathised with him. It was tough, and he'd only been separated two weeks. He was freshly hurt, newly raw. 'Sad,' I thought, 'but he'll do all right.' He was handsome and obviously well off. He'd be a great catch for some lucky woman. I had no doubt he'd find happiness.

After we finished the champagne it was time to go. I needed to get some rest. The man had told me his name was Philip. I said my goodbyes (I hardly talked to the other two men) and I left. We did not exchange numbers. I imagined him getting into a Porsche and driving home. 'How refreshing,' I thought, 'to meet such a nice person, who bought me champagne and didn't want anything in return.' I really enjoyed our conversation and he didn't even hit on me, or ask for my number. I took a taxi home, downed a Rohypnol and went to sleep. I assumed I'd never see the man again. I put the night behind me, as a deep velvety blanket of sleep engulfed my conscious mind.

The next day I had a few meetings in town, and when I got back to Nigel's flat in the late afternoon the red light was blinking on the answering machine. The message was from Nigel's manager's secretary. 'Hello, Brixie, I'm sorry to call you at home, but I've had a gentleman on the phone who would like very much to get in touch with you. Apparently you met him last night at Harvey Nichols. His name is Philip Start and he left this number, and would like you to call him back.'

I called him back and said, 'You tracked me down! I can't believe it. What can I do for you?'

Then he explained, 'I so enjoyed talking to you last night. You seem like a sweet person. I would like to take you out.'

'You're asking me on a date?' I was stunned. I had never been pursued like this before. My mind, which had been focused on Murray, was not prepared for this. I thought for a moment, and weighed everything up. Philip Start was also very handsome, grown-up and cultured (with taste). He might turn out to be a boring rich businessman, but so what?

Philip was keen to go out that week. But I was busy for two weeks, recording gigs for the live album. I was due to spend the next week in Manchester (I'd also invited Murray to come up with me and stay in the hotel), so I made the date with Philip, for when I was back in London.

The night before my date had been a heavy one. I had partied hard and had fallen asleep, in a numbed-out stupor with Rohypnol, in the late morning. I didn't wake up until 7 p.m. I scrabbled around getting dressed and grabbed one of Nigel's old jackets from off the floor. I threw it over my outfit. I ran outside, hailed a taxi and arrived at the Kensington bar forty-five minutes late. Philip was not pleased. I was surprised that he had waited for me. My time-keeping was dreadful back then; my clock was permanently set to the rock and roll time zone. After I apologised profusely, he seemed to relax a bit. We had a drink and the conversation warmed up. I had no intention of really dating him. I must have been giving off hard-to-get vibes. The thing is, sometimes being hard to get only makes men want you more. Especially men who are used to getting what they want in life, as Philip obviously was.

We left the bar and went to a restaurant where Philip had booked a table for dinner. He drove us there in his navy blue Porsche 911 convertible (exactly as I imagined). We arrived at a restaurant called the First Floor, above the Market Bar in Notting Hill. We sat down to a meal, and I ordered steamed vegetables with no butter or oil. I was in one of my anorexic phases, on a mission (again) to get and remain as thin as I possibly could. Our conversation was easy. Philip was so easy to talk to, the evening disappeared in record time. There was never a lull in our dialogue and, before we knew it, the restaurant was closing. Neither of us was ready for the night to end. Philip invited me back to his house, in Holland Park, for a drink.

Philip's house was one of the loveliest houses I'd ever seen in London. It was huge and Georgian, but remodelled in a modern way, retaining the best of the old with the elegance and minimalistic vibe of the new. He looked at me and asked if I would like a smoke. I said yes, at first believing him to mean a cigarette. He got up, and reached into a kitchen drawer, from which he pulled out the biggest lump of black Afghani hash I had ever seen. It was bigger than a man's fist. He wasn't as straight as I imagined. This night had just gotten very interesting indeed.

We stayed up all night talking. When morning came we went to breakfast. We spent most of the next day together. The next night I slept over in his guest room. But at some point in the night I snuck downstairs and crawled into bed with Philip. There was definitely something brewing between us, and being in his company was seamless and addictive. We talked about having sex. I insisted we both go for AIDS tests. I was spending my days off with Philip, and sleeping with Murray during the nights. I was juggling. I felt guilty . . . a bit. I wasn't completely honest with either of them. I figured it was my business, and I'd deal with it, when the time came. I was a free agent.

After two weeks of this pattern, Philip, who was by no means stupid, sat me down at a restaurant and had a heart-to-heart with me. It was crunch time, I could feel it. My time in the UK was coming to an end. I was due to fly back to LA for a few months and pick up my life there. I would come back to the UK and Europe in the summer. The Fall were booked to play some big festivals and a few dates. I was dreading leaving both Philip and Murray. I had already changed my ticket once, to stay longer. Philip looked me straight in the eyes and said, 'I know you are seeing somebody else. I want to give you one hundred per cent, but you have to give me one hundred per cent.'

'Wow,' I thought. That was so direct and to the point. Nobody had ever said anything like that to me before. I felt embarrassed that he had known I'd been two-timing him with Murray all along.

I thought about what Philip said for a minute, and then replied, 'I'd be happy to give you a hundred per cent of me, after you go out and fuck anybody you want to. You've been in a relationship for a long time. I don't want to commit to you if you are going to play the field. You go, get it all out of your system, and when you're finished, I'll be here, waiting. I just don't want to go through it. I don't think I can handle it.'

Then he said words I'd never thought I'd hear. Words I'd always wished to hear but had given up any hope of hearing: 'I've been around a long time. I know what I want. And I want you. Break up with him.'

My eyes filled with tears. 'OK,' I said.

Two days later, I stood in the Atlantic Bar and Grill with Murray, in almost the exact spot where I'd met him. I explained the situation. I was emotional. I loved Murray. I loved both of them. Philip, however, was a healthy choice. He was the man I'd been waiting for all my life. I knew it. I'd kissed a lot of frogs before I found my prince. If I hadn't been in relationships that were difficult and destructive I would never have realised what a good relationship felt like. Thank goodness for dualities.

Murray was amazing about the whole thing. I think he loved me too. He loved me so much he let me go. We embraced. We cried in each other's arms.

Then I left the Atlantic Bar, and got into Philip's car, where he was waiting for me, to begin our life together. We have been together for over twenty years. We are partners in every way, and I love him very much. At last I made the right choice.

During a break from shows I went back to LA, and I was reunited with my pug Satchmo. Philip and I talked every night on the phone for hours. We had a transatlantic love affair. Unable to be apart, Philip planned to come to LA and see me. I was to return to the UK three months later, so we decided to cut the time apart in half with Philip's visit.

In the meantime, I continued my mega diet. I ate as few calories as I could, and ran for an hour each day. I was getting painfully thin and the bones in my chest were now protruding, which I thought was great, but I must have been looking like the *Cerebral Caustic* cover without the clown nose. When Philip arrived, I introduced him to Susanna Hoffs and Lisa Feder, along with my other friends, Robin Ruzan and Suzanne Todd. They all approved. Even though Philip was almost seventeen years older than me, which raised a few eyebrows, they all adored him.

I introduced Philip to my grandmother, who took us out to the Friars Club in Beverly Hills for brunch. Sadly my grandfather had by then passed away from a stroke. My grandmother adored Philip and I was thrilled they got to meet. Philip was gobsmacked by the old-school Beverly Hills opulence of the club. It was a special day for me. I like to believe that my grandmother thought I was at last happy, and in safe hands.

After Philip left, I began to feel unwell. I was exhausted. At first, I thought I was lovesick, and possibly depressed again. But I was so debilitated I couldn't walk down the block. I began to worry. I could barely get up to go to the kitchen. I slept all the time and would wake up drenched in sweat. My sheets were wet. I checked my temperature and was running a low-grade fever, constantly. I began to vomit. I called Susanna and told her something was wrong. She told me to go to the doctor. I had a blood test. It wasn't good news. My liver was enlarged and inflamed; the doctor told me she suspected I had hepatitis. 'How could I have hepatitis?' I thought. 'I've never used a needle in my life.'

Susanna was worried about me and called her father. Josh Hoffs, being an eminent psychiatrist, had connections in the medical world. He referred me to a friend of his who was a specialist in diagnosing illnesses. I had a battery of tests. When the results were in, I was diagnosed as having a very rare virus called 'fifth disease', or human parvovirus B19. I was sure my dieting had caused it. I had depleted myself of crucial nutrients, and gotten too thin. I had weakened myself and caught the virus. I spent the next six weeks in bed eating as healthily as I could. I was riveted to the TV. I watched the O. J. Simpson trial round the clock.

Eventually I willed myself better. I wasn't completely well, and still exhausted, but I flew back to England to meet Philip and begin what would become (although I didn't know it then) my last stint in The Fall.

1996

We recorded *The Light User Syndrome* in Brixton at the beginning of 1996. This was the first record I'd make in The Fall without Craig. My new pug puppy, Gromit, came to the studio every day. Philip had bought her for me after Satchmo had sadly died of a catastrophic seizure. You can actually hear her barking on the album.

In the old days Mark would be in the studio all the time during recording. He'd nip out to the pub for a couple hours, but he'd be there every day. On this album it seemed that he didn't show up until he was properly drunk, and he would put his vocals down and then mess with whatever we had done. He'd come in and say, 'Take off that, put on that, do this', and re-orchestrate everything. Some days he wouldn't show up at all. He did most of his vocal parts on the final night.

Somehow, there are some great songs on that record. I loved singing the cheerleader backup on 'He Pep!', another one of Mark's odes to speed mixed with a rant about record companies. Julia did great keyboards on that track. Mark and I showed we could still come up with some magic together. 'Spinetrack' is a great song. I have no clue what it is about.

But there were some songs on the album that I thought so heinous I couldn't think of parts to add to them. I refused to play on 'Secession Man' and 'The Ballard of J. Drummer'. The record also had fifteen tracks – if it had been boiled down to the best nine it would have been more palatable. It's not like we were getting paid by the song. So the result is a few great songs, surrounded by pink fibreglass filler.

June 1996, and *The Light User Syndrome* had been released about two weeks earlier, with little fanfare. The tour had started off fine at the Astoria in London – a warm-up, basically, to a series of summer festivals. We were on our way to Denmark to play to 115,000 people at the Roskilde Festival, alongside Björk, Red Hot Chili Peppers, Pulp and David Bowie. On the plane I kept to myself and read a book. Mark apparently drank for the entirety of the flight. We were met in the Copenhagen airport by these sweet, young assistants to the Danish promoter. They were there to collect the bands and drive them to the hotel. They were chirpy twenty-year-olds, all smiles, with ruddy cheeks and blonde hair. They were so excited to meet The Fall. The band responded by being sullen and monosyllabic, heads down, not communicating. I was trying to be a human face and chatty. We got in to this white transit van. I was towards the back, sitting next to Steve Hanley. Mark was near the front and said, 'Right, let's go. Come on. Come on. *Raus.*'

Mark doesn't know German at all, but that doesn't stop him from speaking it. I think he learns it from Nazi war movies. Our current album featured the lyric, '*Das Vulture Ans Ein Nutter-wain*', which meant absolutely nothing. In the van he's screaming, '*Schnell! Schnell!*' He's getting louder. 'Come on, you cunts. Drive the van!' And the little happy chappy turned around and said, 'No, we have to wait for the other band to arrive.' Mark was incredulous: '*What?* This is our van. David fucking Bowie doesn't have to wait for any other band! Drive! Go! Leave them!'

Steve and I slinked down in the chairs and hid our faces. I was dying inside, but the worst was yet to come. They had to wait, but Mark was getting more and more irate, falling into a fugue of rage and paranoia and ego. Thunderbolts were emanating from him and the mangled German morphed into a litany of curses. It was like he was possessed. The driver was a nervous wreck, then the other band approached the van carrying their luggage. They were a mixed-race rap group; they were all very large and imposing. One of them came up smiling, and opened the door.

'*Get away from the fucking bus, boy!*' Mark bellowed. We were all stunned. The moment he said it I convulsed. Steve and I looked at each other and then I just floated above the situation and detached myself. There was no way to diffuse it, no way to reason with Mark, and no way to placate this band, who had been deeply offended (and rightly so).

I don't believe that deep inside Mark is a racist. I think he was just at the nadir of his John Galliano public spiral; the synapses in his brain were disconnecting and zapping poison charges – and he was drunk and barely able to walk while reaching, Tourette's-like, for the most offensive thing to say. This, crossed with his natural predilection to cause chaos and pit people against each other, and the fact that he was leading up to a seizure . . . He was extremely unwell and should have been in hospital .

But what he said was so bad. I just started crying. I begged the innocent cherub driver, 'Please! Go! Just drive away!'

The band, still trying to get on the bus, were beyond incensed. The driver realised the magnitude of the situation – that someone was going to get hurt – and peeled away, leaving them behind. The ride to the hotel was silent, or at least I think it was. We drove to where we were staying and I saw that it's called the Friendly Hotel, so I start laughing (while still crying). It was like a cosmic joke. I got out of the bus and we all checked in. Of course, I discovered I was rooming with Julia, because Rimmer did the booking assignments.

At the check-in I ran into two music agents I knew. I was still crying and upset, and they asked what was wrong. I told them and they were shocked. I went into mine and Julia's room. Philip had given me a mobile phone, so I called him and in between sobbing and hiccupping I said, 'I hate him, and want to come home now. I can't be in this band, it's tarnishing me as a human being.'

While I was on the phone there was a violent rapping on the door. I opened it and Steve Hanley was the most agitated I had seen him since we had met in 1983. 'Get out, right now!' he said, like there was a murderer in the attic. 'We're moving hotels.' We grabbed our things and ran back to the bus and went to another hotel. It turns out that the band had checked in to our hotel as well and we had to leave because they were on the warpath, hunting for Mark.

We still had to play the festival. The van took us to the backstage area, and we were being filmed that night for MTV. I wanted to go home to Philip and live a normal life. But we had obligations. Different MTV factions from all over the world were there to film us, but Mark was nowhere to be found. After the interview, Steve and I sat down and wondered if he was even going to turn up. We wrote the set-list, which is what we were used to doing by now. It was no longer this precious, divine scroll that only Mark could pen. He didn't give a fuck. Sometimes, at the last minute, he'd scribble things out and add songs which were done in my 'walking in the desert and serving pancakes' period, as he put it, so I would have no clue how to play them. It's a festival, so we filled the set-list with more upbeat numbers like 'Pearl City' and 'US 80s–90s'.

Our onstage time was approaching, and by this point we were unable to talk. Mark was still MIA, and festivals are big-money gigs. There was so much stress and tension, and 115,000 people screaming in the crowd. It went past the time we were due to go on – then Mark nonchalantly walked in. On stage, I was playing my guitar and it was sounding great. We had a power. The chaos was harnessed. I was losing myself in the music, in playing, in connecting with the other musicians – and I looked at Mark and I thought I was hallucinating. He had the snout of a mouse. It was like Mark E. Smith had visited *The Island of Dr Moreau*. I tried not to miss a note, but I inched closer and focused on his face. I could see that his face had been mangled to such a degree that, indeed, he had a snout. Some of his already precarious teeth had been knocked out. The offended band had found him and exacted their revenge. They tracked him down and beat the shit out of him.

But Mark was on stage singing and inspired. It was a great gig. He got all the way through without leaving the stage, and did all the songs. He rose to the occasion despite being beaten senseless.

I hated being the only guitarist. Craig and I had played off each other, and our differences were what created the sound. Without Craig there, it felt empty. The European tour ended in Barcelona. Rimmer had roomed me and Julia together again. We had a night off and the two of us went out and had some drinks at an outdoor bar overlooking a harbour. It was in a weird modern complex that looked like a surreal car park mixed with a golf course. We had a nice time together then went back to the hotel.

When we got back to our room, Mark had obviously been listening out for us. He came to the door of our hotel room and pounded and kicked it in frustration. It was late at night and other hotel guests called the front desk and complained. Security was called and Mark retreated to his room, and Julia, feeling bad and probably worried for her job, followed him. When she came back to our room there had been some kind of altercation, but she wouldn't go into detail.

Again, we still had yet to play the gig. Before the tour Mark and I had made an agreement that I was to be paid in cash (£500) every night after a show. I was paid after the first concert only. He claimed it was because all the advance money went into an account in Manchester, and I would be paid at the end of the tour. I was frustrated and said that that was not the deal, but I had no choice.

Philip flew in the next day to see us play. We were backstage, and I complained to him about how Mark hadn't paid me. Philip said, 'I'll deal with it.' Philip went into Mark's trailer, looked at him, rolled up his sleeves as if he were getting ready to punch Mark's lights out, and demanded that he pay me. I got my money. After that Mark only referred to Philip as 'the greengrocer', because he owned shops.

After the Phoenix Festival in July we had a break, until a UK tour in late September. Things deteriorated. Mark became more and more unhinged. He was violent, incoherent. I spent my whole time avoiding him. It was, I assumed, alcoholism and amphetamine psychosis. In a lovely country house hotel in Chiltern he turned all the paintings around so they were facing the wall. He said the paintings were speaking to him and spirits were coming out of them.

The substance abuse worsened. I would say, 'Look, this is so bad. You need to go somewhere and clean up and get everything out of your system.' He would thank me for being honest and then tell me to fuck off. He would call me a 'fucking bitch', 'tramp', 'cunt', everything. Our rider consisted of forty-eight cans of lager, forty-eight cans of bitter, one bottle of scotch, one bottle of vodka, one or two bottles of French champagne (which was for me), lime, Diet Coke and a juice. Everyone was drinking beer, continuously around the clock, and Mark would drink whiskey. If you were to walk into the dressing room you would turn right around because the vibe was so bad. It was like Mark was the abusive father and we were the huddled kids.

After every show Mark would give us what one would in theatre call 'notes'. That's a very polite way of describing his diatribes. He would turn and let us have it about who did what wrong. Once in a while somebody did something good. But mostly it was criticism about everything. Occasionally, it was a temper tantrum. Sometimes there would be a kernel of truth buried in his paranoid, different take. We would just sit there and take it.

The gigs were only shit when Mark would just abruptly leave the stage, which happened quite frequently. By this point, all I felt was anger towards him – as well as the heartbreak of seeing someone you once loved doing this. There was also self-preservation: I was trying to stay away from him and do my job, but I was furious at him for sabotaging what was so good. For most of the tour I had my own driver and wouldn't travel with the band. I couldn't be near Mark. It was awkward for the group, but I think they understood. We all have to do what we do to survive. I was constantly on the phone to Philip.

Steve and I were now officially in charge of doing the set-list every night. It was beyond Mark. Quite often he would be in his own dressing room, and we wouldn't see him until the show. More than once, I would have to go in there, just before our set time, and he would be passed out with his face on a table, drool coming out. It was my job to wake him up to get him on stage, because nobody else wanted to prod the lion.

SCABS

Scabs are endlessly fascinating to me. The remarkable way that the human body can knit its wounds is like magic. It's like watching time-lapse footage of a flower blooming and then dying: the ugly sandpaper melding of dried blood and skin cells morphing into a new soft, smooth surface. Sometimes the scars are visible. Sometimes they are invisible. They are always remembered, however, cellularly and psychologically. The scab stage I am most fascinated by is that of itching. When you know they are actually healing, but you can't seem to stop picking at them, worrying them, challenging them. The delicate pain of quiet self-harm.

Cheltenham, Saturday 5 October 1996. The last full day I spent in The Fall started like so many others. I rose with an early-morning wake-up call from the hotel reception. I was groggy, dopey and vibrating with a low hum of dread. ('Just get through it, just get through it.') By this time I was seriously dependent on sleeping pills. After years of touring – after hundreds (maybe thousands) of hotel rooms, endless, copious amounts of stress, and massively disturbed sleep patterns – I had succumbed to the only thing that could put me out. We had a lengthy five- or six-hour drive ahead of us that day, from Cheltenham to Motherwell. I dressed in a miniskirt, tights, Doc Martens and a comfy Voyage jumper, and headed to the hotel breakfast room. I ordered coffee, toast and gagged down an egg, for my own good. Bleary-eyed and sullen, I galvanised myself for the day ahead.

I remember seeing a roadie and the driver at another table. No other band members had managed to make it to breakfast. Instead, they preferred to roll out of bed and straight on to the bus, usually without showering, still reeking of last night's toxins. Tensions within the band were at their height. We sat separated in the bus keeping ourselves to ourselves. I sat in the back, hunkered down, immersed in my Patricia Cornwell crime novel, trying to blot out any brewing dramas. Everyone else was basically listening to music on headphones, sleeping, playing cards, smoking cigarettes.

Mark's mood swings, which were already the stuff of legend, had increased dramatically. Worst of all, he had begun having grand mal seizures. I lived in fear of him having a fit on stage. Thankfully, that never happened during my time in the band. Often he would turn up to a gig with a blackened tongue or a bruised face, from where he'd smacked it while thrashing and writhing on the ground. To watch someone you once loved, and still cared about, go through something so debilitating and scary was one of the most difficult things I've ever dealt with.

Although I never found out what caused the seizures, I suspected a long-term diet of amphetamines and alcohol played a large part. We all walked on eggshells around Mark. We gave him a wide berth on the bus, and did our best not to engage with him for fear of setting him off. The drive to Motherwell seemed endless. I was at my breaking point. Emotional, angry, depressed, on edge and exhausted.

I was scared about my future. The fear of the unknown. What would I do with my life if I left The Fall? I was now living with Philip. Still, as comfortable as that was, I needed to be able to take care of myself and not rely on someone else. A clever man like Philip wouldn't respect or fancy me for very long if all I did was live off him as a dependent. If I had learned anything over the years about relationships, it was that strong, intelligent, successful men (the kind I was attracted to) liked women whom they respected, and who had their own lives.

Finally, we arrived at the Motherwell Concert Hall, a gloomy, sad, monolithic cement theatre-cum-bingo hall. The sky was grey, heavy, overcast and oppressive. Mark passed me one last time on his way from washing his hands, yet again, in the sink. I noticed his hands had dark spots on them. Mark rarely turned up for the soundchecks any more. Long gone were the days of having a laugh and jamming on random un-Fall-like cover versions. The first thing we did during a soundcheck was mic up both drum kits and check the sound of each drum. We always placed a 'dummy' mic in front of each bass drum. During a show, one of Mark's favourite ways to torment us was to remove the bass drum mic, thus pulling the heartbeat out of the band and making it much more difficult to keep time and lock into sync with each other. And he still infuriatingly messed with the settings on all our amps mid-show. Sometimes we'd spend hours getting the sound just right, especially, for instance, if the venue had tricky acoustics. In the end we'd have to mark out our settings with gaffer tape on our amps each night, in case of sabotage.

The next instrument we'd check was Steve's bass. Then Julia's keyboards and guitar and, finally, my guitar and vocal mic. Someone, usually Steve, tested Mark's mic to make sure the sound was OK, and his monitor was working. A shitty monitor sound could result in instant meltdown.

The final detail of any soundcheck was to make sure the stage area was clear of any old pieces of gaffer tape used by previous bands to secure their leads. All pieces of old tape had to be physically scraped and peeled off the floor. These remnants of tape would send Mark into a furious rage. Only then were we ready to start soundchecking.

Sitting in my dressing room with my head in my hands, I took in the smell of stale beer and old pizza, combined with the sickening aroma of deodorising carpet cleaner. This was the scent of many a venue. (It would take me fifteen years to set foot into any music venue again. Every time I smelled that smell, my sense memory would take me back and slam me into an instant anxiety

THE RISE

attack.) Cigarette smoke clung to the walls. Lewd graffiti of penises and hairy balls, deftly scribbled on the walls by previous bands, couldn't even lighten my mood. I stared at the swirling purple and black carpet that vaguely reminded me of the carpet in mine and Mark's first flat together on Rectory Lane. How had things got this bad? We were plummeting.

The soundcheck started normally enough, but the tension in the air and the vibes were bad. With Mark still on the bus, I took my place on the stage with the others. I checked my guitar sound. I checked my vocal mic. I checked my monitors. All good. I set my levels on my amp and marked them with gaffer tape. All seven of my customised pink 'BRIX' plectrums (Dunlop USA 77 mm) were lined up and taped to my mic stand. (I was very OCD about this, and taping them was a ritual superstition.) I used to hand out my plectrums to avid Fall fans between songs as souvenirs.

We all started to play together, running through numbers to get the sound right for the engineer, who was setting the levels for the front of house.

About three songs in, Mark ambled cockily on stage. Looking like an extra from *Dawn of the Dead*, he was in a steaming mood. We all held our breath. 'Right! What the fuck is this monitor sound? It's SHIT! Right! You fuckin' cock, you fix this bleeding sound, you cunt!' With that, Mark picked up his mic stand, pulled it apart and hurled it spear-like at the poor bewildered monitor man standing innocently at the side of the stage. The man ducked and it missed him by inches.

I exploded. The fury of years of suppressed anger boiled up inside me like a raging torrent of devil's sputum. I yelled, 'DON'T YOU EVER DO THAT TO ANOTHER PERSON! You can't treat someone like that. He's just doing his fucking job.' The rest of the band stared, gobsmacked, jaws hanging. Mark turned on his heels and grabbed my handbag, which I had put to the side of the stage by my amp. He took it and threw it with all his might across the stage. The entire contents of my life scattered and strewed across the stage for everyone to see: mobile phone, tampons, lipsticks, a jewelled dog collar for Gromit, sleeping pills.

Now I was shaking with a rage I had never felt before. I vibrated with pure black fury. I grabbed my pink paisley Telecaster by the neck, the same one Elvis's guitar player Scotty Moore used, and I swung it like an axe. With all my might I ran at Mark, swinging it in hysterics. Then bellowing at the top of my lungs (*Auf der Lungen. Auf der Zungen*), 'I WILL SMASH YOUR HEAD IN LIKE A PUMPKIN!'

At this point things became blurry. We were separated by the others. Someone grabbed me. They pulled me back. Someone else grabbed Mark, who had gone nuclear, and was screaming, 'YOU BITCH! YOU AMERICAN PSYCHO-BITCH! YOU CUNT! YOU TRAMP! YOU FUCKIN' SHITBAG FROM LA! GET THIS PSYCHO BITCH AWAY FROM ME! Assault! ASSAULT! Call the police! CALL THE FUCKING POLICE! I'M BEING ATTACKED BY A PSYCHO AMERICAN BITCH!'

My guitar was wrenched from my hands. Mark wrestled out of the arms of his captors and grabbed my guitar. He smashed it to the ground and threw it off stage. I was sobbing, shaking and broken. Mark was ushered off stage back to the bus. Someone was trying to calm him. He was intent on calling the police and having me charged with assault. I never actually touched him, physically. Afterwards they told me they wished I had landed a blow.

The next thing I remember was sitting alone with Steve, sobbing. We sat in the foyer of the theatre near the main bar. I told Steve I couldn't go on. I couldn't deal with Mark any more. I couldn't deal with this craziness and the stress and tension. I couldn't condone the things he did, and how they reflected on me – us – as human beings. I started reeling off the list of unpleasant incidents – moments when Mark's lapse in sanity caused me to feel a deep shame within my soul. Steve calmed me, and sat with me like a father might do. This big pillar of a man was listening to me, understanding me. I knew he wanted me to stay.

I started on my Mark rant again, bringing up every unhinged incident and weird moment of behaviour. 'Anyway, Steve,' I said, carrying on with my tirade, 'did you see him on the bus? Washing his hands constantly? What's all that about? Did you see all those black marks on his hands?'

'Don't you know, Brix?' Steve asked. 'Don't you know why he keeps washing his hands?'

'No,' I said. 'Why?'

'Well, do you remember the second date of the tour? Back at King's Lynn Corn Exchange? After the show, a fan came backstage to meet Mark. She was in a wheelchair. Mark shook her hand. Ever since then he's been washing his hand obsessively, believing he caught her "disease".'

I sucked in my breath, shocked and dumbfounded. I stopped sobbing.

Steve went on, 'He washed and washed and washed his hands, but the "disease" would not come out, so he BIT IT OUT. The black marks on his hand are scabs from trying to bite out the "disease", so it can escape.'

It was the scabs that got me in the end. The realisation of how troubled Mark's mind had become. I knew then that I could no longer safely stay in this environment. I could not control this. It was unfixable. My gut instinct (Mother) told me to get the hell out of there, and fast. Don't look back. Don't think. Just go. Run. The only thing I could control now was myself. Nothing is better than something that's bad (Father, biological).

I grabbed my belongings, including my guitars, and asked the promoter to call a taxi for me. I went to the nearest airport, which was in Glasgow, and took the next flight to London. I never played the gig. I left them all in a pit of chaos and misery. I quit. But in quitting I saved myself. My scabs were going to heal.

The Fall played two remaining dates without me. In Worthing, an audience member tied Mark's shoelaces together and he fell down on stage. The final show of the tour was the next week in London. Pete Nash, our agent, called me and said, 'Brix, please come back and do London. You don't have to talk to him, just get on that stage and do it. They need you to do it or they're going to go down.' He begged me, and I said, 'Fine.' I turned up at the Forum in Kentish Town and Mark had no idea why I was there. I don't remember him speaking to me. Inside, I felt that there was a part of him relieved that I'd come back to do the show, but he wasn't going to tell me. I knew it was my last time on stage with them. Instead of saying, 'Good night', which is what I always used to say to the audience, I said, 'Goodbye.'

NOTTING HILL

Periods of transitions in life are seldom easy – my transition from The Fall back into real life certainly wasn't. Philip was going through changes too. He had recently sold his fashion chain, Woodhouse. He was now in the final stages of divorce from his wife, and to raise the money he was forced to sell his beloved house on Addison Avenue in Holland Park.

Eventually, we found a small terraced house in Notting Hill, on Westbourne Park Road. We bought it with Philip's remaining money, and moved in. It was a lovely house, but Philip hated it. Nothing it seemed would measure up to the splendour of the Holland Park home. For three years we lived in Notting Hill. I pursued my solo music projects and pushed myself to keep writing. I managed, somehow, to get one EP out called *Happy Unbirthday*. I did this with Marty Willson-Piper and one of The Fall's old producers, Mike Bennett. One track on it I particularly liked was the cover version of David Bowie's 'Space Oddity'. I actually had high hopes for a song called 'Orangina', which was inspired by a salacious story Mike Myers once told me about a girl's vagina. (I still think 'Orangina' is a hit waiting to happen.)

Marty and I had an entire album of demos we had written and recorded during my downtime in LA. A friend of Marty's called Dare Mason had a studio in Penzance, Cornwall, and invited us to come down record at his studio. He generously said he would produce the album for us. In Penzance we recorded the entire album properly. The album included the songs 'Star', 'Super Softy', 'Hooves for Hands' and 'The Joys of You' among others, but music began to fade away into the background of my life, and my feelings about it began to change. My relationship to music was like that of a relationship to an old lover. Not only was I no longer attracted to it, I felt myself begin to sour towards it. I know this was my self-preservation instinct kicking in. Because I had hit a brick wall with my musical career (yet again, and possibly the final wall in my astrological chart prediction) I guess I had no choice but to turn my back on it completely.

The music business had consumed me. Now I wanted nothing to do with it. I shoved my guitars in the closet. I stopped going to any gigs, and I rarely listened to records, or the radio. I didn't care. Once, at a dinner party, the person seated next to me asked what I did, and I replied, 'Nothing.' I saw Philip visibly cringe. The fact was I was doing nothing. I was at a place in my life where I had no direction. The strands of my life as a musician that I had tenuously pulled together in LA – and carried on with during my second time in The Fall – had slipped through my hands like wet noodles. This time, though, it wasn't a man who broke my heart, it was the music business itself.

For me, the music had died. I put The Fall firmly behind me. I never told anyone what I did. I simply didn't discuss it. I tried to erase my memory banks. I didn't want to be one of those sad musicians who live off their past glory, talking endlessly about a band they used to be in. The thought of re-joining The Fall ever again was abhorrent. The mental image of myself standing on stage at the age of fifty, playing the guitar, was unthinkably hideous. 'Who would want to see that?' I reasoned. I made a conscious decision to retire from music. Chapter closed.

Even though there were many moments of joy in my life, I slowly slipped into another depression, without realising it. Unbeknownst to anybody, including Philip, I spent the bulk of the day lying on the couch and watching daytime TV. I slept a lot and vegetated. I hid this from Philip. As soon as I knew he was on his way home from work, I'd pull myself together, spruce myself up and pretend I'd been productive. In actual fact, I was barely keeping it together. I was functioning, but only just. It was only after my close friend Kate Holmes suggested that I might be suffering depression that I broke down in tears and sought help.

Sadly, my old Jungian therapist Eva Loewe had passed away from breast cancer while I was living in LA. Philip's family GP referred me to yet another shrink, and my depression was diagnosed. I was promptly put back on Prozac, which helped to alleviate some of the grief I felt about leaving The Fall and quitting music. I rekindled my old friendship with the dancer/TV presenter Katie Puckrik. Katie was now a well-known public face. When I saw her on TV, I got a very strong feeling. The same feeling I used to get as I teenager watching bands playing live on stage. 'I can do that too. I should be doing that. I'd be good at that.'

I decided to reinvent myself as a TV presenter.

THE WEDDING OF THE CENTURY

My first TV job came in a roundabout way. I was introduced to the journalist Cathy Wilson, from the *Daily Telegraph*. She was the style director at the *Telegraph* magazine at the time. We formed a friendship. Along with another friend of hers she was starting up an all-female production company. They needed a presenter, and gave me a shot. They had very close ties to Channel 4, and were hired to produce some fashion content to be included in the coverage of the Cheltenham Festival. We filmed an interview with the race-horse trainer Henry Cecil at his home and stable yard, where I spoke to him about his fashion style. On the day of the actual races I did a live piece to camera, discussing all the fabulous frocks and glamorous people at the race track. It was stressful but exhilarating. We also filmed at London Fashion Week. I reported live from the catwalk on the Robert Cary-Williams show. This was not broadcast on the channel but was, in fact, streamed live over the internet. It was one of the first times Channel 4 had ever attempted anything like this, with groundbreaking new technology.

After five years together, Philip and I decided to get married. This was more important to me than him. I had been sensitive about our age gap, and felt judged by people who assumed I was his midlife-crisis plaything. I was still insecure, having been burnt so badly in the past. I wanted to feel legitimised. I rang my mother and Marvin in Chicago, and broke the news. They were overjoyed and we began to plan the wedding. My mother and Marvin generously offered to pay for the whole thing. We decided that it would take place in Italy. My mother and Marvin had done very well over the years. Marvin was one of the foremost experts in

America on Iran and the Middle East. His expertise in risk analysis of emerging markets had propelled him from university professor to public speaker and nightly news expert. He advised everybody from the state department to oil companies. My mother, having retired from her job as the head of the state of Illinois film commission, was now managing Marvin's hugely successful career.

They'd decided to invest some of the money they made in property. One of the properties they purchased was called San Pietro. It was an eleventh-century church and farmhouse, half a mile up a mountain in Umbria. It was stunning, with panoramic views over the Umbrian countryside. They'd bought San Pietro in 1989 from the Catholic church, who owned most of the property and land in the area. It had been abandoned, and the buildings were practically ruined. Marvin and Mom lovingly restored the buildings and planted wild gardens and built a glorious pool. The whole place was spectacular (*spettacolare*, as the Italians would say). Mom and Marvin had vacationed every summer there since they bought it – as had I – and some Christmases too. This was great for me. It allowed me to spend more time with them, since they were now partially based in Europe.

San Pietro was to be the scene of my forthcoming wedding. My mom donned her old 'producer's cap' and set about putting together *un matrimonio spettacolare*. Over the next year, I flew back and forth between the American embassy in Rome, the commune in Città di Castello (where our house was in Umbria), and London, trying to sort out the reams of paperwork and official documents needed to get married legally in Italy. Because I was a US citizen, and a UK resident – and Philip was a British subject – it was all incredibly complicated. Whilst I was in Italy, my mom and I made pilgrimages to caterers, venues, florists, photographers and a range of hotels, *palazzi* and B&Bs. We were helped by our dear friend Patrizia, who acted as an interpreter and organiser for us. Eventually we settled on everything, and booked it all up.

I had asked another good friend, Angel (Dunn) Radcliffe, to be my matron of honour. She helped me with all of my preparations, including the wedding dress and bridesmaids' dresses. I had decided to ask our friend Desiree Mejer, the designer and owner of FAKE LONDON, to make my dress for me. Desiree was a wild and fun Spanish woman who had hit it big with her label of mostly recycled cashmere. Angela and I would drive out to East London, where Desiree lived and worked. FAKE was located in a huge industrial loft in Wapping, overlooking the Thames. We talked to Desiree about what I wanted, and then returned periodically for fittings. I loved where Desiree lived. East London was not yet gentrified. It was edgy and cool like SoHo in New York had been in the eighties. There was a creative energy there. It was a different way of living than in West London. It was more bohemian and artistic.

On the day of the final fitting, Angela and I drove out east. I was excited to see the finished dress. We both were. The dress was actually in two parts. The top was a pale pink cashmere halter top, decorated with three-dimensional roses made out of cashmere in pastel colours of blush, cream and pink. The top was backless and tied with silk ribbons. It was dotted discreetly with Swarovski crystals. The skirt, also dotted with crystals, was made of white shredded silk tulle. It was the sort of dress a punk princess-cum-waif ballerina might wear. It was delicate yet irreverent.

As we got back into the car after the fitting, Angela turned to me and said, 'This is one of the hardest things I've ever had to say to anybody – but you are one of my best friends, and I have to be completely honest with you. Please don't be upset. I'm so sorry, Bree [her nickname for me], but you cannot wear that dress . . . It's just not good enough.'

Angela was a top model. She had modelled for Yves Saint Laurent and Hardy Amies, among others. She knew her stuff when it came to fashion. She was, and still is, my go-to person for fashion and styling advice. Her nickname is '1-800-ANGELA'.

She has amazing taste and is very cultured in social and fashion etiquette. She explained to me that for an occasion such as this particular wedding, that dress was so casual, too rock and roll, and not nearly elegant enough for the occasion planned.

I cried. I panicked. 'What should I do?' I wailed. I had only five days left before I was due to leave for Italy to start my final wedding preparations. I was also devastated for Desiree. We both were. She had worked so hard on the dress. We struggled with how to tell her. She would be coming to the wedding, and I would be walking down the aisle wearing someone else's dress. It was a fashion disaster of major proportions.

We decided to ask Jan Marie von Giebelhausen, who was making my pre-wedding dinner dress and all the bridesmaids' dresses, if she could use the same pattern she had cut for the pre-wedding dress to make a wedding dress. If she could, we would just have to pick the fabric.

She could, and we did. I chose an off-white silk-satin fabric, covered partially with white cream chiffon, which dripped off my shoulders. My back was exposed, and down one side of my back Jan Marie sewed huge champagne-and-white silk flowers. The dress itself was cut like a flamenco dress. It was slit very high up my leg and ruffled at the edges. I showed a lot of leg when I walked. My body was perfectly honed from all the yoga I had been doing to fill my days. I'd never been in better shape in my life. I wore white Gina sandals with glittering buckles. The dress Jan Marie made was sheer perfection. She was also a model, and a trained couturier. She was still putting the final touches on my dress on the morning of my wedding.

Before I left for Italy, there was one thing left to do, and that was to have a hen night. Kate Holmes threw me the hen party. It started out in the Primrose Hill record company offices of her husband, Alan McGee of Creation Records. I had a group of about ten girls, including Angela, Gráinne Fletcher, Cathy (Wilson) St Germans,

Patsy Kensit, the novelist Freya North, Murphy Williams, Desiree and Ruth (Mayer) Day. We started out with champagne and sushi, and then headed to the newly opened private club Home House, on Portman Square. Kate was a member. Things got a little crazy there, and I remember one guest, not named above (and who shall remain nameless), performing a party trick to end all party tricks.

She opened a bottle of champagne with her vagina!

The morning of the wedding was bathed in sparkling sunshine. At the appointed time, one in the afternoon, Marvin drove me in the 'wedding mobile' (our cool, black Alfa Romeo sedan) to the eleventh-century commune building in the centre of Città di Castello. He escorted me out of the car and up the ancient sloping steps to the 'courtroom', where everybody was assembled, including Angela, my maid of honour, and my seven bridesmaids, who included Michelle Lineker and Marvin's daughters, Nadia and Leah. Marvin's mother, Grandma Clara, my only living grandparent, who was ninety-three at the time, had travelled all the way from Boston.

My mother was also, of course, waiting for me, with tears in her eyes. Rocky, Philip's son, walked my mother down the aisle to her seat. Tellisa Clarke, the daughter of my friends Lesley and the hairdresser Nicky Clarke, was my flower girl.

I walked in to the sound of a string quartet playing, first, Bach, and then 'Here Comes the Bride'. Philip was waiting by the altar, wearing a white suit and white Prada shoes. He looked devastatingly handsome. We were married by the mayor of the Città di Castello. My stepsister Nadia, who was fluent in Italian, translated for the guests. Philip and I were given the key to the city and made honorary citizens. My wedding day was one of the happiest days of my life.

After the formal part of the wedding was over, the guests were driven by minibus to a castle we had hired in Tuscany for the champagne reception. Il Castello di Lippiano was a very special place.

Marvin again drove the wedding car, with me and Philip in the back. The reception was held in the upper grounds of the castle. We had a selection of hot hors-d'oeuvres, including my favourite: deep-fried zucchini blossoms. As the sun set, and night fell, the castle was lit by hundreds of candles. The dinner took place on the lower castle grounds, where tables were set up and named after my favourite places in the world. My table was St Barths. I had worked very hard on all the table arrangements and seat placements. One table, I remember, was the Rock and Roll table. Seated there were Alan McGee and Kate Holmes, the music journalist James Brown (who had done the first interview with me when I'd joined The Fall sixteen years previously), Nick Laird-Clowes from The Dream Academy, Liam Gallagher from Oasis and Patsy Kensit. Also on the table were Andy Fletcher from Depeche Mode and his wife, my friend Gráinne.

Alan McGee and Liam Gallagher had graciously offered to DJ for the night. The first song they played to kick off a night of dancing was 'Guns of Brixton' by The Clash. It was 14 August 1999, and we partied like it was 1999.

The next day, the final day, was relaxed and chilled out. We held an all-day party and buffet in our gardens at San Pietro. Everyone joined us at our home for swimming, hiking and eating. My mother had done an amazing job organising the wedding. It was perfect. Every single moment of it. Patsy Kensit told me I was the most beautiful bride she'd ever seen. Angela Radcliffe dubbed it 'The Wedding of the Century'.

PIONEERS

Following the release of the movie *Notting Hill* property prices in the area had doubled. We were asset-rich, but cash-poor. After our wedding, we began to discuss downsizing. We thought it was a good time to change our life, and start afresh somewhere else. Philip never loved our house, and by selling it we could release some much-needed cash. I didn't relish the thought of leaving Notting Hill. All my friends were there. It was a small village where I felt comfortable.

But one day, as Philip and I were driving out to see Desiree Mejer at FAKE LONDON HQ in Wapping, something caught my eye as we headed down City Road, near the Old Street round-about in Shoreditch. It was a big banner hanging from a massive red-brick building: 'Loft for sale'. There was a telephone number printed on the banner. I wrote it down. 'Look, Buddy [my nickname for Philip], there's a loft for sale. I think we should go and take a look.'

The building, which was an old factory, was equidistant from Islington and Shoreditch. It was a superb location. I felt I was definitely being guided. My skin tingled and rose with goosebumps as I punched in the number on the phone. When things in life are meant to be, they move easily, with no resistance.

As it happened, the estate agent was free, and just around the corner. We pulled our car over and waited by the big industrial gates of the old factory. The loft we were going to see was, in fact, a penthouse. It was over 2,800 square feet and had a 1,000-square-foot roof terrace. It was bigger than our whole four-floor house in Notting Hill. As we entered the loft, I was surprised to see it was truly a shell. The entranceway and common parts had already been done to a tastefully high standard. I had wrongly assumed all the units had been done up too. Although some had, the one we were being shown hadn't. The space inside the loft was virtually uninhabitable. There were no individual rooms, of course, just one huge space. There was not a single pipe, no bathrooms, and no internal walls. The floor was filthy, made up of cracked, uneven cement. There were pigeons living on the inside of the loft, their feathers and shit in mini-heaps on the floor. The ceiling was high – so high that light flooded into the space from the massive, industrial glass windows that surrounded the apartment on three sides. The apartment was a corner unit, and benefited from light coming from the south and from the east.

As we stood in the vast room of the loft and looked up, we looked straight into a void. Here, the ceiling was double-aspect. It soared more than thirty feet above our heads. Light from the glass roof at the top of the loft illuminated the space even more.

There was a second floor, and a roof terrace, but there were no stairs. There was an old rickety ladder leaning against a brick wall. We had to angle it through the gap in the ceiling, and rest it precariously against the cement ledge of the floor above. I was too scared to go all the way up. Isobel, the estate agent, and I held the ladder for Philip, so he could climb as high as he dared, to get a better look at the space. 'You've got to get up here,' he said. 'You will not believe how great it is up here.'

The developers, the Manhattan Loft Corporation, had put architectural structures made of metal and glass on the roof of every penthouse, which allowed light to flood in, creating über-modern conservatories. It didn't matter to me that it was in Shoreditch, which had once been a slum. Philip and I looked at each other, and decided there and then to buy it. Philip made an offer on the spot.

THE SEED WAS PLANTED

The raw space of our loft was like a blank canvas on which we could create the home of our dreams. Philip had a vision for what he wanted, and he knew what he did not want: a typical utilitarian industrial loft, one with kitsch furniture, and bicycles hanging from the walls. His inspiration was, instead, that of an elegant, minimal, but luxurious New York penthouse: lots of rich wood, glass and stainless steel to offset the exposed brick walls. We hired Colin Radcliffe, my friend Angela (Dunn) Radcliffe's husband, to design and build the interiors for us. Colin used walnut for the floors, kitchen and bathroom. He built a floating staircase to the second level, where he installed a glass floor, which let light pour through from the glass roof above it. We turned the terrace into a roof garden, with a flower-covered pergola under which we could seat up to twelve people. The view from our rooftop garden over the City of London was panoramic. Philip furnished the house with twentieth-century modern furniture, and his impressive art collection. Colin also designed the flat so it was photographer-friendly. It was used for both photo-shoots and filming, which eventually generated an income stream for us. Our kitchen was used by chefs Jamie Oliver and Gary Rhodes for both of their TV shows.

For the six months that our apartment was being built, Gráinne and Andy Fletcher lent us their weekend home in Marlow, Buckinghamshire, on the banks of the Thames. It was blissful and calm. Their house was located on a private island, with no direct access for cars. Philip, who commuted to London every morning, parked his car off the island on a nearby street. As the flat neared completion, Philip decided he didn't want to work for the company he had created. He was no longer a majority shareholder, so he sold off his remaining shares and cut his ties to Woodhouse for ever. The sale of his shares gave us some money to live off . . . for the time being.

We would both have to find jobs in the future. The question was: what would we do? What could we do? I was dead, musically speaking, and retired. TV work so far was unpaid and decidedly sparse. Although I still believed I would crack it at some point, the reality was . . . it wasn't happening yet, and might never happen. Philip too needed a complete reinvention.

After our wedding, I had received some devastating news. My half-brother Jon had been diagnosed with multiple sclerosis, the same disease my father suffered from. He was no longer able to work as a graphic artist in New York and had had to move back to LA, where he would be closer to Maggie and my father. That way he could be cared for if and when the time came. I needed to see him and give him my love. He was in his twenties. I wondered if it was genetic. I also wondered if perhaps this disease had been affecting my father's mental health all along? Perhaps it could explain much of his behaviour? Maybe it was time to cut my father some slack?

I decided to call him and bury the hatchet. It was time for me to reach out to him like an adult. With Philip by my side I felt stronger. I no longer needed to cling to the fantasy that my father would come through for me and take care of me. I stopped worrying about whether my father loved me, and decided to love him, no matter what. I wanted to forgive him, and see if I could try one last time to have some sort of relationship with him.

Philip and I started our holiday in LA, staying at the truly romantic Hotel Bel-Air for a few days. This hotel was one of my all-time favourites; since we hadn't had a honeymoon, I thought a few days at the Bel-Air would be a special treat. I invited my father over to join us for breakfast. I assumed the front desk would call me when my father arrived, which would give me time to come out, and greet him on my own. I could make my peace privately with him, and then Philip could join us after we'd had a chance to talk.

Philip was in the bathroom getting ready when there was a knock at the door of our bungalow. I opened the door to find my father standing there, unannounced. I was marginally caught off guard. I had been anxious even to call him, but I was trying, and that's what was important. My father had aged. His hair was now white. He had put on weight; he looked like my grandfather. He had swapped his cowboy boots for Birkenstocks. He wore jeans and a linen shirt. Thankfully, he wasn't wearing a kilt. He burst in the room and hugged me. He sat down on the bed. After making himself at home, he began to pour his heart out.

Sobbing, with tears streaming down his face, he apologised for being a terrible father to me, Jon and Karina. He said he'd realised he'd mentally fucked us up. He went on to say he had done the best he could, and begged my forgiveness. He then listed a multitude of things he'd done wrong, both as a parent and a man. He owned up to his past mistakes and the damage he had wreaked on his children. At one point he even said he should never have had children.

Philip, who had been listening behind the bathroom door, was stunned. He came into the room and hugged my father. Philip was blown away by what he had overheard my father telling me. He told my father how courageous it was for him to come here and 'own up' and speak so honestly with me. Unfortunately, I'd heard my father's impassioned speeches one too many times in my life. Still, I believed he meant it; every single word of it. And it was important for me to hear those words. I felt deep in my father's soul that he needed to say them. My father's confession was a release for both of us on some level. Still, I wondered if anything would change?

After the conversation, I asked my father about the vintage stove I had left with him while I set up my new home with Philip. It contained all of my music memorabilia – press cuttings, photographs, everything. I wanted him to send it all to me.

'What memorabilia?' he replied. 'I thought you were never coming back for the stove so I gave it to the neighbour.'

I didn't know what to say. All the mementos of my life and my career up to that point were gone . . . for ever. I had promised him I would come back for it. I was incredulous.

After we finished breakfast, we said goodbye to my father. I waited for weeks, then months, for him to pick up the phone and call me. I had wanted to believe he would stay true to his word. I waited and I waited. It was his turn now. I'd done my bit. I'd done it multiple times over the years. My hopes would always be crushed, even though I tried not to have hope. Years went by . . . I turned forty . . . then fifty . . . No call ever came.

After the meeting with my father, the rest of the trip was a breeze. We stayed with Candice Hanson, my lawyer, for a few days, and Aunt Susie and Uncle Fred in Brentwood. We hung out with all my friends, and visited my brother, who was doing well, considering his debilitating illness. We decided to tour around LA and check out the great shops and hot restaurants. Philip, a retailer at heart, wanted to see the best and coolest shops Los Angeles had to offer. We spent an inordinate amount of time in Fred Segal on Melrose. Philip loved the café there, the healthy Californian cuisine. Fred Segal had always been one of my favourites too. My mother had taken me there as a kid. It was the go-to place for jeans: they had one of the best selections in the world. The shop was a boutique emporium, a destination store. Philip found it inspirational. Unbeknownst to us, a seed had been planted, in both our minds.

We returned to England after our eventful trip and moved into our new loft. Reunited with our pug, Gromit, we set out to gauge the lay of the land and finally get our heads around our future. We could not afford to live a life of leisure for much longer.

STARTING AGAIN

Our loft was a sensational place. But Shoreditch was not. The transition from the leafy, charming neighbourhood of Notting Hill to the urban wasteground of Shoreditch was proving hard. We made frequent trips back to West London to see our friends, dine and shop. We even took Gromit to Kensington Gardens for her walk. Old habits died hard.

Frequently we were invited to dinner parties, always in West London, since we didn't know anyone in Shoreditch. I've always thought it polite to take the host or hostess of a dinner party a small gift. One morning I woke up, grumpy. The first thought I had was that I was going to have to go all the way to Selfridges to buy a hostess gift. Lying in bed, I turned to Philip and complained, 'There's nowhere to buy anything around here.'

Philip thought for a while, and then he looked at me and said, 'Why don't we build a shop in Shoreditch, and fill it with everything we love?'

According to Plato, 'necessity is the mother of invention', and so it was with us. The necessity of buying a hostess gift gave way to us starting a shop. We just felt: if you build it they will come. That very day, Philip set about scouring Shoreditch for the perfect location for our shop. He found a small empty estate agent's office near Hoxton Square. The empty office was on a dirty back street called Rivington Street. There were only a handful of retail businesses open in the area at the time: the famous Bricklayer's Arms pub, which was the heart of old Shoreditch; the SCP furniture shop; Tommy Gun's hairdressers, who pioneered the famous Hoxton-fin haircut; and, as luck would have it, the executive head chef of the

Ivy, Mark Hix, was opening his first restaurant, the Rivington, on the same street. Philip instinctively knew the area was ripe and rife; he felt it. He made an offer on the empty estate agent's office. It was accepted.

We were introduced to a talented artist and shop-fitter who was also an expert in lighting. Philip Oakley and Philip (Start) would design the shop together. The shop was on two floors. We divided it into men's and women's. The basement, which was tiny, would be the women's department. My domain. I was so excited. I couldn't wait to do the buying and create an environment in our little shop. It didn't matter that I'd never done it before. I went into it blind, with enthusiasm. I loved clothes: I'd been an avid shopper all my life, I'd been to the best stores in the world. How hard could it be? I figured that if I filled the store with clothes that I loved, other people would love them too. Besides, I had Philip, with thirty years of retail experience behind him. He was a visionary in menswear, and helped to revolutionise men's retail in the UK. He was beloved and respected by all who knew him in the fashion industry.

Before we started the buying process, Philip told me it was crucial to identify our market, our customer base. Shoreditch was a burgeoning creative hub. Architects, graphic designers, PRs and the beginning of the tech industry were all starting to move into offices in the neighbourhood. The area was home to a vibrant art and music scene. There were multiple art galleries, artists' and photographers' studios, DJs, nightclubs and recording studios already ensconced.

It was also important that we had a point of difference from other stores. It was vital to invent ourselves as a destination shop. It was do or die. We would curtail our stock to appeal to this market. These were the customers that would be our focus. We would cater to their needs.

With that in mind, we began to visit showrooms, and pick up fabulous street brands: Maharishi, original Adidas, including vintage trainers, and a complete leather tracksuit, which the DJs freaked out about. We also did something that very few shops were doing at that point. We began work with artists on collaborations and one-off customisations. We had cool pieces that were unavailable anywhere else. We also made it a point to work with local artists, and graffiti artists such as Pure Evil, who took vintage army jackets and customised them by painting his fang-tooth logo-face on the back.

All of this was done with the money Philip had left from the sale of his shares of Woodhouse. We never had any outside investment. This was a pressure, so we simply had to make it work. The shop was due to open in October 2002. We still needed to get the interiors finished and fill the shop with clothes before that could happen.

We decided to fit out the shop in a modern way, but decorate it with interesting antiques, like the three huge Venini chandeliers, and old cabinets from the V&A Museum, once used to display artefacts but now full of our accessories.

Fred Segal was our inspiration, and for me it was all about the denim. I longed to see the best edit of denim all in one place. I wanted to know about cool new jeans brands as well as the big boys like 7 For All Mankind. Philip also clearly identified denim as being all-important. Jeans became an 'it' item. So we decided to build our business around jeans. We would create the 'go-to boutique for denim', both men's and women's.

As a woman, I had always found buying jeans a soul-destroying experience. Excited about the purchase, believing I'd found the 'perfect pair', I'd enter the changing room with high hopes, only to look at myself wearing the jeans in the mirror, and find my hopes dashed. I'd end up being more depressed about my body after trying on the jeans than before I went in. I realised I was not alone. There were millions of women experiencing the same depressing routine I had. I decided to become an expert on jeans. I wanted to understand fit, fabrication, the art of abrasion and the science behind it. I was hell-bent on being able to create a wonderful experience for women, and fit them in the perfect pair of jeans for their body.

We made appointments with all the hippest showrooms and clothing agents in London. We targeted the most up-and-coming and sought-after names in denim at the time, like Paper Denim and Cloth, 7 For All Mankind, Joe's Jeans and True Religion. These showrooms also carried other brands of clothes, so we picked interesting pieces to go with the jeans. That way we could up-sell, creating whole looks for customers. We looked for garments other buyers might not have chosen. We wanted our shop to be unique. The edit was all-important. It was our vision, our taste.

On 11 October 2002 we opened the doors to START, 59 Rivington Street. We decided to call our shop START, because it was our surname, and it was the start of our new life; a fresh start for us. 'Start' is such a positive word. We opened the doors with no fanfare or publicity, just word of mouth. There was, however, a buzz in the street. The first day we were open, we expected a few curious people, but we couldn't believe our luck. By the end of the day we'd taken over £1,000. As the last customer was leaving, he turned to us and said, 'I guess you are closing up for the weekend?' 'No,' Philip replied, 'we are opening the whole weekend, including Sunday.'

The man looked at us like we were crazy. 'There's no one around here,' he said. 'Everybody closes up for the weekend.'

It was with trepidation that we approached Saturday. When we arrived at our shop in the morning, we were horrified at the state of the street. It was trashed. Friday night had been a big night in Shoreditch. We used our feet to kick the beer cans, plastic cups and chicken bones out of the way. When we approached the front door of our shop we were dismayed to find someone had urinated on it. The council wouldn't be around to clear it up, so Philip swept the street himself. The area was quiet. Tumbleweed quiet.

We wondered if we had made a disastrous mistake opening a shop in Shoreditch. Friends had always been sceptical. It was dead that first Saturday morning. Shoreditch was slow to wake up, but somehow, very gradually, people began to find us. We also discovered a new category of customer we weren't expecting, one that didn't fit our initial profile of young creatives who worked in the area. These customers were wealthy locals with good taste who'd been bereft of anywhere to shop in the east. They were thrilled to have a boutique near them, selling clothes they couldn't even find in the West End. We hadn't even known these people existed. They became a big part of our clientele and proved to be champions of our shop.

In the first few months, our customers were primarily men. From the outside looking in through the window, START looked like a men's shop. When loyal male customers realised we also did clothes for women, they started to bring in their cousins, wives and girlfriends.

I would sit downstairs in my women's department and welcome them. I would start by showing them the jeans we had. We had an unrivalled selection of denim. I had chosen each style especially to cater to the different needs of women and their body types. When I went on buying appointments, the showrooms usually had models to try the jeans on. The jeans always looked amazing on the model – they had perfect bodies. The real test was how they looked on me. I was a real woman with hips and an ass. Plus I was a healthy size 29 in jeans. I road-tested every single pair of women's jeans we bought for the shop myself. I discovered, like me, most women were desperate to look good in jeans. I began to appraise women's bodies. I studied them. Everybody was different, but one thing was the same: they all had parts of their bodies that they hated. I learned very quickly how to play up their strong parts, while disguising their negative ones. I learned how to gauge their jean size just by looking at them. I'd ask them a few key questions before I'd begin a fitting. Most importantly, what did they want, or need the jeans for? What job did they need the jeans to do? Were they looking for an all-rounder, a pair for every day that they could dress up or dress down? Were they after a sexy going-out jean, a 'pulling jean'? Or maybe they were looking for a smart jean they could wear to work? I asked them if they preferred stretch or not. Some people felt very strongly about stretch. (Denim purists detested it.) Did they want a dark or light wash? Abrasions or clean? Were they comfortable in a skinny jean, or were they after straight-leg or boot-cut? Once I knew the answers it was easy.

We also began to offer 'a full jeans service'. We did alterations and shortenings; we would take in the waistband to eliminate the 'gape' for those women who had a minute waist but curvy hips. Sometimes these women could never find jeans that fit because the waistband gaped due to their curves.

Once they had their jeans, I then presented them with tops, jackets, shoes and accessories. They would walk out of the store ecstatic. They would tell me that it had been the best jeans-buying experience they'd ever had. They were going to tell all their friends. START was the best place in London to buy jeans.

The time I had put in learning about denim had paid off. My understanding of my own vulnerabilities as a woman also helped me to understand those of my customers. People seemed to love the looks I put together for them. They also loved the way I used colour to complement and enhance their natural palette. Before I realised it, I had become a stylist. Women seemed to love my taste, and my empathy. They trusted me.

Something else was happening too. Other stores, both independent and department stores, were sending over people to spy on us. Word had reached other buyers, and they began to make the trek east to check out START. They wanted to see what brands we had discovered that they had missed. Other stores were inspired by the unique way our shop looked. I began to see other people using similar old-fashioned fittings in a modern and artistic environment.

Starting off small, with little-known designers, selecting pieces we loved and believed in, had paid off. We had captured the cool factor, and the big boys were sitting up and taking notice. I had no idea what a competitive business fashion was, but I was about to learn.

KITCHEN BITCH

Kitchen Bitch was a cooking chat show unlike any other at the time. It was a show for culinary cheaters. Each week there would be a different guest and we would use food, and their likes and dislikes and eating habits, as a way to 'open' them up, to talk about their life.

Most everybody feels comfortable talking about food. Since I was retired from music and my priorities in life were now the shop and cooking dinner for my new husband every night, I had become a 'kitchen bitch'. I knew real cooks did everything from scratch, but I became an expert in putting together great meals by cutting corners and using ready-made sauces and doctoring them. I was able to pull together a three-course dinner party with two hours' notice. My friends were impressed, never guessing I'd cheated, that I'd 'kitchen bitched' them!

I also wondered about other creative people's relationship with food. Mine had been stormy. I loved to eat but had had body and control issues since childhood. I'd had numerous episodes of anorexia and bulimia. I wanted to know what other people ate or cooked for themselves. I anticipated that their answers would shed a huge amount of light on who they were as a person. The setting for *Kitchen Bitch* would be my new kitchen in our loft in Shoreditch. I would invite a guest to come round and 'cook' and 'bitch' with me. By the end of the show we would have knocked up a dish to eat together, and we would have probed the depths of the guest's psyche while doing it. *Kitchen Bitch* was a great idea for a show. The production company decided to film a pilot. Alan McGee agreed to be my first guest.

This was before the series *Desperate Housewives*, but there was a feeling of Doris Day on acid about the whole thing. It was strangely surreal. Gromit was wandering around the whole time, snatching scraps off the floor, while I 'cooked'. Alan McGee was pathologically afraid of dogs at this time, so that made for a bit of screen tension. But I was very pleased with the whole thing, proud of what I had created.

Unfortunately it didn't get commissioned. But I had managed to take an idea from a dream, and get it made into a pilot. That in itself was an accomplishment and gave me hope and determination for the future.

Many, many TV projects fail at the pilot stage. That is normal. There are various reasons for it. In the case of *Kitchen Bitch*, I don't think it was ever pitched to the right people.

START was doing very well. We were well into profit and our shop was constantly busy. It was clear to us that we had outgrown the women's department downstairs. On a Saturday, when jeans-shopping was at its frenzied height, there was hardly room to move. Philip decided to look for another shop. It was time to expand. He always had an ear to the ground in the neighbourhood. He had made it his business to make friends with the local estate agents, both commercial and residential, as well as landlords and business owners. He put the word out on the street that we were looking for bigger premises.

In an unbelievable stroke of luck I can only attribute to destiny, we were told that number 42 and 44 Rivington Street were both coming up for rent in the next month and that the tenants, a sheet-music publishing company, were vacating the premises. These were two medium-sized shop units that we could knock together to create one large shop over two floors. The best part of it was that it was directly opposite our existing shop. The two shops would face each other. Number 42–44 would become our women's lifestyle boutique. Besides clothing we were going to be selling a bigger selection of shoes, bags, jewellery, accessories (wallets and key rings), gifts, make-up, skincare and beauty products. We would create a mini-department store. It was, again, the lack of being able to access these items in Shoreditch that made it seem like a no-brainer to offer that shopping experience to our customers in the East End.

My life was complicated at this time. I was juggling the immense pressure of buying clothes on a grander scale. Now I had to learn how to buy beauty products, including make-up, and how to stock a proper shoe department. These were specialised fields and required new skills.

At some point in the midst of this frenetic time I was on the internet and came across an announcement of pug puppies for sale. Unable to tear myself away from the pictures of the litter, I rang the phone number on the web page and made arrangements to drive down to Hampshire to see the puppies face to face with my friend Victoria. I came home with the most beautiful fawn pug I had ever laid eyes on. Pixie.

'I am Brixie, you are Pixie,' I would say to her. She was my 'mini-me' and followed me everywhere. Gromit was in love with her, and instinctively mothered her. Pixie also gave Gromit a new lease of life. She was now nine years old and getting on a bit. Pixie made our little family complete.

Both Gromit and Pixie worked in the new shop. They patrolled the shop floor and greeted customers and charmed their children. Soon customers' kids were begging to go to START just to see the pugs.

Before long, the new shop was up and running. In one fell swoop, we effectively trebled the size of our business. Our plan for success was to up the ante of the brands we had on offer. We made a conscious decision to go for bigger-named designers and higher-priced pieces to raise the level of our playing field, to properly compete with the best independent boutiques in the country, as well as the department stores. Included in this plan was our fledgling online business. We realised very early on how important online retail was to become.

There was one brand at that time that was my absolute favourite. To me it was the holy grail. If I could have had only one brand to wear personally, it would have been Miu Miu.

After talking to my best customers and asking them what designers they'd like to see in START, the name Miu Miu came up again and again. Philip made the call to the Prada head office in Milan (Prada owns Miu Miu). He told them about our store. He pitched to them: he talked them through the mix of designers that we stocked, including the special one-off artist collaborations. He explained to them that Shoredtich was the up-and-coming new hip area of London. The first three times he called, he only made it halfway through his selling pitch before the man on the other end of the line said brusquely into the phone, 'No more doors in London', before unceremoniously putting down the receiver. Finally, the third time Philip called, a woman answered the phone and listened to what he had to say. Somehow Philip managed to convince this woman at Miu Miu that we were the right store, and that Shoreditch would be the perfect place for their brand. We were given the green light to buy. We knew with the acquisition of Miu Miu we could then get almost any brand we wanted. Miu Miu was the key. We booked our seats and flew to Milan.

The Prada head office and showroom in Milan looked like an art museum. We gave our names at the front desk and were told to sit on a couch in the foyer and wait for the head of sales to meet us. The walls were covered with priceless artwork. The place was white, light-filled and vaguely intimidating. I was foaming at the mouth to get in the showroom and start selecting pieces from the collection. I was most excited about the shoes. Getting Miu Miu shoes for our shop would be a game-changer. The shoes were totally covetable, very commercial and were not too expensively priced.

We waited for about half an hour. Nobody spoke to us. The employees were very serious and I noticed stress in the air. There wasn't a lot of joy to be had at the Prada head office.

I felt in my bones something was wrong. Both Philip and I had a bad feeling.

Eventually, a woman turned up. She explained to us that there had been a mistake. We were not allowed to buy Miu Miu. She was curt and straight to the point. Philip and I looked at each other. We went ballistic at the same time. We stood up, made a scene, and raised our voices. We steadfastly *refused* to take no for an answer. We fought for Miu Miu as if our livelihood depended on it. And to us, it did.

In the end we came to an agreement. We agreed to take Miu Miu menswear, which we did not want, and knew would be difficult to sell, in order to get Miu Miu womenswear, which was of course what we wanted more than anything. Philip called it 'a sprat to catch a mackerel'.

The buy was hard. The showroom was bigger than any I'd been in previously, as big as an airplane hangar and jammed with other buyers from shops around the world. All the buyers were fighting for the best samples, the must-have pieces.

We were under pressure. In order to definitely secure Miu Miu we had to quantify our order there and then. The books were closing at the end of the day. We had to commit ourselves one hundred per cent. There would not be any room for leeway, or changing our minds. We had to give our final size scales, and quantities, for men's and women's clothing, shoes and accessories. We did not have the luxury of going back to our hotel room and taking the evening to juggle numbers. Miu Miu had a minimum spend, which was already more than we had budgeted for. We had to nearly double that, to include the menswear, which we had not budgeted for at all. After twelve eventful hours, we submitted our order. We had secured Miu Miu, but had ended up spending more money than we were comfortable with. It was a gamble.

With Miu Miu on the way, we went on to get Stella McCartney, Alexander McQueen accessories, Phillip Lim, Helmut Lang (for women) and my two favourite under-the-radar designers, David Szeto and Charles Anastase. We were up and running. Our iconic brown craft START bags, with red rope handles, were now a common sight on the neighbourhood streets. We had taken Shoreditch.

ADVENTURES ON THE SMALL SCREEN

At that time in the UK different production companies were trying to get fashion-related shows commissioned by the major channels. I was filmed for casting tapes for at least six different shows, on multiple channels. Not only did I now have fashion credentials as a buyer, retailer and stylist, but producers realised I was a trained and skilled performer too. In other words, I was able to talk about fashion from the inside, as well as being trained to be on camera. Two different strands of my life had collided. Two roads I had followed, at totally different times, had now merged.

One of those taster tapes I was filmed for was for a new series on Channel 4. I remember being interviewed by a young producer. I didn't hear anything back for ages, and assumed the show had not been commissioned, or they had cast someone else. I focused on my day job, the shop and the buying. Buying season had come round again, and with it came the relentless treadmill of fashion.

Philip and I left Gromit and Pixie with Jan, who was our dog-walker. 'The girls' loved Jan. She had looked after Gromit since we had moved to Shoreditch. I remember standing on the street in Milan. We had just been to see the brand Car Shoe. My mobile rang. I had a panicked Jan on the other end.

'It's Pixie,' Jan stuttered. 'We can't get her out from under the bed. She's been under there for forty-five minutes.'

'What's she doing?' I asked.

'She's shagging,' Jan shrieked. 'I'm sorry, Brix. We can't keep them apart.'

'Who is Pixie shagging? Who can't you keep apart?'

'She's shagging Bonce, a black pug.'

It was weird. I had wanted to breed Pixie, and I knew she was in season. I had never had a dog that had had puppies, and it had always been something I'd dreamed of. I had arranged a date for Pixie to meet a fawn pug after I returned from buying. Pixie had beaten me to it. Unbelievably, she even went for her own breed. If she was pregnant, so be it. She had made her own choice. Only time would tell. When we returned home Pixie jumped up on the bed with Philip for a cuddle. She promptly threw up. I knew then that she was knocked up, for sure.

A local estate agent approached Philip with some secret news. A shop on the corner of Charlotte Road and Rivington Street was coming up for rent. This was a premises that Philip had had his eye on for ages. It was perfect for our fourth shop. We discussed what we would sell in the store. We thought about street wear, and kids' clothes, but Philip had an epiphany: tailoring – something he'd known a thing or two about since his Woodhouse days. Yet again he'd spotted a trend. Men's fashion was moving away from casual denim and T-shirts to a more sophisticated way of dressing. We had already been working, in a small way, with a specialised suit manufacturer, creating pieces under our own label, Rivington. It was therefore quite easy for Philip to expand what we had already been doing into a contemporary ready-to-wear tailoring collection. The fourth shop became Mr START.

Mr START or, as we called it, 'Shop Four', looked different to all the other shops. It was elegant and felt like a private men's club, with references to the art world. As we had with our first shop, we simply opened the doors on day one. Somehow by the end of the day we'd taken £6,000. Mr START became the most profitable single brand we had in any store, and the good news was: it was our own.

I began to prepare myself for the birth of Pixie's puppies. I read everything I could about delivering puppies and their aftercare. I visited our vet and picked his brains, asking the same questions over and over again. What was clear from everything I'd read was that pugs were notoriously bad mothers. I would have to give Pixie a lot of help. I hoped the birthing would take care of itself, naturally, but I had an emergency kit prepared just in case. I bought a blow-up kids' pool, and lined it with towels for the delivery. Pixie's pregnant belly was so swollen with pups it touched the floor when she walked. Pixie looked like a pig–pug.

We planned a massive party at the shop to celebrate the opening and success of Mr START. We hired the hip Shoreditch fashion PR agency, Relative, to create the guestlist and put out the word. The night before the party, Philip and I got into bed to go to sleep. Pixie, who sometimes slept at the foot of our bed, was agitated. She was up at the top of our bed, manically digging at the pillows. I realised she was trying to make a nest for her babies. I'd read about this in the books. It didn't mean she would give birth there and then, but she was preparing to do so, and it could last up to forty-eight hours.

I took Pixie into the guest bedroom, so Philip could get some sleep before the big opening party. He would need to be on form to greet all the customers and press. It would be his big day – our big day. Pixie kept digging. She scratched and pawed the pillows the whole night. Not only did she dig and paw, but she began to pant too. It was like she was possessed, or had OCD. I got zero sleep.

The next day, 3 April 2008, I went to work at the shop for a few hours and then came home to check on Pixie. She was still digging, and I checked her temperature: it was up. According to the books, this meant she would deliver soon. The party was due to start at 6.30 p.m., and go on all evening. There was no way I was going to miss the party. I had to be there at least for some of it. I called a friend to come and watch Pixie and monitor her. They were given strict instructions to ring me the moment anything changed. I headed off to the party. I wore nude-coloured Nike Cortez trainers instead of heels. I knew I might need to run home at any time.

The party was insane. So many people turned up, the mass of bodies stopped traffic on both Charlotte Road and Rivington Street. Mark Hix's Rivington restaurant provided drinks and nibbles. All of our favourite loyal customers turned up, including the East End glitterati and art crowd. Many publications were there. There were paparazzi in the street to snap the celebs. At 9 p.m. I received a call on my mobile. The voice said, 'Get home, it's happening.' I sprinted the three quarters of a mile home. When I got there, Pixie was in the birthing pool bearing down. Her eyes were wild. I had decided that if Pixie had a girl I was going to keep her and name her Gladys, after Philip's beloved aunt, who had just passed away.

The first puppy out was a black girl. Gladys. I delivered Gladys at 11.55 p.m. Pixie, not understanding and fearful of her pup, backed away. She looked at her as if she were an alien. It was down to me to clean her up, rub her with a rough towel and aspirate her lungs, which still contained fluid. Eventually, I got Pixie to lie still for one minute for Gladys to nurse. Then Pixie was up again. There was more work to be done. By 9 a.m. I'd been up for forty-eight hours since Pixie had started her pre-delivery nesting. We had five adorable pug puppies: two boys and three girls, all of them jet-black.

Pixie eventually – reluctantly – did take to mothering, but by then it was too late. Two of the girl puppies had died. Thankfully not Gladys, though, who was strong and wilful from the get-go. I took two weeks off work to help Pixie. She wouldn't feed her pups willingly, so I had to calmly hold her on her side so the three surviving pups could latch on. I had to do this every two hours. I was sleep-deprived and depressed from the passing of the two pups that I could not save, although I tried. We eventually gave the two boys to my friend Victoria. We had made a pact early on. Philip and I kept Gladys.

Maybe it's because I delivered Gladys myself and was the first person to touch her; the first person she smelled? Perhaps it's because I cleared her lungs so she could breathe? But in all my life, with all the wonderful animals I've been blessed to have, I've never been so close and connected with any as I am with Gladys. We have a very special bond. I feel like I've known her spirit through many lifetimes.

Soon enough, I went back to work at the shop. Gladys, Pixie and Gromit came with me every day. With all the puppy drama behind me, I began to concentrate on fashion again. I was also booked to film and present a pilot for a new TV series with Claudia Winkleman and Jo Whiley about clothes swapping. I was looking forward to it. That show, and the shop, were my focus.

But, completely out of the blue, I received a phone call about another TV show, one that would change my life again, and prove to be my big break. The producer who rang was from a show called *Gok's Fashion Fix*.

FASHION FIX

A woman's disembodied voice on the end of my mobile phone informed me that I had been cast in the new prime-time Channel 4 series *Gok's Fashion Fix*. I didn't quite understand my role but, according to the producer, I was to be on the show every week. They wanted to use my shop START as a location to film, and they wanted me to style outfits from the shop. They asked about my availability for the next couple of months, and if I would be ready to film the following week. I said I would. I agreed there and then, because I didn't want to lose the job, but I knew I needed to find an agent to look after my best interests, to negotiate the (always) complicated television contract. I needed to move fast.

Television, like music, can be a nasty, tricky, cut-throat business. If a production company can get away without paying you, they will. Nine times out of ten, most people are so happy to be on TV they do it anyway, regardless of the money.

When I found out exactly what I would be doing on the show, I was desperate to be included. Not only would I be working on TV, but the role would benefit our shop. The opportunity to appear on the show could potentially be priceless. The amount of advertising and recognition would put START on the map . . . globally.

The show starred a stylist called Gok Wan. He had come from another successful show called *How to Look Good Naked*. He was a tall gay Chinese man with an edgy haircut and glasses. The nation had taken him to its heart. He had been marginalised for being overweight as a teenager, and he was empathetic to the feelings of all marginalised people. He helped women who normally had little dress sense or confidence to look and feel better about themselves.

He made fashion accessible and enjoyable to those people who may have once been intimidated by it.

The new show was to be co-hosted by Gok Wan and Alexa Chung, who was a model and It Girl. I knew Alexa and liked her very much. She shopped with me at START, and we both had a love for the French designer Charles Anastase.

Each week the last third of the show would be devoted to a cat-walk face-off between high-street and designer clothes. Gok would style four looks from the high street, while four top buyers from London's best boutiques and department stores would style the same four looks with designer clothes. The catwalk face-off would take place in front of a live audience. The models and looks would be mixed up. The audience would vote with coloured paddles for which looks they liked best, not knowing if the looks were from the high street or the designers.

The other buyers on the show were from Harrods, Selfridges and Browns. I was in good company – great company, in fact. After opening START only six years before, I was now being included with some of the best buyers and stores in the world. Philip and I had really created something special with our shops. The producers of *Gok's Fashion Fix* had no idea who I was, or what I had done previously, though. They did not know I had been in The Fall, that I had written hundreds of songs, or that I had trained as an actress. They were completely ignorant of my past. They accepted me instead for my present. The director of my segment was a young woman in her early twenties. She was blonde, smart and hilarious. We laughed so hard sometimes we couldn't get through a take. Hannah Springham captured my sense of humour and my electric energy. She also had the good sense to film my dogs.

Each week the crew would come to START and Hannah would film me running round the shop pulling clothes for a look 'to beat Gok'. As I'd run like a maniac around my shop, grabbing armfuls of glorious garments, Gromit and Pixie would trail in my wake, trying to keep up (Gladys was still too young). I'd also turn to the dogs to ask their opinions about what they thought would constitute a 'Gok beater'. I spoke to my dogs as if they were humans, and some people thought I was actually bonkers. I did this instinctively and thought it added comedy value.

Eventually, on a Friday, which was the day they filmed the catwalk face-off in front of the live audience, I'd pack up my looks for that week and send them down to the studio to be fitted on a model for the show. Selfridges, Browns and Harrods would all do the same. Then our looks would go head to head against Gok's looks from the high street . . . and lose.

Every single week.

None of us buyers knew what each other was doing. Nor did we know what Gok was doing. I assumed, and so did they, that the beauty and simplicity of a brilliant cut, the movement and drape of expensive fabric, and the quality of the craftsmanship of the designer – and, finally, the pureness of the inspiration itself – would show through to anyone who understood clothes. Wasn't that obvious? The answer was . . . no. Not on TV, at any rate.

Television styling is very different from editorial or red carpet. The camera and the screen do things to the vision. They bend and emphasise certain angles and aspects of a look. This can happen when filming the human body as well. That's why some actors look gorgeous on screen, but blend into the crowd in real life. The lens of a camera is like a powerful opinionated eye. It sees things in its own way. To be a great television stylist you have to study the image of the garment on the monitor, not with the naked eye. To be a great TV stylist you first have to see through the eyes of the TV.

Gok was miles ahead of me. He also had a team of top TV stylists helping him. Not only that, he had a certain look to his own styling that was very recognisable. I hadn't realised any of this yet. I was simply putting lovely dresses down the catwalk and hoping for the best.

Week after week this went on. I would film my part at the shop, selecting the outfit, running round the shop, roping the dogs in. Then, every Friday, I'd watch it lose, along with all the other buyers' designer outfits. We had zero control once we sent the outfit off to the studio. No one was there to uphold our vision or tweak the outfit at the last minute.

The other buyers were getting angry. They were putting up big-name designers against the high street and losing every week. This was potentially brand-damaging both to the designer and to the shop. I suspected they were regretting their decision to appear on the show in the first place.

One night, I was sitting in bed. It was getting late, around 10 p.m., when unexpectedly my mobile rang. It was Colette Foster, the executive producer of the show. She asked me if I was free the next day, to go down to the live studio and co-present the show with Gok. She asked me if I would take Alexa Chung's place. I assumed Alexa had been contracted to do something else that week. I explained that I had an important buying meeting at START in the morning and that I would be free after 11 a.m. 'Great,' she said. 'The car will be waiting for you at eleven. Oh, and bring the dogs.'

At precisely 11 a.m. a black Mercedes pulled up to the shop. I got into the car with Pixie. I'd decided to bring Gladys too. She was only four months old, but I was so close to Gladys I actually hated to be apart from her. Something told me even though she was a pup, she'd be fine and well adjusted in a bustling TV studio. She was calm, chilled and imperious. She focused me, and kept me grounded.

The studio was chaotic. Crew and staff were rushing everywhere. I had no dressing room. I could feel immense time pressure, as an assistant producer shoved a script into my hand. I was rushed into make-up. The make-up artist was Gok's long-time friend Charlie Duffy. She did a wonderful job on me, using MAC. She put MAC Reflects on my eyes and they glittered like diamonds. Then I was taken to meet my models and get them dressed in the four different looks sent over for that week's show by the buyers.

I thought it wise to befriend the models, motivate them and educate them about the gorgeous clothes they would be dressed in. I figured if they felt great about what they were wearing they would project extra positivity when walking the catwalk. My girls would be wearing dresses worth thousands of pounds; Gok's girls would be wearing dresses that cost less than £100.

It was then I was introduced to Gok. He was very tall and thin, and reminded me of a cartoon character from Dr Seuss. He immediately made a comment about me using Gladys to accessorise myself. I think he said, 'Your handbag has a pulse.' He welcomed me to the show. He told me not to be nervous. He was cordial, polite and professional. I could detect some underlying tension, though I couldn't put my finger on what it was. Perhaps he was under pressure about something from Channel 4? Perhaps it was his normal pre-show anxiety, or maybe he didn't really want me there? Whatever the case, I knew instantly that the guy was intelligent. I also knew he was driven and a fighter. The last thing he would ever do was willingly let me win. It was his name above the door. The clue was in the title, *Gok's Fashion Fix*. I was here to lose. That was my role.

I asked the boss, Walter Luzzolino, what he wanted from me, what he needed me to deliver performance-wise. He asked me if I knew the character Wilhelmina Slater, played by Vanessa Williams on *Ugly Betty*? He said he wanted me to be like Wilhelmina. He wanted me to be fabulous and fierce. He wanted me to own it, to stand up to Gok, who was a seriously strong character. Walter told me that it was he who had seen something special about me on tape, and it was his decision to bring me down to the studio to co-host the show with Gok for the day.

Of course, designer lost to high street that day. It was always going to happen. I had done the best I could do, and I'd loved the experience. I didn't expect it to lead anywhere. I assumed I'd be going back to my regular role the next week as a buyer-contributor.

The first season of *Gok's Fashion Fix* ended. It was a big hit. The audience loved it when the affordable clothes beat the exclusive, expensive ones. The show was recommissioned for a second series. It was decided, for series two, there would be a change in the format and a change of presenter. It appeared, at last, that I'd made it – for series two it was just me and Gok. Alexa had left after landing a huge show in New York. The producers had decided to make the weekly catwalk face-off a head-to-head battle. Gok versus Brix.

Most of the show consisted of Gok talking about styling, and making over some lucky viewer. My part was expanded. I was now not just shopping in START for my designer looks, but trawling the best shops in London and 'spending thousands of pounds' to get those Gok-beating garments. Cameras filmed me racing down Bond Street like a lunatic, laden down with designer shopping bags, Gladys and Pixie trailing behind me. The producers also gave me my own strand: 'Best of British', which was my favourite part of doing *Gok's Fashion Fix* – one of my favourite things I have ever done on telly. On it I travelled the length and breadth of Britain looking at iconic British fashion brands. I visited factories, and shed light on the artisanship and craftsmanship that goes into making items. I interviewed the craftsmen and women, who in some cases were different generations of the same family. I visited tartan factories, cashmere factories, Mulberry-handbag and specialist-brogue makers, Dents gloves and Mackintosh raincoats. I explained to the public why these designer items cost so much, and that sometimes generations of skill had gone into creating them. I justified the expense of these iconic items, and supported British manufacturing at the same time. The strands of Best of British were like mini-documentary films in themselves.

For the beginning of series two I decided to give myself a new look. I cut my hair into a pixie style and bleached it platinum.

The producers were not thrilled. The look was hard, not soft and appealing. I wanted to come out fierce, like a fashion warrior, and show that I meant business.

Series two catwalk face-offs were filmed in London, in an empty building off Savile Row. The production company built a set inside the building, including a pink catwalk. Now that I was officially the new co-presenter, I sat Gok down and explained to him that I wanted to work together with him, to make the show the best it could be. At the time, I didn't realise how much I hated to lose, and how badly I would take it after each loss. During the first half of filming series two, I continued my losing streak. No matter what I did, the audience voted against my looks. I couldn't beat Gok and it was beginning to get to me emotionally. Even when I was sure my looks were better, and couldn't lose . . . I'd lose.

I believe even Gok was beginning to feel sorry for me. I know there were a few times he seriously thought I should have won. He was so popular and loved, it felt like everyone was on his side, and he was unstoppable.

As the second series began to air, my losing was evident to all who watched . . . and those numbered millions. I began to get recognised as I walked down the street, especially if I had 'the girls', Gladys and Pixie, with me. Strangers would rush up to me at a red light, or grab me in the supermarket or corner me at the Starbucks counter. They all had the same thing to say. 'Why do you always lose? Your clothes are better than Gok's. Why does no one vote for you? We all vote for you in our house.'

I was hardly ever recognised on this kind of level when I had been in The Fall. This time, though, I was recognised as a loser. I felt embarrassed when strangers would pour out their frustration at my losses. I felt doubly embarrassed for the designers, whose reputations I was desperate to uphold. I wondered if I was perhaps damaging my credibility and that of START by being on this show. But the public loves an underdog. Everyone who was approaching me was doing so with love. They were empathising with me. My frustration was their frustration. Even though I was championing high-priced designer clothes the average person could not afford, and the general public's alliance was obviously with the high street, something I was saying was resonating with the viewers.

Halfway through filming the live catwalk face-offs something changed. Philip came and watched the show from the audience. He watched as I lost again. He made some mental notes and observed. He hung around backstage before the show, just watching. He saw how I worked with my team of two, my fashion producer Helen Boyle and our assistant. He watched how Gok worked with his team, a virtual fashion army, a cast of many. I had lost every single face-off I had ever appeared in. I believe the score was Gok 9, me 0. I was beginning to take it personally – how could I not? When we got home, Philip turned to me and calmly said, 'I know how you can win. I've watched everything, and I know what he's doing. The key to everything is in the accessorising, Brix. He puts a belt on everything. Plus he has an entire team to help him.'

Gok maxed out every look by overloading it with accessories. When he thought there were enough accessories on the model, he added more. He styled the plain, inexpensive clothes with attitude. He blinded the viewer with bling. If I was to beat him, I needed to think like him.

I called the producers and explained that I needed one more assistant to help me. The producers agreed, because they were worried that my losing every week was becoming boring for viewers. I called START and spoke to Saranne Woodcroft, a talented young stylist who worked for us doing visual merchandising and window display (she went on to style for *Vogue*). I hired Saranne to comb every shop for the most interesting and creative accessories. I told her to be bold in her choices, and think outside the box.

The first week Saranne came to join my team, we almost won. We were so close I could taste it. We lost by one or two audience votes. It was a moral victory, though. It was the best we'd ever done. The next week we upped our accessorising game even more. I made sure the accessories we used had movement and depth, that they glittered and seduced. Even when I knew, taste-wise, I'd over-egged it, I egged it even more, and then, I covered it with meringue.

As I walked out on to the catwalk in front of the live audience, I clutched at the golden envelope in my hands. In my heart I thought that it might be. Graciously, I ripped open the envelope. I dropped to my knees and shed a tear on TV. I'd won. I'd done it at last.

Gok's Fashion Fix was commissioned for a third time. I vowed to do better. I picked myself up off the floor. I licked my wounds and soothed my battered ego. Now I knew what to do.

Series three was by no means easy. Gok also had the bit between his teeth. There was no way he was going down without a fight. His reputation and show depended on it. The stakes were high and the tension higher. On series three I won a few more, but Gok took the series again, at 5–3.

By series four, I really did feel my reputation was on the line. For the previous three series I'd done everything by the book, I'd been a team player. Now I felt an element of desperation creep in, as well as an element of anger. I redoubled my focus and dug down deep. At night I lay in bed and let my imagination run riot. I closed my eyes and visualised all the looks for the coming week. I did this every single week of series four. As I lay there, breathing deeply, inspiration struck. I noted down what I had imagined, what I had seen in my mind. Then I followed up on it, and recreated these gifts of inspiration for the catwalk. One example of this visual inspiration occurred during the filming of an episode in Leeds. The look both Gok and I had to create was 'oriental inspiration'.

For my look, Helen and I had managed to borrow a £26,000 glittering navy mandarin coat encrusted with thousands of tiny Swarovski crystals from Shanghai Tang. The coat itself was a showstopper, and came alive on the catwalk. It was bedazzling. When I closed my eyes and visualised the coat, I also saw something else: the most glorious accessory to go with it. The only problem was I had to create it. It existed only in my imagination. In my mind I saw the model carrying a birdcage instead of a handbag. Helen and I found the perfect birdcage and went about recreating my vision.

The birdcage was white and delicate. I filled it with lifelike silk butterflies and a pretend bird, with real feathers. Then I covered the outside of the birdcage with small white fairy lights. I wound them discreetly around the bars, and I lit the lights with a hidden battery pack. It was spectacular.

Unfortunately, although Helen and I tried to keep our secret weapon hidden until the final second, someone in the production caught sight of it. They took it away. Claiming I had broken the rules. 'What rules?' I thought. Was I not allowed to use my imagination?

Although it stung, I put that loss behind me and went on to win more. I used my visualisation technique to guide me through the rest of series four. When it came to the final show, the stakes were the highest they'd ever been. The show took place in Canary Wharf in East London – my 'hood.

I could no longer win the series outright, but Gok still could. He was one up on me in the score tally. The best I could do would be to tie. And I could only do that if I won the last show. Both Gok and I went at it hammer and tongs. This competition was very real, and not just for the cameras. The final look was 'fairytale'. My model wore a handmade silk dress of white chiffon, by the designer Matthew Williamson. In my Best of British segment that night we had watched the fabric for this dress be hand-drawn then digitally printed. We had visited Matthew's atelier and watched the dress being stitched together. The viewers and I had been on this fashion journey together. The cameras had captured every step of it. The dress was called 'the parachute dress' because, as the model walked, the train of the dress billowed out on the gentle wafts of air behind her, creating an exquisite parachute. It was feather-light, ethereal; it was angelic. The dress itself created its own delicate drama.

Clutching the golden envelope for the last time, I walked to the end of the catwalk. The crowd was roaring. I could feel the love. I ripped open the envelope. I looked up at the audience. My voice shook with emotion as I read the writing on the card: 'The winner is BRIX.'

THERE'S A MOUSE IN MY HOUSE

As I stood on Rivington Street, between the four START shops, I blinked my eyes, and then wiped them. I pinched myself hard. Yes, I was awake, but I could have been dreaming. I watched as Mickey Mouse exited the Mr START shop and walked past me. He entered my shop, the women's shop, number 42–44, for a night of partying.

I had done this. I had made it happen. I had brought together my childhood fantasies with my adult realities. Never had I known 'the Mouse' to leave 'the park'. Certainly not to attend a private function – not officially, anyway.

My notoriety as a stylist, my high profile on television and in the press, had put me in line for an amazing job. I was hired to curate the British representation of the Mickey Mouse Ears exhibit at Paris Disneyland. It was Mickey's birthday, and Europe was celebrating. Each country in the EU had submitted a collection of customised Mickey Mouse ears, designed by each country's top fashion designers and celebrities. I curated the British contingent. Not only was I being paid a large amount of money to do this, I was also invited to the park for the unveiling weekend, as were all the designers and celebrities from each country that participated. This was such a special occasion: on the evening of the opening of the exhibit, Disneyland Paris would be shut to the public.

After the exhibition closed in Paris, it was written into my contract that the British collection of the Mickey Mouse hats would travel to London. The hats would then go on display at START. We would have a big party to celebrate the hats, and Mickey's birthday . . . and Mickey Mouse himself would be the guest of honour.

There was a lot of red tape. Disney had strict rules regarding Mickey Mouse. We had to comply with everything. We had to bend over backwards and turn sideways. It was serious stuff. At times I doubted that it would happen. Just doing the job and being involved with Disney, and designers, had been enough for me. But, in the end, it did happen. Mickey Mouse stood in the centre of the shop floor at START, in the boutique that I had helped create. He stood against a Disney branding board. The clothes I had carefully selected for the shop had been moved aside, out of view. In his arms, Mickey held a dog. It was not a Disney dog, or a themed toy. It was my dog, Gladys.

I had had a long history with the Mouse. Not all of it good. At times throughout my life the Mouse had represented safety and consistency. At other times, his very presence and chirpy demeanour, as if by contrast, flared up like a reflection of darkness. The Mouse seemed to have a power, a life force. But when I really examined him, and saw behind the costume . . . he had not been a mouse at all, nor even a man . . . but a girl . . . just like me.

The moment was surreal. My worlds had collided. The seemingly separate strands of my life had become unexpectedly connected. I had, without a doubt, made my own dreams come true.

EPILOGUE

EPILOGUE

MARK E. SMITH

The last time I spoke to Mark E. Smith properly was in a dream. He came to me one night in my sleep, to say goodbye. I wondered where he was going. He didn't say, but the dream was very real and, on waking, left me disturbed. A few days later, as it happened, I was in Manchester on work-related business. Upset by my dream, I plucked up the courage to visit Mark one last time. Not knowing where he lived, nor having had any contact with him for years, I took a chance, and knocked on our old front door, the door of the house we had bought together.

I heard muffled noises from inside the house. Then, from behind the door, I heard the unmistakable resonant grumbling of Mark E. Smith.

'Who's there?' he mumbled.

'It's me, Brix,' I said.

'Who?' he asked (seemingly in disbelief).

'It's me, *Brix*,' I said again. 'Your old wife. I'm so sorry to bother you, Mark, but I'm in Manchester for the night, and I wanted to come by and say hello. It's been so long. I don't want anything from you, and I'm not here to give you anything. I just wanted to say hello, and see you, after all this time. I know I've probably caught you by surprise. I didn't have your phone number. I'll give you some time to get yourself together. I'll wait for you to open the door. If you don't, it's your choice, and I'll respect that. I'll go away and I'll never bother you again.'

I waited for while. The door never opened. I left with a heavy heart and a profound sense of sadness.

MUSIC

In the summer of 2014, I picked up the guitar for the first time in fifteen years. Philip had urged me over the years to play again. To try again. To write again. I'd basically laughed in his face. I told him I wanted nothing more to do with music. But I hadn't realised I was missing a piece of my soul.

Secretly, while alone in our flat, with only Gladys and Pixie as witnesses, I pulled Whitey out of his dusty case, and began to strum. What happened then was nothing short of extraordinary. A piece of a song, an entire verse, fully formed, flowed through me. It was as if it had been waiting in the ether for fifteen years. The song presented itself to me: chord structure, melody and words. As I began to sing I realised my voice sounded different. My voice was powerful, forceful and rich. It was vulnerable and delicate in places. Most of all it was bewitching in its honesty. A lifetime of living had honed it without me realising it. The cocoon walls had cracked. I had denied myself this pleasure, this vital part of who I was, who I am.

I was rusty, yes, but even the clumsiness of my movements brought me pleasure. Practising seemed to nurture my very being. I played every day for hours, until I was soothed, until I was better, more confident and connected, to the wispy threads of inspiration than I had ever been.

After weeks of playing only for my dogs, I plucked up courage to play for Philip when he returned home from work one evening. The first song I played him was the first song I'd written after all those years of silence. It was called 'The State of Alaska'. Philip was stunned, and emotional. He too commented on my new voice. Where had it come from? he wondered.

I continued to write and write. I was unable to stop. Playing felt like the only thing that mattered. I could think of little else. I started playing for a few friends; they were gobsmacked. Some had never heard me sing or play guitar since they'd known me. They described a happiness and contentment they'd never seen before come over me. I kept writing, and more songs emerged, so many I could have filled two albums.

A few months after I picked up the guitar and rediscovered my music, I received an invitation. It was to attend a book launch party in Manchester. Steve Hanley, The Fall's bass player (who had by now also left) had written a book. At first I didn't want to go. It had been eighteen years since I'd seen anyone from the band except Marcia and Simon Rogers. To see them again would surely open up old wounds and painful memories. But the timing of the invitation seemed too synchronistic. Throughout my life I'd learned to follow these signs, to be open to them. Unable to face going alone, I roped Marcia into it. Together we took the train to Manchester for a Fall reunion of sorts.

When I saw them again they were noticeably older, but so was I. The main thing that stuck me was that they were happy. Steve Hanley, Paul Hanley, Simon Wolstencroft, Craig Scanlon . . . they were smiling, sorted, and whole. They had passed through the fire and lived to tell the tale.

That night Steve and Paul put together a band to play at the party. They played a few songs, including some old Fall songs. When they played 'Mr Pharmacist' I felt something inside me pop. It was almost as if my fever had broken, or a curse had been lifted. It was all I could do to remain in my seat. I was desperate to join them. I was surprised and taken aback by the force of the feeling.

After the show, I asked Steve why he hadn't asked me to play with them.

'I never thought you'd do it,' he said.

'I would have, I would have,' I told him. 'I'm playing again. I'm writing again.'

I couldn't get the words out quick enough. Steve thought for a moment. Then he turned to me, and quietly said, 'Why don't we play together sometime . . . just for fun?'

We kept in contact, and a month or so later met up with our instruments. The first song we played together was 'US 80s–90s'. Both of us got goosebumps. From that point on, things moved very quickly. We put together a band, with me playing guitar and singing, Steve playing bass, Paul Hanley on drums, Steve Trafford and Jason Brown on guitar. We called our band Brix and the Extricated. When a promoter got wind of our new band, we were offered our first gig, at the Ruby Lounge in Manchester, in December 2014. This was a big deal for me. It was the first time since my single gig with The Adult Net that I had stepped on the stage as a front person, a lead singer.

It was also the first time that we took control of the Fall songs we'd written, airing some amazing songs that had not seen the light of day for thirty years. We did this for the love of our music. We played a mixture of classic Fall songs, and a few of my new songs. When we played 'Hotel Blöedel', which had never been performed live before, I was told members of the audience wept.

START

For everything that has a beginning, so too must there be an end. That was the case with our shop START. In the summer of 2015 we closed the shop's shutters for good. This was not a decision we took lightly, nor was it an easy one. After thirteen successful years we decided that it was time for a change.

There were many factors involved in making our decision. For me, the overwhelming factor was not so much that I'd fallen out of love with the business, but that I had fallen in love with performing. Both my re-found passion for music, and the various TV shows that came after the success of *Fashion Fix*, filled me with joy. I still love fashion, and will continue to work in it. The last few years the shop was open, I designed a label called Gladys & Pixie, named after my pugs. This was primarily a cashmere range, and became a bestseller. I loved being creative within fashion, but I no longer wanted the responsibility, stress and ups and downs of running a large business.

The later years had been tough – tougher than at the beginning. I instinctively felt it was time to change tack. So did Philip. We decided when the lease came up for renewal on the women's shop not to renew. We both wanted to do something else, and could not see ourselves running the shops for another ten years.

MY BIOLOGICAL FATHER

The last time I saw my biological father was at breakfast at the Hotel Bel-Air – the occasion he informed me he had given away my stove containing a lifetime's worth of photographs, press clippings and memorabilia; the physical manifestation of my entire career. It would take me fifteen years to pick up the phone to ring him. By then he was ill, very ill, and possibly dying. I called him and forgave him once again. I told him I loved him, but this time I meant it. I had learned to accept him, for him – not what I expected him to be. I released him from the confinement of my feelings about how he should behave. I allowed him to be himself. I finally realised, you cannot change someone into what you want them to be, or think they should be. If you accept them for what they are, you free both yourself and the other person.

According to my aunt Susie, my father cried for three days after my phone call. The fatherly love I had received from Marvin, and the emotional love from Philip, helped make it possible for me to heal. The combined love of both of these stalwart male figures in my life has helped to fill the void left by my father, a void I've lived with since childhood.

On 19 October 2014, Philip and I flew to Chicago, where we met my mother and Marvin. Together as a family we drove to the Cook County courthouse where, standing before the presiding judge, Marvin legally adopted me.

In the end, love is always the answer.

THE WORD

I let my eyes relax. Pupils soft. Fields and trees blurred into long, stream-
ing bands of colour as the train streaked through the English countryside.
Already I felt my skin loosen, like the air between the layers of an onion.

Shedding-time was near. The shedding of the protective armour of
my thoughts, lazy, rusty, cumbersome stuff.

A lifetime's worth of exhaust pipes and hubcaps.

I knew I was closer to the knowing.

I could feel the quickening, though I couldn't put a name to it.

The room was packed with eager faces. Faces with name tags pinned
to their bodies.

I knew only one person in the room. The girl I had come with. Yasmin.

Like freshly beached fish we twitched, awkward in the uncomfort-
able air.

The room was full of twitching fish. We had all been beached
together,

belched from the same body of water,

and connected by one mind.

We lay on the floor. Looking up at vaulted ceilings. The gentle
unravelling began.

Dust motes came alive as they filtered through the high glass win-
dows in the fading afternoon light. The particles began their dance.

I closed my eyes and saw colours.

Deep resonant blue of a healing variety.

Finally a stream of green coursed from my heart.

It spread out like a blanket, and lowered itself to cocoon my breath-
ing frame. It was the music I heard first. A single note. It was high
and celestial.

Then I heard an orchestra, delicate and barely perceptible, because I heard it with my mind not my ears.

It was elusive and ephemeral. I quieted my thoughts and relaxed, trying to commit the notes to memory.

But it was impossible.

It was as if the music were coming from another dimension.

My best guess was heaven.

As I tuned into the music, I began to hear words.

The words were separate from the music. The words were the important thing.

The music was a means to allow me to hear the words.

The words were soothing and familiar.

So familiar, they felt like my own.

I knew then, it was the Indian.

He had never left my side, even though I'd forgotten his existence.

His voice had simply become my own.

It was he who had whispered guidance and wisdom to me.

He who had lit the deadened roads with alternate trails. He who had kept my heart filled with hope, while the parched fields of my life lay raped and barren.

I was at last able to hear again.

The connection had not been severed, nothing so catastrophic.

It had simply become blocked with life-junk.

Fifty people breathing in unison.

Fifty figures wearing white, their masks were in pieces on the floor.

They were unprotected.

At last I could see their colours.

They were beautiful, like mine.

It was then I was given the word.

The word that would become the key to the rest of my life.

The word that I'd come to understand, instinctively.

A word that I could feel.

It linked everything I ever knew, learned or would learn.

It linked sound, colour, feeling and
Energy.
The word was my safety net.
The word would be the golden rope that would pull me from the depths.
The word was . . .
Vibration.

ACKNOWLEDGEMENTS

The first time I held a copy of this book in my hands, I cried. I couldn't believe I'd done it. I tried to write my story a few times over the years, and failed. Insecurity, the daunting task of actually writing a book, and finding a publisher, ate away at me like the rot on a withering apple core. The accomplishment of writing a book felt like climbing a mountain. It was a concrete and solid achievement. Now I held the proof in my hands.

I did it.

The words on the paper between the covers of this book are actual pieces of my essence, strung together like the bones of my skeleton. Being so honest in public was/is scary. Being so honest with myself has been *life-changing*. Writing this book unearthed many buried feelings and experiences, which rose like noxious gases though the layers of my subconscious. I was forced to look at these unpleasant and uncomfortable aspects of myself in the harsh light of day, and make peace with them.

I would like to thank those people who helped me to make this book a reality:

My husband, Philip Start, and my parents, Lucy Salenger and Marvin Zonis, for their unwavering support, love and guidance.

My literary agent, Matthew Hamilton, who took me on as a client the day he met me and has truly nurtured me through the whole process. His belief in me as a writer convinced me I *was* a writer.

William Van Meter, my friend, mentor, inspirer and literary adviser, whose encyclopaedic knowledge of The Fall could rival anyone's and filled the gaps in my own.

Lizzie Walker and Andrew Weatherall, who shoved Viv Albertine's book into my hands and told me, 'You should do this.' Then they introduced me to Faber & Faber . . .

At Faber, I'd like to thank Stephen Page and everybody who has helped with this book, especially my wonderful editors, Lee Brackstone and Dave Watkins. Lee 'Magic Pen' Brackstone surgically excised nearly half the 800 pages I delivered to him . . . without me needing an anaesthetic. I am eternally grateful to Dave for his patience and perfectionism, for sitting with me for hours and days, and for holding my hand while walking me over the hot coals of my own words. Thank you too, Dan Papps, Head of Publicity. You are amazing, beloved and intelligent, as well as being devilishly handsome. Working with you has been a gift.

Thank you to Elaine Foran, my manager and friend. Thank you Candice Hanson, my lawyer and friend. Thank you to my comrades-in-arms, ex-Fall members Steve Hanley, Paul Hanley, Marc Riley, Marcia Schofield, Simon Rogers, 'Funky Si' Wolstencroft and Steve Trafford.

Thank you to *The Fall Online* for keeping such meticulous records. I couldn't have done it without your amazing website. Thank you Jason Brown from the Extricated, and Nigel Kennedy.

Thank you to my entire family for spending hours on the phone comparing memories with me, including the Salengers, Uncle Fred, Aunt Sue, Jon and Karina. Thank you Maggie Haywood, Lisa Serwin and Jill Kane, and my sisters Nadia Zonis and Leah Harp.

Thank you to Jeff Veitch, Paul Cox, Kerry Curl, Gerrard Gethings, James Maszle, Kevin Cummins and Mark Blundell for allowing me to reproduce their photographs.

Thank you to *all* my friends who gave me a writing retreat outside of London: Kate Holmes and Alan McGee, Michelle Lineker, Saskia Wickham and Robert Bierman, Penny and Roger Palmano, Gráinne and Andy Fletcher, Richard and Pauline True, Fiona Knapp and Michael Pearce.

Thank you to Ella Duncan and Leah Lawry-Johns at Aitken Alexander; you will never know how much your encouragement meant to me. Thank you to everyone at MAC Cosmetics and to Cher Webb for creating my onstage look, 'warrior couture'. Thank you Anna Bartle and Martin Bartle for your support and enthusiasm.

Thank you Angela Radcliffe, Sarah Cox, Melanie Rickey and Yasmin Sewell, Tolley Casparis and Amy Flicker Jaffe, Margaret Pope, Suzanne Todd and Robin Ruzan. Thank you Stephen Duffy, Murray Lachlan Young and Freya North (who planted the seed). Thank you Kerry Shaw and Amelia Troubridge.

A special thanks to my dear, dear friend and first bandmate, Lisa Feder Castenskiold.

Thank you to my loyal pugs, Gladys and Pixie, who were my constant companions while writing this book.

Thank you to Sandwa, for *everything*.

Thank you to my music angel and BFF, Susanna Hoffs.

This book was written in bed(s).